Queer i
the Choir I

Queer in the Choir Room

Essays on Gender and Sexuality in Glee

Edited by MICHELLE PARKE

McFarland & Company, Inc., Publishers
Jefferson, North Carolina

Library of Congress Cataloguing-in-Publication Data

Queer in the choir room : essays on gender and sexuality in Glee /
  edited by Michelle Parke.
        p.   cm.
    Includes bibliographical references and index.

      ISBN 978-0-7864-9593-1 (softcover : acid free paper) ∞
      ISBN 978-1-4766-1695-7 (ebook)

      1. Glee (Television program) 2. Homosexuality on television.
  3. Sex role on television.   I. Parke, Michelle, 1975– editor.
  PN1992.77.G5558Q73 2014
  791.45'72—dc23   2014029130

British Library cataloguing data are available

On the cover: Chris Colfer as Kurt Hummel in *Glee*, 2012
(Fox Broadcasting/Photofest)

Printed in the United States of America

McFarland & Company, Inc., Publishers
  Box 611, Jefferson, North Carolina 28640
    www.mcfarlandpub.com

*For Gleeks everywhere
and for Cory*

Acknowledgments

Thank you to the wonderful contributors to this collection. A big thank you to my Carroll colleagues Jody Nusholtz and Siobhan Wright for their support and encouragement, and an extra thank you to Jody for suggesting the title for this book—it was much more creative than anything that I could have come up with. Finally, thank you to the creators and cast of *Glee*.

Table of Contents

Acknowledgments   vi

Introduction: Why Glee?   1

I. The Narratives of Coming Out:
"I have to just be me"

Coming Out: Challenging Portrayals of Diverse Sexualities
   • TRACY L. HAWKINS •   11

Forced Out of the "flannel closet": The Coming-Out-Gay Imperative
   • TAYLOR COLE MILLER •   24

II. The Intersectionality of Queerness and
Other Identities: "I'm not interested in any labels,
unless it's on something I shoplift"

Race and Ethnicity

"The only straight I am is straight-up bitch": Santana, Kurt, and
   Discursive Constructions of "Post"-Identity Ideology
   • BENJAMIN PHELPS •   39

Defying Blackness: The E(race)ure of Mercedes Jones
   • ANITA M. DEROUEN •   54

"We're all freaks together": White Privilege and Mitigation of
   Queer Community
   • M. SHANE GRANT •   69

Religion

The Princess and Her Queen: A Queer Duet
  • RACHEL E. SILVERMAN •   84

Going Beyond Grilled Cheesus: *Glee* and Queer Theology
  • ERIN KATHLEEN MARSHALL •   97

Disability

"I still have use of my penis": Disability and Queer Sexuality
  • MEREDITH WIGGINS •   107

Sexualities

"So, is this the part where you judge me?" Adolescent Sexuality
  • NIALL NANCE-CARROLL •   125

Let Me Get This Straight: Attraction and Actions
  • CHRISTINE L. FERGUSON •   137

No Substitute for Comprehensive Sex Ed: Analyzing Sexual
Ethics
  • JANE B. MEEK •   150

The Musical Theatre Performer

Glee and the "Ghosting" of the Musical Theatre Canon
  • BARRIE GELLES •   167

**III. The Complexities of Gender—Overachievers,
Good Girls, Bad Girls, and Tough Guys:
"That attitude starts in high school"**

Gold Stars and Slushies: The High Cost for Overachieving Girls
  • KASEY BUTCHER •   187

"I'm a Slave 4 U" but Only When I Want to Be: Female Sexual
Agency
  • MELISSA ESH •   200

"The Power of Madonna": Unleashed?
  • REBEKAH LOBOSCO •   215

Doppelgängers in Lima: Gendered Identities and Divided Selves
  • SHERYL LYN BUNDY •   229

IV. "I know what *Glee* is. I'm a total Gleek": The Cultural Reach of *Glee* and the Many Roles of Its Fandom

Glee Literally Means Glee: The Queer Art of *Community*'s Parody
  • NICHOLAS ALEXANDER HAYES •   243

"Everything is Klaine and nothing hurts": Klaine Fandom and
  Explorations of Teen Sexuality by Female Fanfiction Writers
  • EMILY HAMILTON-HONEY *and* AMY PATRICK •   255

About the Contributors   269

Index   273

Introduction

Why Glee?

MICHELLE PARKE

"This silly little show about a show choir means something much more than jazz hands and diva battles to so many people."—Dorothy Snarker ("Let's Get It On").

In simple terms, this epigraph from blogger Dorothy Snarker answers the question "Why compile a collection of essays on *Glee*?" But, as the contributors to this collection show, it is not that simple; *Glee* is not just a "silly little show" about Ohio teenagers singing covers of Journey and Katy Perry songs. Rather, *Glee* confronts issues of gender and sexuality alongside and against subjects such as race, religion, disability, education, and, of course, music. And, among current quality and complex television shows, it is certainly one of the queerest.[1] It is at these intersections that this collection has its impetus.

At its beginning in 2009, the musical comedy-drama from creators Ryan Murphy, Brad Falchuk, and Ian Brennan received frequent praise from critics. The *San Francisco Chronicle's* Tim Goodman asserted, "'Glee,' one of the season's best and most anticipated new series, delivers on both counts—and more. It's a quirky, sweet, humorous, nonpartisan funfest." Heather Havrilesky of Salon.com observed, "'Glee' is deliciously mean-spirited behind its fluffy, 'Up With People' facade. In fact, [...] it's like a tequila chaser to the squealing, soda-pop madness of its fall time-slot precursor, 'So You Think You Can Dance.' [...] 'Glee' is bold, silly, demonic and addictive—one full hour of very good (but not very clean) fun." As the seasons progressed, the reviews became more varied, even after the show snagged Emmys and Golden Globes while also topping the Billboard Singles chart.[2] In addition to tackling a variety of topics (intentionally and unintentionally), the Fox hit also works through a maze of narrative challenges that are often at the fore of this criticism: "Glee in a nutshell. Flashes of genius. Long stretches of why is this happening. Giant sinkholes of logic. And some real asshole moves" (Snarker "What Doesn't Glee You"). The authors included in this collection address these components with insight, nuance, and rigor.

The collection addresses—or begins to address—the numerous and intersecting concerns of gender and sexuality on the Fox hit program, focusing only on the first three seasons. Because of the ensemble cast, multiple storylines, and the prominent use of music, *Glee* invites examination as a unique television text. Of course, ensemble casts and multiple storylines are not novel on television.[3] *Grey's Anatomy* is perhaps the most comparable network television program to *Glee* in these respects, for example. However, *Glee* distinguishes itself in three (and arguably more) key ways: its focus on adolescents and young adults, its use of music as both a performative element and an aspect of narrative, and its combination of adolescent search for identity and queerness. The latter opens opportunities for a range of analytical approaches. Matters of race and ethnicity, religion, disability, and class intersect in dynamic ways with a variety of gender and sexuality issues. Those convergences can be further complicated with the added component of music, and on *Glee*, this includes everything from Sondheim to Streisand, from Schwartz to Spears.

Furthermore, the variety of identities, use of this musical range, and the familiar setting have created a passionate fandom. Mirroring the show itself, the fandom is queer, and its responses to their (nearly equally) beloved and maligned show are just as multifarious. The *Glee* fandom and the program interact in rather new and compelling ways, again reflecting the various representations of queerness within the show's diegesis.

"And here's what you missed on *Glee*"

The premise of the show appears simple enough: a group of teenagers from different social groups, of different abilities and talents, and of different identities form a struggling glee club called New Directions at McKinley High School in Lima, Ohio. Given the setting, there is certainly a familiarity with many of the characters and storylines on the show; however, *Glee* strives to address some recognizable tropes of teenage television shows from new or problematic angles. Some of these many issues include teen pregnancy and adoption, gay bullying, teen suicide, sexual awakening and identity, religious differences, funding for the arts in schools, graduation, college and career choices, death of loved ones, and texting while driving.

The ensemble cast began with a core group of characters and expanded over the course of the show's five seasons. Some of the authors in this collection address the ways in which many of these characters, young female and gay in particular, are represented. The founding members of New Directions include Rachel Berry (Lea Michele), Mercedes Jones (Amber Riley), Tina Cohen-Chang (Jenna Ushkowitz), Artie Abrams (Kevin McHale), Kurt Hummel (Chris Colfer), and Finn Hudson (Cory Monteith). Will Schuester (Matthew Morrison), choir director and Spanish teacher, advises and leads the group.

Eventually, three members of the national championship cheerleading squad, the Cheerios, Quinn Fabray (Dianna Agron), Santana Lopez (Naya Rivera), and Brittany S. Pierce (Heather Morris), join New Directions, initially as spies for coach Sue Sylvester (Jane Lynch) but then become full and participating members. And, Finn recruits other football players to join, including Noah "Puck" Puckerman (Mark Salling) and Matt Rutherford (Dijon Talton), which begins a familiar narrative arc on teenage programs: the clash between the popular kids and the "losers."

Over the course of the show's run, members have joined and left New Directions. Rutherford did not return in Season 2, but Mike Chang (Harry Shum, Jr.), a dancer, joins and becomes a key member of the group in subsequent seasons. Sam Evans (Chord Overstreet), a football player and guitarist, signs up with New Directions in Season 2, and after Kurt's transfer to Dalton Academy following the gay bullying by closeted football player Dave Karofsky (Max Adler), Puck recruits a reluctant Lauren Zizes (Ashley Fink) to serve as the necessary twelfth member the club needs to compete. We also get to know student Becky Johnson (Lauren Potter) much more in Seasons 2 through 4. She becomes Sue's sidekick and assistant and faces many of the same issues as her peers, such as dating troubles while also navigating McKinley as a student with Down syndrome.

In Season 3, Blaine Anderson (Darren Criss), the lead singer for the all-male Dalton Academy Warblers, transfers to McKinley to be with boyfriend Kurt but immediately joins New Directions. *Glee Project* winner Samuel Larsen was cast as Joe Hart, a Christian student who is attending public school for the first time, and Vanessa Lengies joined as Sugar Motta, an earnest young woman who cannot sing but has a rich father who occasionally supports the glee club financially. Finally, in Season 4, with many of the New Directions members graduating and moving on to college and careers, including Rachel, Finn, Kurt, Mercedes, Mike, and Santana, *Glee* added new characters, including Marley Rose (Melissa Benoist), Jake Puckerman (Jacob Artist), and Wade "Unique" Adams (Alex Newell). Dean Geyer was cast as Brody Weston, a potential love interest for New York Academy of Dramatic Arts (NYADA) freshman Rachel. With such a large and changing cast, *Glee* successfully and unsuccessfully intertwines the multiple plotlines and develops compelling characters within a short amount of narrative space.

A small cast of adults, in addition to Will, surrounds the teen characters and functions as adversaries and advocates. Sue Sylvester, most often, serves as the primary antagonist to the glee club as a group, finding ways to sabotage their hopes at different competitions, for example, and to individual members, which includes her own kind of bullying (e.g., throwing sticks at Mercedes or rigging Santana's and Brittany's lockers to explode with dirt upon opening). Jayma Mays' Emma Pillsbury, McKinley's guidance counselor and Will's on-again, off-again love interest, occasionally advises students regarding relationships and their futures, and she guides Will to do what is best for the students, asserting her role as one of their advocates. At the same time, Emma battles Obsessive-Compulsive Disorder, which affects her relationships and her job.

Burt Hummel (Mike O'Malley), Kurt's father, is one of the most positive adult characters on *Glee*. He supports Kurt as he comes out and endures the violence of bullying; Burt becomes a vocal advocate for not only Kurt but also other LGBTQ teens at McKinley. Another voice of support for New Directions comes from football coach Shannon Beiste (Dot-Marie Jones), who desires harmony between her team and the glee club. Substitute teacher Holly Holliday (Gwyneth Paltrow), though a small role in only three episodes, is a sex education teacher who challenges Will and Emma's perspectives on sex while also functioning as a guidance counselor of sorts to New Directions members, Santana and Brittany in particular.[4] The few adult characters on *Glee* are often just as compelling as the teens in terms of their connection to issues of gender and sexuality, as some of the authors in this collection will reveal.

There are, of course, many more characters who have moved in and out of the *Glee* world over the course of its five seasons. The guest star list perhaps reads longer than the show's cast list and has been the target of criticism and praise.

As previously mentioned, the multiple storyline structure of the show has often been a focus of critics: "Glee gets so many things wrong. Continuity, consistent characterization, coherent plot progression, comprehensible Glee Club budgets" (Snarker "Time Makes You Bolder"). Salon.com critic Peter Finocchiaro also points out that the show has been labeled a "schizo drama." As such, *Glee*'s plot is more difficult to delineate than the cast; the authors in this collection will address many of the key storylines, including those that focus, of course, primarily on issues of gender and sexuality, such as Santana's and Kurt's coming out stories, female empowerment in two of the artist-centered episodes ("The Power of Madonna" and "Britney/Brittany"), and the evolving friendship between Rachel and Kurt.

Regardless of some of the narrative flaws, the subjects tackled on the show, whether done effectively or ineffectively, open the door for scholarship and for larger discussion across boundaries. As Snarker asserts:

> What [*Glee*] does well it does so achingly well you want to catch it in a jar and put it on your nightstand and watch it slowly dance before you as you gently drift into slumber. But what it does badly or, even worse— heavy handedly—it does so badly you want to throw said jar against the nearest wall and watch it crash into a million little pieces, each of which represents an infinitely frustrating missed opportunity ["What Doesn't Glee You"].

In many ways, the scholars in this collection address the range Snarker articulates here and demonstrate the many ways in which gender and sexuality are often at the center of this narrative disparity.

"I'm just keepin' it real"

The essays in the collection are organized into four parts, each focusing on a particular topic. The challenge was organization because these essays overlap with each other across disciplines and methodologies; therefore, they could be put together in a number of different ways. My hope is that the structure I settled on shows readers other ways to consider these essays. The breadth of subjects covered herein is remarkable and proves that the discussion about *Glee*—and its attention to issues of gender and sexuality—is only beginning.

Critics and fans alike give much attention to the coming out stories on *Glee*; the essays directly focusing on this particular narrative serve as useful entry points to the collection. In "Coming Out: Challenging Portrayals of Diverse Sexualities," Tracy L. Hawkins argues that coming out narratives on television historically have been problematic, but *Glee* offers storylines that disrupt and shift this complicated television narrative. Taylor Cole Miller, in "Forced Out of the 'flannel closet': The Coming-Out-Gay Imperative," takes a different tack regarding the coming out narrative on *Glee* by examining it as an imperative on network television and its connection to representations of bisexuality (or its erasure). Both essays provide useful and often divergent approaches to the coming out narrative on the Fox program, which represents the larger conversation about this specific narrative on television and in culture at large.

The second part features essays that focus on issues of queerness as it relates to race, religion, disability, and musical theater. Benjamin Phelps, in "'The only straight I am is straight-up bitch': Santana, Kurt, and Discursive Constructions of 'Post'-Identity Ideology," examines the storylines of Kurt and Santana within the context of the "white male narrative" and critiques the post-race, post-gender constructs that he sees operating on *Glee*. In "Defying Blackness: The E(race)ure of Mercedes Jones," Anita M. DeRouen challenges *Glee*'s representation of race within the context of a system of meritocracy that she asserts is evident on the show. This system veils the "problem of the race/ethnicity-gender intersection," ultimately resulting in the "erasure" of three of the show's women of color. M. Shane Grant, in "'We're all freaks together': White Privilege and Mitigation of Queer Community," interrogates the problem of how the "white racial identity of the non race-based minorities effectively undercuts the queer potential of the glee club's community" and looks at the representation of four minority categories evident on the show: race, disability, sexuality, and body size.

Next, Rachel E. Silverman investigates the intersection of gay and Jewish identities in the form of the relationship between Rachel and Kurt; in "The Princess and Her Queen: A Queer Duet," she asserts that this relationship and its visibility affirm *Glee* as "a transgressive space for understanding identity on television and creating social change." In "Going Beyond Grilled Cheesus: *Glee* and Queer Theology," Erin Kathleen Marshall examines the representations of Christianity, focusing on three particular characters and storylines, through the lens of queer theology.

Then, Meredith Wiggins, in "'I still have use of my penis': Disability and Queer Sexuality," interrogates the problematic intersection between representations of disability and queer sexuality and argues that, more often than not, the disabled characters uphold heteronormative standards.

As is evidenced in many of the aforementioned essays, sex and sexuality hold prominent and often ambiguous as well as fraught places on *Glee*. Three authors further consider the various ways that this program explores issues of sexuality, specifically adolescent sexuality, asexuality, and secondary sex education as represented on television. Niall Nance-Carroll begins, in "'So, is this the part where you judge me?' Adolescent Sexuality," by examining the ways in which *Glee* explores adolescent sexuality, addressing claims from both sides of the political and cultural aisle about the show's morality and immorality in these representations, and considers the effects of such depictions on a teen audience. Next, in "Let Me Get This Straight: Attraction and Actions," Christine L. Ferguson analyzes the character Emma Pillsbury to address issues of asexuality and how, she argues, the program often reinforces cultural prescriptions about how to navigate relationships and how to value sex. Then, Jane B. Meek, in "No Substitute for Comprehensive Sex Ed: Analyzing Sexual Ethics," examines, through the lens of sexual ethics, *Glee*'s influence on its teen audience regarding sexuality and sex with a particular focus on issues of gender and queerness.

Finally, Barrie Gelles, in "*Glee* and the 'Ghosting' of the Musical Theatre Canon," examines the character Kurt, the use of Broadway songs and the effects of the ghost of the original Broadway show, and how the traditional interpretations of these songs can be "subverted to foreground issues of gender and sexuality."

The following section primarily centers on gender issues and *Glee*'s female characters. In "Gold Stars and Slushies: The High Cost for Overachieving Girls," Kasey Butcher analyzes the character Rachel Berry as an overachieving young woman who shows female teen audience members a "highly-capable, highly-driven girl in her successes" while also revealing some of the sacrifices and negative attention that she receives for being this type of character. Butcher asserts, however, that the "inverse relationship" between achievement and popularity on *Glee* might undermine Rachel's positive example. Next, Melissa Esh, in "'I'm a Slave 4 U' but Only When I Want to Be: Female Sexual Agency," explores what she contends is the nuanced portrayal of female sexual agency on the show, which resists binary constructions of sexual desire and instead presents female characters who possess a variety of attitudes and values about sex.

In "'The Power of Madonna': Unleashed?" Rebekah Lobosco shifts our attention to two specific episodes of *Glee*, "The Power of Madonna" and "Britney/Brittany," and examines the representation of feminism, feminine power, and sexuality within the scope of the show's claims that Madonna offers female empowerment whereas Britney Spears does not. But, for the young generation of the New Directions members, Lobosco argues, the outcomes regarding female empowerment differ widely in each episode. Finally, Sheryl Lyn Bundy closes the section with "Doppelgängers in Lima: Gendered Identities and Divided Selves" in which she investigates the characters Quinn Fabray and Blaine Anderson and their performance of two selves that represent gendered archetypes: Quinn's Good Girl/Bad Girl and Blaine's Sweet Boy/Tough Guy. She asserts that the performance of the "right" self on *Glee* translates to acceptance by others and by oneself.

The collection ends with a shift towards the cultural reach of *Glee* to include a discussion of the parody of the show on NBC's *Community* and the diverse and divergent fandom. Nicholas Alexander Hayes analyzes *Community*'s parody of the Fox hit in "*Glee* Literally Means Glee: The Queer Art of *Community*'s Parody," and he asserts that it challenges *Glee*'s "musical depiction of emergent identities" and this mode of identity formation. And, Hayes contends, that when *Community* critiques *Glee* via satire and parody, it, in fact, "critiques itself, revealing the non-normative, queer, impulse of the parody." Emily Hamilton-Honey and Amy Patrick conclude the collection with a study of how fan fiction writers explore sexuality in Blaine and Kurt ("Klaine") fan fiction, in "'Everything is Klaine and nothing hurts': Klaine Fandom and Explorations of Teen Sexuality by Female Fanfiction Writers." They argue that many of these writers, who express sexual attractions towards the characters, use their stories to explore what they desire in a relationship, and "girls can use gay crushes as a way to safely understand their own desires and wants," which, in this case, can be "safer" than real-life crushes.

Conclusion: Don't Stop Believin'

The goal with this collection is certainly multi-faceted. First, we desire to bring *Glee* into the larger conversation about gender and sexuality issues on television, situating it alongside comparable scholarship about programs such as *Buffy the Vampire Slayer, Lost, Dr. Who, Sherlock Holmes* and *Supernatural*, among others. *Glee* demands such investigation and scholarly attention, as the contributors demonstrate.

Second, and in a similar vein, we want to locate *Glee* fully in the study of popular culture, affirming that it deserves legitimate scholarly attention from a range of disciplines. At its core, it is about outcasts and misfits; the reception of the show, both popularly and critically, mirrors this central narrative. Our hope with this collection is much the same as the New Directions members when they wrote "Loser Like Me" for regionals, which is about being bullied and teased: "You may say that I'm a freak show/(I don't care)/But, hey, give me just a little time/I bet you're gonna change your mind" ("Original Song").

Next, with regard to queer identities and adolescence, we hope to contribute to the discussion about the reception of such storylines and characters among particular demographics, such as teenage girls and questioning young adults and teens, which can have significant psychological and emotional impact on these audience members. Many of the authors in this collection directly discuss reception while others certainly gesture towards such a conversation. Also, the epitexts and branding of *Glee*, including the concert tour, the movie, the use of social media by the cast and creators, fandom conventions, and cast appearances for and affiliations with political organizations such as It Gets Better and GLAAD, invite exploration of the reception of storylines centering on queer identities, gender representation, and adolescence.

Finally, we aim to show that *Glee* is more than a show with snarky one-liners and teenage angst with some Broadway and pop numbers thrown in for good measure and that it is, instead, one of those complicated, frustrating, and, dare I say, gleeful programs that makes television fascinating and compelling not only to watch but to study. The study of *Glee* can be challenging and vexing, satisfying and maddening, but exploring the nuances and the complexities of the show, as demonstrated in this collection's essays, can be the best part of a popular culture scholar's day, in much the same way that New Directions functions for one of the more (initially) cynical characters on the show, Santana Lopez: "Okay, look, believe what you want, but no one's forcing me to be here. And if you tell anyone this, I'll deny it, but I like being in Glee Club. It's the best part of my day" ("Sectionals").

We hope that this collection of *Glee* scholarship further opens the doors for critical discussion about this "silly little show about a show choir."

Notes

1. The application of "queer" is meant in the broadest scope, embracing the idea of boundary-blurring identities that can extend beyond sexuality and sexual identity and encompass gender identity as well. For this collection, "queer" reflects how creators Ryan Murphy, Brad Falchuk, and Ian Brennan have characterized the show itself and the characters: the outsider or the misfit who does not conform to the norm. The individual authors within the collection certainly adapt the word for their respective arguments, but generally, "queer" is applied expansively.

2. For example, in his review of the second season, *Variety* critic Brian Lowry comments, "Ah, 'Glee'—what a magnificent, aggravating, uplifting, unruly beast you are. The

unlikeliest of hits, Fox's sophomore sensation returns with a spring in its step and chip on its shoulder, as well as a couple of new cast members to alter the relationship dynamics and create new conflicts. Mostly, though, it's the same old show, which is to say a series characterized by operatic highs (literally, in this case) and irritating excesses. At this point, one can complain or succumb, and given the undeniable benefits, the latter impulse finally overpowers the former."

3. Jason Mittell's notion of narrative complexity comes to mind here. However, I would argue that *Glee* falls short of truly adhering to Mittell's definition of the newer mode of television narrative. In terms of the intricate blending of episodic and serial form, *Glee* does not reside alongside programs such as *The Wire, Buffy the Vampire Slayer,* or *Lost.* However, it could be argued that the privileging of character development over plot is evidenced on *Glee,* though perhaps not to the degree that Mittell suggests occurs in narratively complex programming.

4. Broadway star Idina Menzel was cast as Shelby Corcoran, rival show choir director of Vocal Adrenaline, Rachel Berry's birth mother, and adoptive mother of Quinn's daughter. Initially an antagonist, Shelby soon becomes the director of McKinley's short-lived all-girl group the Troubletones. She eventually develops tenuous relationships with Rachel as well as with Quinn and Puck (the father of Quinn's baby). In season four, Rachel encounters mentor/tormentor dance instructor Cassandra July (Kate Hudson), and Kurt finds a true mentor in his Vogue.com boss, Isabelle Wright (Sarah Jessica Parker).

References

"Blame It on the Alcohol." *Glee: The Complete Second Season.* Dir. Eric Stoltz. Writ. Ian Brennan. Perf. Lea Michele, Dianna Agron, Cory Montieth, and Chris Colfer. Twentieth Century–Fox, 2011. DVD.

Finocchiaro, Peter. "Why Does Everyone Want to Fix 'Glee?'" Salon.com. Salon Media Group, 25 May 2011. Web. 18 Aug. 2012.

Goodman, Tim. "TV review: 'Glee' has all the right ingredients." Rev. of *Glee. San Francisco Chronicle* 9 Sept. 2009. Web. 18 Aug. 2012.

Havrilesky, Heather. "'Glee' Could Be Great—If It Weren't So Awful." Salon.com. Salon Media Group, 9 Oct. 2010. Web. 18 Aug. 2012.

Lowry, Brian. "Glee." Rev. of *Glee. Variety* 20 Sept. 2011. Web. 18 Aug. 2012.

Mittell, Jason. "Narrative Complexity in Contemporary American Television." *Velvet Light Trap* 54 (2006): 29–40. Web.

"Original Song." *Glee: The Complete Second Season.* Dir. Bradley Buecker. Writ. Ryan Murphy. Perf. Lea Michele, Dianna Agron, Cory Montieth, and Chris Colfer. Twentieth Century–Fox, 2011. DVD.

"Sectionals." *Glee: The Complete First Season.* Dir. Brad Falchuk. Writ. Brad Falchuk. Perf. Lea Michele, Dianna Agron, Cory Montieth, and Chris Colfer. Twentieth Century–Fox, 2010. DVD.

Snarker, Dorothy. "Let's Get It On." *Dorothy Surrenders.* Blogspot.com. 7 Nov. 2011. Web. 18 Aug. 2012.

_____. "Time Makes You Bolder." Dorothy Surrenders. Blogspot.com. 9 March 2011. Web. 18 Aug. 2012.

_____. "What Doesn't Glee You." *Dorothy Surrenders.* Blogspot.com. 23 Feb. 2012. Web. 18 Aug. 2012.

I. The Narratives of Coming Out:
"I have to just be me"

Coming Out
Challenging Portrayals of Diverse Sexualities

Tracy L. Hawkins

Coming Out on Television

On April 30, 1997, viewers watched ABC's sitcom *Ellen* with rapt attention as they waited for Ellen Morgan (Ellen DeGeneres) to make the announcement that they knew was coming. So, when Ellen accidentally spoke into the airport intercom microphone and said, "Susan ... I'm gay," audiences knew that they had just witnessed the first portrayal of someone going through the process of coming out on television. The reaction was very mixed, and while the episode was widely watched, a backlash ensued, and the show was canceled after only one more season. Despite the show's lack of continued success, however, it made an important step forward in opening the possibility for other coming out storylines to be explored.

We should note that shows prior to *Ellen* had characters who were depicted as lesbian, gay, bi-sexual, or transgender (LGBT), but this essay will focus on shows that depict characters in the process of coming out. With that focus in mind, we can easily observe that since *Ellen*, viewers have watched many characters in a variety of different television genres come out. We have seen characters come out on shows like *Buffy the Vampire Slayer*, *Dawson's Creek*, *Gossip Girl*, *Brothers & Sisters*, *Bones*, *The L Word*, *Law & Order*, *Happily Divorced*, and *Friends*, just to name a few. We have also seen characters remember and re-live their coming out moments on shows like *Will & Grace* and *Modern Family*. In each of these cases, coming out is (or was) an important moment because it gives both other characters and the viewers a deeper understanding of the character involved.

Because we have seen coming out storylines appear in such a wide variety of shows, we may be tempted to think that these portrayals have worked to increase the acceptance of LGBT people and to empower them in their coming out process. Upon further analysis, however, that might be a somewhat optimistic conclusion. While it is the case that these portrayals have increased the visibility of issues surrounding coming out, it is not at all clear that these portrayals have made it easier or less necessary for people to go through the often painful process of coming out. In fact, in this essay, I will argue that the patterns that television has established for portrayals of coming out are quite problematic. Despite those problems, however, I believe that recent portrayals are beginning to move in a better direction. Namely, I contend that Fox's *Glee* helpfully breaks with those established patterns and offers some new messages that may prove to be quite helpful and empowering.

Established Coming Out Tropes Are Problematic

With all of the examples of coming out narratives mentioned above, we might believe that these stories have been portrayed from a variety of perspectives and with a great deal of variety in context; unfortunately, that it is not quite the case. Instead, while the exact details of each of these stories has been somewhat different, television's portrayals of coming out have largely conformed to one of two patterns: (1) neither the other characters nor the audience knows that a character is LGBT, so when the character finally reveals her or his sexuality, the other characters respond with shock, rage, or disgust and the audience may feel that the storyline was too contrived or (2) the characters and the audience have known all along that the character was LGBT and there is a moment when the tension and secrecy are finally resolved.[1]

There are many examples that follow the first pattern. For example, on *The Office*, when Oscar was outed to his co-workers ("Gay Witch Hunt"), they were all shocked. On *Greek*, Calvin is portrayed as a stereotypical frat guy, so his coming out is a huge surprise ("Black, White, and Read All Over"). On *Gossip Girl*, Eric is outed to his mother by a friend of his sister in a shocking conversation at the dinner table and then comes out himself to a party full of surprised friends and to Gossip Girl herself ("All About My Brother"). Additionally, in *Brothers and Sisters*, when Saul, who is in his early 70s, comes out even his openly gay nephew is very surprised

("Moral Hazard"). In all of these cases, the audience feels the surprise along with the other characters. Though somewhat less common, several examples of the second pattern also easily come to mind. For example, on *Suburgatory*, it is clear to several characters that Mr. Wolfe is gay before he officially comes out, and the same applies to Marshal on *United States of Tara*. There are many other examples of shows that have followed these patterns, but listing them is outside the scope of this essay.

Instead, the point here is that while the number of coming out stories has dramatically increased, they have not varied much in their content. They have, instead, closely followed these two established patterns. Because of this, while these stories have been helpful in bringing visibility to LGBT experiences, their ability to help and encourage people in the coming out process has been limited. In fact, more than simply limiting their ability to empower people, I believe that these established patterns have begun to embed some problematic messages into these coming out storylines. While I'm sure there are others, I find three particularly problematic messages that deserve attention.

First, despite the number of series that include some type of coming out storyline, the plot movement of these patterns rests on the minority status of the LGBT character. These patterns require that shows rarely include more than one LGBT character. Occasionally, shows may include two LGBT characters (particularly if they are in a relationship with each other), but unless the show is particularly about an LGBT community (like *The L Word*[2]), there are almost never more than two LGBT characters within the group of characters on a given show. Because of this, these shows demonstrate to viewers that LGBT sexualities are minorities that are very uncommon, perhaps even an anomaly within in the larger population.

Second, the stories based on these patterns repeatedly show that we can (and should?) make assumptions about people's sexuality from cursory observations of their appearance and behavior. If the first pattern is followed, the characters react with shock because they have made the assumption that the LGBT character is straight and news that the character does not meet that expectation is alarming. Or, if the second pattern is followed, characters have made judgments based on the character's dress or interests to conclude that he or she is closeted and therefore when the character does come out, the characters respond with a sentiment along the lines of "Well, I'm glad you finally realized it." In either case, these patterns gain their impact from the assumptions of the surrounding characters. Because of this, viewers see these assumptions, which are not so far away from stereotyping, as acceptable and commonplace. We may ask whether the portrayal of these assumptions mirrors the way real people already act or whether real people continue to make these assumptions because they see them play out on television (and my suspicion is that it is some of both); however, regardless of which comes first, the point is that these portrayals do nothing to discourage these assumptions.

A third message conveyed by these patterns is that the sexuality of LGBT people requires a public element, while the sexuality of straight people may remain private. These shows continue to suggest that LGBT characters must publicly come out in order to be authentically themselves and to have honest relationships with those around them. Before characters are out, there is a sense of hiding or even deceit (either to the audience or to the other characters) because the character does not meet the unspoken expectations of society. Because of this tension, closeted characters, whose sexuality is still private, cannot be in harmony with their surrounding and that harmony can only be achieved by outing oneself. Since this social tension requires a public (or at least semi-public) pronouncement about the character's sexuality, the subtext suggests that straight sexuality may remain private while LGBT sexualities must enter the public sphere in order to be authentic or free of tension. Straight people can live their whole lives without ever having to publicly or explicitly express their sexual preferences, and they are not seen as being deceitful or as hiding something if they never talk about their sexuality with their parents or their non-romantic friends. Conversely, LGBT sexualities cannot go un-discussed; instead, they must publicly identify themselves and submit themselves to the reactions of their friends and family in a way that heterosexual people are never expected to endure.

Because the established patterns for coming out stories express these three problematic messages, I claim that the increasingly common television portrayals of coming out stories may have actually done more harm than good. These portrayals have concretized the assertion that LGBT sexualities are so uncommon as to be anomalies, and they have served to encourage people to make assumptions about other people's sexuality. Furthermore, these portrayals have served to make LGBT sexualities necessarily public in a way that straight sexualities are not. Despite the prevalence of these messages, I believe that shows can break away from those patterns, and I assert *Glee* has begun to do so.

Glee Builds from the Established History

As we have seen, these patterns have become the conventional way to approach coming out storylines, and *Glee* had to begin from within that history. As a result, *Glee*'s first coming out storyline was fairly familiar.

From the beginning of the series, Kurt Hummel was presented as a well-dressed, Broadway-obsessed, sensitive teenager who rivals the main female characters for soprano solos.

Following the second pattern, most of the characters in the show (and most viewers) assumed that he was gay before he explicitly identified his own sexuality. Kurt's sexuality is first explicitly addressed in the third episode of the first season. In that episode, Mercedes begins to develop romantic feelings for Kurt and is lead to believe that Kurt feels the same way about her; the two even start "hanging out" together. Midway through the episode, however, Tina and Rachel step in to inform Mercedes that Kurt is gay, but Mercedes responds with indignation and insists that he is not gay even though he dresses so well. Nevertheless, when she later asks Kurt to make it official that they are dating, he rejects Mercedes and quickly claims to be in love with Rachel, which makes Mercedes angry and jealous. Later in the episode, however, Kurt decides to tell Mercedes that he isn't in love with Rachel, and that he is in fact gay. He claims that he couldn't tell her before because he has never told anyone and does not have the confidence to be out. Mercedes is surprised, but ultimately responds by saying that Kurt should not be ashamed and should feel free to express himself. This storyline seems to encompass both of the established patterns. Some characters are surprised, but most have assumed Kurt's sexuality before he self-identified.

However, this is not the end of Kurt's coming out story, and his sexuality is important in the next episode as well. At the beginning of the next episode, Kurt explicitly tells Finn that he is not gay, which suggests that while Kurt understands his own sexuality, he is still not ready for his sexuality to be made public. This inner conflict and outward concealment demonstrate the tension that undergirds that problematic message that LGBT sexualities must be made public in order to be authentic. More explicitly addressing that message, later in the same episode Kurt says, "I don't want to lie anymore" and comes out to his father ("Preggers"). His father endearingly responds by saying, "I know … I've known since you were three. All you wanted for your birthday was a pair of sensible heels" ("Preggers"). This second coming out scene for Kurt is again somewhat familiar, and as Kurt's sexuality enters the public sphere, the tension that grew from hiding his sexuality is resolved.

In these two instances, Kurt's story followed both of the established patterns and in many ways did express the three problematic messages discussed above—his father and viewers made assumptions about his sexuality, the tension in his life was only resolved by coming out thus making his sexuality public in a way that it would not have needed to be if he were straight, and Mercedes's reaction established gay sexuality as the unexpected minority. In fact, if we stopped our analysis here, we might conclude that *Glee* is fairly similar to all the shows that came before it. But, let's not stop here.

I believe that Kurt's story actually accomplishes something a bit different than what was accomplished by those same storylines in other shows. As mentioned above, coming out stories often appeared in other shows as "the" LGBT storyline. In a series with six or seven seasons, there might be an episode or two devoted to a character coming out, and that short arc would serve as a bit of plot movement but really did nothing to change the tenor of the rest of the show. Importantly, however, Kurt's coming out storyline serves a different purpose and does change the tenor of the show. Namely, Kurt's story demonstrated to audiences that *Glee* was going to directly and purposefully address issues of sexuality. Kurt's story eased audiences in to the topic of sexuality with patterns that were familiar, but *Glee*'s plan to break with the established patterns was foreshadowed by the show's repeated use of both established tropes in the same character's experience. Kurt's coming out episodes moved audiences through all the standard plot lines and left the door open for moving into new territory. *Glee* had to build on the history that came before it, but it also demonstrated that it was not going to stop at duplicating those same patterns.

After Kurt's storyline opened the topic, coming out narratives were more frequently portrayed on *Glee*, and I believe that the context and content of each of these coming out stories helpfully challenges the established patterns. In fact, I claim that *Glee*'s portrayals challenge all three of the problematic messages conveyed by those established patterns of coming out.

Glee Challenges the Idea That LGBT Sexualities Are a Minority

As we saw above, the established patterns for coming out storylines have made characters who come out into anomalous minorities; however, I believe *Glee* breaks with that pattern in some important ways.

First, the sheer number of people who come out on *Glee* means that people who come out are not really a minority population. Of the thirteen main high school characters, five of them have gone through some type of coming out storyline.[3] Additionally, several supporting characters, notably Dave Karofsky and Rachel's dads, have come out or been portrayed as LGBT. All in all, LGBT sexualities are shown to be quite common in the community of characters on *Glee*, and I believe this conveys an important message: that each viewer probably knows an LGBT person.

Additionally, the minority status of LGBT sexualities is challenged because straight people must negotiate and discuss their sexualities, too. It is not only LGBT people who must come out. For example, the members of the glee club assume that Sam is gay, but he does not identify as such and instead comes out as straight ("Duets"). In fact, most of the characters in the show are still figuring out their sexualities, and those sexualities are still malleable. Because of that, in some ways everyone is still trying to articulate her or his own sexuality. I believe that this helpfully conveys the message that all people must "come out" (if only to themselves) as they figure out their own sexualities. Because of this common struggle, coming out does not necessarily serve to inscribe minority status on individual characters.

Because *Glee* challenges the message that LGBT sexualities are minorities, I believe *Glee* helps change society's underlying belief that LGBT sexualities are rare and therefore are deviant.

Glee Challenges the Idea That People Can Make Assumptions About Sexuality Based Only on Appearance or Interests

Glee's portrayal of straight characters, like Sam, having to come out not only challenges the idea that LGBT sexualities are minorities, but it also challenges the established acceptance of making assumptions about people's sexualities. This challenge is accomplished by repeatedly showing that characters' sexualities do not necessarily match with what might be expected from their dress and behavior.

As mentioned above, in Season 2, Sam is initially thought to be gay, even by Kurt, because of his interest in glee club and his other personality traits. He breaks with the glee club's assumptions, however, and comes out as straight. This is the most direct challenge to the trend for people to make assumptions about sexuality based on appearance or interests, but others exist as well.

Both Sue Sylvester and Coach Shannon Beiste are portrayed in ways that could lead audiences to assume that they are lesbians, and Sue even has to deal with being assumed to be a lesbian in her congressional campaign in Season 3 ("I Kissed a Girl"). Breaking with that expectation, both characters have storylines with male romantic interests. Likewise, Dave Karofsky was portrayed as a manly-man football player, but eventually comes out as being gay. In all of these instances, the sexuality of the character breaks with what might have been expected based on their other characteristics.

By including these types of storylines, I believe that *Glee* is suggesting that society should refrain from making these assumptions at all. *Glee* disentangles a person's clothing style and hobbies from sexuality, and I believe this is very helpful in combatting the harmful assumptions and stereotypes that have arisen in contemporary society. While "gay-dar" is sometimes valued for showing understanding and inclusion in LGBT communities, it seems to me that assuming a person's style or interests is necessarily related to her or his sexuality is a very limiting and dis-empowering practice. Would it not be better to allow people to dress or be interested in any number of hobbies without that necessarily being indicative of their sexual preferences? By disentangling style/interests from sexuality, I believe we would open space for people to dress as they wish or be involved in the activities that interest them without fear of being outed, stereotyped, or misunderstood. Furthermore, it seems to me that this approach would give people (especially youth) the space to articulate their sexualities in whatever ways seem most fitting to them, free from the pressure of expectation and assumption.

Glee Challenges the Idea That LGBT Sexualities Must Enter Public Space

In addition to the ways that *Glee* challenges the idea that LGBT sexualities are minorities and the trend for people to make assumptions about sexuality based on appearance or interests, *Glee* also challenges the message that LGBT sexualities must enter public space in a way that straight sexualities do not need to. On *Glee*, characters have the ability to make public or keep private their sexual preferences and behaviors, whatever those preferences may be.

The primary example of this is found in Brittany's character. Her sexuality is very fluid throughout the show, and she never feels compelled to publicly identity herself as straight, lesbian, or even bi-sexual. Though she is romantically involved with several characters on the show, including Santana and Artie, and mentions that she has made out with nearly everyone in the school ("Bad Reputation"), her sexuality never enters public space, and she barely even discusses it with her intimate partners. She does not feel that she is hiding or lying about her sexuality, and there is no tension created from her sexuality remaining private. She simply lets her sexual preferences play out over time, and that is fine with both her and the other characters. Additionally, as we saw above, the show includes scenarios where straight sexualities enter the public space when they break with the expectations of the other characters.

By showing that a variety of sexualities may be called on to enter public space and by showing that non-straight sexualities may stay private, *Glee* challenges the expectation that LGBT sexualities (and only LGBT sexualities) must enter public space in order to be authentic. While it is the case that several LGBT characters do feel compelled to have their sexuality enter public space via some coming out expression, the overarching message of *Glee* is that sexuality is a complicated and fluid aspect of personhood, one that changes over time and must be articulated and re-articulated both to intimate partners and to non-romantic relations. I believe this is a helpful challenge to the message conveyed by the established patterns because it shows that all sexualities can and should have equal ability to remain private or be made public at the choice of the individual.

Glee's New Message: People Do Not Have to Accept the Labels Assigned to Them

I have explained several ways that I believe *Glee* challenges the messages of previous coming out storylines, but I also think that *Glee* also offers a new message: that individuals have agency to define, articulate, and label (or not) their own sexualities. Many of the characters on *Glee* carefully negotiate being labeled by others and claim the right to label or reject labels for themselves, and I believe this offers a helpful new message to viewers about the way that both individuals and society can approach sexuality.

In *Giving Account of Oneself*, Judith Butler claims that people are forced to label themselves in order to make themselves recognizable and understandable to those around them. In short, Butler claims that people are forced by society to adopt familiar identities so that people can understand them, and she claims, in the process of that adoption, individuals must submit to social norms. As a result of this, these norms of recognition become constricting, perhaps even oppressive. However, individuals are not merely victims to this process. Instead, Butler goes on to suggest that people can push back against the constriction of these norms through subversive repetition. What she means by this is that people will still need to adopt these familiar identities in order to be recognizable and understandable, but that they can perform those identities in a slightly new (and subversive) way. Then, over time, these new subversive performances will begin to break down the strength of the norms.

The established patterns of coming out on television certainly demonstrate the constricting power of these norms. The patterns suggest that LGBT characters must follow certain processes for coming out and must dress and act in certain ways in order to be understood as gay or lesbian, etc. Combatting that power, I think *Glee* works to highlight the potential of subversive repetition.

This potential is primarily seen through the ways that Santana and Brittany work to negotiate their sexualities. Though we know from the beginning of the show that Santana and Brittany are sexually involved, neither of them identifies as lesbian.[4] During Season 1, Santana dates and sleeps with several male characters, including Puck, Finn, and Sam. She seems to present herself as straight, and her sexual activity with Brittany is certainly never a defining characteristic of her personhood, even when her feelings for Brittany start growing. Throughout Season 2, however, Santana can no longer ignore her feelings and makes a heart felt confession of her love for Brittany ("Sexy"). Brittany responds that she reciprocates Santana's love but also loves Artie and wants to be with him for the time being. Brittany tells Santana that if her relationship with Artie ends, she would proudly be with Santana; however, Santana is very hurt that Brittany does not choose to be with her immediately. In expressing her feelings to Brittany, Santana comes out, in the sense that she must explicitly articulate her sexual preferences because they do not meet people's expectations. This again challenges the idea that you can make assumptions about people's sexuality based on their appearance or even their previous behavior. However, despite her romantic feelings, Santana, at least initially, rejects the label (re: lesbian) that her own desires inscribe on her. Brittany also refuses to use commonly understood labels and instead identifies herself as "bi-curious." In this scene, both characters demonstrate their own agency for self-labeling and for understanding the sexualities of those around them.

In the next episode, in response to Brittany's rejection, Santana starts dating Dave Karofsky but with the explicit acknowledgment that they are functioning as each other's beards ("Born This Way"). In that episode, the Glee members are asked to make T-shirts with words that acknowledge some part of themselves that they are insecure about. Santana originally makes a shirt with the word "Bitch" on it, but Brittany makes her a second T-shirt that says "Lebanese" (both Santana and the audience understand that Brittany meant for it to say "Lesbian") and encourages her to wear it for their performance. With reluctance, Santana does eventually wear the shirt that Brittany made, but she refuses to participate in the performance while wearing it and instead sits in the audience next to Karofsky. In this way, we see that Santana acknowledges her affiliation with lesbian identification, but we also see that she still refused to be publicly identified that way. More analysis about Santana's motivation for accepting this label may be necessary, but it is clear that Santana only accepts the label in her own time and in her own way. After accepting the label privately, Santana faces the challenge of making that private identification public. In Season 3, she comes out to her parents and her grandmother ("I Kissed a Girl"). In both cases, she identifies herself as lesbian and in both cases feels a sense of resolved tension after the period of being closeted. This trajectory is in fairly stark contrast to Brittany's (as discussed above) constant refusal to submit to the labels and norms of lesbianism or bi-sexuality.

These two characters, who are interestingly portrayed as alternating between the strongest and the weakest characters on the show, challenge traditional understandings of coming out because they do not merely accept the labels that others would inscribe on them. Butler would call this a subversive repetition because they go through the "coming out" process but deny its power over them. Santana denies its power by coming to terms with the label lesbian in her own unique way, and Brittany denies its power by refusing to submit to the term at all. By depicting the ability of these characters to negotiate the labels that are inscribed on them, I believe *Glee* empowers young people to see that they have agency and that they do not have to merely accept whatever labels people place on them. Though it may take time for this contribution to impact changes in the lives of real LGBT youth, this seems to be an important contribution to changing the way that individuals may self-identify and the way that society views and discusses LGBT sexualities.

Glee Also Shows Some of the Inner Turmoil Faced by LGBT Teenagers

In addition to challenging the messages of previously established patterns and alongside the new message of empowered label negotiation, *Glee* also directly and unabashedly addresses the struggles and pain that real LGBT youth endure. While other shows have shown these scenarios briefly or through flashbacks, *Glee* is the first show to directly and repeatedly depict these struggles.

The longest story arc that addresses the struggles of LGBT teenagers is the story of Dave Karofsky. Viewers first meet Karofsky as a bully to Kurt; Karofsky makes Kurt's life so miserable that Kurt transfers to a different school for a while. Later in the series, however, we learn that Karofsky is really in love with Kurt and only bullied him as a way to deny his feelings and establish a straight identity for himself. That is unsuccessful, however, and as his sexuality becomes public, he begins to be bullied himself. As a response to the bullying, in Season 3, Episode 14, "On My Way," Karofsky tries to commit suicide. This episode is very moving, and *Glee* does not sugar-coat or dodge the pain of the situation.

Additionally, as mentioned above, in "I Kissed a Girl," after coming out to the supportive glee club and her parents, Santana decides to come out to her grandmother. Santana explains to her grandmother that she has only really started to understand love by being with Brittany, and the scene is very tender and heartfelt. Her grandmother, however, responds very negatively and tells Santana to leave her house and never come back. This clearly hurts Santana deeply.

By clearly depicting the pain of Kurt, Karofsky, and Santana (and Blaine also discusses being bullied in the past), *Glee* shows several situations where LGBT youth can and do experience distress and trauma. Furthermore, because this pain is shown through a number of episodes and from the perspectives of a variety of characters, *Glee* demonstrates the frequency and gravity of these situations in real life and call attention to the fact that something be done to prevent this type of unnecessary suffering. While showing these painful stories may not change the underlying assumptions or the modes of discussion about LGBT sexualities in contemporary society, I believe (and hope) that this contribution can have a more direct impact on contemporary society. Furthermore, this more direct message may be easier for casual viewers to absorb.

Glee Contributes to Changed Media Portrayals and Changed Assumptions

In summary, while Kurt's coming out somewhat followed the established patterns, I believe that the coming out stories on *Glee* demonstrate that those patterns are not all encompassing and that other trajectories should be considered and explored. *Glee* suggests that LGBT sexualities should not hold the minority status that they have been given, that people should not make assumptions about sexuality based on appearance or interests, and that LGBT sexualities should not be required to enter public space differently than straight sexualities. Furthermore, *Glee* empowers people to see that they have the ability to negotiate the labels that society wishes to inscribe on them and calls attention to the fact that society needs to address the great suffering that is caused to LGBT youth by bullying and intolerance. In these ways, I believe *Glee* makes an important step away from problematic portrayals of coming out stories on television and, more importantly, contributes to changing the ways that these topics are addressed in contemporary society. Though *Glee* is not primarily about LGBT empowerment, it has moved us a long way from *Ellen* and from the harmful message of other common representations. Because of that, I believe that we can hold out hope that future shows will continue to move us toward more empowering television portrayals and toward a more whole and accepting view of a variety of sexualities.

Notes

1. The summary of these patterns is adapted from ideas in Mary Gary's book *Out in the Country: Youth, Media, and Queer Visibility in Rural America.*

2. Even in cases like *The L Word*, where most of the characters are lesbians, the character who comes out is still understood to be the minority because she is the only one still figuring out her sexuality while the rest of the characters already understand their sexualities.

3. Of the main high school characters (Artie Abrams, Blaine Anderson, Rachel Berry, Mike Chang, Tina Cohen-Chang, Sam Evans, Quinn Fabray, Finn Hudson, Kurt Hummel, Mercedes Jones, Santana Lopez, Brittany Pierce, and Noah Puckerman), Blaine, Sam, Kurt, Santana, and Brittany have come out. It should be noted that Sam came out as straight.

4. Their sexual relationship is first mentioned in Season 1, Episode 13, "Sectionals."

References

"All About My Brother." *Gossip Girl*. Writ. Paul Sciarrotta. Dir. Janice Cooke. Warner Home Video, 2008. DVD.

"Bad Reputation." *Glee*. Writ. Ian Brennan. Dir. Elodie Keene. 20th Century–Fox, 2011. DVD.

"Black, White, and Read All Over." *Greek*. Writ. Patrick Sean Smith, Anne Kenney, and Carter Covington. Dir. Perry Lang. Buena Vista Home Entertainment, 2008. DVD.

"Born This Way." *Glee*. Writ. Brad Falchuk. Dir. Alfonso Gomez-Rejon. 20th Century–Fox, 2011. DVD.

Butler, Judith. *Giving Account of Oneself*. New York: Fordham University Press, 2005. Print.

"Duets." *Glee*. Writ. Ian Brennan. Dir. Eric Stoltz. 20th Century–Fox, 2011. DVD.

Gary, Mary. *Out in the Country: Youth, Media, and Queer Visibility in Rural America.* New York: New York University Press, 2009. Print.

"Gay Witch Hunt." *The Office*. Writ. Greg Daniels. Dir. Ken Kwapis. NBC, 2007. DVD.

"I Kissed a Girl." *Glee*. Writ. Matthew Hodgson. Dir. Tate Donovan. 20th Century–Fox, 2012. DVD.

"Moral Hazard." *Brothers and Sisters*. Writ. Sheri Cooper-Landsman and Jason Wilborn. Dir. Michael Morris. Buena Vista Home Entertainment, 2008. DVD.

"Preggers." *Glee*. Writ. Brad Falchuk. Dir. Brad Falchuk. 20th Century–Fox, 2011. DVD.

"Sexy." *Glee*. Writ. Brad Falchuk. Dir. Ryan Murphy. 20th Century–Fox, 2011. DVD.

Forced Out of the "flannel closet"
The Coming-Out-Gay Imperative
TAYLOR COLE MILLER

In the wake of the recent string of gay teen suicides and the resulting tens of thousands of "It Gets Better videos," *Glee* (2009—) creators Ryan Murphy, Ian Brennan, and Brad Falchuk honed a specific trajectory for the second season of the show: to take gay bullying to task and advance an ethos of acceptance for homosexuals. In so doing, they quickly shuffled in two new gay male characters representing a spectrum of more normal masculinity in comparison with the original, overly-flaming Kurt Hummel, to articulate an "any kind of gay is OK" after-school- special message. By the third season, three of *Glee*'s main characters were explicitly outed and several more were tagged as exclusively homosexual. To date, little room is left for the true development of bisexual characters, those questioning their orientation, or those who prescribe to a queer sexual fluidity that resists essentialism.

Among the show's cast of characters in New Directions, the fictional McKinley High School glee club, two seemingly-straight supporting cheer-leaders, Brittany S. Pierce and Santana Lopez, are off-handedly involved in a sexual relationship that many of *Glee*'s queer viewers praised as the show *finally* portraying the bisexual hue in its rainbow of sexual identities. With the narrative's shift toward gay bullying, however, the changing por-trayal of bisexuality or queered anti-essentialism turned Santana into yet another self-hating homosexual just itching to be saved from her identity struggle. Although the new plot trajectory excited some viewers who saw their struggle personified, many of *Glee*'s younger bisexual and queer fans were devastated by the erasure of her bisexuality and what that meant for their own identity politics.

On the one hand, the presence of multiple gay characters in one primetime American broadcast show targeted toward family audiences represents a decades-long cultural struggle for the gay community to combat invisibility in the media. As Richard Dyer has argued, "making gayness visible had to overcome the fact that, apart from sexual acts, homosexuality is not something visible, something that can be seen (or of course heard...). But the gay project wanted a more secure visibility, it wanted to make widespread the face, literally of homosexuality" (15). This is a battle that, despite being bogged down by offensive-to-some stereotypes (or perhaps because of them), has largely been won. Bisexuality, on the other hand, has had to combat something much more sinister than just invisibility: erasure. As law professor and cultural critic Kenji Yoshino argues, "both self-identified heterosexuals and self-identified homosexuals have overlapping interests in the erasure of bisexuality that lead them into an 'epistemic contract' of bisexual erasure [including] (1) the stablization of exclusive sexual orientation categories; (2) the retention of sex as an important diacritical axis; and (3) the protection of norms of monogamy" (353).

An illuminating portrait of modern-day bi-erasure can be found in the second season episode "Blame It on the Alcohol," in which an intoxicated Blaine Anderson, Kurt's boyfriend, has a moment of sexual identity confusion—that is, a bisexual moment—when he kisses the female lead, Rachel Berry, and likes it. "I'm sorry this hurts your feelings or your pride, but it's more confusing for me," Blaine explains to an exasperated and biphobic Kurt. "You're sure about who you are. I'm searching, honestly trying to figure out who I am."

Several of the show's bi, pan, and queer fans were excited by this moment and the prospect of a Bi-Blaine but ultimately critical and disappointed in his bi-erasure. As one viewer explains:

> This [would have been] a major opportunity for the *Glee* writers and producers to reach out to a marginalized, and often ignored or exploited minority [that] lacks any real, relevant role models in the media. This would have been ground-breaking in ways we never dreamed. But none of this is going to happen [D.A.K. n.p.].

A response to this article regarded this "negative" treatment of possible bisexuality as in line with *Glee*'s overarching ideology (and American broadcast television in general), which I have come to call its coming out imperative. "It doesn't surprise me that a show that promotes positivity in gay males is full of fail when it comes to other groups in the LGBT spectrum. It sounds like the argument is in the same breath as the 'choose a side already' argument that those of us not entirely straight or gay have become accustomed to" (Ibid. n.p.). Conversely, fan uproar about Blaine's bicurious confusion left many gay viewers "screaming, ranting and about to give up on their favorite show, because a fictional character MIGHT possibly go from gay to bisexual" (Williams n.p.).

PerezHilton.com quoted Murphy as placating his supposed gay-friendly fan following: "Blaine is NOT bi. He is gay, and will always be gay. I think it's very important to young kids that they know this character is one of them" ("Ryan Murphy Clears Up Rumors" n.p.). Murphy's "one of them" quotation annoyed viewers who saw the comment as biphobic, and who were again let down in the third season when Santana as a queer character was forced out of the "flannel closet" by Finn:

> Kurt's biphobia annoyed me, but the bi erasure of Santana struck me. *Glee* fans often rationalize it as "Santana was always a lesbian; phases happen in real life." Yeah, bisexuality can be a phase for some lesbians in real life, but staying bi for a lifetime happens in real life too. So why do writers, producers, and directors show that very scarcely in comparison to the ever so realistic phase? Brittany is bi, but she doesn't have her own story. Bisexuality is invisible on *Glee* ["Regarding *Glee*" n.p.].

At the end of the episode, Blaine assures Kurt not only that he is gay, but that he is "100 percent" gay, quelling any hope of his being a well-adjusted bi character and bowing to a coming out imperative with an exclusive declaration. In one episode, Blaine's character toys with the idea of bisexuality, as do most media representations, only to reaffirm the stability of his homosexuality begging the questions this essay seeks to address: If, as most sexuality studies suggest, the incidence of bisexuality is in fact greater than or comparable to the incidence of homosexuality, why does broadcast television contain so few bi-representations? Why has the coming out imperative become such a critical axis for queer characters on television? What precedents have informed and governed these representations? And how have critics and viewers responded to Santana's coming out story arc?

The Erasure of Bisexuality from Prime Time Network Television

Although I am chiefly interested in the fictional program of *Glee*, I feel it's important to situate televisual bisexuality within its cultural history in the tabloid talk show circuit, to acknowledge how these first deployments continue to govern televisual representations. In his book *Freaks Talk Back* (1998), sociologist Joshua Gamson argues that *The Phil Donahue Show* (*Donahue*) began programming episodes dedicated to bisexuality and transgenderism as a way of amping up controversial issues to compete with daytime soaps and game shows of bigger budgets. Viewers hungry for controversial television sought out syndicated talk shows willing to do what networks wouldn't and as GLAAD sent more and more "normalized," straight acting white men to talk shows like *Donahue* and *The Oprah Winfrey Show* as "representatives of the community" preaching about the monogamy of homosexuality, the less controversial and confrontational it eventually became. "Over time, the talk shows have managed to do for their audience what no one else has," Gamson writes. "Through their continual exhibition of the most colorful sideshow figures, [they] make 'deviance' seem 'normal.'" But the *new normal*, as *Glee* creator Ryan Murphy's new show suggests, is the monogamous, family-oriented gay man that eventually became boring for talk show audiences, effectively ushering in new forms of tolerance for a gay/straight binary. It was thus sexual promiscuity that became subversive which bisexuality inherently invoked. Indeed, because of the danger it poses to the stability of monogamy, bisexuality has frequently become tied to deceit and bisexuals are represented as cowardly, self-hating, closeted homosexuals yearning to come out.

An example comes from a 2004 episode of *Oprah* about men living on the "down low." The episode began with an introduction by Oprah that worked to scare her female viewers with statistics demonstrating how AIDS was being spread to women: "Today you're going to hear many reasons why AIDS is on the rise again [and] why so many women are getting AIDS. Their husbands and their boyfriends are having secret sex with other men" ("Men Living on the D.L."). Many such episodes depended upon the stability of the gay/straight binary to demonstrate how bisexuality was inconceivable. "It's not straight or gay," as Oprah introduced bisexuality in a 1995 episode, "it's both and neither" (qtd. in Gamson 151–162).

Largely under the influence of talk show pioneers like Oprah and Donahue, our relatively recent media culture has come to represent "coming out" as a great moment of personal achievement—a sort of bourgeoisie notion of psychological wholeness or self-actualization after which (and only after which) we can become our true, complete selves. This trope is then used to justify our demand that celebrities (and by extension our culture of celebrity mimicry) come out of the closet for their own good. Thanks in part to talk shows like *Oprah* and *Donahue*, the lie we tell ourselves now is that we come out for ourselves, when in reality, we're mostly supplying the demand by a hetero(homo)normative monogamous imperative.

As Yoshino writes, bisexual erasure occurs "because the two dominant sexual orientation groups—self-identified straights and self-identified gays—have shared investments in that erasure. It is as if these two groups, despite their other virulent disagreements, have agreed that bisexuals will be made invisible," in order to secure the notion of a stable sexual orientation and defend the norm of monogamy (361–362).

George Gerbner and Larry Gross point to the dearth of gay characters in the late seventies, remarking, "representation in the fictional world signifies social existence; absence means symbolic annihilation" (182). But the erasure of bisexuality throughout network fictional programming is far from symbolic. At the time of their writing, 1976, gay characters or one-off episodes featuring mostly gay men had already become fairly common in the sitcom realm.[1] *All in the Family* did it first in 1971 with a sympathetic portrait of one of Archie Bunker's old football buddies ("Judging Books by Covers").

Rodriguez Rust argues that the historically shifting conceptualization of sexual identity began to rely on heterosexuality and homosexuality as "distinct forms of sexuality, predicated upon concepts of men and women as opposite genders" which rendered bisexuality as "simultaneously conceivable and inconceivable" (180–181). Writing about representations of sexuality in literature, Ritch Savin-Williams in 2005 similarly posited nine different archetypes of bisexuality that are commonly represented of the emerging adulthood era, only the first three of which network television frequently uses, and all three of which are constrained by heteronormativity and are thus only fleeting and ephemeral identities.

In (1) *situational bisexuality*, heterosexuals engage in bisexual behavior because of extenuating circumstances preventing them from heterosexuality of which prison sex, often represented in *Oz*, is a possible example. (2) *Chic bisexuality* (or *heteroflexibility*) is when heterosexuals engage in same-sex behavior as a way of mining cultural cool points or being socially acceptable, an example of which is found in Katy Perry's "I Kissed a Girl." Michaela D. E. Meyer argues that the heteroflexible individual "eventually defers to powerful heterosexual norms, their 'openness' serving as evidence that bisexuality is a fictitious concept rather than a valid identity category" (371). And finally (3) *transitional bisexuality*, as perhaps the most represented form of "disordered" bisexual identity, is seen as the bridge between hetero and homosexualities upon which one travels to discover or accept himself/herself as actually homosexual. Although Santana (and to a lesser degree Blaine) are among the best examples of this from recent years, reverse examples stretch all the way back to the late seventies and early eighties such as Jodie Dallas from *Soap* or Steven Carrington from *Dynasty*, both of whom claimed to be homosexual even while engaging mostly in heterosexual relationships. In these various bisexual models, the individual uses "bisexual behavior as a liminal space" but is ultimately recuperated into an essentialist identity either as purely hetero or homosexual (Ibid.).

Although a number of queer or straight characters in American network history could be read as one of a variety of these ephemeral identities, one the first explicit primetime representations of bisexuality is a 1988 episode of NBC's *Midnight Caller* (1988–1991) entitled "After It Happened" when a bisexual man with AIDS is depicted as having sex with women to deliberately infect them with the disease (Tropiano 101–103). The episode is another startling illustration of the threat bisexuality is thought to pose to monogamous (straight) communities.

As Meyer argues, contemporary representations of bisexuals, mostly in the last five years, are "typically female, portrayed by non–White actors, thus signifying a cultural struggle over the matrix of oppression through gender, race and sexuality. Ultimately, these characters operate as intersectional hybrids that serve hegemonic and counter hegemonic functions simultaneously" (367). Examples include Callie Torres from *Grey's Anatomy* and Kalinda Sharma on *The Good Wife*. By lumping sexuality in with a variety of other marginalized identities, the struggle for bisexual identity is contained to raced bodies in a way that ultimately makes it less threatening to white male patriarchy and masculinity.

"Do I smell like a golf course?!" Santana Lopez as Transitional Bisexual

Originally cast alongside Brittany S. Pierce as the bitchy back-ups to head cheerleader Quinn Fabray, Santana and Brittany enter the series and the glee club as moles for Cheerios' coach Sue Sylvester—to destroy the glee club from within. Santana is tied to promiscuity from the beginning, sleeping with several men in the school, including Puck ("Acafellas," "Mash Up," "Hairography") and Finn, whose virginity she "steals" ("The Power of Madonna"), as well as a revelation in the first season that she and Brittany occasionally engage in sexual activity, though the remark is off-handed ("Sectionals"). When the trajectory of the show became more focused on the issue of gay bullying during the second season, Santana's character was promoted to full lead, and the producers developed Santana's penchant for "sweet lady kisses" and "all that scissoring" to suggest she was actually a struggling, closeted lesbian ("Duets"). Thus, Santana begins the shift from the situational bisexuality presented in the first season to the transitional bisexuality of the second season bridging the gap between her heterosexual and new homosexual identities.

As Santana's storyline continues to develop, Brittany post-coitally suggests the two sing a Melissa Etheridge duet for a glee assignment, which Santana rejects, illustrating Christina Belcher concept of the "shameful lesbian musicality" of one of the most famous American lesbian musicians. Belcher compares the queer theorist's privileging of urban and punk sub-cultures as more progressive to suggest that "it is little wonder that lesbian musicality, associated with women's music of the lesbian separatist movement, becomes something of a drag on *Glee*" (412). Here *Glee*, as it so often and skillfully does, uses references to popular cultural icons to both identify but also commodify its characters as archetypes of musical identities. So while Rachel is positioned as Barbara 2.0 and Mercedes as belting black diva, Brittany's use of Etheridge begins to tie Santana to a lesbian musical identity, a label that she is both uncomfortable and ashamed to appropriate. After the two do perform a duet of "Landslide," Santana acknowledges her love of Brittany while explicitly denying an essentialist sexuality. "Let's be clear here: I'm not interested in any labels, unless it's on something I shop lift" ("Sexy").

While I argue that this statement is true of the still-side character Brittany, who seems not to be necessarily resistant to labels but childishly unaware of them, *Glee*'s creators employ Santana as a device of identity, introducing new antagonisms to contemporary notions of identity struggle both within the diegesis and in the real world. As Kurt always already served as the flamboyant gay archetype for *Glee*'s supposed gay fan following and a generation of liberal-minded women,[2] Santana's character becomes the token lesbian of the show—a model through whom to portray the tenuous process and struggle of coming out in emerging adulthood, especially as a queer body of color. Conversely, because Brittany is both a white, able-bodied character and the comic relief, she is allowed to maintain a label-less sexual fluidity that Santana cannot as a character upon whom labels are always foisted "based upon her ethnicity, economic position, gender, social status, perceived sexuality, etc." (JJ n.p.). While Brittany is allowed not to define, Santana continues to struggle with the new label of "lesbian" with which she has begun to identify and discusses with Brittany:

> I'm a bitch because I'm angry. Because I have all of these feelings. Feelings for you that I'm afraid of dealing with, because I'm afraid of dealing with the

consequences. And Brittany ... I can't go to an Indigo Girls concert, I just can't.... I want to be with you, but I'm afraid of the talks and the looks. I mean, you know what happened to Kurt at this school ["Sexy"].

In this conversation, Santana reveals the central ideology the gay trajectory of *Glee* (and the televisual medium in general) depends on: the imperative of the coming out ritual in order to live one's authentic and true self. While Santana is positioned as understanding her homosexuality but afraid to articulate it, for the other characters, her resistance to coming out is seen as a betrayal of her sexual orientation and identity; after all, if Kurt can come out and deal with the backlash of homophobia (and surely it is worse for him in the minds of the three gay male creators), she owes it to him and to herself to do the same. It is apparent from *Glee*'s employment of Kurt's gay-bashing (and secretly-gay) bully, Dave Karofsky, that closeted homosexuals on *Glee* are treated as deceitful and self-hating— indeed, the closet is a dangerous place to be.[3] The two team up as each other's mutual "beards" to run for Prom King and Queen, a title he wins, but she loses to Kurt in a cruel joke by their classmates ("Prom Queen"). After it is revealed that Kurt has been selected as McKinley High's Prom Queen, both Kurt and Santana storm out of the gymnasium for separate scenes with their homosexual love interests to reveal their anguish about the debacle.

Subsequent interlacing shots of both Kurt's and Santana's "crying hysteria" represent the former as understandable and the latter as contrived. While Kurt's serious-as-a-heart-attack scene demonstrates *Glee*'s opposition to real-world hate and homophobia, Santana's plight reads less relevant and, indeed, her own fault for failing to accept (and/or disclose) who she is. "They must have sensed that I was a lesbian, I mean they must have," Santana says. "Do I smell like a golf course?! ... I [have] to be an outsider my whole life; can't I just have one night where I'm queen?" ("Prom Queen").

In a moment of strange lucidity, Brittany suggests Santana might have won the title had she only been honest with herself (and everyone else) about her orientation: "They don't know what you're hiding. They just know you're not being yourself. If you were to embrace all the awesomeness that you are, you would have won" ("Prom Queen"). Slightly placated by Brittany's words, Santana asks Brittany what she should do. "Go back out there and be there for Kurt. This is going to be a lot harder for him than it is for you" ("Prom Queen"). Although several of *Glee*'s fans read the scene not as Santana's superficial discontentment over losing the title but as a portrait of her inner struggles (and every bit as serious as Kurt's outer ones), the show and its creators continuously and problematically portray the journey of the homosexual man as vastly more difficult than that of the homosexual woman. They do this through the voice of Brittany, another supposed "deviant" sexuality, who implicitly suggests that Santana is following in a lineage of stereotypically hysterical and melodramatic female media figures. *Glee* thus responds to Santana's aforementioned worry that her outness will be treated as Kurt's as inappropriate.

Santana's identification struggle continues into Season 3 when she and Finn, the straight white able-bodied male protagonist of the show, become involved in a battle after Santana leaves the glee club (New Directions) to join the school's other vocal group (the Trouble Tones). ("Mash Off"). After her departure, Santana becomes increasingly critical. In his response, and to "get her back," Finn echoes *Glee*'s ideology of outness by confronting Santana in the hallway in the presence of other students at the school:

> Hey Santana, why don't you just come out of the closet? You know, I think I know why you're so good at tearing everybody else down. It's because you're constantly tearing yourself down because you know that you're in love with Brittany, and she might not love you back. That must hurt not to be able to admit to everyone how you really feel. You know what I think you are? A coward ["Mash Off"].

For me and many other LGBTQ-identified critics, this is *Glee*'s ickiest moment because it not only positions Finn as being right and allowed to criticize her for not coming out but also for representing Santana as someone who "deserves it." Later in the episode, when conservative- leaning Cheerios' head coach Sue Sylvester launches a political campaign, her competitor runs a television ad smearing her as homosexual-tolerant because she promoted a lesbian to head cheerleader. As the show's central villain, *Glee* often employs Sue in its gay bullying schema as a metric to measure the acceptable amount of evil a character can possess. In other words, even though Sue is explicitly evil, not even *she* would sink to true gay bashing outside of a few insulting nicknames. Indeed, she often becomes a de facto ally and source of strength for gay characters in the show; it is Sue who delivers the news about the ad to Santana in the presence of Kurt's father, Burt (who is also running a political campaign), as well as glee coach William Schuester. Santana is devastated and begins to sob, revealing for the viewers that she is actually a sympathetic and vulnerable soul. The result is heartbreaking: "I can't believe this is happening. I haven't even told my parents yet" ("Mash Off").

After singing an emotional mash-up of Adele's "Rumor Has It" and "Someone Like You" Santana slaps Finn across the face for outing her in public, and it is she who is then suspended for being in the wrong. Luckily for her, Finn is right there to ride in on his white piano bench and save her from suspension, from her secret, and from her self-hate by once again asserting the coming out ideology of *Glee* and helping her finally accept (and disclose) who she *really* is ("I Kissed a Girl"). Even after her *abuela* (grandmother) disowns Santana for her revelation, saying it would have been better *not* to disclose, Santana is still gleeful about living a newly-free and honest life, and gives Finn a big hug to show her appreciation.

"Bisexuality is invisible on *Glee*": Critical and Queer Reception of Santana's Sexuality

In Season 2 when *Glee* creators Murphy, Brennan, and Falchuk developed Santana's sexually-queer storyline and her relationship with Brittany, critics and fans together rejoiced that Santana rejected essentialist orientation. Lux Alptraum, a queer critic for the feminist site *Jezebel*, praised her non-essentialist "queer-cheer" attitude:

> Brittany and Santana probably aren't lesbians—their numerous dalliances with boys make that pretty clear—but they're definitely not straight. [But] whatever they are, it's definitely a bit queer. And as a girl who's been attracted to men, women, and everything in between, it's thrilling to see this sort of sexual fluidity represented on one of the most popular shows on television [n.p.].

Many straight critics also celebrated Santana's transition into a homosexually-identified character, even if they were critical of *how* the "truth" was revealed. *AV Club* reviewer Todd VanDerWerff wrote that he generally believed Santana's story, struggling with her homosexuality, is the show's most compelling work in Season 3. But, VanDerWerff's grief with the episode is that she is confusingly happy when her friends stand up for her in a scene that suggests "being a lesbian isn't a choice with a song [Katy Perry's "I Kissed a Girl"] that's all about straight girls choosing to put on lesbian costumes to titillate their boyfriends (n.p.). VanDerWerff was also confused at why the show chose to turn "what should be a big moment— both sad and glad—for Santana into a musical number seemingly designed to play up the potentially arousing aspects of lesbianism [and that] the point of view character for this number seemingly become[s] Finn."

JJ, a straight female blogger and self-described Brittanalyst (from the portmanteau of Brittany's and Santana's relationship), responded positively to another episode in which the glee clubbers are supposed to wear a shirt with a word that shames them. Although Santana originally chooses the word "bitch," Brittany makes Santana a shirt that reads "Lebanese" in what JJ described not as Brittany's stupidity, but as a way to point to but *not* identify Santana's *actual* orientation. JJ also claims that by doing so, Brittany argues that "Santana cannot change the fact that she is a lesbian anymore than she could change her own ethnicity ... like if she were Lebanese, for example" (JJ n.p.).

However, the taste of happiness many viewers felt at Brittana's queer relationship quickly turned bitter when the label of homosexual continued to be thrust upon Santana by many of the show's straight characters as well as her own girlfriend. In the comments section of VanDerWerff's review of "I Kissed a Girl," one viewer wrote: "As a queer girl in my early 20's, I tend to identify with [Santana] more than other characters. [But] even taking off those goggles, even after trying to find something good tonight, I couldn't. I just hated this episode." This commenter was also critical of Santana coming out and being disowned by her *abuela* because of the way it contains homophobia to raced bodies. "I'll call her Abuela Enchilada because she was pretty much the most stereotypical Hispanic Grandmother possible," the viewer wrote, summing up the scene: "'Abuela, I love girls like normal girls love boys.' 'Ay Caramba Santana! Don't you know little baby Jesus [pronounced Hey-zeus] cries little baby tears when you kiss girls and like it? NO SALSA FOR YOU.'"

Another commenter was livid because of the show's erasure of Brittany from an episode about Brittana's relationship. "Brittany does absolutely nothing in this episode ... beyond hugging [Santana]. Fucking Finn Hudson is the catalyst, and Santana and Brittany don't even have a single scene to themselves to talk about their relationship" which the commenter also referred to as "awfully inconsequential all season." A third commenter shared this concern: "[Santana's] in love with Brittany, but Finn is the one to guide her on her journey to coming out? What the fuck?! The guy who outed her?! It makes zero sense."

In the *Glee* world, however, it makes perfect sense. *Glee* positions Finn, the straight, white, able-bodied jock, as Santana's guide because it needs to find ways to allow hegemonic heteronormativity seem approving of homosexuality to advance its activist intentions. Nothing is as seemingly normal (and vanilla) as Finn's sexuality, and so he becomes a stabilizing and normalizing figure for Santana's new homosexuality. As with my discussion of the way in which bisexuality or closeted homosexuality works in the talk show circuit, *Glee* has adapted its own ideology of the coming out imperative in order to proclaim that it is not Santana's homosexuality that marks her as a failure, but her inability to come out of the closet. Positioning Finn as an accepting audience is the show's way of making "heteronormativity" a character itself—and so by failing to come out as Kurt successfully, though painfully, did, she is literally called a "coward."

A reviewer for the lesbian and bisexual website AfterEllen.com was also critical of Santana's coming out moment:

> It's rad that Finn wants Santana to feel free to be her unicorn loving self. It's cool that he knows how sometimes people turn their aggression inward when they're so full of anger. But come on, man. He feels sorry for her? HE FEELS SORRY FOR HER? That's condescending to a face-punching degree [Hogan n.p.].

Another commenter on VanDerWerff's review pointed to Murphy as the culprit for the way in which Santana as a woman was allowed to be treated by the male protagonist: "The more I watch his shows, the more I think Ryan Murphy is the kind of gay man who never spends time with any women, much less queer ones." For many such viewers, *Glee*'s constant positioning of Kurt's storylines as a gay male being more serious and dangerous than Santana's is an example of the way in which Murphy, Brennan, and Falchuk's approach to Santana's story is considered misogynistic. This can be read in Santana's own rejection in the "shameful lesbian musicality" of "dykons" like Etheridge and The Indigo Girls as Belcher argues, as well as the way in which *Glee* used a Katy Perry song as both the title of Santana's coming out episode and the title song of Santana's defining moment.

In VanDerWerff's review of the episode "Mash Off" one viewer responded to the next episode's tease (featuring the Katy Perry song) as offensive: "There are SO MANY excellent songwriters who are actually out that it strikes me as a travesty that they passed up in favor of Perry's drivel. I mean Tegan and Sara aren't exactly unknown. For that matter, neither are Melissa Etheridge or KD Lang." The commenter was worried that *Glee* would employ the song during Santana's pivotal coming out scene to her parents which was erased entirely from the episode as it took place off camera—another major critique of the episode.

Although they explicitly create an ethos of anti-bullying in response to the cultural climate with Kurt, some viewers argue that the show bullies Santana (and other bisexuals) in a similar regard *out of* the closet. One commenter felt Santana's outing as a lesbian was not only biphobic, but did not make sense in terms of the plot. In the episode after Blaine's potential bicuriousness, "Santana starts questioning her sexuality and the sex-ed teacher asks her if she's a lesbian [instead of asking her if she's bisexual, since she's always been boy-crazy yet had feelings for Brittany...]" ("Regarding Glee"). The commenter said after *Glee*'s treatment of Blaine they stopped watching the show because "I was so sick to my stomach for months about *Glee* that I couldn't get myself to watch it again." They also believed that the reason bisexuality is excised from *Glee* is because of Murphy's own activist move toward making homosexuality acceptable, which is, as I discuss in the first section, done by portraying homosexuality as an acceptable foil to heterosexuality, while bisexuality is always already promiscuous.

"You do realize you're trying to force me out of the flannel closet?" Conclusions and Observations

Bisexuality has been portrayed rarely on television outside of ephemeral moments of indecision that reify and naturalize hetero and homosexuality as acceptable, genuine identities. In the talk show circuit, episodes began revolving around bisexuals when homosexuality became too tame to generate controversy and ratings. In primetime, bisexuals were erased because of the need to create stable, monogamous archetypes for characters that bisexuality implicitly challenges. Such programming strategies create an ethos of acceptance for homosexuality by tying deviance to promiscuity. Because of the absence of stereotypical bi traits outside of sex attraction to multiple bodies, unlike the flaming fag or the butchy dyke, bisexuality is thus tied to deviance through its supposed lechery.

In their attempt to combat gay bullying, *Glee* creators Murphy, Brennan, and Falchuk crafted a "gay trajectory" for Santana, who originally served as an model of queerness by being unidentified, resistant to essentialism, and marked only as a sexually-fluid queer raced body that was more developed than her ditzy dancing partner, Brittany. By sending her on a coming out journey, however, *Glee* alienated many such queer and bi fans who received the new storylines as the continued variety of bi-bullying and bi-erasure they have experienced with potential televisual representations since TV's inception.

Notes

1. See the 1971 *All in the Family*'s episode "Judging Books by Covers."
2. For more, see Taylor Cole Miller, "Performing Glee: Gay Resistance to Gay Representations and a New Slumpy Class," *flowtv.org*, July 6, 2011.
3. For instance, one commenter read Santana's homophobic grandmother as a closeted homosexual because of her reaction to Santana's outing (VanDerWerff "I Kissed a Girl" n.p.).

References

"Acafellas." *Glee.* Fox. 16 Sept. 2009. Television.

"After It Happened." *Midnight Caller.* NBC. December 3rd Productions. 13 Dec. 1988. Television.

Alptraum, Lux. "Why *Glee*'s Brittany and Santana Are My Queer Icons." *Jezebel.* 1 Oct. 2010. Accessed 8 April 2012. Web.

Belcher, Christina. "'I Can't Go to an Indigo Girls Concert, I Just Can't': *Glee*'s Shameful Lesbian Musicality." *Journal of Popular Music Studies* 23.4 (Dec. 2011): 412–430.

D.A.K. "Fuck You, Ryan Murphy. #glee #biphobia #spoilers." *Pardon My Sarcasm...* 15 Feb. 2011. Accessed 5 May 2012. Web.

Gamson, Joshua. *Freaks Talk Back.* Chicago: University of Chicago Press, 1998. Print.

glee.wikia.com.

"Hairography." *Glee.* Fox. 25 Nov. 2009. Television.

Hogan, Heather. "'Glee' Episode 307 Recap: I kissed a girl—sort of." Afterellen.com. 30 Nov. 2011. Accessed 8 Apr. 2012. Web.

"I Kissed a Girl." *Glee.* Fox. 29 Nov. 2011. Television.

JJ. "'I'm not interested in any labels': On Brittany, Santana, Labels, and the Uncertainty Principle." *Lima Heights Adjacent, themostrandomfandom.tumblr.com.* 8 Jan. 2012. Accessed 8 April 2012. Web.

"Judging Books by Covers." *All in the Family.* Tandem Productions. CBS-TV. 9 Feb. 1971. Television.

"Laryngitis." *Glee.* Fox. 11 May 2010. Television.

"Mash Off." *Glee.* Fox. 15 Nov. 2011. Television.

"Mash Up." *Glee.* Fox. 29 Oct. 2009. Television.

"Men Living on the D.L." *The Oprah Winfrey Show.* Syndicated. 16 April 2004. Television.

Meyer, Michaela D. "Representing Bisexuality on Television: The Case for Intersectional Hybrids." *Journal of Bisexuality* 10 (2010): 366–387. Print.

Miller, Taylor Cole. "Performing Glee: Gay Resistance to Gay Representations and a New Slumpy Class." *flowtv.org*, July 6, 2011. Web.

"The Power of Madonna." *Glee.* Fox. 20 Apr. 2010. Television.

"Prom Queen." *Glee.* Fox. 10 May 2011. Television.

"Regarding Glee." *Sexuality, Women, and LGBT Concerns christineleem.tumblr.com.* December 2011. Web. Accessed 8 Apr. 2012. Web.

"Ryan Murphy Clears Up Rumors about Blaine's Sexuality." PerezHilton.com. 14 Feb. 2011. Accessed 5 May 2011. Web.

Savin-Williams, Ritch. *The New Gay Teenager.* Cambridge: Harvard University Press, 2005. Print.

"Sectionals." *Glee.* Fox. 9 Dec. 2009. Television.

Sedgwick, Eve Kosofsky. "How to Bring Your Kids Up Gay." *The Children's Culture Reader.* New York: New York University Press, 1998. Print.

"Sexy." *Glee.* Fox. 8 Mar. 2011. Television.

Tropiano, Stephen. *The Prime Time Closet: A History of Gays and Lesbians on TV.* New York: Applause Theatre and Cinema Books, 2002. Print.

WanDerWerff, Todd. "I Kissed a Girl." *TV Club A.V. Club.* 30 Nov. 2011. Accessed 5 May 2012. Web.

_____. "Mash Off." *TV Club A.V. Club.* 16 Nov. 2011. Accessed 5 May 2012. Web.

Williams, Adrienne. "'One of Them': *Glee*'s Ryan Murphy Shows Unity of Biphobia to his Gay Base, Outrages Bisexual Community." bisocialnetwork.com. Web.

♦ *Race and Ethnicity* ♦

"The only straight I am is straight-up bitch"

Santana, Kurt, and Discursive Constructions of "Post"-Identity Ideology

BENJAMIN PHELPS

In "Heart," Episode 13 of the third season of the popular Fox television series *Glee*, the members of the newly formed Christian "God Squad" are discussing their plan to deliver singing telegrams to their classmates on Valentine's Day. Santana Lopez (Naya Rivera), a Latina female and out lesbian, requests a telegram for her girlfriend, Brittany Pierce (Heather Morris), a White female peer. Although three of the four God Squad members have no objections to the request, they want to make sure Joe Hart (Samuel Larsen), a new male student and very observant Christian—as evidenced by his Bible salesman father, his Bible verse tattoos, and his knowing only Christian songs—feels comfortable singing for a gay couple. Mercedes Jones (Amber Riley), a Black female and the de facto leader of the group, explains why she feels the need to get Joe's approval before delivering the telegram: "I don't want to hurt Santana's feelings, but I also don't want to make someone do something they're not comfortable with."

In the world of *Glee*, Mercedes' explanation serves to equate Santana's ostensible right to express her feelings for her same-sex partner—at a public school, no less—to Joe's right to freedom of expression and religious choice. Lost in the discussion is that Joe's right to exercise religious freedom has become collapsed with the exercise of denial of others' freedom. By allowing one person's personal "feelings" about homosexuality, and thus level of comfort, to carry the same weight as another's feelings about a same-sex romantic partner, the show adheres to a framework of formal equality that gives both parties the same rights to individual freedom, at least on paper. As Lani Guinier explains, under this framework, "treating individuals differently based on the color of their skin [or, in this case, sexual orientation] was constitutionally wrong" (93). Formal, legal barriers to full participation have been removed, and thus all individuals are seen to be on an equal playing field. In *Glee*, Joe and Santana are positioned equally, such that his potential discomfort with her homosexuality is not portrayed as discriminatory or prejudiced; it is simply a natural feeling that deserves as much protection as her own desire to send her telegram. However, not expressed by the show is the fact that deciding against Santana would be supported by a dominant ideology that subordinates homosexuality. If Joe were to declare his discomfort with Santana's request, he would be expressing not only his personal sentiments, but also those of dominant society, which systematically privileges heterosexual relationships.

This brief storyline epitomizes the way *Glee* reproduces the same dominant ideologies that it, on the surface, claims to counter. It adopts a liberal and progressive image, yet contributes to the production and reproduction of inequity through the images and messages presented in the series. In this essay, I will specifically problematize the neutrality and normalization of the White male narrative within *Glee*'s LGBTQ discourse by comparing Santana's characterization and story arc with those of Kurt Hummel (Chris Colfer), the gay White male character. In doing so, I demonstrate that *Glee* positions the two as analogues—they may have different racial/gender locations, but they are both made, simply, gay,[1] by the fact that they are attracted to people of the same sex. Yet, they are not both simply gay, as Kurt's narrative consistently trumps Santana's by drawing on unnamed dominant identity tropes. This universalizing discursive strategy erases important intersectionalities and (re)produces "post-identity" (post-race, post-gender) ideologies that ultimately serve to redeem and restore dominant identities (Whiteness, maleness) to their full value atop their respective hierarchies by ignoring them as power categories. I critique the post-race/gender constructs exhibited in *Glee* by analyzing Santana's coming out storyline in relation to Kurt's, arguing that, while the series has garnered praise for the latter, attempting to essentially repeat the storyline with Santana further marginalizes her as a lesbian of Color, which then reifies the hegemonic position of the gay White male. That this is being constructed inside the popular media narrative of gayness is particularly complicated, as it is functioning within a facade of liberalism and rights.

Post-Racialism and *Glee*'s Production of "Difference"

In this essay, post-racialism, as theorized by Critical Race scholar Sumi Cho, serves as an umbrella framework for the intersection of marginalized identities. As Cho describes it, post- racialism "is a twenty-first-century ideology that reflects a belief that due to significant racial progress that has been made, the state need not engage in race-based decision-making or adopt race-based remedies, and that civil society should eschew race as a central organizing principle of social action" (1594). Particularly after the 2008 election of Barack Obama as president—one year before *Glee* premiered—post-racialism allows for the claim that U.S. society is now "beyond race," and that any explicit consideration of race is itself racist. It is defined by four distinct features: a belief in racial progress and transcendence; a race-neutral universalism that refuses to link race to power; a moral equivalence that places those who draw attention to racism on the same moral footing as those who practice it; and conscious distancing from civil rights activism, political correctness, and Critical Race scholarship, which are seen as regressive. While a single instance of post-racialism does not require all four of these features to be present, they work in interaction to produce a complex ideological system that has grown increasingly popular.

Post-racialism also differs slightly from the ideology of colorblindness, addressing some of the logical fallacies inherent in the claim of not seeing color, and is able to appeal to "moderate-to-liberal whites who suffer from 'racial exhaustion'" (Cho 1599). Although post-racialism and colorblindness share many of the same features and objectives, especially around the "retreat from race imperative" (Cho 1599), post-racialism is set apart in that it is not simply aspirational, and actually uses a transcendent event to authorize that retreat (1598). Under post-racialism, race may be "seen" and acknowledged, but it assumes a level playing field in which any racial discrepancies are due to individual choice, reducing issues of power to the interpersonal level. The "retreat from race" and racial progress narrative are made even more believable due to the increased presence of people of Color in the public eye. However, rather than signify a truly more equitable society, this increased diversity reflects that, as Patricia Hill Collins argues, "we've gone from politics that protects racial privilege through maintaining all- white spaces to a multicultural, colorful politics that relies on allegedly color-blind mechanisms to reproduce the very same racial privilege" (47). By framing policies and legal decisions as "universal" and "neutral," colorblind practices assume Whiteness as the standard, which allows it to become more deeply entrenched while going unmarked. Under the ideology of post-racialism, it is acceptable to acknowledge race as a characteristic of people and culture, if not an organizing principle of society. Thus, when Collins writes, "To function, color-blind racism needs *visible* representations of blackness and brownness simultaneously to claim the universal, social justice ethos of the *Brown* [*v. Board of Education*] decision while deflecting attention away from the *Brown* decision's failures" (70), it perhaps makes more sense to think of her "color-blind racism" as post-racialism. Under this ideological system, people of Color *must* be visibly represented in order to prove that racism is no longer a barrier to full enjoyment of society. *Glee* does just this, presenting characters that vary along lines of race and ethnicity as a demonstration of diversity, multiculturalism, acceptance, and tolerance. And while race is acknowledged—though only among students of Color, allowing Whiteness to continue unmarked—it is never pointed to as a reason for differential treatment. Race may become fodder for a joke or an ostensibly comedic storyline, but it is never handled as a serious topic that actively plays a role in constructing students' lives.

This post-racial framework also allows for an understanding and interpretation of *Glee*'s erasure of intersectionalities, due to the alleged equality of all identities—yet, the elision of meaningful difference serves only to privilege the unnamed dominant identity categories. Because a post-racial ideology needs visible representations of difference (i.e., "Color") to demonstrate that such difference no longer has societal implications, *Glee* provides them in myriad ways—characters not only from different racial/ethnic backgrounds, but also from various positions of class, gender, sexuality, and ability. Although post-racialism takes race as its focal point, these other social identity categories are important to consider as well. As Kimberlé Crenshaw explains, intersectionalities—that is, the varied and multi-contextual ways in which categories of identity and power intersect—cannot be ignored, as doing so only conflates intragroup differences and erases the diverse experiences of, for instance, women and people of Color (1242). However, in having such a large cast and attempting to represent seemingly every type of "difference," *Glee* essentializes difference and reduces many of its characters of Color to racial tokens, pushing them to the margins of the show. This type of essentialism thereby reifies dominant identity categories because simply having characters from underrepresented groups takes the place of substantive representation, and those who mirror hegemonic norms remain at the center. A comparison of Santana and Kurt highlights the intersectionalities of identity that are largely ignored and rendered invisible in *Glee*'s post-race, post-gender ideological framework—namely, how Santana's experience differs from Kurt's due to their respective racial, gender, and sexual locations.

Political and Ideological: A Textual Analysis of Pop Cultural Hegemony

In this essay, I conduct a textual analysis, which aims, as Alan McKee explains, not to determine how accurate or correct a text is, but rather to understand how to make meaning of a particular text within a specific temporal, political, historical, and cultural context. In performing a textual analysis on *Glee*, and particularly on Santana and Kurt's respective coming out narratives, I "make an educated guess at some of the most likely interpretations that might be made of that text" (McKee 1), considering the current post-identity ideological and discursive context. Although the representations I am analyzing may not have meaning in and of themselves, "they are the vehicles or media which *carry meaning* because they operate as *symbols*, which stand for or represent (i.e., symbolize) the meanings we wish to communicate" (Hall 5, emphasis in original). Thus, this essay deconstructs Santana's character in relation to Kurt's, illustrating how both are written to highlight their sexuality in a post-race/gender power vacuum while ultimately recentering and reprivileging dominant identities.

It is important to remember that popular culture is more than a form of mass entertainment—it is also, as Hall, Kellner, and Storey, among others, have each argued, an instrument of hegemony, whereby texts naturalize certain political and ideological positions. Considering its reach and accessibility, popular media maintains an inordinate amount of power with which to produce knowledge that becomes accepted as natural and normal. As a highly-rated, award-winning television series, *Glee* fits both the theoretical and more literal definitions of "popular," and has garnered particular acclaim for its portrayals of teen sexuality vis-à-vis LGBTQ youth. *Entertainment Weekly* writer Jennifer Armstrong celebrated the show for "changing hearts, minds, & Hollywood," and various cast members have filmed PSAs for the viral It Gets Better Project, further politicizing *Glee* as a vehicle for LGBTQ rights. However, this mainstream praise and activism eclipses the question of which LGBTQ identities and stories the show is promoting and protecting, and so discursively bolsters dominant ideological positions. Particularly, *Glee* positions Kurt Hummel as the hegemonic queer individual, whereby the gay White male character and story become neutral and the norm. *Glee* discursively collapses nor-

malized gayness with Whiteness, maleness, and all that is culturally privileged, yet decouples those identity categories from differential power.

Santana Lopez has appeared on *Glee* since its pilot episode but was
a minor character throughout the first season. In the second season,
though, Rivera is promoted to series regular status, and Santana takes on
a more prominent role in the show. Her key storyline over Seasons 2 and
3 involves her realization and acceptance of her lesbian identity, which
involves the development of a casual sexual relationship with her friend
and fellow glee club member, Brittany, and culminates in her coming out
to her friends and family. The Season 3 episodes "Mash Off" and "I Kissed
a Girl" are arguably the most important and most problematic in Santana's
"coming out" arc. Over the course of the series, Santana had been questioning her sexuality, with an implied sexual relationship between her and
Brittany, but she had not come out to her peers or her family as a lesbian.
In "Mash Off," she comes out but not due to her own actions or agency;
rather, Finn Hudson (Cory Monteith), the straight White male lead of the
glee club and of *Glee*, outs her in the middle of the school hallway, telling
her she is too afraid to come out of the closet and be herself. Once Finn
has outed Santana, there is a marked tension between the two. At the end
of a musical performance in which Santana is singing the lead, Finn leans
over to Rachel Berry (Lea Michele), his girlfriend and the straight White
female lead of the group, and whispers something in her ear. Santana
jumps off stage and angrily asks him what he just said. He claims he was
praising her performance, but she does not believe him. Instead, she
blames him for outing her, and slaps him across the face. As I will explain,
this series of events contains many of the features of post-racialism and
illuminates the broader post-identity discursive stance of *Glee* when compared to Kurt's own coming out arc.

The "coming out imperative" and Post-Racial Erasure of Intersectionality

Dominant discourses around sexuality and coming out have constructed an in/out binary that "tend[s] to offer no moral alternative BUT
to come out" (Rasmussen 146), yet this strict framework fails to recognize
or allow for complexities of individual and institutional identities, instead
assuming a norm that applies to all. Mary Lou Rasmussen calls this the
"coming out imperative":

> There is an imperative for lesbian and gay identified people to come out in
> educational settings, and I have argued this imperative can place people in an

invidious position. When coming out discourses are privileged, the act of not coming out may be read as an abdication of responsibility, or, the act of somebody who is disempowered or somehow ashamed of their inherent gayness [146].

Santana's positioning in the "Mash Off" storyline clearly places her in this binary structure. Indeed, the "imperative" is so strong for LGBTQ-identifying students to come out, that a classmate forces her out of the closet. Finn sees Santana as "too afraid" to come out and embrace "who she really is," but because coming out is seen as a necessity for all LGBTQ-identifying students, he takes it upon himself to push her out of the closet. However, while strongly advocating for this universal coming out imperative, drawing a discursive link between the coming out process and a sense of personal empowerment and freedom, *Glee* not only fails to interrogate the different institutional and individual contexts for coming out, but also "may have the reverse effect of reinforcing heterosexuality because of its tendency to underpin the heterosexual/homosexual binary" (Rasmussen 148). By stripping Santana of her agency, and by ignoring the specificity of a Latina female coming out into a predominantly White, heterosexual school environment, the show further marginalizes Santana while claiming to do the opposite. She must follow the rules and stipulations set by those in power, yet the race- and gender-neutral context—evident through its invisibility—ensure her continued disempowerment by refusing to take non-dominant positions into consideration.

In fact, it is Santana, not Finn, who is punished under the school's zero tolerance policy against violence—yet, this erases any power differential between Finn and Santana, whether relating to sexual orientation, race, or gender. Finn's position as straight White male is placed on the same level as Santana's position as a gay Latina female. Finn's verbal outing of her and her slapping of him are both measured in a power vacuum, without consideration of the marginalization of her multiple intersecting identities within both the school and broader society. Although the situation is not explicitly or primarily about race, it is couched in post-racial ideology and discourse concerning the decoupling of race and power. Finn's actions are not just morally equivalent to Santana's, they are actually morally superior—he was "helping" her achieve the imperative to come out and she responded with violent resistance. Finn uses his multiple privileges and positions of power over Santana to effectively determine who she is, and what is and is not moral. He is presented as simply assisting her in doing the right thing, yet he is able—and, even *thinks* he has the right—to do so because of his privileged position relative to her. And by refusing to question the symbolic violence of Finn's action itself—which, as Charles Lawrence explains in the context of racist speech, may have the effects of psychic injury, reputational injury, and the denial of equal educational opportunity—*Glee* abdicates responsibility for other forms of violence against LGBTQ people of Color and reifies the entitlement and power of the dominant group.

In the imagined world of *Glee*, the power Finn holds over Santana is inconsequential because she just needs to come out and accept "who she is." Even though Santana points out to Finn that he basically forced her out of the closet, her loss of agency is not presented as problematic because she is now out. Finn's explanation to her exemplifies the show's views on coming out: "The truth is, I think you're awesome. And when you hide part of who you are, you hide your awesomeness with it." There is no power of any type attached to that statement—no reflection on institutional structures, cultural norms, or even interpersonal relations. Instead, Santana should just come out because she is "awesome," but she cannot truly be awesome until she shares every aspect of her identity with everyone. This captures the race-neutral universalism of Cho's post-racialism, which holds that race is not a power category and is no longer a significant organizing feature of society. Extended to a post-identity framework that also encompasses gender, Finn's comments to Santana represent a power-neutral discourse that ultimately does little to change her subordinated position. The statements are made within the popular liberal discourse of coming out, yet Santana is not actually safer when her sexuality is forcibly made public, and the storyline is driven by Finn's and the school's respective actions. Thus, the effect is that Santana—and consequently other LGBTQ students of Color—remains marginalized, while Whiteness, maleness, and heterosexuality are redeemed thanks to Finn's "selfless" act.

Dominant discourses about coming out also tend to overlook the complexities of intersecting identities, privileging a White male position within LGBTQ discourse. Indeed, as Kathryn Snider argues, the "failure to see gender and race (if you are male and White) as mitigating factors in the process of revealing sexual orientation ... exposes the power differential between those who are able to discount multiple 'other' subject positions and those who are not" (297). This is particularly evident when comparing Santana's coming out storyline to Kurt's and contributes to the discursive construction of a post-racial position in the show. In the episode "I Kissed a Girl," Santana comes out to her parents, but the action happens off screen—all the audience sees is a happy Santana, telling the rest of the group that her parents were very accepting of her. Besides violating the basic "show, don't tell" principle of screenwriting, this approach to Santana's coming out downplays its significance and serves to draw parallels between Santana's and Kurt's respective processes of coming out to their parents. Kurt came out to his father in Season 1, with a number of scenes across multiple episodes focusing on his father's acceptance, yet Santana's coming out to her own parents is worth only one throwaway line with no visual back-up. Whatever the reasons for this approach—a runtime issue, a desire not to essentially repeat the coming-out-to-one's-parents storyline the show had done with Kurt, or something else entirely—the effect is a diminishing of the importance of Santana's decision to come out to her family and a privileging of Kurt's own storyline. Because his is the only one we see, it has a universalizing effect that implies Santana's story would be only superficially different and thus not worth showing. But, this universalizing is a false one and bolsters a hegemonic normalization of White gay maleness.

Indeed, the relative placement and telling of Santana and Kurt's coming out stories serves to reinforce the dominant position of White men within coming out and LGBTQ discourses, as Snider explains, while ostensibly placing them on equal footing. Santana, then, becomes a tool for what Cho describes as race-neutral universalism, as her story is written as superficially similar to Kurt's. Her race and gender are not given as reasons she may have resisted coming out, nor are they presented as unique challenges when compared to Kurt. This race-neutral universalizing has the effect of redeeming and further privileging Whiteness (and maleness), though, as it refuses to challenge racism or sexism within LGBTQ discourses. As Snider argues, "Perhaps homophobia is the only systemic deterrent to achievement for gay, White youth. However, without also challenging racism, nothing has been accomplished for many lesbian and gay youth of color except a demand to hierarchize oppressions" (299). Thus, the equating of Santana and Kurt's coming out stories serves to position oppression based on sexual orientation hierarchically above that based on race but does so by neutralizing and stripping race of its power. Because of its position in a larger discursive and ideological context where race is no longer an organizing principle, *Glee* is able to focus solely on sexuality, without attention to race or intersectionality. This lack of attention normalizes a single coming out narrative—Kurt's—while dismissing the specificity that other identity markers contribute.

Moreover, the association between *Glee* and campaigns such as the It Gets Better Project, which "was created to show young LGBT people the levels of happiness, potential, and positivity their lives will reach—if they can just get through their teen years," erases multiple intersections and obscures the point that it does not actually "get better" for every person who identifies as LGBTQ, nor is coming out as LGBTQ always a viable or desirable option, as Rasmussen and Snider have both argued. For Santana, it does seem to get better, but the improvement of her situation functions as a way to hide both the hostile school environment into which she was forced to come out and the impacts of race and gender, rather than as a reflection on any true universality to the claim "it gets better." That both Santana and Kurt's situations improve reflects *Glee*'s stance that it is merely individual bullies and homophobes who are the problem and that anyone, regardless of any other positionality or context, can be happy and accepted as who they are once the effects of those bullies are overcome. This focus on the treatment of homosexuality rather than the investigation of heteronormativity not only allows heterosexuality to go unmarked and to retain its normal, natural, and privileged position, as Deborah Britzman and Kevin Kumashiro have argued, but it also redeems dominant identities and the power they carry. *Glee*'s universalizing discourse around coming out eliminates intersectionality, complexity, and specificity, continuing the marginalization of women and people of Color—and women of Color—within a post-race, post-gender context. And, while sexuality has supplanted race and gender as an actual "issue," its narrative treatment continues to privilege only a specific form of homosexuality without recognition that it is, in fact, specific and non-universal.

Representing Post-Racial Cultural Difference

Some differences that highlight intersections of identity *are* drawn between Santana and Kurt's coming out experiences, yet they are presented in a power vacuum and serve more to do the work of representing cultural difference that Ann Arnett Ferguson describes as a key part of reproducing racial inequality. The two characters face different interpersonal levels of bullying and discrimination. Kurt is harassed repeatedly by one particular student, David Karofsky (Max Adler), to the point that Kurt transfers to another school for much of the second season to avoid the constant harassment. When Karofsky kisses Kurt in Season 2's "Never Been Kissed," it is revealed that Karofsky's anti-gay bullying is, in fact, a manifestation of his own closeted sexuality, and he threatens to kill Kurt if he reveals this secret. It is after this and several more acts of intimidation that Kurt decides to transfer to the all-male prep school, Dalton Academy, which some TV critics, including Seitz, and online commenters nicknamed "Gay Hogwarts" for its seemingly idyllic tolerance and acceptance of LGBTQ students. This storyline serves the dual purpose of buttressing the "It Gets Better" narrative and demonstrating that Kurt is not free from homophobia and harassment, even with his privileged racial and gender identities. First, Kurt's situation is dramatized as so unsafe that he fears for his life and must leave McKinley High. However, at Dalton, and upon his eventual return to McKinley, all of the bullies are gone and he is in a completely safe environment. Although he had to make some changes and adapt, his situation did get better, and he was eventually able to "go back to normal" at his old school with his old friends, with no more problems. Second, even though Kurt is a White male, he is still bullied and harassed for his being gay. This accomplishes the work of post-racialism/gender by indirectly arguing that bullying is a universal difficulty faced by LGBTQ youth, while simultaneously supporting the "coming out imperative"— that LGBTQ youth should come out, even if doing so will temporarily bring more problems, because it will eventually get better and result in empowerment and greater personal happiness. The message *Glee* sends is that for LGBTQ youth, there is a race- and gender-neutral universalism—an even playing field when it comes to race and gender—and homosexuality is a uniting facet of identity that trumps all others.

The bullying Santana faces, on the other hand, is presented as much more limited, and thus more benign. After being outed, Santana is approached by a male rugby player who calls her "smokin'" and states that he views her as a challenge to "make normal." Although the other glee club girls rebut him, telling him that being a lesbian is not a choice—and that, even if it were, he would be her last choice—this reinforces essentialized notions of sexuality. As Rasmussen explains, sexual identities change and transform over time, yet *Glee* supports the dominant discourse that LGBTQ youth are simply "born this way"—a narrative reinforced in their episode "Born This Way," borrowing its title from the Lady Gaga song that has itself been called a "gay anthem." This example also underscores the heterosexual/homosexual binary and highlights that Santana never considered that she might be bisexual, even though she had many sexual relationships with men. Consequently, she is not only forced out of the closet by Finn but also forced into a binary that denies a possibility for a sexual identity that does not fit within those narrow confines. However, *Glee* only emphasizes Santana's brief encounter with her apparently heterosexual male bully in order to lead into a literal rendition of Katy Perry's "I Kissed a Girl"—a popular song, sure to sell iTunes singles the next day—and to segue into her sharing with the group that she came out to her accepting parents.

Thinking back to Kurt's own experience being kissed by Karofsky, both Kurt and Santana are sexually harassed, which serves to erase any racial or gender power differentials by showing that any LGBTQ-identifying person can be equally sexually objectified. If anything, because of the cumulative effect of his bullying, Kurt's experience is positioned as worse than Santana's and a sign that White males may actually be victimized *more*. Crenshaw argues that the importance of intersectionality is not to rank oppressions, but rather to understand the complexities and interactions of power on multiple levels. But, *Glee* takes the reductive approach, not only ranking, but giving the "disadvantage" to the privileged group. It is not suggested that Kurt is bullied *because* he is a White male but because he fits the hegemonic image of a gay teen and his storyline follows the popular narrative of LGBTQ bullying—and, significantly, because Santana does not—Whiteness and maleness retains the center. Gayness, and the harassment it entails, are presented as universalizing for LGBTQ youth, yet the gay White male character and story still take up a relative majority of the screen time and are positioned to elicit the bulk of the viewer's sympathy.

Additionally, *Glee* makes the suggestion that because Santana is a Latina who is strong-willed and a self-defined "bitch"—and those characteristics are tied to her racial/ethnic identity—she is immune from greater harassment. She is still drawn from various stereotypes, as she is the hot-headed and hyper-sexualized Latina that Isabel Molina-Guzmán describes, having been known to have sexual relationships with at least two of the boys and one of the girls in glee club, but in her post-racial construction those stereotypical traits are stripped of historical context and are attached to material advantages. In *Glee*'s post-racial world, Santana may be the "hot Latina," but this works only in her favor. As Molina-Guzmán and Angharad Valdivia argue, "Latina beauty and sexuality is marked as other, yet it is that otherness that also marks Latinas as desirable" (213). Santana becomes an object of desire to both men and women, though, not because she is Latina, but because she is "hot" and sexually aggressive. These characteristics are portrayed as natural, and are the reason she would receive any sexual harassment after she has come out of the closet. Her ability to also be a "straight-up bitch" is constructed as natural, as well, and it is this behavior that allows Santana to protect herself against unwanted advances. Unlike Kurt, who is shown to be scared and largely powerless against the larger jock Karofsky, Santana can use the aggressiveness and fiery personality she just "happens" to have in order to avoid prolonged and severe bullying and harassment. Of course, by not characterizing Finn's actions or Santana's near-suspension as acts of bullying in and of themselves, *Glee* promotes the idea that only homophobic, sexually motivated individuals can be bullies. The post-racial racialization of Santana makes sense, then, as her ability to use her natural behavior to protect herself. She just happens to be hot, fiery, and aggressive, while also happening to be Latina. The two parts are not joined, and the individual characteristics are presented as beneficial and positive, serving to neutralize any racial or gender differences.

However, this variation on the "positive stereotype," though decoupled from any systematic power, is nonetheless problematic. Rather than suggest that gay Latina women face specific forms of sexual and racial harassment and discrimination on both interpersonal and institutional levels, Santana's characterization and her placement in *Glee*'s narrative imply that she is able to fully protect herself and does not face much harassment to begin with. This frees up both resources within the show's fictional world and screen time on the show as a real-world production to instead devote to Kurt, which ultimately reprivileges those identities that are already culturally privileged, despite *Glee*'s claims to equality.

Conclusion

Although *Glee*'s viewership and critical acclaim are in decline, those drops can be attributed more to haphazard narrative choices and inconsistent characters than to the problematic discursive constructions of post-identity ideology. *Glee* has been and remains a bona fide cultural phenomenon, and apart from its iTunes singles, concert tours, and reality spin-offs, one of its most visible contributions to the cultural landscape has been its discourse and awareness-raising around LGBTQ issues. Many, including Don Gorton, have cited the existence of Kurt as a main character who is openly gay, as well as his subsequent relationship with Blaine Anderson (Darren Criss), as part of the show's main appeal and as positive forces in raising awareness about anti-gay bullying and coming out. However, while these may be positive characteristics of *Glee*, and valid reasons for its widespread embrace, because the series raises these issues within a front of liberalism and rights that garners mainstream praise and awards, it insulates itself from criticism regarding whose experiences are being substantively represented, and, consequently, whose are being left out.

By adopting a post-racial, post-gender ideological stance and discursively diminishing important intersectionalities, *Glee* ultimately maintains hegemonic ideas of culture, identity, and power. While it may deserve to be applauded for its efforts to resist the status quo, we must also resist its post-identity discourse and challenge the show's writers and producers to both recognize and demonstrate that there are, indeed, power differentials associated with collective group identity that continue to exist—although they are both gay, Santana and Kurt are no more the same than Rachel and Mercedes or Finn and Brittany. *Glee* may have a diverse cast, but in many ways, it is no better than those shows Vincent Brook describes as "lily white" if it pretends that differences across race, class, gender, sexuality, ability do not matter. Television is a powerful tool, but in *Glee*'s case, that power is being used to promote a false ideology under the guise of progressivism.

Note

1. I choose to use gay rather than queer throughout as a reflection of the show's own terminology—LGBTQ characters on *Glee* do not identify as queer, nor do others refer to them as such. Additionally, queer implies a more overt and conscious political orientation and while *Glee* as a cultural phenomenon does engage politically (e.g., It Gets Better), within the text it is more concerned with gayness as an indicator of sexual preference than as a sociocultural facet of identity.

References

Armstrong, Jennifer. "Gay Teens on TV." *Entertainment Weekly* 28 Jan. 2011: 34–41. Print.
"Born This Way." *Glee*. Fox. 26 April 2011. Television.
Britzman, Deborah P. "Is There a Queer Pedagogy? Or, Stop Reading Straight." *Educational Theory* 45.2 (1995): 151–65. Print.
Brook, Vincent. "Convergent Ethnicity and the Neo-Platoon Show: Recombining Difference in the Postnetwork Era." *Television & New Media* 10.4 (2009): 331–53. Print.
Cho, Sumi. "Post-Racialism." *Iowa Law Review* 94.5 (2009): 1589–1649. Print.
Collins, Patricia Hill. *Another Kind of Public Education: Race, Schools, the Media, and Democratic Possibilities*. Boston: Beacon, 2009. Print.
Crenshaw, Kimberlé. "Mapping the Margins: Intersectionality, Identity Politics, and Violence Against Women of Color." *Stanford Law Review* 43.6 (1991): 1241–99. Print.
Ferguson, Ann Arnett. *Bad Boys: Public Schools in the Making of Black Masculinity*. Ann Arbor: University of Michigan Press, 2000. Print.
Gorton, Don. "How Popular Culture Can Combat Bullying." *The Gay & Lesbian Review* 18.1 (2011): 4. Print.
Guinier, Lani. "From Racial Liberalism to Racial Literacy: *Brown v. Board of Education* and the Interest-Divergence Dilemma." *The Journal of American History* 91.1 (2004): 92–118. Print.
Hall, Stuart. *Representation: Cultural Representations and Signifying Practices*. London: Sage, 1997. Print.
"Heart." *Glee*. Fox. 14 Feb. 2012. Television.
"I Kissed a Girl." *Glee*. Fox. 29 Nov. 2011. Television.
It Gets Better Project. Savage Love, LLC, 2010–2012. Web. 8 May 2012.
Kellner, Douglas. *Media Culture: Cultural Studies, Identity and Politics Between the Modern and the Postmodern*. New York: Routledge, 1995. Print.
Kumashiro, Kevin K. *The Seduction of Common Sense: How the Right Has Framed the Debate on America's Schools*. New York: Teachers College, 2008. Print.

Lawrence, Charles R., III. "If He Hollers Let Him Go: Regulating Racist Speech on Campus." *Duke Law Journal* 1990.3 (1990): 431–83. Print.

"Mash Off." *Glee.* Fox. 15 Nov. 2011. Television.

McKee, Alan. *Textual Analysis: A Beginner's Guide.* Thousand Oaks, CA: Sage, 2003. Print. Molina-Guzmán, Isabel. *Dangerous Curves: Latina Bodies in the Media.* New York: New York University Press, 2010. Print.

Molina-Guzmán, Isabel, and Angharad N. Valdivia. "Brain, Brow, and Booty: Latina Iconicity in U.S. Popular Culture." *Communication Review* 7.2 (2004): 205–21. Print.

"Never Been Kissed." *Glee.* Fox. 9 Nov. 2010. Television.

Rasmussen, Mary Lou. "The Problem of Coming Out." *Theory Into Practice* 43.2 (2004): 144–50. Print.

Seitz, Matthew Zoller. "Can 'Glee' Be Saved?" *Salon.* Salon Media Group, Inc., 14 Feb. 2011. Web. 8 May 2012.

Snider, Kathryn. "Race and Sexual Orientation: The (Im)possibility of These Intersections in Educational Policy." *Harvard Educational Review* 66.2 (1996): 294–302. Print.

Storey, John. *Cultural Studies and the Study of Popular Culture: Theories and Methods.* Athens: University of Georgia Press, 1996. Print.

Defying Blackness

The E(race)ure of Mercedes Jones

ANITA M. DEROUEN

In the episode "Asian F," the *Glee* audience—both on screen and off—witnesses the final showdown between the group's two female vocal powerhouses: Rachel Berry and Mercedes Jones. Mercedes, tired of lingering in Rachel's shadow, decides to audition for the school's musical production of *West Side Story*, going head to head with Rachel for the lead role of Maria. When he happens upon two of the three co-directors of the musical discussing casting issues, Will Schuester, the director of the glee club, seems surprised to discover that Mercedes is even a contender for the role. This moment, remarkable for several reasons, reveals what can only be called a blind spot in Will's teaching when it comes to Mercedes. By the start of the third season, Mercedes is nearly invisible to Will, and their interactions revolve around her as a troublemaking presence, not as a key and original member of the club. It might be surprising to consider her this way until we look back to *Glee*'s first episode, "Pilot," where the audience sees Will's reactions to the auditions of each of the initial members of New Directions save one: Mercedes Jones. In Season 2's "Rocky Horror Glee Show," Will is unable—and unwilling— to conceive of Mercedes as an appropriate Dr. Frank-N-Furter. These and other moments may slip by unnoticed, but in light of Will's response to Emma and Shannon's casting dilemma in "Asian F," the absence of Will's reaction to Mercedes' initial audition becomes simply the first moment in a three-season string of erasures.

By the close of the third season, Mercedes, who in the first season referred to herself as "a strong black woman," has been defeated in her attempt to assert herself outside the context and confines of the safe mainstream glee community. No longer seeking a moment in the spotlight, Mercedes recedes into the safety of the competitive performance background. She's been defeated—soundly—by her former teammates, and while no reason is given for the defeat of the Trouble Tones in Season 3's "Hold Onto Sixteen," the implied one is that her best wasn't good enough to best the New Directions—even without Rachel. Mercedes competes on what appears to be the field of merit and loses. Were the field a fair one, we could perhaps see our way to a positive reading of this narrative, but as comparison of the narrative treatment of the two divas-in-training will demonstrate, merit is a mythical being. Her blackness, seen by Mercedes as a strength throughout Season 1, is implied over and over again to be a hindrance in a system that's stacked against her. In this essay, I examine the way in which the character's experience with a supposedly meritocratic system allows the show's writers and producers to uphold a veneer of equality in a system that is anything but equal. First, I establish the concept of merit as a necessary lens through which we need to view the various opportunities encountered by the characters. Next, I demonstrate how merit works to mask the problem of the race/ethnicity- gender intersection, resulting in the upholding of the supremacy of one white-reading female character. Finally, I examine the way that upholding this one character denies the claims of three women of color to the same.

Critical race theory's critique of liberalism pays particular attention to the concept of meritocracy, which Margaret Zamudio, et al., in *Critical Race Theory Matters: Education and Ideology* explains "assumes a level playing field where all individuals in society have an equal opportunity to succeed. [It] also assumes one's work ethic, values, drive, and individual attributes such as aptitude and intelligence, determine success or failure" (11). For the critical race theorist, the idea that people advance based on individual merit or "worth" is predicated on the notion that everyone begins at the same point—that, for lack of a better description, all babies are born to equal opportunity to prove their merit. Continued discussion and analysis of the deep-seated structural inequities in U.S. social, political, and economic life demonstrates that merit is at best an inspiring fiction and at worst a benevolent jailer for many who exist under the burden of centuries of oppression. One of its more deleterious effects is to uphold the promise of colorblindness, which can easily become the rallying cry of those who refuse to acknowledge or address the ongoing impact of racial discrimination that is cooked into the very systems often assumed to be level fields. In the educational system, merit and colorblindness afford politicians, administrators, instructors—and even parents and students—an easy way to turn a blind eye to the often overwhelming evidence of structural inequity (disparities in physical infrastructures, resource allocation, graduation and retention rates, test scores) and lay the failure of students of color to achieve directly at their feet.

Zamudio goes on to point out that

> while liberal educational reformers believe that education provides a means to equalize the disparities of wealth and poverty by providing individuals with the opportunity to compete and rise to their natural potentials, the Marxist perspective of Bowles and Gintis posits that schools in fact reproduce the inequalities of the broader society. The organization of schools into a hierarchy—the instruction of some pupils in technical and operational skills, the emphasis on obedience and authority, and the reproduction of the liberal ideology designed to accommodate the capitalist economy rather than to challenge it—structures education to serve the profit imperative of capitalism rather than to serve the egalitarian purpose of the personal development of students [18].

Turning momentarily to the subject of our analysis, we can easily consider the concept of structural inequity in relation the representation of the educational opportunities afforded to/expected for Mercedes and Rachel. By the end of Season 3, Rachel is off to hone her craft in the favored "high culture" arena, while Mercedes has been packaged and commodified, pursuing her education through "extension courses at UCLA" while working as a backup singer in a recording studio thanks to Sam's YouTube video ("Goodbye"). It took a village of teachers and students and parents to get Rachel on her way—an entire community galvanized to make her dreams come true—while it took one impoverished boy with a dream to support Mercedes in the pursuit of hers.

In addition to the cumulative effect of the structural inequities present,

> students of color are allowed to enter the classroom but never on an equal footing. When they walk in, they are subject to the same racial stereotypes and expectations that exist in the larger society. Students of color do not have the advantage of walking into a classroom as individuals; they walk in as black, brown, or red persons with all the connotations such racialization raises in the classroom [Zamudio 18].

Students of color can never forget that they are, indeed, students of color, and they are subjected to the same microaggressions[1] that plague persons of color on a daily basis. As Mercedes notes in Season 2's "Born This Way," "at this school, the thing that makes you different is the thing that people use to crush your spirit." Microaggressions serve as constant reminders of difference and, often, markers of inferiority. Even on a show like *Glee*, where the titular club is meant to be a safe haven for the marginalized performer, characters of color[2]—and, by extension, audience members of color as well—cannot escape these constant and unwelcome reminders of the inequalities plaguing contemporary life.[3]

The glee club operates on a thin veneer of meritocracy. From the outset, students sign up and audition for the club; that initial audition sequence introduces several of the club's initial members. Mercedes Jones is first to sign up for an audition, and hers is the first student voice the audience experiences as Will Schuester listens to the students' auditions. While the song that she sings, Aretha Franklin's "Respect," can serve as a theme for the club's narrative arc for all three of its seasons, it is Mercedes who is most vocal in her pursuit of respect for her voice and talent on what is supposed to be an equal playing field.

The audition sequence and the subsequent inaugural glee club performance establish key themes in the relationships between characters. After Mercedes's audition, we see Kurt Hummel's and Tina Cohen-Chang's auditions, each followed by a shot of Will's reaction to their performances. After Rachel introduces herself and her audition piece, Will says, "Fantastic. Let's hear it," and at the end of her audition and voiceover monologue, he affirms her performance, saying, "Very nice, Rachel." Later, after Rachel storms out of their first club rehearsal, Will appeals to her merit to bring her back ("You're the best kid in there, Rachel. That comes with a price"). What may be missed on first viewing is that the audience is not privy to Will's reaction to Mercedes; the audience is introduced to the character and hears her sing, but gets no response from Will, who at this moment functions as an audience identification character.

The hierarchy is thus established. During the first half of the first season, Rachel, Kurt, and Tina are each presented as possible front persons for the group (as potential soloists), while Mercedes' position is clearly established by the fifth episode, "The Rhodes Not Taken," where she performs as a member of the ensemble, providing the last—and amazing—note during the group's performance of Queen's "Somebody to Love." I might call what I'm doing here nitpicking, but further consideration of the interactions between Mercedes and Will in subsequent episodes in the first season suggest that this is just the beginning of things to come as he repeatedly puts off her requests for performance opportunities. In the first half of the first season, both Tina and Kurt are presented as potential soloists (in "Preggers" and "Wheels," respectively), while Mercedes' requests are put off or denied.

The students contest for the spotlight against the assertion of Rachel's merit, which is established when we first meet Rachel Berry in "Pilot." In a voiceover monologue, Rachel runs down the details of her preparation for a life of stardom; from her fathers' selection of "potential surrogates based on beauty and IQ" to her enrollment in a variety of artistic enrichment activities to her diligent use of whatever means available to "keep [her] talent alive and growing," it's clear that Rachel Berry has had—and taken—every advantage she could. Yes, she's lonely, friendless, and socially awkward, but there is no denying that Rachel's life—particularly her artistic life—has been one of privilege, and this privilege is what positions her to command the spotlight for the first three seasons of the show. In the glee club, Rachel can easily invoke the familiar narrative of merit; while that invocation is frequently met with friction from Will and the glee club members, the narrative arcs surrounding the majority of the competitive performance moments (particularly the Sectional, Regional, and National competitions) frequently operate to reinforce the idea that Rachel is the most deserving of featured performances because she's the hardest worker and, therefore, the most talented.[4]

In the end, Mercedes' conflict with Rachel and her merit are implicitly framed in the context of race. In "Asian F," Mercedes' expulsion from the club comes after an extended rant on her perception of Mr. Schuester's favoritism toward Rachel; the end result of that rant is a performance of "It's All Over" from *Dreamgirls*. This performance, framed as a dream sequence that Mercedes has during the argument, pits her against everyone in the club, highlighting the way in which her continued insistence on an opportunity to shine makes her feel as though she is marginalized inside of a group of the marginalized. From her lament that "Mr. Schue was supposed to love me" at the number's opening to her isolation on the stage at its close, the audience witnesses the cost of Mercedes' engagement with merit. While race is not a stated factor in the conflict at this point (having long been dropped as a vocally claimed identity marker for Mercedes), the placement of the scene in "Asian F," an episode otherwise overtly preoccupied with issues of racial identity and racism,[5] as well as the use of the song from *Dreamgirls* to dramatize Mercedes' exit from the group, brings race into the foreground as a significant element of both the cultural sphere in which she operates and her own perception of her experience in the community.

The *West Side Story* casting plot further exacerbates the race issue. Rachel references the role as "iconic" during the episode, and the dialogue between Will and the two teachers involved in casting the show, Emma and Shannon, suggests that she is the clear "fit," with Emma going so far as to note that "Rachel is Maria. Isn't she?" As Will discovers throughout the conversation, though, Rachel is no longer the prima facie or de facto

Maria because Mercedes' audition has disrupted the expected outcome. The audience witnesses the disruption for Will most clearly, as Mercedes has not registered in his mind as a contender, even though the character's intention to audition for the role is made clear in the choir room during the season's opening episode, "The Purple Piano Project." Emma's and Shannon's subsequent lines in the scene provide the rationale for the difficulty of their decision, and their conversation masks the issue of casting against type. Rachel "is Maria" in the most crudely visual sense; Lea Michele's long straight dark hair, olive complexion, and slender build more closely align her to Natalie Wood, the Maria most likely to occupy mainstream consciousness, than Amber Riley's curly hair, darker skin, and fuller body. That Shannon recognizes Mercedes as "the more exciting choice" further reinforces the idea that Rachel is the expected choice. In the end, Emma and Shannon, along with the third director, student Artie Abrams, decide to double-cast the role even after a callback audition where Rachel admits (to Finn) that "[Mercedes] was better." The audience watches as the system supposedly resting on merit gives way to privilege, and Mercedes is completely released from her ties to the glee club's structure. Throughout the episode, Mercedes is framed as the better performer, while Rachel's strength lies in her tenacity, her single-minded championing of her superiority, and her knowledge of the theatre and its casting conventions.

This episode has the potential to function as a turning point in the way the two characters are engaged and perceived by the students and teachers who come into contact with them, and to a limited extent, this is true: in subsequent episodes, the glee club laments Mercedes' departure ("Pot of Gold") and identifies her new group as a potential threat ("Pot of Gold," "Mash Off"). While Will refuses to acknowledge Mercedes' importance to the group, the audience and Finn witness his shocked and concerned response to the first Trouble Tones performance ("Pot of Gold"). In the end, however, the Trouble Tones prove only a pseudo-threat to New Directions in the Sectionals competition as they lose, and while the end result of the arc is that the Trouble Tones are welcomed back into the group with the promise of a featured spotlight in future competition performances, this move further relegates Mercedes—along with Santana and Brittany—to ensemble roles while Rachel continues to receive solo performance spots in competition in deference to her supposed merit.

While Santana's departure provides another example of a woman of color leaving New Directions to chase greener performance pastures, Tina Cohen-Chang's blowup in "Props" most clearly reveals the extent of the show's narrative investment in upholding Rachel's merit. At the start of the episode, the audience sees Rachel making the latest in an alarming number of phone calls to Carmen Tibideaux, the recruiter from the fictitious New York Academy of the Dramatic Arts (NYADA) who denied Rachel admission to the school after she choked during her audition ("Choke"). Rachel's focus on getting into this program is presented as her destiny, and she pursues the program in the face of denial with a zeal that hearkens back to the first episodes of the first season. Tina, tired of continually being relegated to the background, challenges the group assumption that Rachel will perform a solo at Nationals and makes a move to leave the group; like Mercedes and Santana before her, Tina is tired of being in Rachel's shadow. After Tina walks out, Mike confronts her, calling her "selfish" for demanding the spotlight and suggesting that "[she'll] get [her] chance next year" ("Props").

Hot on Mike's heels is Rachel, who initially offers Tina a bribe to "let this all go until after Nationals." When Tina refuses, Rachel follows up with an appeal to the familiar narrative of hard work and merit and echoes Mike's argument that "[she'll] have [her] chance next year" ("Props"). On the surface this seems like a reasonable request, particularly when one considers the grade-related hierarchical structure of the U.S. high school; student organizations are frequently led by senior members, with the baton being passed on to the next group in line once those students graduate. On closer inspection, though—and when we factor in the intersectional complications of race—the idea that Rachel is somehow more deserving of this moment, that because "[her] entire future depends on [them] being amazing" the team members must sublimate their individual wants and desires to help her achieve her dream, we may begin to wonder whether merit is a raw deal for anyone who doesn't identify as white ("Props").

And so we arrive at a consideration of the complications of communicating across multiple identity positions. Intersection theory, a key component of black feminist thought, insists upon examining the interlocking and often tangled web of marginalizing forces at play when agents of varying racial or ethnic backgrounds interact. While the theory was initially posited and is frequently used to draw attention to inequity in the marginalization of the concerns of women of color in matters of jurisprudence, social justice, and violence against women, intersection theory can also prove instrumental in helping readers and viewers articulate the intricacies of the narrative representations of interracial relations. As Kimberle Crenshaw argues in "Mapping the Margins: Intersectionality, Identity Politics, and Violence against Women of Color," "[the] focus on the intersections of race and gender only highlights the need to account for multiple grounds of identity when considering how the social world is constructed" (1245). Crenshaw urges us to resist the impulse to flatten identity along binary oppositions and, when engaging issues of cultural representation, to "[consider] the ways in which ... images are produced through a confluence of prevalent narratives of race and gender" (1283). Crenshaw's work engages the very real ramifications of identity intersection in the legal sphere, and her recognition of the role of cultural representation in the continued oppression of marginalized groups underscores the importance of attendance to that representation in order to effect meaningful cultural change.[6] Its diverse cast and educational setting in many ways makes *Glee* an ideal spot for just this sort of dialogue at identity intersections.

Unfortunately, *Glee* habitually splits conversations that might be productively held across intersectional lines. One such conversation deals with the issue of non-conventional casting; on two separate occasions (Season 2's "The Rocky Horror Glee Show" and Season 3's "I Am Unicorn"/"Asian F"), the show explicitly engages the issue of casting against expected type in the storyline associated with Kurt while almost loudly ignoring the same issue in the storyline associated with Mercedes. While the intent may be that the explicit conversation surrounding one (the white gay male) will naturally apply to the situation of the other (the black straight female), as Crenshaw notes, "when one discourse fails to acknowledge the significance of the other, the power relations that each attempts to challenge are strengthened" (1282). When we look at the audience's experience of the commercial and televised representation of the school production of *West Side Story*, this is most certainly the case; while on screen they auditioned for the lead roles of Tony and Maria, neither Chris Colfer nor Amber Riley performed or recorded any of the songs from the musical; instead, all performances and commercial releases from the musical songbook are performed by those actors actually cast on screen in those roles. The audience is invited to imagine these actors/characters in these roles (called "iconic" by Rachel Berry in "Asian F"), but the narrative refuses to give either an aural or visual referent to explicitly serve or support that possibility. That Kurt has an actual conversation with his father about the casting situation further erases Mercedes' blackness; we witness Kurt struggling with the connection between his identity and desired roles before coming to his own decision about the sorts of roles he will pursue and are denied a similar moment for Mercedes, the narrative choosing to leave her non-traditional casting story in the realm of the on-going conflict between her and Rachel.[7] The silence surrounding the questions Mercedes poses during "Asian F"—about Rachel's supposed merit, about the powers-that-be's reluctance or refusal to "hurt her feelings" by denying her what she demands—deafens after the previous episode's treatment of Kurt's similar narrative. In a cultural moment where we see a decline in representation of racial minorities in mainstream television, the absence of dialogue about casting against expected type solely in the case of the black character renders the problem of black cultural representation invisible.[8]

The erosion of Mercedes' claim to her black identity begins early in the first season. In the episode "Throwdown," Sue Sylvester uses marginalized identity categories to divide the glee club as part of her plan to destroy them from within. After escalating the division to the point that only three of the twelve club members—one white male, one white female, and one white-presenting Jewish female—remain, Sue and Will have a heated and personal argument in front of the students. Finn halts the argument, and Mercedes follows up.

> Finn: Enough. I'm sorry, Mr. Schue, Ms. Sylvester, but if we wanted to hear mom and dad fight, those of us who still have two parents would just stay home on payday.
> Mercedes: I agree. Glee Club is supposed to be fun. And furthermore, I don't like this minority business. I may be a strong, proud, black woman, but I'm a lot more than that ["Throwdown"].

The end of Mercedes' identity statement—"but I'm a lot more than that"—is exemplar of the type of self-identification that Crenshaw finds problematic, the statement serving to "[achieve] self-identification by straining for a certain universiality ... and for a concomitant dismissal of the imposed category ("Black") as contingent, circumstantial, nondeterminant" (1297). While Crenshaw's analysis affirms the validity of these types of identity statements, she correctly points out that "the most critical resistance strategy for disempowered groups is to occupy and defend a politics of social location rather than to vacate and destroy it" (1297). Sue's plan to divide and conquer doesn't work in the manner she intends it to, and it further serves to explicitly render Mercedes' blackness a non-issue as the narrative progresses. I specify Mercedes' blackness here because other characters—particularly Santana and Tina—more readily call out racist and ethnically biased or demeaning circumstances, while Mercedes' blackness diminishes as an explicit point of identity.

With a better understanding of what is at stake when we consider multiple identity positions in conversation, we return to "Props" to see how lack of consideration of intersectionality coupled with merit and colorblindness serves to detrimentally erase the unique experiences of the marginalized. After her initial argument with Rachel, Tina falls and hits her head, sparking a dream where everyone in the glee club has switched places and she is now Rachel. In her dream, Tina gets a solo—as Rachel and only in her head—and the experience leads her to help Rachel convince Carmen Tibideaux to give her another chance at her failed audition. When we take into account the racial and ethnic subject positions of the three women involved in the conversation, we can begin to understand the importance of attention to the intersections. After accepting her proper place in the hierarchy, Asian American Tina pleads with African American Carmen to give White/Jewish Rachel yet another chance to prove herself worthy of the desired prize. Tina's plea leads to White/Jewish Rachel reminding African American Carmen that she, too, had to continually knock on doors to get her start, the show itself all the while missing or ignoring the elephant in the room—that Carmen Tibideaux's journey to stardom must have begun in a far less advantaged place than Rachel's privileged one, and that Rachel must rely on the appeal of the marginalized to the marginalized to get another chance. Given the missed opportunity of Mercedes' failed audition in "Asian F," this moment could have served—in a small way—to do for blackness what episodes like "The Spanish Teacher," "Wheels," and Kurt's coming out storyline, did for other marginalized groups. Instead, the appeal works and upholds the narrative of Rachel's merit: Carmen comes to Nationals to give Rachel one more audition, and Rachel performs her solo in the middle of an otherwise fairly well-blended display of the group strength of the glee club and secures her spot at NYADA.

The cumulative weight of three seasons of this narrative trajectory[9]—the elevation of Rachel over other voices in the club—makes Tina's intervention with Carmen Tibideaux (not to mention the narrative elements employed to orchestrate that plea) ring false. The concept of merit as the deciding factor in the allocation of scarce educational/performance resources is appealing, but this concept is a myth. Merit operates as the central narrative means for upholding Rachel as the star performer, but in ways both explicit and implicit, Rachel's actual merit is continually called into question. Tina's plea to Carmen on Rachel's behalf can just as easily be seen, then, as a plea to entitlement, the idea that because Rachel works hard she deserves yet another opportunity to prove her merit. Tina's eventual acceptance of her "proper place" in the glee club hierarchy now that she's accepted Rachel's claim to hard-work-as-evidence-of-merit helps to maintain the myth of meritocracy, locating Tina's frustration in the less valid emotions of jealously and impatience. Tina's failure to secure a solo or spotlight, then, is hers and hers alone; to prove her merit, she must acquiesce and be patient.

Santana Lopez and Mercedes Jones, on the other hand, are anything but acquiescing or patient, but by the close of the third season, they, too, have given in to Rachel's supremacy. For both women, the move to the Trouble Tones means that their opportunities for the spotlight in competitive performances are confined to the spotlight they can take in their own subgroup. Santana, Mercedes, and Brittany only return to New Directions on the condition that the Trouble Tones—the group, not the individuals—will be featured in subsequent competitions. By the time the team performs at Nationals, the Trouble Tones have made room for both Tina and Quinn, essentially making them the New Directions' girls choir—absent Rachel Berry, who must, of course, have a solo with which she can revisit her failed audition. That Santana, Mercedes, and Tina are happy with this arrangement—an arrangement that essentially returns them to their starting places as part of the ensemble, albeit an ensemble of their own making—and are willing to cede the spotlight to Rachel so that she can pursue her dreams suggests that they, too, see the supremacy of Rachel's merit over their own.

It may be easier to understand Santana's willingness to stand aside; her public outing in Season 3's "Mash Off" combined with her featured performance in Season 2's "Special Education" and the lack of an expressed desire to make a name for herself in vocal music make a compelling argument for a simple lack of genuine investment in her stated desire to have that particular spotlight shine in her direction. By "Saturday Night Glee-ver," it's clear that Santana is interested in fame but hasn't identified a particular domain in which she'd like to be famous. Mercedes' situation is more complicated.

For Mercedes, the quest for the spotlight necessitates a battle with Rachel on the false field of merit. From their first glee club rehearsal, Rachel's actions frame the performance space through a lens of heterosexual, able-bodied white superiority.[10] While the happy band of misfits who constitute the club present a buffet of diversity for the mainstream viewing audience, the story at the heart of the narrative primarily centers on the white and/or the straight. In the end, to merit stardom in the group, Mercedes has to somehow overcome that which makes her other to Rachel—her race, her physical size, and, to a lesser extent, her gender. This transcendence is impossible due to what Patricia Hill Collins terms "dichotomous oppositional difference," the characters' whiteness and blackness "invariably [implying a relationship] of superiority and inferiority" (S20). No matter how good she is, Mercedes can never be "not black" and the narrative's continued insistence upon Rachel's merit upholds this unequal difference. As the audience experiences it, then, the story of Mercedes' high school experience demands she submit to an erasure and sublimation of self under the guise of finding a "place" where she can engage starring roles. The end result is the character's movement from "loud and proud" claims to her black identity; to questions about the connection between that identity and her failure to advance; and to a final acceptance of her supporting role when she eschews traditional higher education to pursue an offered spot as a studio backup singer. This transformation is framed as a maturing of her character, the "sassy" diva peddling a white-imagined "blackness" early in Season 1 finally giving way to a more subdued young woman for whom race is no longer an expressed identity marker.[11] As her quest for the spotlight further enmeshes her in the trap of meritocracy, Mercedes becomes, if not colorblind, color-silent, a silence that denies both the character and the audience an opportunity to see the sham of equal opportunity at play before their eyes.

As I close, I'm struck by the way in which Mercedes recedes into the background within the confines of my own essay; as I've written and structured this argument, I've found it difficult—if not impossible—to carve out a space of her own. Perhaps it is a testament to *Glee*'s ability to so deftly interweave the plotlines involving its ensemble cast that I cannot gather enough distance to focus solely on Mercedes, but I'm reluctant to let go so easily. Instead, I believe the difficulty of isolating Mercedes in this discussion is indicative of the way in which her character never fully emerges from the confines of the group. Even when she is most isolated, to understand her isolation we must engage with her role in the group dynamic.

Notes

1. I draw from Derald Wing Sue et al.'s work in clinical psychology to define racial microaggressions as "brief, everyday exchanges that send denigrating messages to people of color because they belong to a racial minority group" (273). Sue's work identifies three types of microaggression: microassault ("an explicit racial derogation characterized primarily by a verbal or nonverbal attack meant to hurt the intended victim through name-calling, avoidant behavior, or purposeful discriminatory actions" [274]); microinsult ("characterized by communications that convey rudeness and insensitivity and demean a person's racial heritage or identity" [274]); and microinvalidation ("characterized by communications that exclude, negate, or nullify the psychological thoughts, feelings, or experiential reality of a person of color" [274]).

2. At this point I should note that while my analysis hews to issues of race and, briefly, ethnicity, many of these arguments could easily be extended to address the variety of discriminatory statements and microaggressions faced by characters in other marginalized groups. Given the scope of this essay, however, I wish to maintain a clear focus on one particular marginalization.

3. In "Throwdown," for example, the audience witnesses the following exchange:

WILL: As we head into Sectionals I wanna get some feedback. Like, what kinda stuff you guys would like to be doing. Is there anything, any music in particular that you guys wanna do? Mercedes: Could we maybe try something a little more ... black?

KURT: I agree, we do an awful lot of showtunes. Rachel: It's glee club, not crunk club.

MERCEDES: (to Rachel) Don't make me take you to the carpet

WILL: (over Mercedes) Fantastic. Thank you, Mercedes, Kurt. Duly noted. Anything else? Mike: [raising hand] I can pop and lock.

WILL: [looks at ceiling] Not really what we're going for, Mike, but noted. Noted, yes.

This exchange exemplifies a typical set of character interactions: Will presents an openness to difference while denying the requests of students of color, Rachel maintains the supremacy of showtunes (as representative of high culture and being of the greatest merit) while denigrating other genres of music, in this case categorizing Mercedes' request to do something "more black" with crunk, her tone suggesting cultural inferiority. Later in this same episode, Will categorizes the song performed by "Sue's kids" (Jill Scott's "Hate On Me") as a song about hate, demonstrating his surface level misunderstanding of a song clearly seeking to empower the marginalized.

4. Even in moments where the narrative might productively question Rachel's merit—like Rachel's decision to eliminate another woman of color, Sunshine Corazon, from competition for the spotlight by sending her to an (admittedly inactive) crack house (2.1 "Audition")—the exposure of the tenuous nature of Rachel's merit is quickly covered up by the narrative's return to assert her supremacy.

5. In "Asian F," we meet Emma Pillsbury's "ginger supremacist" parents and Mike Chang's parents, his father a doctor with high expectations for his son's future path, his mother Mike's secret supporter as she can relate to his desire to follow his talents and dreams. Mike Chang's father is the one who invokes the term "Asian F," thereby giving license to the show's white writers/producers to use the term—which could be read as a positive and yet derogatory stereotype—for the episode's title. Interwoven with these two plotlines is the main one—Mercedes' challenge to Rachel's assumed position as the lead in the school musical, *West Side Story*.

6. Sociologists have demonstrated that lack of attention to intersection theory in real-world quantitative studies can underplay the importance of the intersection. Two such studies are Seth Ovadia's "Race, Class, and Gender Differences in High School Seniors' Values: Applying Intersection Theory in Empirical Analysis" and Marla H. Kohlman's "Intersection Theory: A More Elucidating Paradigm of Quantitative Analysis."

7. Tina Cohen-Chang's acknowledgment and seeming acceptance of only ever having a chance at lead roles clearly identified as Asian females further supports my argument that the absence of conversation in the particular case of Mercedes' blackness serves to further hide the problem of black representation in the media ("Asian F").

8. Lee H. Rachel cites data gathered from the Screen Actors Guild demonstrating that "the number of jobs for nonwhite actors dropped to 27.5 percent of total roles cast in 2008 from a high of 29.3 percent in 2007" with African Americans "[losing] the most ground."

9. Three women of color challenge Rachel for featured performance spots. In Season 1, Mercedes is chosen as the first soloist—by the group when Will is barred from coaching the club—but gives up her solo in favor of Rachel when the team discovers that Sue has shared their set list with an opposing team ("Sectionals"). In Season 2, Santana Lopez gets a solo spotlight performance—without having to audition—when Emma suggests to Will that his performance lineups are becoming stale and predictable (2.9 "Special Education"). Tina is featured—though not as soloist—during Season 3's "Hold on to Sixteen" due to Rachel's suspension from school for stuffing a ballot box (3.8). Each of these moments occur at the Sectionals competition, the first in the established road to the National stage. By locating the spotlight performances for the "also-rans" at this stage where the competition is, in theory, weaker and more local, the narrative creates a space to highlight less frequently heard voices while reserving the more plum competitive performance spots for Rachel (during Regional and National competitions). That the New

Directions go head to head against the Troubletones in this particular moment of competition, then, combined with the other narrative machinations—Will's teaching suspension, Emma's intervening suggestions, Rachel's suspension—reinforces the idea that Rachel is the assumed lead soloist for the group and any deviation from the norm will only occur due to outside intervention and/or extraordinary circumstances.

After the group's rehearsal of "Sit Down, You're Rocking the Boat," Rachel questions Will's decision to give the lead solo to "the boy in the wheelchair." This question—perhaps meant to make a joke about the fact that Artie is already sitting—also suggests that Artie's disability makes him unfit to have the solo in the song. This reading is reinforced by the group's later rehearsal of "The One That I Want," where Rachel comically eliminates every other in the group (Kurt, Tina, and Mercedes) by physically pushing them away as she makes her way across the stage to Finn ("Pilot"). That the remaining members of the club at this point are each in some way other—Mercedes is black, Kurt is gay, Tina is Asian—indicates that Rachel should be the clear lead soloist in the group.

In fact, by the third season, references to blackness are more likely to be made by one of Mercedes' two love interests; Shane Tinsley makes reference to "cocoa babies" ("The Purple Piano Project") and Sam Evans strips under the moniker "White Chocoloate" ("Hold on to Sixteen") and asks Mercedes if her refusal to date him is "because [he's] white" ("Yes/No").

References

"Asian F." *Glee: The Complete Third Season*. Writ. Ian Brennan. Dir. Alfonso Gomez-Rejon. 20th Century–Fox, 2012. DVD.

"Born This Way." *Glee: The Complete Second Season*. Writ. Brad Falchuk. Dir. Alfonso Gomez-Rejon. 20th Century–Fox, 2011. DVD.

"Choke." *Glee: The Complete Third Season*. Writ. Marti Noxon. Dir. Michael Uppendahl. 20th Century–Fox, 2012. DVD.

Collins, Patricia Hill. "Learning from the Outsider Within: The Sociological Significance of Black Feminist Thought." *Social Problems* 33.6 (1986): S14-S32. Print.

Crenshaw, Kimberle. "Mapping the Margins: Intersectionality, Identity Politics, and Violence against Women of Color." *Stanford Law Review* 43 (1991): 1241–1299. Print.

"Goodbye." *Glee: The Complete Third Season*. Writ. Brad Falchuk. Dir. Brad Falchuk. 20th Century–Fox, 2012. DVD.

"Hold on to Sixteen." *Glee: The Complete Third Season*. Writ. Ross Maxwell. Dir. Bradley Buecker. 20th Century–Fox, 2012. DVD.

Kohlman, Marla H. "Intersection Theory: A More Elucidating Paradigm of Quantitative Analysis." *Race, Gender & Class* 13.3–4 (2006): 42–59. Print

"Mash Off." *Glee: The Complete Third Season*. Writ. Michael Hitchcock. Dir. Eric Stoltz. 20th Century–Fox, 2012. DVD.

Ovadia, Seth. "Race, Class, and Gender Differences in High School Seniors' Values: Applying Intersection Theory in Empirical Analysis." *Social Science Quarterly* 82.2 (2001):340–356. Print.

"Pilot." *Glee: The Complete First Season*. Writ. Ryan Murphy, Brad Fulchuk, and Ian Brennan. Dir. Ryan Murphy. 20th Century–Fox, 2011. DVD.

"Pot of Gold." *Glee: The Complete Third Season*. Writ. Ali Adler. Dir. Adam Shankman. 20th Century–Fox, 2012. DVD.

"Props." *Glee: The Complete Third Season*. Writ. Ian Brennan. Dir. Ian Brennan. 20th Century–Fox, 2012. DVD.

Rachel, Lee H. "Minorites Lose Ground." *New York Times* 26 Oct 2009: C2. Web.

"The Rhodes Not Taken." *Glee: The Complete First Season*. Writ. Ian Brennan. Dir. John Scott. 20th Century–Fox, 2011. DVD.

"Rocky Horror Glee Show." *Glee: The Complete Second Season*. Writ. Ryan Murphy and Tim Wollaston. Dir. Adam Shankman. 20th Century–Fox, 2011. DVD.

"Special Education." *Glee: The Complete Second Season*. Writ. Brad Falchuk. Dir. Paris Barclay. 20th Century–Fox, 2011. DVD.

Sue, Derald Wing, et al. "Racial Microaggressions in Everyday Life: Implications for Clinical Practice." *American Psychologist* 62.4 (2007): 271–286. Print.

"Throwdown." *Glee: The Complete First Season*. Writ. Brad Falchuk. Dir. Ryan Murphy. 20th Century–Fox, 2011. DVD.

"Yes/No." *Glee: The Complete Third Season*. Writ. Ross Maxwell. Dir. Eric Stoltz. 20th Century–Fox, 2012. DVD.

Zamudio, Margaret, et al. *Critical Race Theory Matters: Education and Ideology*. New York: Routledge, 2011. Print.

"We're all freaks together"

White Privilege and Mitigation of Queer Community

M. Shane Grant

To borrow from the logos of Facebook, "Shane Grant is in a relation-ship with *Glee* and it's complicated." I love to hate it, and I hate that I love it. My ambivalence about *Glee* stems from the show's representations of LGBTQ youth. I admire *Glee* for the frequency with which it includes and often foregrounds storylines dealing with issues faced by young queers: coming out, outing, bullying, dating, and even sex. I also appreciate the program's most prominent theme—the battle of the underdog, made apparent by their signature song: Journey's "Don't Stop Believing." Without question, the club's diversity contributes to the underdog theme. At the time of this writing (three episodes into Season 4) nineteen characters inhabiting fictional McKinley High have, at some point or another, par-ticipated in glee club. Those nineteen include characters who are Jewish (Rachel and Puck), Asian (Mike and Tina), black (Mercedes, Wade/Unique, and Matt), Latina (Santana), disabled (Artie), fat (Lauren), gay (Kurt, Blaine, and Wade), lesbian (Santana), bisexual (Brittany), and transgen-dered (Wade/Unique). The straight, white, able-bodied glee club members (Finn, Sam, Quinn, Sugar, Joe, and Marley) constitute less than one-third of New Directions' population since the show began airing in fall 2009.

Indeed, the glee club consists of so many different categories of "oth-ers" that it becomes easy to view New Directions as a queer community—perhaps too easy. Despite all this seeming diversity there are still a lot of white people in that glee club. Yes, the show contains representations of four minority categories: race, disability, sexuality, and body size. However, the gay, disabled, and fat characters are all, with only one exception, white. The fact that almost all the othered characters exist from only one minority identity position provides much of what I find so frustrating with *Glee*: the white racial identity of the non race-based minorities effectively undercuts the queer potential of the glee club's community. I build my case first by examining how New Directions can be read as a queer community; I then move on to illuminate that whiteness serves to make non-white, othered characters less threatening to a mainstream audience by refusing multiple identity positions to characters of color; and I end my discussion by examining how *Glee* uses whiteness as a force to produce an assimilationist, anti-queer docility (in the Foucauldian sense of the term) within the queer characters of New Directions.

In his 1999 book *The Trouble With Normal: Sex, Politics, and the Ethics of Queer Life*, queer studies scholar Michael Warner reveals that the term queer need apply not only to individuals or communities of sexual/gender difference. Warner points out that "queer scenes are the true *salons des refusés*, where the most heterogeneous people are brought into great intimacy by their common experience of being despised and rejected in a world of norms that they now recognize as false morality" [emphasis Warner] (35–6). According to Warner queer communities consist of heterogeneous people, which certainly applies to the variously othered students of New Directions. Diversity alone does not constitute queer community, however. In addition to heterogeneity, the individuals that comprise the queer community experience an intimate knowledge of each other not based solely on sexual difference but rather their rejection of normative ideals. This rejection of normative ideals in no small part contributes to the queer community's commitment to inclusion that supports heterogeneity.

The students in New Directions attitudes and actions (both individually and collectively) often contribute to strategies of inclusion that force students to confront hegemonic forces. For example, in the ninth episode of Season 1, "Wheels," school officials refuse to pay the extra fees for a wheelchair accessible school bus, requiring Artie find alternate transportation to a competition. At first, his classmates see no problem with Artie traveling separately, chauffeured by his father. However, after being forced by their teacher, Mr. Schuester, to use wheelchairs three hours a day for a week, and learning the choreography to a musical number performed entirely in wheelchairs, the students receive a small taste of how often Artie finds himself excluded from the group's day-to-day activities.

Although the students participate in an offensive bit of disability tourism that nowhere nearly communicates an accurate experience of disability, their enlightenment leads them to raise funds for the accessible school bus rental, and– perhaps more significantly—call upon school administration to improve wheelchair access throughout the school's facilities ("Wheels").

We see another example that supports the notion of queer inclusivity in one of the numerous times Kurt finds himself bullied and harassed at school. In Season 1, Episode 20, "Theatricality," Mr. Schuester wants group members to embrace their individuality, so he instructs them to find a song by Lady Gaga that they feel expresses themselves. While in Gaga drag, Kurt draws the ire of then-closeted David Karofsky and another football player, who threaten to beat him up in a bathroom. This storyline coincides with Finn discovering that he and his mother will move in with the man she's been dating (Kurt's single father, Burt). Clearly uncomfortable living under the same roof with Kurt, Finn finally explodes when Kurt reveals their ornately redecorated shared bedroom. During Finn's rant against Kurt's "faggy" décor, Burt storms in to protect his son from Finn's homophobic vitriol. Finn lamely defends himself by stating that calling Kurt's decor "faggy" is not the same thing as calling Kurt a fag. Burt cuts Finn off, acknowledging his own (Burt's) youthful homophobic attitudes. Burt's discussion of his own homophobia successfully forces Finn to realize and admit that his (Finn's) language is hateful, hurtful, and used with the purpose of oppression. Finn, who initially refused to participate in the Lady Gaga assignment, embodies his newfound outlook by donning a red plastic dress and, with the help of his fellow Gaga-bedecked members of New Directions, defends Kurt when the bullies attack a second time. After fending off the threat, Finn overtly acknowledges the queerness of the group, stating, "We're all freaks together" ("Theatricality"). As was the case with Artie's accessibility needs, the club pulls together in staunch support of their individual differences.

Queerness also exits in opposition to fixed, normative traditions. As queer theorist David Halperin explains in his 1997 book *Saint Foucault: Towards a Gay Hagiography*, "Queer is by definition whatever is at odds with the normal, the legitimate, the dominant. There is nothing in particular to which it necessarily refers. It is an identity without an essence. 'Queer,' then, demarcates not a positivity but a positionality vis-à-vis the normative" (62). This lack of particularity Halperin identifies directly contributes to decentered, unstable aspects of queerness. New Directions demonstrates its queer instability through the unfixed, fluid nature of its membership. When the show began in 2009, the glee club consisted of only five students: Rachel, Mercedes, Artie, Kurt, and Tina; Finn joined them by the end of the first episode. Because "official" rules dictate, as part of the show's fiction, that clubs must consist of at least twelve members in order to compete, we see new members join the club for various reasons over the next few episodes. Finn convinces three of his fellow football players to sign on under the guise that "chicks dig dudes who can sing" ("Showmance"). Additionally, the school's cheerleading coach, Sue Sylvester (who openly seeks the glee club's destruction), instructs three of her cheerleaders to join the group so they can act as spies. Toward the middle of the first season Finn quits days before the first sectionals competition when a love triangle between himself, Quinn, and Puck explodes.[1] One member short of the required twelve, a random student, Jacob, agrees to join on the condition that all he has to do is mouth the words, stand in the back, and sway.

Season 2 begins with the loss of one of the football players, Matt, and introduces a new student, Sam, who takes Matt's place on the football team and in glee club. Next, Kurt leaves when he transfers to a private school in reaction to escalating bullying at the hand of David Karofsky ("Furt"). Lauren Zizes, the "fat girl," fills Kurt's spot. Shortly before the second season ends, Kurt returns to McKinley High, restoring the group's openly gay contingent. At the beginning of the third season Quinn has quit, but quickly returns to, New Directions as part of a brief rebellious bout signified by her pink hair and goth-esque attire. Quinn's rebellion plays a part in Santana leaving the club for two episodes when Quinn throws a lit cigarette on a purple piano the Cheerios doused with lighter fluid. Mr. Schuester blames the fire on Santana, who claims responsibility for the vandalism in the name of "political protest" ("The Purple Piano Project"). In the same episode, Lauren announces her departure from the club, disappearing from the show's narrative entirely. "Asian F," Season 3's third episode, shows a frustrated Mercedes breaking from New Directions to found a new all-girl glee club, the Trouble Tones, a group that will ultimately also include Santana, Brittany, and the new character, Sugar Motta. The fourth episode recoups those losses in part by introducing another new character, Irish exchange student Rory Flanagan. After defeating the Trouble Tones at sectionals, New Directions absorbs the group. The only other major change to membership before the third season finale occurs when Sam returns halfway through the season, having left McKinley High and Lima while his parents struggled with unemployment. The last episode of the season, "Graduation," provides the most recent major shake-up of New Directions' membership, the permanent departure of graduating seniors Rachel, Finn, Santana, Mercedes, Kurt, Puck, and Mike.[2]

Looking beyond already-aired episodes, it appears the club's membership will remain in flux for Season 4 with new additions to compensate for the loss of the graduated seniors. Such instability of membership requires the students to continually alter, adjust, and renegotiate their relationship and position within a constantly destabilized organization. The frequent comings and goings of students also reinforces the group's queer inclusivity— with only two exceptions, no student is ever thrown out or denied membership, yet new additions are always welcome.[3]

Although the fluctuating membership and student commitment to defending difference do work toward building queer community, the choice to cast the non-race-based minorities predominantly with white actors undercuts the sense of inclusiveness as well as the queer destabilization created by the club's population shifts. In the introduction to his seminal book *Reading the Popular*, media scholar John Fiske points out that successful media in pop culture simultaneously contain progressive ideologies while reflecting traditional norms (2). Fiske goes on to claim that "popular culture is the culture of the subordinate who resent their subordination" (7). We certainly see characters from underrepresented groups resent their subordination throughout *Glee*, yet in order to achieve mainstream success the show's writers and producers must temper the resentment so as not to alienate too many viewers. In short, the progressive aspects of the show must be made, to some degree, safe and familiar. *Glee* achieves this familiarity by allowing only the white characters in the glee club to possess identity positions in addition to their race. With only one exception, the students in New Directions marked by race find themselves denied the opportunity to identify with and look from more than one minority perspective. The show allows characters to be white and gay, white and disabled, and white and fat, but *Glee* does not afford such multiplicity to characters made different by race.[4]

In his foundational book *White: Essays on Race and Culture*, film scholar Richard Dyer addresses issues of visibility in representation, pointing out the obvious that "being white is a passport to privilege" (44). Dyer goes on to illuminate a paradox, stating, "visual culture demands that whites can be seen by whites. Yet there is a problem with such visualization ... whiteness also needs to be not visible" (44). Since the majority of the television audience is white (for another decade or two, anyway) white characters must be present for viewing while their whiteness continues to go unacknowledged. This unremarkable quality of whiteness affords characters the opportunity to become marked with an additional identity category (such as disability, sexuality, or body size). Even though the characters are white and gay or white and disabled, whiteness affords viewers the opportunity to see only a disabled or abject sexual identity. As Dyer points out,

> In Western representation whites are overwhelmingly and disproportionately predominant.... Yet precisely because of this and their placing as norm they seem not to be represented to themselves as whites but as people who are variously gendered, classed, sexualized, and abled [3].

So, if the character isn't white and something else, they are only something else—gay, disabled, or fat (in terms of the characters in New Directions). Furthermore, the presence of an "other" identity position renders their whiteness even less visible, making the character comprehensible within a single identity category. In making their identity singular (and not white), the othered character becomes less threatening to mainstream audiences because they can be easily categorized and comprehended. In becoming so easily categorized characters lose some of their queer potential to exist in opposition to traditions and norms.

However, for viewers who see the white characters' whiteness, and in instances such as this one right now where white identity becomes the subject of scrutiny, any white characters who have the opportunity to also look from a non-racial minority position become what I call "white and...." They can be seen and examined as white and disabled, or white and fat, and so on. In the introduction to *Postcolonial Whiteness: A Critical Reader on Race and Empire* (2005) postcolonial English scholar Alfred J. Lopez points out that regardless of which branch of postcolonial theory an individual subscribes to, there is a common goal among each branch: "critiquing the privilege and power associated with whiteness, and exposing the ways in which whiteness has historically been used to suppress and marginalize its others" (2). Interestingly, "white and..." representation suppresses and marginalizes both its racial and non-white others. The whiteness portion of the "white and..." equation marginalizes the "and" via its ability to remain invisible, thereby relegating the "white and..." subject to the realm of their "and" identity position. In order to retain supremacy over the non-racially abject, whiteness must continue pretending that its figurative invisibility is actually literal. Whiteness, at least as it occurs in *Glee*, also operates in a way that allows for white supremacy to oppress racial minorities in a most postcolonial fashion: by refusing them the opportunity of being "black and..." or "Asian and...."

A prime example of this theory in practice can be seen in the seventeenth episode of Season 2, "A Night of Neglect," in which Lauren Zizes reduces Mercedes' identity to only black instead of black and fat. Prior to Lauren joining New Directions, two episodes establish Mercedes as black and fat. In the first instance, Mercedes faints in the lunchroom after severely cutting her calories when Sue insists she lose ten pounds if she wants to be a member of the Cheerios. Later, Quinn pulls Mercedes aside, encouraging Mercedes to value herself as is, which works; the episode ends with Mercedes singing Christina Aguilera's anthem "Beautiful" ("Home"). The second instance takes place during Season 2 when the school bans tater tots from the lunchroom; denied her beloved side dish, Mercedes stands atop a lunch table, thrusting a crude sign in the air that reads: "tots," à la Sally Field as Norma Rae ("The Substitute"). In these moments Mercedes claims her "black and fat" identity. In "Night of Neglect" the new, white, considerably larger Lauren Zizes works to "help" Mercedes become the diva she deserves to be (and make sure people treat her that way). Mercedes becomes, at Lauren's instruction, rude, self-serving, and almost brings a performance to a halt when her diva demands are not met. By the end of the episode, though, Mercedes drops the stereotypical diva attitude after realizing that divas achieve their status by overcoming difficult struggles and strife. Importantly, Diva-dom remains Mercedes' long term goal. Because the moniker of "diva" is so often considered a common personality trait of black women, Mercedes' identity as "black and fat" slims down to simply black, all at the hands of a white and fat girl. Not only does Lauren's "white and..." status afford her the opportunity of multiple identity positions, she also has the power to revoke Mercedes' "black and..." status. This refusal of multiple identity positions for non-white characters undercuts the potential for queer community through its insistence that non-race-based otherness be associated only with whiteness. Once paired with whiteness, which has the potential to disappear, the abject identity position becomes marked, making the gay, fat, or disabled character easily comprehended, categorized, and therefore less queer.

The notion that characters can be culturally understood as "white and..." but not "black and..." or "Asian and..." allows us to examine an intersection between postcolonial whiteness and disability theory: the issue of access.[5] A common discussion in much of disability studies revolves around the notion of accessibility—that able-bodiedness practically guarantees not only easy physical access to every space, but affords social and cultural access often denied those stigmatized by their disability status. One argument in disability theory states that lack of access serves as a marker of disability. For example, in the Season 3 episode "Big Brother," Artie convinces the newly and temporarily wheelchair bound Quinn that amusement parks are not a fun place for the disabled in part because people who use wheelchairs find themselves continually re-marked as disabled due to the assistance they need getting on and off of rides. Taking the issue of access into account, a healthy number of shows nowadays contain representations of lesbian and gay characters, and, to a lesser extent, characters who are fat, or have a disability (with fatness often being portrayed as a disability). In almost all cases, though, the fat, gay, or disabled character's racial identity is white.

Well, what about Santana?[6] As a Latina lesbian, surely she contradicts the notion that the New Directions community remains steadfastly dedicated to incorporating characters with only a single, othered identity position. Not necessarily; there is a strong relationship in *Glee* between whiteness and the act of coming out, outing, and being out. Santana maintains little agency over her sexual identity, reducing her ability to act (and speak) from her lesbian identity position. For instance, although Santana's same-sex inclinations appear early in Season 1, Santana resists the label of lesbian for almost two full seasons, suggesting her Latina identity cannot make room for a second identity position. Richard Dyer explains, "White people, in their whiteness, however, are imaged as individual and/or endlessly diverse, complex and changing" (12). Santana's Latina identity prevents character complexity or change, thus enabling her to resist the moniker of "lesbian" over such a long period of time. The lack of agency over her own sexuality presents itself most strongly when Finn outs her in the halls of McKinley High. Because Santana seems unwilling or unable to claim her lesbian identity a white, straight, able-bodied man must do it for her. Yes, in moving from closetedness to outness Santana gains a second identity position, but that privilege exists only because a white man bestows it upon her—she did not achieve it herself.

Another aspect of coming out mediates the radical potential of Santana's multiple minority identity positions. In the world of *Glee*, each character that moves from closeted to uncloseted becomes more docile, in the Foucauldian sense of the term. In his essay "Docile Bodies," postmodern theorist Michel Foucault uses the example of seventeenth century French soldier training to explain how social institutions, such as schools, and their inhabitants regulate the ways in which people deploy their bodies; in other words, how people behave. Foucault defines a docile body as one "that may be subjected, used, transformed, and improved" (180). Prior to officially coming out Santana is known in no small part for a wit that ranges from acerbic to near lethal, her sharp tongue often functioning as a form of rebellion or resistance against Finn and Rachel, the characters who receive the most narrative attention. Yes, Santana's status as a cheerleader makes her more popular in the world of the show (high school), but the show's narrative almost always privileges Finn and Rachel (individually and as a couple) despite the fact that *Glee* frames Naya Rivera's

Santana as a more capable singer and dancer than Finn. Cory Monteith, the actor who plays Finn, is arguably the least skilled singer and dancer on *Glee*, and the show continually works that into Finn's narrative.

In the Season 3 episode "Mash Off," the episode in which Finn outs Santana, Santana continually jabs away at Finn as they each prepare for a contest between New Directions and the Trouble Tones. The "trash talk" begins between these two characters early in the episode as the separate choirs argue over whose group is better. During this argument, Santana responds to Finn's statement that the two choirs can "compete without being enemies, we don't have get vicious" by stating, "Oh, I think we do, soft serve. You see, The Trouble Tones are 'three F': fierce, femme, phenomenal. Oh, and guys, hurry up and go get some moist towels. We have to keep Finn wet before we can roll him back in the sea" ("Mash Off"). Although not a strong dancer, Cory Monteith cannot accurately be classified as fat; he maintains the fit physique Hollywood requires of a young TV star. The trash talk continues in a later scene when Santana approaches Finn in a school hallway with a more than usually harsh, litany of insults: "I'm sorry that you sing like you're getting your prostate checked and you dance like you've been asleep for years, and somebody just woke you up. Have fun riding on Rachel's coat-tails for the rest of your life" ("Mash Off"). While Santana's use of fat bias as a method for attacking Finn is troubling and problematic, the majority of Santana's tirade calls into question Finn's supremacy as the character who leads the glee club despite the fact he neither sings nor dances as well as most everyone else.

Finn immediately retaliates:

> Hey, Santana. Why don't you just come out of the closet? You know, I think I know why you're so good at tearing everybody else down—it's because you're constantly tearing yourself down because you can't admit to everybody that you're in love with Brittany.... That must hurt, not being able to admit to everyone how you really feel ... I think you're a coward ["Mash Off"].

In this moment, *Glee*, via Finn, equates Santana's sharp-tongued resistance to Finn's supremacy as unhappiness stemming from her closetedness— implicity concluding that coming out will make Santana a nicer person. Because this is television, the two make up during the next episode, and their reconciliation barely precedes the absorption of the Trouble Tones into New Directions. As a member of the losing team, Santana capitulates to Finn's primacy (which has been reinforced by New Directions' win).

Upon agreeing to "play nice" after being outed, Santana does soften some. She retains her acerbic wit, but uses it less frequently. When her harsher comments do resurface, she employs them in defense of the glee club. We see this change in Santana when a member of another rival glee club, Sebastian, injures Blaine by throwing a slushy loaded with rock salt in Blaine's face. Santana later confronts Sebastian, employing her biting wit as a tactic, and elicits Sebastian's confession. Unbeknownst to Sebastian, Santana records their conversation and uses the tape to shame Sebastian in front of the other Warblers. Once used as a tool to resist the unearned authority of her colleagues, Santana refocuses her method of resistance after her being outed and uses it as a tool to protect the interests of the club as a whole, even those that maintain their privilege over her within the group. In outing Santana, Finn does afford her access to multiple identity positions, but doing so serves the purpose of making Santana more docile, less rebellious, and therefore less queer.

Like Santana, David Karofsky finds himself outed by his peers, and, also like Santana whiteness plays a part in making him abject. In a Season 3 two-episode arc ("Heart" and "On My Way"), Karofsky's football teammate, Nick, spies Karofsky at Breadstix with Kurt on Valentine's Day. Assuming the two are on date, Nick's pointed dialogue clearly succeeds in shaming David. In the episode that follows, David enters the locker room to find the word "fag" spray painted on his locker. David flees, narrowly avoiding a physical confrontation with the "friend" that outed him, Nick. Although both the actors playing Nick and Karofsky read as white, the actor playing Nick reads as whiter than Karofsky. As Dyer points out, "There are also gradations of whiteness: some people are whiter than others" (12). Dyer goes on to say that

> a shifting border and internal hierarchies of whiteness suggest that the category of whiteness is unclear and unstable ... the sense of a border that might be crossed and a hierarchy that might be climbed have produced a dynamic that has enthralled people who have had any chance of participating in it [19–20].

Dyer's discussion here reveals that the pale complexion of blonde-haired, blue-eyed Anglos and Nordics exists as the ideal center of whiteness, while other Caucasian ethnicities, such as the Irish, Italian, Greek, and even people of Latin or Jewish descent exist within outer circles of whiteness whose degrees of white privilege and access remain constantly in flux (18–24). In addition to ethnic variation, sex and sexuality also contribute to hierarchies of whiteness. Dyer claims that in western society sexual "drives are typically characterized as dark" (28). This association of sex/uality with darkness proves particularly insightful because *Glee* makes no direct mention of Nick's sexual proclivities—Nick's asexual quality increases his whiteness, and his privilege, by not staining him with the milder darkness of heterosexual desire. The actors' appearance, as these characters, also contributes to the white privilege Nick wields over David. The blonde-haired, blue-eyed, tall and lean Aaron Hill, as Nick, conforms more to the Anglican body aesthetic associated with ideal whiteness; while the shorter, stockier Max Adler, as Karofsky, with his brown hair and eyes exists within less stable areas of whiteness.

Also like Santana, David is made docile after transitioning from closetedness to outness. This occurs in "On My Way" when Kurt visits David in the hospital and, as a means of comfort, provides David with a heteronormative vision of the future. Prior to his suicide attempt, David appears in two brief scenes that imply he's having sex with other men. In the fifth episode of Season 3, conveniently entitled "The First Time," Kurt and his boyfriend Blaine unexpectedly run in to David at a local gay bar, Scandals. In reaction to Kurt's surprise at seeing him in a gay bar, David explains that he likes Scandals because he "feels accepted" there and the other patrons "like him." Tellingly, the only reason David offers as to why he's liked is that he's a "bear cub," a designation that places emphasis on sexual attraction and fulfillment, intimating that David could be sexually active. The second, and last, time we see David at the bar he asks Sebastian for advice about how to "get" guys, implying that David pursues romantic and/or sexual encounters.[7] These scenes at the bar demonstrate a young man who, at least to some degree, is on the prowl. Back in the hospital scene, Kurt employs every "It Gets Better" tactic in order to console his former bully. When David, through tears, says he "can't go back to that school," Kurt responds with "Then go to another school!" Through his own tears Kurt goes on:

> I'm not gonna lie to you, it ... it isn't gonna be easy. And they'll be some days when life just sucks. But you're gonna get through this. 'Cause I'm gonna help you. And so is everyone else who loves you and accepts you for who you are. And if they can't accept that, then ... screw 'em! Right? ["On My Way"].

Kurt then leads David through a visualization of David's future, beginning in a "fantastic" office (David decides he's a sports agent). There's no work in this vision, though, as David's partner and their son (a toddler) arrive so that the husbands can take their kid to his first baseball game. The exercise produces the intended effect and ends with David saying, "I'm so happy right now." According to Kurt, the key to David's future happiness can be found by earning lots of money while working in a fancy office, monogamy, childrearing, and family trips to sporting events. Over the span of only a few appearances, David goes from a closeted gay bar bear cub hottie on the prowl to being out, proud and married with child—a docile and less queer state of being. Envisioning David heteronormatively also serves to increase his whiteness, as the dark stain of sex/uality lightens when one moves from meeting guys in bars for sex to a monogamous relationship.

Unlike Santana and David, Kurt chooses to come out, preventing anyone from exerting white authority over his decision to mark himself. However, whiteness does work to reduce the darkness associated with Kurt's
same-sex attractions, thus also mitigating his potential to queerly disrupt
normative sexual mores. Surprisingly, the rules regarding white womanhood
work toward rehabilitating Kurt's sexual stain, particularly as they relate to
his nickname, "porcelain." In his discussion about gender and whiteness,
Dyer notes, "the construction of white female sexuality is different from
that of the male. The white man has—as the bearer of agony, as universal
subject—to have the dark drives against which to struggle. The white woman
on the other hand was not supposed to have such drives in the first place"
(28). This ideal, that white women should lack a sex drive, relates directly
to female images of whiteness—the more chaste the lady, the purer, and
therefore whiter, she becomes. In associating the show's primary gay male
character with porcelain, an object so brilliantly and delicately white, Kurt
becomes simultaneously more pure (white) and more feminine. The result,
a gay male character who, like white women, ideally lacks a sex drive.

Glee wastes no time in putting Kurt's new white, pure, and sexless
potential to work. As it turns out, Kurt receives his "porcelain" nickname
in the very same episode in which he transfers from McKinley High to
Dalton Academy. Already enamored with the openly gay star of Dalton's
glee club, Blaine Anderson, the increased contact they experience as classmates only fuels the fire of Kurt's passion. Sure enough, seven episodes
later, Kurt and Blaine begin dating after Blaine kisses Kurt. Sadly, the
beginning of their relationship, for all intents and purposes, ends their
sex lives. Other than some hand-holding or a few brief little pecks here
and there, the kiss that initiated their relationship appears to be the most
physically intimate interaction between them. Before he got a boyfriend,
and his porcelain moniker, Kurt lusted after boys. Once Kurt started dating
Blaine, however, any hint of Kurt as a sexual creature flies out the window.
After Sue nicknames Kurt, but before he and Blaine become a couple, we
learn Kurt has never had a sexual encounter of any kind. In a particularly
annoying scene Kurt appears "grossed out" by the idea of sexual acts while
claiming devotion for the de-sexed romance of golden-age Hollywood
films ("Sexy"). Furthermore, the night Kurt and Blaine emerge from Scandals after running into Karofsky, Blaine tries to get Kurt to have sex with
him in the back seat of the car. The scenario clearly disgusts Kurt, who
blames this unseemly breach of seemliness on Blaine's drunkenness ("The
First Time"). Kurt's increased whiteness, via the porcelain image, reduces
his queerness by associating him with idealized white female sexuality.[8]
This, in tandem with a relationship that adheres to values based on het-

erosexual ideals, produces a more docile, desexed Kurt. Interestingly, the same forces of whiteness that regulate Kurt also increase Blaine's whiteness, docility, and desexualization. "Sexy," the episode that produces much of Kurt's prudery, also reveals that Blaine, prior to dating Kurt, was sexually active. Blaine's sexual history and his attempt to bed Kurt align Blaine with associations between white men and sex. As Dyer explains, white men should simultaneously experience desire but strive to resist their carnal longings (27–8). By yoking Blaine and his sexual desires to the insistently chaste Kurt, Blaine's dark stain of sex/uality fades. The stain never disappears, but because Kurt moves Blaine from a sexed place (Blaine being single) to an unsexed place (Blaine dating Kurt), results in a more white, docile, and less queer Blaine.

I must admit that I find whiteness' power to reduce queer instabilities in a way that produces docile bodies fascinating. Perhaps one of the strongest implications of my analysis here lies within the notion that an individual's ability to exist in queer opposition to normative sexual mores might be mitigated by the very process of coming out. Is it possible that the resounding cries to "come out, come out, wherever you are" that pour forth from both LBGTQ people and our allies contributes to more docile or complacent LGBT communities? Do we lose our ability to radically and progressively challenge oppressive sexual standards by rendering ourselves both visible and comprehensible to the white, heterosexual, patriarchy whiteness depends on for its power? The answer might be, "yes," but I hope only in part. Even though whiteness and its associated privileges work to undermine the potential for both queerness and queer community in *Glee*, and perhaps the world at large, the possibilities for queer revolution remain. Yes, white privilege intersects with postcolonial, disability, and queer theories in ways that sustain white supremacy in the interest of reducing degrees of difference that produce more docile, well-behaved, and safe bodies. Difference, though, still exists and is actively celebrated within *Glee* in ways that erode hegemony. Unfortunately, erosion is most frequently a long process; one that produces noticeable change only by centuries (decades, if we're lucky). But, as an admittedly ambivalent viewer, I remain a bit like those plucky little glee clubbers: I "don't stop believing!"

Notes

1. Finn has a change of heart, rejoining the group only hours before they perform.
2. Brittany's 0.0 GPA prevents her from graduating. Additionally, numerous and contradictory rumors abound as to what degree the graduated students will remain part of the show's narrative.

3. Becky, the first exception, is co-captain of the Cheerios and Sue Sylvester's minion. Mr. Schuster denies her membership because New Directions is too close to a competition to add new members; he does encourage Becky to join "next year" (Season 4). The second exception, Sugar Motta, is denied membership because she cannot sing. Apparently her experience in the Trouble Tones improves her voice a bit as she is allowed entre into New Directions when they absorb the Trouble Tones after sectionals.

4. Santana is the exception, and I address her later in the essay.

5. Tina, who is Asian, spoke with a stutter, but admitted it was an affectation early on in the series.

6. Unique/Wade Adams joins New Directions in the first episode of the fourth season with at least three identity positions, black, gay, and transgendered. After only a few episodes into Season 4, however, Wade appears to be fading while Unique is seen more frequently. Should this continue throughout Season 4, Glee will, once again, take steps to reduce or minimize multiple identity positioning. Should Glee render Wade/Unique as only female, there exists a potential to view Unique more normatively (female and heterosexual) than transgendered and gay/queer. I feel it is a bit premature to assess Unique/Wade's representation since, at the time of this writing, only three episodes of the fourth season have aired.

7. After learning of David's suicide attempt in that same episode, Sebastian recalls his previous interaction with David at Scandals.

8. As an image, "porcelain" contains the potential for an association directly oppositional to that of feminine delicacy and refinement—the toilet. Because Kurt desires other men, the image of the toilet carries with it dirty, non-white associations of excrement and anal sex. Associating Kurt as such seems antithetical to his characterization on the show. Kurt maintains a creamy, clear complexion; his fashion sense is also neat and clean, and, ultimately, he doesn't have sex. While the porcelain association of the toilet remains a possibility, Kurt's semiotics largely resists such imagery.

References

"Big Brother." *Glee: The Complete Third Season.* Perf. Matthew Morrison, Lea Michelle, Jane Lynch, Cory Monteith, and Chris Colfer. DVD. 20th Century–Fox, 2012.

Dyer, Richard. White: *Essays on Race and Culture.* London: Routledge, 1997.

"The First Time." *Glee: The Complete Third Season.* Perf. Mathew Morrison, Lea Michele, Jane Lynch, Cory Monteith, and Chris Colfer. DVD. 20th Century–Fox, 2012.

Fiske, John. *Reading the Popular.* Boston: Unwin Hyman, 1989.

"Furt." *Glee: The Complete Second Season.* Perf. Matthew Morrison, Lea Michele, Jane Lynch, Cory Monteith, and Chris Colfer. DVD. 20th Century–Fox, 2011.

"Heart." *Glee: The Complete Third Season.* Perf. Matthew Morrison, Lea Michele, Jane Lynch, Cory Monteith, and Chris Colfer. DVD. 20th Century–Fox, 2012.

"Home." *Glee: The Complete First Season.* Perf. Matthew Morrison, Lea Michele, Jane Lynch, Cory Monteith, and Chris Colfer. DVD. 20th Century–Fox, 2010.

Foucault, Michel. "Docile Bodies." *The Foucault Reader.* Ed. Paul Rabinow. New York: Pantheon, 1984.

Lopez, Alfred J. "Introduction." *Postcolonial Whiteness: A Critical Reader on Race and Empire.* Ed. Alfred J. Lopez. Albany: State University of New York Press, 2005.

"Mash Off." *Glee: The Complete Third Season.* Perf. Matthew Morrison, Lea Michele, Jane Lynch, Cory Monteith, and Chris Colfer. DVD. 20th Century–Fox, 2012.

"A Night of Neglect." *Glee: The Complete Second Season.* Perf. Matthew Morrison, Lea Michele, Jane Lynch, Cory Monteith, and Chris Colfer. DVD. 20th Century–Fox, 2011.

"On My Way." *Glee: The Complete Third Season.* Perf. Matthew Morrison, Lea Michele, Jane Lynch, Cory Monteith, and Chris Colfer. DVD. 20th Century–Fox, 2012.

"Purple Piano Project." *Glee: The Complete Third Season*. Perf. Matthew Morrison, Lea Michele, Jane Lynch, Cory Monteith, and Chris Colfer. DVD. 20th Century–Fox, 2012.

"Sexy." *Glee: The Complete Second Season*. Perf. Matthew Morrison, Lea Michele, Jane Lynch, Cory Monteith, and Chris Colfer. DVD. 20th Century–Fox, 2011.

"Showmance." *Glee: The Complete First Season*. Perf. Matthew Morrison, Lea Michele, Jane Lynch, Cory Monteith, and Chris Colfer. DVD. 20th Century–Fox, 2010.

"The Substitute." *Glee: The Complete Second Season*. Perf. Matthew Morrison, Lea Michele, Jane Lynch, Cory Monteith, and Chris Colfer. DVD. 20th Century–Fox, 2011.

"Theatricality." *Glee: The Complete First Season*. Perf. Matthew Morrison, Lea Michele, Jane Lynch, Cory Monteith, and Chris Colfer. DVD. 20th Century–Fox, 2010.

Warner, Michael. *The Trouble with Normal: Sex, Politics, and the Ethics of Queer Life*. New York: Free Press, 1999.

"Wheels." *Glee: The Complete First Season*. Perf. Matthew Morrison, Lea Michele, Jane Lynch, Cory Monteith, and Chris Colfer. DVD. 20th Century–Fox, 2010.

The Princess and Her Queen

A Queer Duet

RACHEL E. SILVERMAN

In the fourth episode of Season 2 of *Glee*, the members of New Directions are asked to partner up and sing duets. A duet, Mr. Schuester tells them, "is when two voices join to become one. Great duets are like a great marriage." He continues, "The singers complement each other, push each other to be better." Initially, there is not much of a response, but when the prize of a gift certificate to the elusive restaurant Breadsticks, given to the winning pair, is mentioned, each member of the glee club begins plotting to win. Santana quickly ditches gal-pal Brittany for the better voice of Mercedes; Rachel and Finn, New Directions' "it" couple, assume the win is theirs; and Kurt dares to ask the newest member of the club, Sam, to be his partner. As Tina chides Mike about the monotony of Dim Sum and stresses her desire for a real salad, Rachel decides to, and then convinces Finn they must, throw the competition in order to boost Sam's confidence. Finn, however, is worried that that Sam's duet with Kurt will cause Sam to be ostracized by the school and eventually drop out of glee—ruining the team's chance at the nationals.

Initially, Kurt refuses Finn's demand that he "can't do this" to Sam; however, after Kurt's dad agrees that Finn is right, and that performing with Sam may cause problems, Kurt reluctantly decides to sing alone. In his rendition of "Le Jazz Hot!" from *Victor Victoria*, Kurt performs a duet with himself. Defending his decision and countering Santana's ridicule that duets can't be done alone, Kurt tells the members of glee, "when you're different, when you're special, sometimes you have to get used to being alone." As everyone stands to applaud his brave performance, a look of concern and understanding pans across Rachel's face. In the end, Sam and Quinn win, by a vote of two, and as members of the team respond to their wins and losses, with their partners, Rachel looks behind her to see Kurt alone, again.

Later, in the hallway besides his locker, Rachel approaches Kurt and tells him, "I think you and I are a little bit more similar than you think." Pausing to spray hairspray around his head, Kurt bluntly states, "That's a terrible thing to say." Unfazed, Rachel adds, "I know you're lonely. I can't even imagine how hard it must be to have feelings in high school that you can't act on for fear of being humiliated, ridiculed, or worse, hurt." As Kurt slowly nods in acknowledgment, Rachel reminds him that while he may be lonely, he is not alone. She then asks him if he will sing a duet with her, just for the two of them, and assures Kurt, "I think you'll be really happy with my song selection, it has everything both you and I love." In the final scene of the episode, Rachel and Kurt sing the Judy Garland (Kurt)/Barbra Streisand (Rachel) duet mash-up of "Happy Days Are Here Again" and "Get Happy" ("Duets").

In the days following the episode, television critics from across the country praised Kurt and Rachel's performance; *New York Post* critic Jarrett Wieselman claimed they "redefined show-stopper" and *Time Magazine* critic James Poniewozik described their characters and choice of performance as one that existed "between two real-life divas so appropriate that, had it not existed, *Glee* probably would have had to invent it." For many critics and fans alike, "Duets" was the redeeming episode of Season 2 because it "was a return to that honeymoon feeling, when *Glee* first surprised, scandalized and satisfied you" (Flandez). And, according to Christie Keith, television critic for Afterellen.com, "Duets" was the "queerest episode of any series that's ever been on television."

When Poniewozik noted that Rachel and Kurt's pairing is not only "the strongest" on the show but also that Rachel's "obvious-in-retrospect point that the two of them really are a lot alike," he hints at something well beyond the scope of a *Glee* episode. Poniewozik describes the characters' similarities as "strong-willed, competitive and sometimes [having] a hard time seeing past themselves"; however, the similarities between characters like Rachel and Kurt that is, Jewish and gay characters, have been discussed for well over a century. Furthermore, the pairing of Jewish and gay identities on television is by no means unique to *Glee*; it is in fact a time-tested ensemble.[1] What makes *Glee* unique, and this new pairing worthy of note, is that unlike their predecessors, there is no doubt Rachel is Jewish and Kurt is gay. Previous characters, such as Will and Grace,[2] for example, were often read without these significant identity markers because unlike race or gender, which are most often visible, sexuality and religion cannot be "seen" and gays and Jews often "pass" as not gay or Jewish.[3] But Rachel's and Kurt's identities are seen. In fact, being so out about their differences is exactly what makes them "in"– in New Directions, that is—and creates transgressive space for understanding identity on television and creating social change.

In the episodes following "Duets" that tell the story of teen bullying, *Glee* is the first mainstream television show to deal with the harsh reality of being an openly gay teenager in high school. Kurt's gay identity is placed at the forefront of the narrative, and alongside him is Rachel, who not only notices Kurt's initial feelings of being alone but also actively works to protect him from harm. The friendship between the two characters grows as a result of the injustices done to him and her fight for social justice. Furthermore, the characters grow together as Rachel comes to realize winning is not everything and Kurt finds that fitting in might not feel as good as he expected. That Kurt and Rachel change together, in mutually reciprocal ways, offers some old and new ways of understanding the relationship between Jewish and gay identity. First, Kurt and Rachel's distinct personalities, which help define their gay and Jewish difference, illustrate how both gay and Jewish identities continue to exist on the margins of normalcy. Second, the friendship between Kurt and Rachel works to situate the characters within historical, political, and social pairings that have long existed between gays and Jews. And finally, the storyline wherein Rachel defends and supports Kurt and Kurt comes to understand the different ways he can exist within a community demonstrates the way Jewish and gay identity "complement each other" and can "push each other to be better" both on screen and off.

A Princess and a Queen

Rachel undoubtedly exemplifies the stereotype of a Jewish American Princess (JAP). She is over the top while at the same time grounded, she is as manipulative as she is giving, and she seeks individual attention just as hard as she works for the group as a whole. Rachel describes herself as someone with a "pathological need to be popular" ("Bad Reputation") and says just "like Tinkerbelle … I need applause to live" ("Laryngitis"). However, in the end, she always appears to put the group above herself because she knows that "being a star didn't make [her] feel as special as being [a] friend" ("The Rhodes Not Taken"). However, what is often seen as best for the group is also really what is best for Rachel. Her ironic nature is typical of the stereotype of the JAP, which emerged as part of U.S. popular consciousness in the 1950s and has remerged in characters ever since.[4]

A characteristic Rachel shares with the JAP, which is particularly relevant to her relationship with Kurt, is an inability to perform normative femininity. Jewish feminist scholar Ann Pellegrini claims that the JAP, like the stereotypical Jewish mother, presents a version of femininity contradictory to Western standards of white womanhood; that is, the Jewish woman is overbearing, strong-willed, and demanding, unlike the ideal version of femininity, which is passive and demure. Likewise, the "Jewess" is grotesque with an unnaturally protruding body, particularly her nose and buttocks, unlike the ideal beauty, which is restrained and minimizes space.[5]Rachel demonstrates Pellegrini's claim in her constant failings to mirror the personality and beauty of Quinn Fabray, McKinley High's head cheerleader and a traditional American beauty. Whereas in one episode Rachel laments to Finn, "I'm not Quinn. I don't look like her. And my personality, while excitable and full of surprises, isn't exactly low maintenance" ("Hell-O"). In another episode, she considers a nose job so that she can look "less Hebraic and more Fabray-ic" ("Born This Way"). Importantly, however, it is exactly the Jewish woman's insufficient version of femininity that situates her as the ideal counterpart to gay men, who perform a socially incorrect version of masculinity.[6]

Kurt, the original gay male member of New Directions' is as "queer as a three dollar bill" ("Special Education"). He not only redecorates his bedroom in what Finn describes as a "faggy" décor and every night performs an intensive facial process of cleansing, exfoliating, and moisturizing, but he also, in a moment of despair, recognizes he is "so depressed, [he's] worn the same outfit twice this week" ("Funeral"). Kurt's version of masculinity directly opposes hegemonic notions of masculinity, which expect men to exert power and control, to be dominant forces in society, and reaffirm patriarchal culture.[7] Rather, Kurt offers a stereotypical version of gay identity, wherein he is consumed with topics such as fashion and interior design. Kurt's gayness, in accordance with Hollywood standards, "has been defined in opposition to masculinity" because "gayness is that which is not masculine" (Battles and Hilton-Morrow 90). Similar to Rachel's inability to perform femininity in comparison to Quinn's ideal version, Kurt's identity is clearly gay, when compared to his masculine counterpart Finn. Whereas Finn is captain of the football team, Kurt introduces the football team to Beyonce's dance moves, and whereas Finn's masculinity attracts the sexual attention of many, Kurt spends half of the series single.

Kurt is a revolutionary character for all the reasons that he is different, for all that makes him *Glee*'s queen. And like Rachel, *Glee*'s princess, Kurt's difference is what makes him a critical member of New Directions. Together, Rachel and Kurt offer a new moment in the history and current conceptualizations of gay and Jewish difference on television. More importantly, they offer a glimpse at the possibilities that exist between the LGBT and Jewish communities.

A Brief History of Gay and Jewish Identity

Since the early twentieth century, being gay or Jewish means to be similarly constructed as a societal Other. From medicine, which "invented" homosexuality at the same time as it biologized Jewish difference, to the political construction of gays and Jews as societal "strangers"—due in part to their non-normative gender performances— the construction of gay and Jewish identity as Other is difficult to define yet similarly conceptualized.[8] According to Jonathan Freedman, "the Jewish other and the sexual other" have been "frequently placed in vibrant contiguity" (91). Well before "sexologists or psychologists or race theorists codified that relation" a similarity could be found in "the literary traditions of the West" (Freedman 91). Today, the similarity can be seen on television.

Jon Stratton's analysis of Jewish and gay characters on television suggests that the identities parallel each other in that they often go "unseen," and are able to "pass" as Christian or straight, respectively. Because popular cultural representations rely heavily on normative identity constructions, without obvious visual identity markers, Jewish and gay identity does not materialize as anything different than what is considered normal. As a result, Jews and gays are ostensibly "invisible identities" (Herman 9). As such, gay and Jewish characters enjoy the many rewards of white, heterosexual, Christian privilege. However, at the same time, Jewish and gay characters suffer from the perils of having unseen and unrecognized differences. Passing invites the complementary tension of assimilation and invisibility, which often leads to the loss of claims to selfhood. Self-naming and agency are claimed at the risk of marginality and very real violence— as is the case for both Rachel and Kurt.

While neither Rachel nor Kurt "pass," they do suffer in the moments when their identity is called out and made known. Rachel endures countless quips that denigrate her identity, whereas Kurt suffers from bullying and the fear of death. Whether it is constant attention drawn to her nose and the continuous comments about her needing a nose job or Santana telling her that she "looks like Pippi Longstocking, but Israeli" and that she "should move to Israel" ("Hell-O"), Rachel is regularly ridiculed for her Jewishness. Kurt, however, suffers from much more than ridicule. In the beginning episodes of the series, Puck, along with other members of the football team, throws him into the dumpster; and throughout Season 2, football player Karofsky bullies Kurt for being gay to the point that Kurt transfers school so that he can feel safe.

While the marginality from which Rachel suffers may be nowhere near as physical as the violence Kurt fears, she is, like Kurt, Othered amongst her peers and an outsider at McKinley High. Moreover, Rachel and Kurt's non-normative, mutually reciprocal gender performances and similar outsider status construct them, the princess and the queen, as each other's ally and the best duet on *Glee*. Because when Rachel and Kurt "join to become one" they "complement each other, push each other to be better" ("Duets"), and ultimately exemplify a move toward social change worthy of being mirrored in real life.

From Television to Reality

The enormous power to inform people and influence conceptions of Self and Other is one of the many persuasive potentials of television. Mediated representations of Otherness, such as Jewish and gay identity, create meaning for people. In other words, *Glee* creates meaning about gay and Jewish identity for its watchers. As such, it is important to understand what stories are being told, what information is being conveyed and how messages represent and naturalize social divisions and alliances between identities. For cultural studies theorists, rhetorical critics, and media scholars, understanding the constructions of marginalized groups becomes an act of intervention intended to make a difference in the world. For Lawrence Grossberg, critical theory is "concerned with relations between culture and power because it believes that culture is a crucial site and weapon of power in the modern world" (142). Similarly, John Sloop argues that media "representations work to offer knowledge and subject positions to cultural participants, providing part of the material that allows them to exist while simultaneously constraining their knowledge/understanding" (5). For Sloop, responses to mediated representations are dependent on the cultural knowledge and exposure of the viewer. Likewise, Stuart Hall's work exposes how representations of identity, through the presentation of, and negotiation with, dominant ideologies, convey messages and gain consent from their audience. He claims that television discourse is "a group of statements which provide a language for talking about—a way of representing the knowledge about—a particular topic at a particular historical moment" (291). Furthermore, Bonnie Dow argues for television as a "thing" to be analyzed, as a space of production for certain kinds of identities, which can contribute to larger cultural conversations about the privileging or disciplining of discourses and characters (3–4). As such, television has the potential to influence minorities, such as gays and Jews, and the social world because, as a cultural mirror, television offers an electronic classroom full of representations that viewers, particularly minorities, can mimic.

As a product of U.S. culture, television provides a productive site to explore the making and meaning of identities—such as Jewish and gay identity. For many people, television is the only space where marginalized bodies are encountered. Because what is being said about one group or another will matter in different ways at different times, a show such as *Glee*, which deals with reality of LGBT teen bullying, is ideal for understanding the realities of LGBT teen life and bullying today. As our world becomes increasing cognizant about the lack of rights for LGBT people and the increased bullying of LGBT teens, *Glee* is a space from where change can be seen and, hopefully, change can be learned and mirrored.

Changing Our Social Culture

In the episodes following "Duets," the bullying of Kurt by football player Dave Karofsky begins to intensify. When Kurt finally confronts him, the argument quickly gets heated, Karofsky threatens to punch Kurt, who responds by mocking him for being a "scared little boy [who] can't handle how extraordinarily ordinary [he is]" ("Never Been Kissed"). At this point, Karofsky grabs Kurt and kisses him. Shocked, Karofsky punches the locker and runs out, leaving Kurt on the verge of tears. Later in the episode, Kurt attempts to talk to Karofsky and alleviate his fears of coming out. Kurt assures Karofsky his feelings are normal and he is not alone. Karofsky denies his sexuality and threatens to kill Kurt if he tells anyone else what happened in the locker room.

In both of these scenes, particularly the locker room, Kurt's gay identity is the focus; likewise, many characteristics of and stereotypes about gay identity are highly visible. In the locker room, Kurt specifically addresses the fear that "all [us] gays are secretly out to molest and convert" straight men ("Never Been Kissed"). Likewise, his outfits are particularly fabulous—yellow knee high rain boots and a matching yellow cardigan, a shirred black sweater and red pants, and denim pea coat with a large scarf. More importantly, he repeatedly claims his own identity and reiterates the fact that Karofsky "can't punch the gay out of me (Kurt) any more than I can punch the ignoramus out of you" ("Never Been Kissed"). When Karofsky kisses Kurt, *Glee* intentionally shows how repressing one's identity and denying sexuality, as Karofsky does, is the real cause for predatory behavior and most often the root of homophobia. Kurt, on the other hand, who is open about his sexuality, is shocked by the kiss and moreover, is hurt by the kiss because it was his first kiss and it was stolen by a bully.

As the storyline between Kurt and Karofsky begins to reach a breaking point, and Kurt admits to feeling terrified all of the time, Rachel gathers Tina, Brittany, and Quinn, each of whom has a boyfriend on the football team, and asks them to rally their men to fight on Kurt's behalf. Rachel insists, "we need to defend Kurt, and there is strength in numbers" ("Furt"). When the women are slow to respond and Quinn chides her for having "personally sent the feminist movement back fifty years," Rachel adds, "If something bad happens to Kurt and we didn't do anything to stop it, we'll never be able to live with ourselves" ("Furt"). Unfortunately, when Rachel approaches her own beau, Finn refuses to confront Karofsky for fear that he will get injured on the football field and lose his place as quarterback and captain of the team. Shocked by Finn's response and claims that he can help Kurt "more by staying on top" of McKinley's social hierarchy, Rachel bluntly states, "I've never been so disappointed in you before."

In these series of scenes, Rachel's overbearing and strong-willed nature is used for good, not for her own selfish desires. She fights for what is right when everyone else around her acts as a bystander and passively allows the bullying to go on. Rachel takes the lead in championing for Kurt and in doing so exemplifies a history of Jewish civil rights activism. Kurt also continues to overtly embody gay stereotypes as he is simultaneously planning a wedding while the bullying is happening. An important parallel story occurs in this episode that works to further highlight Rachel's Jewishness, Kurt's gay identity, parallels between the two communities, and the potential for change. Cheerleading coach Sue, in her fantastical ways, decides to marry herself, and her mother, a world famous Nazi hunter, returns to Ohio for the wedding. The repeated mentioning of Nazis juxtaposed with Kurt's bullying and Rachel's attempts to stop the bullying reminds viewers of *Glee* about the history of Jewish oppression—one not so different than what the LGBT community is currently facing—and makes note of the fact that Rachel's Jewish identity is not simply a joke, but a minority status still facing Anti-Semitism. Additionally, the wedding of Sue to herself juxtaposed with the wedding between Kurt's dad and

Finn's mom is a way to highlight the lack of marriage rights for LGBT people. Coach Sue, played by a well-known lesbian actor, spends every episode in a tracksuit—her wedding dress is even a tracksuit cum gown—clothing that plays with stereotypical notions that all female gym teachers are lesbians. The two very different weddings, one which is obviously a joke and one which the audience is meant to take seriously, highlights the perception many Americans have of same-sex marriage—that it is a joke. The ludicrousness of Sue's wedding exemplifies what Kenneth Burke calls "perspective by incongruity," which works to reveal the absurdity in the denial of LGBT rights. By offering a hyperbolic version of "wedding" *Glee* subtly argues for the acceptability and normality of LGBT weddings and reminds audiences that one of the other major issues the LGBT community faces, in addition to bullying, is lack of equal marriage rights. Altogether, the strategic storytelling by *Glee* works to create a narrative of intolerance, discrimination, social justice, and the fight for equal rights.

Eventually, Kurt decides to leave McKinley High because without proof of the violence or death threats the school board cannot expel Karofsky. When he announces to the glee club his decision to leave McKinley and attend Dalton Academy, which has a zero-tolerance bullying policy, Rachel bluntly asks, "Does this mean you're going to be competing against us at sectionals?" which causes everyone to roll their eyes as she is, yet again, rendered self-centered and uncaring ("Furt").

In the following episode, when the storyline reaches completion, the team is headed to sectionals and *will* be competing against Kurt and his new team the Warblers. Prior to the competition, when Kurt is offered the chance to vie for the solo, he approaches Rachel for help. "Even though we hate each other," Kurt admits, "we've had our moments and I could use your expertise" because, he acknowledges, "you're as brilliant and talented as you are irritating" ("Special Education"). Rachel helps Kurt with his solo, and at sectionals when the two see each other, she learns he did not win the solo. "If you didn't get the solo then they [the Warblers] must be really good. We are doomed," she laments, and then, in a moment of growth, says, "Sorry. That was selfish. What I meant to say was that, wow, that really sucks, I'm sure you were really good." Kurt, also recognizing he has changed, admits that singing at Dalton has made "me question things about myself." After his rendition of "Don't Cry for Argentina"[9] didn't work out, and he was told "don't try so hard next time … didn't you notice we all wear uniforms around here? It's about being part of the team" ("Special Education"), Kurt realizes that he might like being different and standing out.

Queering Difference

Kurt and Rachel's moments of recognition about their identities and how they want to be seen are, in a sense, mutually reciprocal. Kurt likes being different and being part of a team made up of unique individuals, not people in uniforms, where sometimes difference may cause pain and feelings of being alone. Rachel realizes that being different isn't necessarily better than fitting in, and that being part of a team and fighting for what she believes in is more important than winning. Their coinciding realizations about finding the balance between difference and sameness and the space of commonality created as a result is here offered as a metaphor for social change.

The friendship between Kurt and Rachel began during what critics called the "queerest episode of any series that's ever been on television" and since then, they have remained one of *Glee*'s most powerful duets. The choice to use the word "queer" opens the door to a plethora of meanings about queer identity, queering identities, and the potential for queer spaces because the history and current usage of the term *queer* has significant political and social potential. According to Annamarie Jagose, queer is "a source" of change (5), and for Moe Meyer, queer "indicates an ontological challenge to dominant labeling philosophies" (1). In this sense, queer is subversive and libratory; it is meant to denaturalize and problematize social norms. As such, the current understanding of queer is as a theoretical move or act of analysis, and the task of queer theory is to identify ways in which people on the margins can resist dominant culture. Within this homology of the term, Rachel, Kurt and the show itself, *Glee*, are queer. That is, they offer a source of change as they regularly challenge dominant labeling philosophies.

To see *Glee*, and within *Glee*, Kurt and Rachel as queer, is to see a space for social change. Because television acts as not only a mirror of our culture but as an electronic classroom, the models of identity and the roles these identities play must be seen as a way to understand the similarities between Jewish and gay difference as well as the potential for social alignment between the two outsider identities. Susan Sontag, in her foundational essay *Notes on Camp*, describes Jews and gays as the "outstanding creative minorities in contemporary urban culture" and suggests they are "the two pioneering forces of modern sensibility" (290). Their vibrant and contiguous relationship has, according to Sontag, shaped American culture via the mix of moral seriousness, aestheticism, and irony. On *Glee*, Rachel and Kurt exemplify these qualities in their characters, their interactions, and their storylines. Just as both Kurt and Rachel offer models of difference and models for change, *Glee,* because of its popularity, offers the potential for the growth of a queer sensibility, which embodies social change, equality, acceptance, and difference.

Notes

1. For other television shows and film, watch *Buffy the Vampire Slayer, Will & Grace, Happily Divorced, Sex and the City, Angels in America, The Bird Cage.*
2. From the NBC hit series *Will & Grace,* which ran from 1998 to 2006.
3. For a more in depth discussion of seeing and passing see Sedgwick.
4. For other JAPs on screen, check out: Rachel Green on *Friends;* Cher Horowitz from *Clueless;* and the characters Gilda Radner performed on *Saturday Night Live.*
5. A further understanding of what it means for femininity to be constrained by space can be had by reading Berger.
6. Both the Jewish woman and the gay man's incorrect performance of gender rely on normative assumptions about gender, which are highly contested. Queer theorists and feminist scholars have long been debating the relationship between sex, gender, and sexuality. Furthermore, as a result of feminist, postmodern and queer theory, it is generally understood that any and all identity labels are a fluid production of individual and collective discourse, rather than a concrete set of personal or behavioral characteristics. For more on this topic see Butler, Fausto-Sterling, or Foucault.
7. For a deeper understanding of different version of masculinity, see Pelias or Connell and Messerschmidt.
8. Gilman, among others, notes that the mid–19th century in Germany was a time where Jews and homosexuals were biologically determined to be Other via their genitals, psychological differences and atypical sexualities. For example, he claims, "being Jewish is analogous to being homosexual—it is an incurable disease" (125). For more discussion on Jewish and gay similarities and differences, see Boyarin, Itzkovitz and Pellegrini.
9. The choice of songs is particularly striking because of both the original singer and its more contemporary cover. Eva Peron, also known as Evita, fought for women's suffrage in Argentina. Her commitment to equal rights won the hearts of many, but also cast her as a woman with too much power and as a result many condemned her as fascist. Years later, Madonna revisited Evita in the self-titled film *Evita.* Madonna is infamous for her support of gay rights, her outspokenness, and for her commitment to Kabbalah—a Jewish form of mysticism.

References

"Bad Reputation." *Glee.* Writ. Ian Brennan. Dir. Elodie Keene. Perf. Chris Colfer, Cory Monteith, Matthew Morrison, Jane Lynch, Lea Michele, Jayma Mays, Dianna Agron, Naya Rivera, Amber Riley, Heather Morris, Harry Shum, Jr., Kevin McHale, Jenna Ushkowitz, Mark Salling, Olivia Newton John, and Iqbal Theba. Fox 4 May 2010. Television.
Berger, John. *Ways of Seeing.* New York: Penguin, 1990. Print.
"Born This Way." *Glee.* Writ. Brad Falchuk. Dir. Alfonso Gomez-Rejon. Perf. Chris Colfer, Cory Monteith, Matthew Morrison, Jane Lynch, Lea Michele, Jayma Mays, Dianna Agron, Naya Rivera, Amber Riley, Darren Criss, Heather Morris, Harry Shum, Jr., Kevin McHale, Jenna Ushkowitz, Mark Salling, Ashley Fink, Iqbal Theba, and Max Adler. Fox 26 April 2011. Television.

Boyarin, Daniel, Daniel Itzkovitz, and Anne Pellegrini. *Queer Theory and the Jewish Question*. New York: Columbia University Press, 2003. Print.

Burke, Kenneth. *Language as Symbolic Action: Essays on Life, Literature and Method*. Berkeley: University of California Press, 1966. Print.

Butler, Judith. *Bodies That Matter: On the Discursive Limits of Sex*. New York: Routledge, 1993. Print.

Connell, Robert, and James Messerschmidt. "Hegemonic Masculinity: Rethinking the Concept." *Gender and Society* 19 (2005): 829–859. Print.

Dow, Bonnie. *Prime-Time Feminism: Television, Media Culture, and the Women's Movement Since 1970*. Philadelphia: University of Pennsylvania Press, 1996. Print.

"Duets." *Glee*. Writ. Ian Brennan. Dir. Eric Stoltz. Perf. Chris Colfer, Cory Monteith, Matthew Morrison, Lea Michele, Jayma Mays, Dianna Agron, Heather Morris, Harry Shum, Jr., Kevin McHale, Amber Riley, Jenna Ushkowitz, Mark Salling, Amber Riley, Chord Overstreet, and Max Adler. Fox 12 October 2010. Television.

Fausto-Sterling, Anne. *Sexing the Body: Gender Politics and the Construction of Sexuality*. New York: Basic Books, 2000. Print.

Flandez, Raymund. "'Glee,' Season 2, Episode 4, 'Duets': Recap." *Wall Street Journal*. 12 Oct. 2010. Web. 7 July 2012.

Freedman, Jonathan. "Angels, Monsters, and Jews: Intersections of Queer and Jewish Identity in Kushner's *Angels in America*." *PMLA* 113.1 (1998): 90–102. Print Foucault, Michel. *History of Sexuality: An Introduction*. New York: Vintage, 1990. Print.

"Funk." *Glee*. Writ. Ian Brennan. Dir. Elodie Keene. Perf. Chris Colfer, Cory Monteith, Matthew Morrison, Jane Lynch, Lea Michele, Jayma Mays, Dianna Agron, Naya Rivera, Amber Riley, Heather Morris, Harry Shum, Jr., Kevin McHale, Jenna Ushkowitz, Mark Salling, Jonathon Groff, Stephen Tobolowsky, Iqgbal Theba, Idina Menzal, and Jessalyn Gilsig. Fox 1 June 2010. Television.

"Furt." *Glee*. Writ. Ryan Murphy. Dir. Carol Banker. Perf. Chris Colfer, Cory Monteith, Matthew Morrison, Jane Lynch, Lea Michele, Jayma Mays, Dianna Agron, Naya Rivera, Darren Criss, Amber Riley, Heather Morris, Harry Shum, Jr., Kevin McHale, Jenna Ushkowitz, Carol Burnett, Dot-Marie Jones, Lauren Potter, and Mike O'Malley. Fox 9 November 2010. Television.

Gilman, Sander. *The Jew's Body*. New York: Routledge, 1991. Print.

Grossberg, Lawrence. "Toward a Genealogy of the State of Cultural Studies: The Discipline of Communication and the Reception of Cultural Studies in the United States." *Disciplinarity and Dissent in Cultural Studies*. Eds. Cary Nelson and Dilip Gaonkar. New York: Routledge, 1996. 131–47. Print.

Hall, Stewart. "Introduction: Who Needs 'Identity?'" *Questions of Cultural Identity*. Eds. Stuart Hall and Paul du Gay. Thousand Oaks, CA: Sage, 1996. 1–18. Print.

"Hell-O." *Glee*. Writ. Ian Brennan. Dir. Brad Falchuk. Perf. Chris Colfer, Cory Monteith, Matthew Morrison, Jane Lynch, Lea Michele, Jayma Mays, Naya Rivera, Heather Morris, Harry Shum, Jr., Amber Riley, Kevin McHale, Jenna Ushkowitz, Jessalyn Gilsig, Idina Menzel, and Jonathan Groff. Fox 13 April 2010. Television.

Herman, Didi. "'I'm gay': Declarations, Desire and Coming Out on Prime-Time Television." *Sexualities* 8 (2005): 7–29. Print.

Jagose, Annamarie. *Queer Theory*. New York: New York University Press, 1996. Print.

Keith, Christie. "'Glee' Episode 204 Recap: 'Don't Go Breakin' Kurt and Brittany's Heart.'" Afterellen.com. Logo. 13 Oct. 2010. Web. 5 July 2012.

"Laryngitis." *Glee*. Writ. Ryan Murphy. Dir. Alfonso Gomez-Rejon. Perf. Chris Colfer, Cory Monteith, Matthew Morrison, Jane Lynch, Lea Michele, Jayma Mays, Dianna Agron, Naya Rivera, Amber Riley, Heather Morris, Harry Shum, Jr., Kevin McHale, Jenna Ushkowitz, Mark Salling, Mike O'Malley, Ashley Fink, and Josh Sussman. Fox 11 May 2010. Television.

Meyer, Moe. *The Politics and Poetics of Camp*. New York: Routledge, 1994. Print.

"Never Been Kissed." *Glee*. Writ. Brad Falchuk. Dir. Bradly Buecker. Perf. Chris Colfer,

Cory Monteith, Matthew Morrison, Lea Michele, Jayma Mays, Dianna Agron, Heather Morris, Harry Shum, Jr., Kevin McHale, Jenna Ushkowitz, Naya Rivera, Iqbal Theba, Ashley Fink, Amber Riley, Josh Sussman, Laure Potter, Amber Riley, Max Adler, Dot-Marie Jones, and Darren Criss. Fox 9 November 2010. Television.

Pelias, Ronald. "Jarheads, Girlyman, and the Pleasures of Violence." *Qualitative Inquiry* 13 (2007): 945–959. Print.

Pellegrini, Anne. "Whiteface Performances: 'Race,' Gender, and Jewish Bodies." *Jews and Other Differences: The New Jewish Cultural Studies.* Eds. Daniel Boyarin and Jonathan Boyarin. Minneapolis: University of Minnesota Press, 1997. 108–149. Print.

Poniewozik, James. "Glee Watch: It Takes Two." *Time.* 13 Oct. 2010. Web. 6 July 2012.

Prell, Riv Ellen. "Rage and Representation: Jewish Gender Stereotypes in American Culture." *Uncertain Terms: Negotiating Gender in American Culture.* Eds. Faye Ginsburg and Anna Tsing. Boston: Beacon Press, 1990. 248–266. Print.

"The Rhodes Not Taken." *Glee.* Writ. Brad Falchuk. Dir. Brad Falchuk. Perf. Chris Colfer, Cory Monteith, Matthew Morrison, Jane Lynch, Lea Michele, Jayma Mays, Dianna Agron, Naya Rivera, Amber Riley, Heather Morris, Harry Shum, Jr., Kevin McHale, Jenna Ushkowitz, Mark Salling, and Kristen Chenoweth. Fox 30 September 2009. Television.

Sedgwick, Eve. *Epistemology of the Closet.* Berkeley: University of California Press, 1991. Print.

Shugart, Helene. "Reinventing Privilege: The New (Gay) Man in Contemporary Popular Media." *Critical Studies in Media Communication* 20.1 (2003): 67–91. Print.

Sloop, John. *The Cultural Prison: Discourse, Prisoners, and Punishment.* Tuscaloosa: University of Alabama Press, 1996. Print.

Sontag, Susan. *Against Interpretation, and Other Essays.* New York: Farrar, Straus & Giroux, 1966. Print.

"Special Education." *Glee.* Writ. Brad Falchuk. Dir. Paris Barclay. Perf. Chris Colfer, Cory Monteith, Matthew Morrison, Lea Michele, Jayma Mays, Dianna Agron, Naya Rivera, Heather Morris, Harry Shum, Jr., Kevin McHale, Jenna Ushkowitz, Mark Salling, Amber Riley, and John Stamos. Fox 30 November 2010. Television.

Stratton, Jon. *Coming Out Jewish: Constructing Ambivalent Identities.* New York: Routledge, 2000. Print.

"Wheels." *Glee.* Writ. Ryan Murphy. Dir. Paris Barclay. Perf. Chris Colfer, Cory Monteith, Matthew Morrison, Jane Lynch, Lea Michele, Jayma Mays, Dianna Agron, Naya Rivera, Heather Morris, Harry Shum, Jr., Kevin McHale, Jenna Ushkowitz, Mark Salling, Amber Riley, Ashley Fink, Iqbal Theba, Mike O'Malley, Josh Sussman, Stephen Tobolowsky, and Lauren Potter. Fox 11 November 2009. Television.

Wieselman, Jarett. "Happy Days are Here Again on 'Glee.'" *New York Post.* 13 Oct. 2010. Web. 5 July 2012.

Going Beyond Grilled Cheesus
Glee *and Queer Theology*
ERIN KATHLEEN MARSHALL

According to a 2007 Barna Group study, the most common word that comes to mind when young people are asked about Christianity is "anti-homosexual." Ninety-one percent of young (16–29) non–Christians held this opinion, as did 80 percent of young Christians (Kinnaman, chapter 2, location 320). So when Ryan Murphy, the openly gay co-creator and show runner of *Glee*, expressed a desire to cast an evangelical Christian during *The Glee Project* ("Sexuality"), it seemed incongruous to add a performer who might find the show's content objectionable. The show explored Christianity in its first two seasons, but the shallow depiction was typical for prime-time television; Christianity was used either to show the hypocrisy of organized religion, or to examine Christian apologetics versus atheism. The casting of Christian actor Samuel Larsen, however, ended up providing *Glee* with a different angle to look at Christianity ("Glee-ality")—a point-of-view familiar to queer theologians.

Patrick Cheng speaks of queer theology being grounded in the idea of radical love: "Radical love, I contend, is a love so extreme that it dissolves our existing boundaries, whether they are boundaries that separate us from other people, that separate us from preconceived notions of sexuality and gender identity, or that separate us from God" (Cheng, *Radical Love*, introduction, location 140). Queer theology can be seen as a theological complement to queer theory, "seeing something in a different light and reclaiming voices and sources that had been previously been ignored, silenced or discarded" (Cheng 1, introduction, location 325). To show a theological narrative that challenges a status quo is unusual on network television, which tends to depict non-threatening views of religion that are acceptable to large portions of the viewing audience; the actual religion of television is mostly about attracting a market share (Blythe).

From its start, *Glee* has been a program about transgressing boundaries, or at least the boundaries of William McKinley High School. The popular kids and the social outcasts come together to participate in the school's glee club. Recognizing the transgressive nature of her participation, popular cheerleader Santana Lopez once told her fellow members: "And if you tell anyone this, I'll deny it ... but I like being in glee club. It's the best part of my day, okay? I wasn't gonna go and mess it up" ("Sectionals"). Later in that first season, popular straight football player Finn Hudson dresses in a red vinyl dress and offers to defend gay character Kurt Hummel from the other jocks at the school ("Theatricality").

While the show addressed religion through a few characters and a "very special episode" in the second season, religion was used to reinforce a status quo, rather than challenge norms. However, in the third season, the dreadlocked, guitar-playing Joe Hart is introduced ("Heart"), and *Glee*'s take on religion took a different perspective. The formerly home-schooled Joe, at first glance, seemed intended as a stereotype of American Christianity, as was the Fabray family in Season 1 and Tammy Jean Albertson in Season 2. But during the episodes "Heart" and "On My Way," Joe becomes an example of inclusivity and boundary-breaking normally associated with queer theology. This essay will introduce queer theology, examine previous representations of Christianity on *Glee*, and finish with the episodes "Heart" and "On My Way," discussing how they demonstrate a queer vision of theology that suits the embracing nature of *Glee*.

Queer Theology

Queer theology is a way of looking at religious theory through a queer lens. Marcella Althaus-Reid writes: "In Queer Theology, the grounding of theological reflection lies in human relationship, for as we have argued in previous chapters, it is in scenes of intimacy and the epistemology provided by those excluded from the political heterosexual project in theology that unveilings of God may occur" (*The Queer God*, chapter 7, location 2673). This is a significant departure from the forms of Christianity that have been dominant since Constantine's conversion, making Christianity the state religion of the Roman Empire and the hegemonic religion of the West, as well as creating an egress for a religion that originally addressed the marginalized people of an occupied country. Queer theology borrows from the language of liberation theology, speaking from the perspective of the world's oppressed, not a theology that originates from the oppressors; it looks at the intersectionality of oppression and says that liberation is not just a matter of race or class, but also of the oppression of all those who can be viewed as outsiders, including sexual minorities. Queer theology finds god in places where love can be so strong and radical that it blurs the lines separating people, embraces their differences, and moves them to closer community (Cheng, *Radical Love*, chapter 3, location 1302).

We can look for instances of queer theology in moments of *kenosis*, where God voluntarily joins humanity, becoming one of us. Divinity becomes dependent on joining the margins and transgressing them (Althaus-Reid, *The Queer God*, chapter 2, location 916). The queer theologian is examining not a religious text but stories from the margins, and ways of knowing that are outside of societal norms. The texts that introduce a queer notion of religion are those that push things beyond the boundaries of convention, finding where God lies outside of the religious texts amongst the queer, the lost, the poor, and oppressed.

The other queer theological perspective we can use to examine *Glee* is Patrick Cheng's rethinking of sin and grace. Traditional Christian theology sees sin as doing wrong, and grace as undeserved forgiveness for those wrongs. Readings of the Lord's Prayer ("forgive us our trespasses, as we forgive those who trespass against us") provide a transactional model of sin and grace, with divine forgiveness being offered in exchange for its human counterpart. As the straight view of theology has cast much of sex to the margins, a queer theology seeks to reclaim human sexuality as a valuable expression of radical love. This model of crime and acquittal has done untold damage to queer people. However, when Christ is queered and moved to the margins, we can look at sin as that which moves us away from God, and grace as that which moves us closer to god. Cheng proposes a rethinking of the seven deadly sins and amazing graces:

1. Sin as exploitation, grace as mutuality;
2. Sin as the closet, grace as coming out;
3. Sin as apathy, grace as activism;
4. Sin as conformity, grace as deviance;
5. Sin as shame, grace as pride;
6. Sin as isolation, grace as interdependence; and
7. Sin as singularity, grace as hybridity [Cheng, *From Sin to Amazing Grace*, Introduction, location 159].

These views of queer theology give us a place to observe the characters of *Glee*. In Joe's journey through two episodes, we can see an analogy for *kenosis*: a home-schooled religious student is removed from his bubble, where the secular or different are not allowed, and joins a community of outsiders. This analogy provides a starting point to demonstrate a queering of traditional theological constructs. By entering this queer space, and exploring and embracing the stories from the margins, Joe finds the sacred outside of the Christian bubble that had sheltered his views.

Religion and *Glee*'s First Two Seasons

In the first season of *Glee*, Christianity mainly exists through Quinn Fabray, president of the Celibacy Club and a believer that physical excitement while showing affection would "make the angels cry" ("Showmance"). The Christianity in Season 1 was a hypocritical religion—Quinn is, first of all, not really celibate; when offering her boyfriend to feel-up her breast in exchange for his quitting glee club, she covers her cross, and she cheats on her boyfriend, which results in pregnancy ("Showmance," "Preggers"). Her likewise Christian parents talk of taking her to the Celibacy Ball (a take on the Purity Balls that are popular in some evangelical Christian circles) but reject her when they discover her pregnancy ("Ballad"). Later, shortly before Quinn gives birth, the hypocrisy of her parents is made evident when Mrs. Fabray reunites with her daughter due to Mr. Fabray's infidelity ("Journey to Regionals"). The Christianity in this season is less about religion and more about status and sanctimony, reinforcing the negative status quo in *Glee*'s Lima, Ohio, and the opposite of the radical love of queer theology. Instead of valuing the stories of the other, the Christian characters of *Glee* seem to exist only to suppress the stories of the "other."

Early in Season 2, the episode "Grilled Cheesus" is largely focused on religion and a lack thereof. Finn, who is meant to be an archetypical "dumb jock," sees the face of Jesus in a grilled cheese sandwich and begins to pray to it. In his mind, the god of the sandwich, or "Grilled Cheesus" as he calls him, is viewed like a genie in a bottle, to the point of treating his prayers like three wishes. His requests are as immature as his views on faith—win a football game, touch his girlfriend's "boobs," and be re-instated as quarterback. When his first wish (apparently) comes true, he requests the glee club honor "Grilled Cheesus" in song. Kurt objects, expressing his objection to belief in God as well as organized religion: "If I wanted to sing about God, I would go to church—and the reason I don't go to church is that most churches don't think highly of gay people, or women ... or science."

Later in the episode, Kurt's father suffers a heart attack. Kurt's atheism leads to a conflict with other students, as he rejects their faith-based support while his father lies in a coma. The writers of the show use Kurt's atheism and McKinley's acerbic cheerleading coach, Sue Sylvester, to address the theological question of theodicy—neither Sue nor Kurt is able to reconcile a loving and caring, and supposedly omnipotent, God who allows evil to exist. Says Kurt: "He makes me gay, and then tells his followers to hate me." A queer theology doesn't seek to repress or ignore the pain of those on the edges. Murphy, who has stated in interviews that he does believe in God, said that he wanted to use the episode to explore the concepts of teenagers working out what faith means to them (Martin).

The theology of the episode begins to draw closer to a queer vision of theology when Kurt is taken to church—not as an act of proselytization, but of caring. Kurt allows his friend Mercedes Jones to help in her own way, and she offers to care for Kurt by fostering community. Kurt doesn't become a believer, but he expresses a belief in the sacredness in community: "I don't believe in God, Dad, but I believe in us. You and me. That is what is sacred to me." When Kurt finds that sacredness his father wakes up from his coma. The episode ends with a cover of the Joan Osborne song "One of Us," reinforcing the idea of *kenosis* — not into a perfect sinless human, but God being just like us.

Later in the second season, the Christianity of the first season is echoed in "Original Song," an episode set around a glee club regionals competition. Celebrity guest judge Tammy Jean Alberston, a Sarah Palin-esque character, is shown to be obsessed with evangelical tribalism and Tea Party touchstones. She approves of the performance meant to pander to her ("Jesus Is a Friend of Mine") and quickly objects to the two gay male characters singing a duet; her characterization is later hammered home when she objects to a performance of a song called "Loser Like Me," saying: "I'm a politician, and when I lost my election, and there will be a recount, I didn't sing songs about being a loser. I Twittered that Obama was a terrorist ... I had to, it's a fact." Another Christian character, Sister Mary Constance, also a celebrity guest judge, is introduced in this episode. A stripper-turned-nun who looked to the convent as "the one place I knew I could stay off the pole," Sister Mary Constance refuses to be pandered to by "Jesus is a Friend of Mine," telling the other judges, "For a nun, I am pretty liberal." Beyond her habit, her Christianity is rarely referenced.

While showing moments that explicitly reject people from the outside, the episode's B- story was one of the more queer-friendly plots. Blaine

Anderson, one of the openly gay characters on the show, realizes he is interested in Kurt, and the two young men share their first kiss. The episode shares another moment of embracing pride and diversity as the glee club sings "Raise Your Glass" by P!nk, a song celebrating those from the outside.

The cited examples show that while the content of *Glee* is often queer, its views on religion are not always the same. The theology of *Glee* is mostly about the status quo and not about challenging things, and while some of the moments in "Grilled Cheesus" hint at a loving God who shakes things up, the majority of the first two seasons display a theology focused on preserving the hegemony, not a theology challenging from the margins.

The Glee Project and the Search for a Christian Character

Speaking with *TV Guide* during the hiatus between the first and second season, Murphy talked about adding a Christian character to the cast of *Glee*: "We've taken a couple jabs at the right wing this year, so what I want to do with this character is have someone who Christian kids and parents can recognize and say, 'Oh, look—I'm represented there, too!' If we're trying to form a world of inclusiveness, we've got to include that point of view as well" (Keck).

This didn't happen during the second season, but during the 2011 summer hiatus, the Oxygen network aired a reality competition called *The Glee Project*, and a Christian contestant, Cameron Mitchell, seemed to interest Murphy ("Pairability"). Despite Murphy's pleading, Mitchell left the show during the "Sexuality" episode, when he realized that acting on the show might bring him into conflict with his religious beliefs. In that same episode, contestant Samuel Larsen spoke of his Christianity, his Christian-themed tattoos, and how his conservative mother might object to his performing a scene with gay content. During an interview after making the final four contestants of *The Glee Project*, Larsen stated that he wanted to show audiences a different version of Christianity (Marti "The Glee Project Finalists"):

> I think something that's very relevant in real life, and that they don't portray enough on TV, is that when you think "Christian" you think "goody two shoes," they have to look a certain way and do certain things—and it's just not true. Some of the craziest people I know, some of the coolest guys I know who party and go crazy and play rock shows and have tons of tattoos, they will still go to church on Sunday and do their best to live that kind of a life. I think that would be very cool to see on TV because that *is* true.

Larsen was one of the two winners of *The Glee Project* ("Glee-ality"). His prize was a newly-created *Glee* character to appear in a seven-episode story arc. Murphy had found a Christian actor around whom he could create the kind of religious character he wanted. Joe Hart would soon be added to the halls of McKinley High.

The Introduction of "Teen Jesus" in "Heart"

Larsen's character was rolled out in the episode "Heart," which aired on Valentine's Day, 2012. Introduced during a meeting of "The God Squad," a group of the known Christian members of the glee club (Quinn Fabray, Sam Evans, and Mercedes Jones) to discuss faith, pray and plan service projects, Joe is a dreadlocked, formerly home-schooled sophomore. Averse to wearing shoes, Joe comes from an almost stereotypical evangelical Christian household where the only allowed broadcast entertainment are hymns and talk radio, and his father is a door-to- door Bible salesman. Quinn comments, "We have our own Teen Jesus." Yet Joe seems uniquely open to the differences in the glee club. This section will discuss how he is initially wary of the group but comes to exemplify a message love that is part of queer theology.

The main focus of this episode is the issue of the show's lesbian characters, Santana Lopez and Brittany Pierce, engaging in public displays of affection. A (presumably) Christian character complains about public kissing, and the young women are brought before the principal for a reprimand. Santana is upset about the "insane double standard" at McKinley, where straight students are allowed overt displays and gay pecks cannot occur without reprimand. The "God Squad" is set to perform singing valentines as a fundraiser, and Santana requests that the Squad perform one for her girlfriend. Joe is uncomfortable by the request—he later states that he has never known any gay people—and the God Squad meets to discuss her request. This produces one of the more bizarre and amusing exchanges, as the "God Squad" wrestles with their feelings about sexuality and Christianity, ranging from a discussion of the Levitical codes to the possible sexual orientation of Jesus's disciples. Quinn ends the discussion with her vision of being a Christian as "looking at the hard issues, and deciding what you really believe," introducing a bottom-up element to her vision of Christianity, rather than the conventional top-down authoritarian vision that is a cultural norm for many societies. The episode concludes with Joe declaring that "love is love," and he would be happy to sing a love song to Brittany.

Using the aforementioned queer theological views of sin and grace, we can examine the messages of the episode. Santana rejects the sin of the closet, demanding to be out. The God Squad, meanwhile, rejects the sin of apathy through their service project. Joe sees the grace in interdependence, and his statement, insisting that love trumps all, engages and brings us to the point that theology should be about love: "Understanding the meaning of love in practice, that is friendship, solidarity, and the political strategies and organization of the social structures necessary to foster a theological praxis of love in action" (Althaus-Reid and Isherwood 303). In a limited, high school kind of way, Joe's actions are about loving enough to see ensure that justice exists. Though initially resistant due to his upbringing, Joe ultimately begins his queer theological journey.

Offering Comfort in "On My Way"

Early in the third season episode "On My Way," Dave Karofsky, a student who had previously bullied Kurt, is outed and himself bullied. A montage of Dave being harassed, ending with a suicide attempt in a closet, is intercut with Blaine Anderson singing "Cough Syrup" by Young the Giant, a song that can easily be read as a cry for help. The staff and students find out about Dave's attempted suicide, followed by the God Squad discussing a prayer for Dave and his family. When Quinn accuses Dave of being wrong and selfish, Kurt challenges Quinn's opinion, explaining that the pain a gay student feels is unique in a homophobic society. When Kurt's presence is challenged by the God Squad on account of his atheism, Joe acknowledges that it was he who invited Kurt. Such an invitation is defined by the character to be less a proselytization, and more as an act of love and comfort to the afflicted, echoing Mercedes' actions in "Grilled Cheesus." Kurt had felt guilt for actions that (he thought) may have contributed to Dave's suicide attempt. In return, Joe offers what he has to give: love.

The location of the suicide attempt can be taken as an easy metaphor for the sin of the closet. It is Joe's inviting Kurt to the God Squad meeting that is the most radical, particularly coming from standard models of Christianity. Joe recognizes that Kurt should not be alone and invites him into interdependence. Additionally, Kurt is given the space to share his vision of the word, and Joe has created a space for a voice from the margin to be heard, not preached at. Unlike in "Grilled Cheesus," where Christianity existed solely as a place for sermonizing against the queer, the vision of Christianity in "On My Way" is a place where Kurt is given the chance to be heard. The healing he receives is not from theology, but an act of healing that comes from his story and his pain. Later in the episode, Kurt is able to offer healing to his former oppressor, as he visits Dave in the hospital.

Conclusion

Joe's journey to a queer theology was not completed in only two episodes; instead, it is only the beginning and a parallel to *kenosis*. He joins the glee club, aligning himself with the marginalized ("Big Brother"), and while helping Quinn with her physical therapy, an inopportune erection (or "in-his-pants feelings") creates a place to explore his feelings about his own sexuality ("Saturday Night Glee-ver"). And while he doesn't immediately jump into sex, he acknowledges that desire and sexuality are parts of his humanity. Finally, Joe's journey to queered perspective becomes even more pronounced when a character mis-genders him: "Joe's really pretty, but I've heard she doesn't shave her armpits" ("Dance with Somebody"). This mis-gendering further emphasizes that Joe has embraced the radical love that blurs the boundaries between gay and straight, male and female, jock and geek.

The aforementioned Barna study highlighted some of the dangers of theology becoming too aligned with anti-gay power structures. It becomes a tool of oppression, not of liberation. *Glee*'s vision of Christianity is challenging such a presumption by offering stories from the margins and creating an avatar for those entering into this space. The world of *Glee* is not a queer utopia; it is a deeply flawed universe that gives space for, and listens to, the stories of outsiders. In later episodes, a gender-queer character of color named Unique is introduced ("Saturday Night Glee-ver"), adding another story from an uncommon perspective, and further expanding the canon of its stories. Althaus-Reid writes, "Queering is also the art of deconstructing laws in search of justice, an art which comes from experiences of love at the margins of lawful, or to use Christian terms outside the redeemable" (*The Queer God*, Chapter 5, location 1842). Joe directly experiences and facilitates that love by singing to the lesbian couple, and by offering comfort to a friend struggling with guilt and inadequacy. The queering of religion in *Glee* is by no means a finished project or a closed text, in that queering can never be finalized, but it is an ongoing saga where characters will continue to add their own queer journeys that challenge and transgress from the outside.

References

Althaus-Reid, Marcella. *The Queer God*. New York: Routledge, 2007. Kindle.
Althaus-Reid, Marcella, and Lisa Isherwood. "Thinking Theology and Queer Theory." *Feminist Theology* 15.3 (2007): 302–14. Print.
"Ballad." *Glee*. Writ. and dir. Brad Falchuk. Fox. Los Angeles, 18 Nov. 2009. Television.
"Big Brother." *Glee*. Michael Hitchcock. Dir. Eric Stoltz. Fox. Los Angeles, 10 Apr. 2012. Television.
Blythe, Teresa. "The Theology of Television." *Beliefnet*. N.p., Oct. 2003. Web. 3 June 2012. http://www.beliefnet.com/Entertainment/Movies/2003/10/The-Theology-Of-Television.aspx.
Cheng, Patrick S. *From Sin to Amazing Grace: Discovering the Queer Christ*. New York: Seabury, 2012. Kindle.
_____. *Radical Love: An Introduction to Queer Theology*. New York: Seabury, 2011. Kindle.
"Dance with Somebody." *Glee*. Ross Maxwell. Dir. Paris Barclay. Fox. Los Angeles, 24 Apr. 2012. Television.
"Glee-ality." *The Glee Project*. Prod. Ryan Murphy. Oxygen. Los Angeles, 21 Aug. 2011. Television.
"Grilled Cheesus." *Glee*. Brad Falchuk. Dir. Alfonso Gomez-Rejon. Fox. Los Angeles, 5 Oct. 2010. Television.
"Heart." *Glee*. Ali Alder. Dir. Brad Falchuk. Fox. Los Angeles, 14 Feb. 2012. Television.
"Journey to Regionals." *Glee*. Writ. and dir. Brad Falchuk. Fox. Los Angeles, 8 June 2010. Television.
Keck, William. "*Glee*'s Blessed Arrival." *TV Guide*. TV Guide, 1 June 2010. Web. 12 June 2012. http://www.tvguide.com/news/glees-blessed-arrival-1019091.aspx.
Kinnaman, David, and Gabe Lyons. *UnChristian: What a New Generation Really Thinks about Christianity ... and Why It Matters*. Grand Rapids: Baker, 2007. Kindle.
Martin, Denise. "The Glee Project Finalists Sound Off on Christianity, Reality TV Editing and Ryan Murphy." *TV Guide*. TV Guide, 15 Aug. 2011. Web. 15 July 2012. http://www.tvguide.com/News/Glee-Project-Finalists-Interviews-Damian-Lyndsay-Samuel-Alex-1036395.aspx.
_____. "Ryan Murphy, Cory Monteith on *Glee*'s Religion Episode, 'Grilled Cheesus'" *TV Guide*. TV Guide, N.p., 4 Oct. 2012. Web. 1 Aug. 2012. http://www.tvguide.com/News/Glee-Grilled-Cheesus-1023969.aspx?rss=news.
"On My Way." *Glee*. Roberto Aguirre-Sacasa. Dir. Bradley Buecker. Fox. Los Angeles, 21 Feb. 2012. Television.
"Original Song." *Glee*. Ryan Murphy Dir. Bradley Buecker. Fox. Los Angeles, 15 Mar. 2011. Television.
"Pairability." *The Glee Project*. Prod. Ryan Murphy. Oxygen. Los Angeles, 17 July 2011. Television.
"Preggers." *Glee*. Writ. and dir. Brad Falchuk. Fox. Los Angeles, 23 Sept. 2009. Television.
"Saturday Night Glee-ver." Matthew Hodgson. *Glee*. Dir. Bradley Buecker. Fox. Los Angeles, 17 Apr 2012. Television.
"Sectionals." *Glee*. Writ. and dir. Brad Falchuk. Fox. Los Angeles, 9 Dec. 2009. Television.
"Sexuality." *The Glee Project*. Prod. Ryan Murphy. Oxygen. Los Angeles, 31 July 2011. Television.
"Showmance." *Glee*. Ryan Murphy, Brad Falchuk, and Ian Brennan. Dir. Ryan Murphy. Fox. Los Angeles, 9 Sept. 2009. Television.
"Theatricality." *Glee*. Writ. and dir. Ryan Murphy. Fox. Los Angeles, 25 May 2010. Television.

♦ Disability ♦

"I still have use of my penis"
Disability and Queer Sexuality
MEREDITH WIGGINS

Almost since its first airing, *Glee* has drawn much ire from disability rights activists, who have critiqued the show for its use of "crip drag" (the practice of casting nondisabled actors in the parts of disabled characters—most notably in the character of wheelchair user Artie Abrams, played by nondisabled actor Kevin McHale) and the unwillingness of its show creators to engage in dialogue with the disabled community. In contrast, the show's depictions of gender and sexuality have met with general acclaim; *Glee* has received widespread, largely positive media coverage for its attention to issues facing LGBTQIQ youth, and the characters of Kurt Hummel, a flamboyant, bullied gay teenager (played by out gay actor Chris Colfer), and Santana Lopez, a lesbian cheerleader, are among the show's most popular. But while *Glee*'s portrayals of gender and sexuality and its portrayals of disability garner a good deal of scholarly and media attention individually, comparatively little work has been done considering the topics together. Given the high degree of visibility that *Glee* provides for queer and disabled characters, groups traditionally underrepresented in popular media, the lack of scholarship addressing the intersectionality between the show's portrayals of disability and its portrayals of queer sexuality,[1] while perhaps unsurprising, feels problematic, especially given that multiple episodes of the show directly link storylines regarding disability and sexuality involving queer characters.[2] Unfortunately, in this respect, *Glee* is the rule rather than the exception, symptomatic of what Anna Mollow and Robert McRuer call the "frequent elision of the queerness of disability" (29).

107

In this essay, I examine the first three seasons of *Glee* and consider the implications of the fact that, although the show contains characters of varying levels and types of disability and characters across the sexuality spectrum, *Glee* allows none of its characters with disabilities to identify as queer. This is particularly troubling because sexuality and sexual expression by disabled people can be considered inherently queer (because nonheteronormative) acts. On the contrary, *Glee*'s physically and developmentally disabled characters often suppress queer potential, frequently serving as the sites of what disability theorist Robert McRuer's *Crip Theory: Cultural Signs of Queerness and Disability* terms "heteronormative epiphanies, continually making available, to the out heterosexual, a sense of subjective wholeness" (12). Defying their potential to act as boundary-destabilizing figures in the dual worlds of McKinley High and Lima, Ohio, disabled characters on *Glee* instead most often act as agents to uphold and reinforce the largely heteronormative and ableist standards that the show implicitly champions.

It may prove helpful here to provide a brief review of the dominant stereotypes surrounding sexuality and disability. The most prevalent of these stereotypes ascribes asexuality to disabled people. As Tom Shakespeare, Kath Gillespie-Sells, and Dominic Davies note, "The prevailing attitude, central to the prejudice faced by disabled people, is that disability and sexuality are incompatible" (9). Put differently, ableist society assumes that the mere presence of disability eliminates or precludes the sexual desires or drives presumed present in nondisabled persons, leading to what Abby Wilkerson has called the "[s]exual marginalization" of disabled people—a chronic and continuing form of disabled oppression which works to deny the full personhood of people with disabilities (198). Interestingly, the other major stereotype about sex and disability directly contradicts the myth of disability as asexuality, labeling the sexuality of disabled persons as excessive and positioning them as dangerous predators. These widespread yet dichotomous cultural representations of disabled sexuality—as what Anna Mollow elsewhere calls "somehow both lack (innocence, incapacity, dysfunction) and excess (kinkiness, weirdness, perversion)" (286)—make plain the damagingly limited model of sexual possibility available to people living with disabilities and suggests the difficulty they might have in redefining the stereotypically heteronormative mold of what sex is or can be.

"I'm in a wheelchair, but I'm still a guy": Artie Abrams

Despite being *Glee*'s original disabled character, Artie's initial role on the show was quite small. Although a founding member of the glee club, he usually had only one or two lines of dialogue each week, and it was not until nearly halfway through the first season, in "Wheels," that he had any major plotlines of his own. Notably, this episode, the first in which there is any suggestion of Artie's romantic or sexual potential, is also one of the first episodes of the series to intertwine significant storylines about disability and queerness: the primary plot of the episode focuses on the glee club trying to raise money to rent a wheelchair-accessible bus to drive them to Sectionals, while the secondary plot concerns Kurt's attempts to audition for the competition solo of *Wicked*'s "Defying Gravity"—a song traditionally sung by a woman—and the harassment he and his father endure along with it.[3] From the outset, then, it would appear that *Glee* recognizes the queerness of Artie's sexual potential, but in fact, despite repeatedly linking disability and queerness on levels both explicit and implicit, *Glee* works tirelessly to contain and constrain—that is, to het-eronormativize—the queer impulses underlying Artie's character and the representation of his sexuality.

It must be said that *Glee*'s portrayal of Artie's sexuality is not without its positive points. He notably escapes inclusion in the major stereotypes about sexuality in disabled persons. Neither asexual nor "excessively" so, he engages in two fairly long-term romantic relationships, one of which includes sexual intimacy, and while his disability does cause some prob-lems (mostly occasional insecurity) during those relationships, it is not necessarily presented as the main cause of either break-up. The show even allows him to express comfortably some minor homosexual desire, as when he reports in "Hold on to Sixteen" that watching Sam perform one of the body rolls Sam perfected during his time as a teenage stripper gave him "light tingles where it's only 50/50 for tingling." Ultimately, however, Artie proves to be one of the show's staunchest representatives of hetero-normative values, even though as a disabled man, he is technically excluded from the strictest representations of those values.

Artie's firm adherence to heteronormativity (or, at the very least, his repeated attempts to adhere to those norms) shows itself in one of his earliest interactions hinting at romantic or sexual potential. After Mr. Schuester declares in "Wheels" that the entire glee club will be performing a number in wheelchairs in order to show solidarity with Artie, Artie takes over the responsibility of teaching his fellow glee club members how to dance in the chairs.[4] After one particularly strenuous practice, Tina stays behind to praise his fortitude in dancing in the wheelchair, providing the first real hint at their future romantic storyline: "I really admire you, Artie," she says, before asking him how he became disabled ("Wheels").[5] Artie reveals that he was in a car accident when he was eight that resulted in the loss of his ability to use his legs, then takes the chance to inform the girl he likes of one other important matter: "I wanna be very clear—I still have use of my penis," he says seriously ("Wheels"). Given that, at this point, Artie and Tina have yet even to kiss, his announcement feels somewhat out of the blue—an impression driven home by Tina's response of somewhat confused silence followed by a quick exit. The moment is obviously intended to humorously convey the marvelous ineptitude of a would-be cool teenage boy faced with the slightly terrifying prospect of a girl he likes, but it also conveys a deeper meaning: for Artie and for *Glee*, Artie's continued "use" of his penis is both the single most important outcome of his becoming disabled, making it possible for him to take part in "normal" sexual activity, as well as the condition that allows the scene to resolve itself on a humorous, rather than tragic, note. Had Artie not retained the use of his penis after becoming disabled, the scene would have taken on a distinctly different feel, if it had even existed at all.[6] Even this early in the series, the message seems clear: as Sarah Smith Rainey writes, "[T]he scripts that surround love are possibilities only for those that can perform in certain physical and emotional ways" (28).

Artie's insistence on trying to fit into fundamentally heteronormative standards manifests throughout the duration of his relationship with Tina, but it becomes particularly noticeable in his Season 2 relationship with Brittany, during which time *Glee* consistently raises the possibility for queer modes of sexual and/or romantic expression only to undercut those possibilities at practically every turn. The basis of Artie and Brittany's relationship is queer not merely in the academic/activist sense of being nonheteronormative, but also in that it has its origins in same-sex desire—namely, Brittany and Santana's sexual relationship, first mentioned in "Sectionals" and made visible in "Duets." As Brittany and Santana kiss on Brittany's bed— which Santana calls "a nice break from all that scissoring"—Brittany suggests that they pair up for that week's glee club assignment and sing Melissa Etheridge's lesbian anthem "Come to My Window" to one another ("Duets"). When the still-closeted Santana refuses, Brittany makes a play for Artie, who has recently been dumped by Tina, instead. Artie is surprised by her attention, but definitely interested in the idea: "So, let me get this straight," he asks, "you wanna be my girlfriend because you like the idea of wheeling me around?" to which Brittany replies, "I just really wanna get you in a stroller" ("Duets").[7] As Brittany pushes Artie's wheelchair past Santana, she turns, points to her breasts, then makes an "off-limits" gesture toward Santana, who looks annoyed.

Artie and Brittany's relationship thus begins with the male partner a pawn for queer, female sexual desire. This pattern continues throughout most of "Duets," with Artie playing the role of the more stereotypically feminine, passive partner to Brittany's more dominant, stereotypically masculine aggressor. Later in the episode, they go to Brittany's house to practice their duet, where, in a reversal of stereotypical gender dynamics, Artie expresses a desire for an emotional connection to go along with the physical attraction he feels toward Brittany. Realizing that he still has feelings for Tina, Artie tries to leave, but Brittany stops him: "You wanna get over Tina, right? Let me help you" ("Duets"). She then lifts him out of his wheelchair and carries him, like a damsel in distress, to the bed, where she straddles him. As Artie nervously asks her, "Am I about to lose my virginity?" Brittany confidently replies, "Before our duet, we're gonna do it" ("Duets"). This decision backfires for her, however, after a jealous Santana tells Artie that Brittany only wanted to be with him because he was a good singer, not because she had any genuine interest in him: "She's using you for your voice. That's the only reason she had sex with you," Santana says, adding, "[T]he only thing you can give Brittany that she can't get somewhere else is super-choice parking" ("Duets"). In retaliation, Artie breaks up with Brittany, who he feels has betrayed him: "I know that sex doesn't mean anything to you, but did you ever think how much it means to me? After my accident, we didn't know if I'd ever be able even to do that. And when I found out that I could, it seemed like some kind of miracle, and you just *walked* all over that" ("Duets," emphasis added). Brittany, clearly chagrined, attempts to apologize, but Artie merely turns and goes, leaving her alone and forlorn in the hallway.

Again, this scene begins with clear queer potential; Artie's apparent desire for their sex to "mean something"—and Brittany's apparent ease with sex that is "just" sex—run counter to the sexual scripts assigned to men and women by culture at large. However, *Glee*'s urge to heteronormativize their interaction quickly takes over; aside from ignoring that heterogenital, penis-in-vagina sexual intercourse is far from the only form of sex available,[8] the show ends up punishing Brittany for her sexual behavior while allowing Artie to escape with no damage done. Artie's indignation over what he perceives as Brittany's sin—that her desire to have sex with him might not have been motivated purely by attraction to him—ignores the fact that he has told her, mere moments before they have sex, that he is having sex with her for other reasons, as well; if she "used [him] for [his] voice," he used her to help get over Tina ("Duets").[9] Furthermore, we see Artie and Brittany in a scene together after they have sex but before he officially breaks up with her, at which point he is apparently content in the relationship—a relationship he has previously revealed has little meaning for him, since he is still emotionally invested in Tina. Artie's contradictory words and actions suggest an unsettling, decidedly un-queer subtext to the scene: that it is fine if sex does not necessarily mean anything to him, but that it is not fine for it not to mean something to her. The end of the scene endorses this impression, as viewers are left with the sight of a teenage girl, abandoned by the boy with whom she has just had sex, apologizing for her behavior and asking for his forgiveness—forgiveness that *Glee* implies she perhaps does not deserve[10]—for the crime of having treated him exactly as he has treated her.

"I'm more than just one thing": Sean Fretthold

One of the most instructive examples of how *Glee* suppresses the queer potential of its disabled characters occurs in the first season episode "Laryngitis," which introduces the character of Sean Fretthold (played by paraplegic actor Zack Weinstein), a friend of Finn's who sustained major spinal cord injuries during a football game and is now quadriplegic. Sean's narrative is written into the show as a counterpoint to the narrative of Rachel contracting a case of acute tonsillitis that causes her to lose her singing voice; viewers meet Sean only because Finn grows tired of Rachel's incessant whining and introduces the two in an attempt to get her to stop feeling sorry for herself. Rachel is visibly uncomfortable throughout their conversation, most noticeably during Sean's attempts at flirtation: "I don't understand," she whispers to Finn, "this isn't funny" ("Laryngitis"). Sean, seeing her discomfort, does his best to assuage her anxiety: "Sorry. They make me see a shrink. He says I compensate with humor..." ("Laryngitis"). Finn then encourages Sean to tell Rachel the story of how he became disabled, which focuses on Sean's anger and frustration over "what [he] lost": "I'm miserable. I miss my body. I miss my friends. I miss girls" ("Laryngitis"). He admits, however, that there is at least one benefit: he no longer feels pressure to define himself only by his talent on the football field, as he once did—or, as he puts it, he has discovered that he is "more than just one thing" ("Laryngitis").

Sean does not appear immediately to fulfill either of the main stereotypes regarding disability and sexuality, but upon closer examination, it becomes clear that he actually manages to fulfill both stereotypes simultaneously—quite a feat, considering he has approximately five minutes of total screen time and is never seen nor mentioned again on the show. Sean clearly finds Rachel attractive, attempting to flirt with her at their first meeting, but his attempts to express his desire make Rachel excessively uncomfortable. She is barely able to speak to him throughout their first meeting, stammering and directing her comments toward Finn, rather than toward Sean himself; after Sean comments drily that he's "got a shot" at dating Rachel, Rachel turns to Finn and whispers, "I don't understand. This isn't funny" ("Laryngitis"). The merest hint that Sean possesses sexual desire is enough to make Rachel profoundly ill at ease, and her body language—shrinking in on herself and cowering away from Sean—suggests an element of fear, as well, thereby rendering Sean's sexuality "dangerous."[11]

From that point on, Sean's sexuality is effectively banished from his interactions with Rachel. When she returns some days later, voice having recovered, to offer him singing lessons, the subject of his attraction to her is never broached; in fact, he barely speaks at all. Instead, Rachel takes the lead, thanking him for "showing [her] that just because [she's] not good at anything other than singing doesn't mean [she's] not any good if [she] can't sing" ("Laryngitis"). A potentially queer moment does arise, however, when Sean asks Rachel to hold his hand. Looking down at their entwined fingers, she asks, "Can you feel that?" to which he replies, "No, but it's weird. I remember what it feels like, and I can see it, so—it's like I can" ("Laryngitis"). Because visual stimulus can cause arousal even in the absence of feeling, Sean's sight of their hands touching can create a sense memory of touch—touch which could be sexual.[12] They then begin singing together to U2's "One," a performance that culminates in Rachel singing with Sean as a single tear slides down her face. In this way, even the erotic potential of their touch is neutralized; rather than examining— or even simply acknowledging—that there is sexual possibility in Sean and Rachel's touch, the show emphasizes his passivity: Sean becomes an object of pity only, the earlier threat of his "excessive" sexuality brushed aside and replaced by a forced asexuality that draws out Rachel's charitable impulses (and her tears) without ever awakening her recognition of his subjectivity.

Not content merely to deny Sean's sexual potential, *Glee* also repurposes Sean as a teaching tool, one designed to direct Rachel toward her correct romantic path. In other words, Sean appears on *Glee* in order to reassure Rachel of her worth as a human being, regardless of whether she is able to sing as well as she is used to (as well as to remind her implicitly of how much worse her life could be), but he only does so in the context of furthering her romantic desirability. Sean's real purpose is to serve as a plot device that will ultimately bring Finn and Rachel closer to pursuing a relationship, a point made explicit by a conversation Finn and Rachel have before meeting Sean, when Finn accompanies the nervous Rachel to the doctor. By this point in the show, Finn is actively pursuing Rachel, who began dating rival show choir star Jesse St. James earlier in the season, and Finn takes the opportunity to urge Rachel again to break up with Jesse: "When are you gonna realize he's not into you like I am? You think he's gonna stick around if you can't sing? If you're a vocal cripple?" ("Laryngitis"). The implication is clear: Jesse might not want Rachel if she became a "vocal cripple," but Finn still would.

Rachel's singing voice does recover, of course, and she returns to assure Sean that he has helped her realize that she can be more than just a singer, if she wants to be. Tellingly, however, *Glee* never shows Rachel realizing any other dream she might pursue in the absence of her singing voice, so what is this "other thing" she might be? Read in dialogue with the earlier scene in the doctor's office, the implication is clear: Rachel will be fine no matter what because she will still have the ability (a word I use intentionally) to be Finn's girlfriend—a point the show drives home by cutting from a shot of Sean and a teary-eyed Rachel singing in Sean's bedroom to a shot of a smiling, happy Rachel and Finn singing to one another as they make full use of their nondisabled bodies to dance and chase one another around the auditorium stage. Sean's whole purpose on the show, his very reason for existence, is thus to serve as a conduit to move Finn and Rachel one step closer to their mutual heteronormative epiphanies. Having done so, he then disappears from *Glee* permanently, his queer potential safely suppressed by the major arc of heteronormative romance.

"I've said good-bye to that part of my life": Quinn Fabray

Intriguingly—or perhaps fittingly—*Glee*'s most recent major plotline about disability involved one of the show's (arguably) least queer characters[13]—Quinn Fabray, the sometime-head-cheerleader, sometime-bad-girl glee club member who loves Jesus and popularity and whose pregnancy during Season 1 sets up a number of the show's major plotlines. Both prior to and following her pregnancy, Quinn espouses a belief in chastity; in her romantic relationships, she represses her sexuality whenever possible, sublimating her sexual desires with desires for popularity and social status,[14] and viewers are reminded multiple times throughout the series that her sexual transgression—sleeping with Puck, the decision that resulted in her pregnancy—occurred only "because [he] got [her] drunk on wine coolers, and [she] felt fat that day" ("Preggers"). Although her characterization varies wildly throughout the course of the series, Quinn's baseline character remains invested in heteronormative ideals—an observation that holds true despite the queer potential that arises through her disability storyline.

Quinn becomes disabled in a car accident that occurs while she is texting and driving in "On My Way," eventually spending several episodes in a wheelchair due to a severely compressed spine. In a speech that seems written specifically to combat the critiques of *Glee*'s representations of disability, which tend to focus on the tragic and/or inspirational, Quinn takes Rachel to task for feeling sorry for her; when Rachel tearfully says that Quinn's injury is "not right" and "shouldn't be like this," Quinn replies, "Well, maybe not, but this is the way it is. My accident—which you did not cause, by the way—does not define me or ruin our senior year ... I'm not gonna dwell on this, and neither should any of you, okay?" ("Big Brother"). But viewers soon learn that Quinn's emotional stability and acceptance is all an act; she has a breakdown when Artie suggests that her condition may be permanent, coldly informing him, "I'm not like you. This isn't my life" ("Big Brother").

Quinn begins to move toward a more genuine acceptance of her situation only in the context of her burgeoning relationship with Joe, a new boy at school. In fact, a significant portion of Quinn's disability storyline is devoted to establishing Joe's character, rather than developing Quinn's in any real way; he joins the glee club at her behest, nearly three full episodes after first appearing on the show, and it is through their interactions that his character begins to develop beyond its initial, somewhat sketchy outlines. They bond over their mutual Christianity, and he offers to help her with her rehab, where sexual tension grows between them; in a montage set to their performance of Whitney Houston's "Saving All My Love for You," viewers see them share flirtatious glances and meaningful stares, even coming close to kissing before Joe pulls away ("Dance with Somebody"). Convinced that her disability has made her unattractive, Quinn takes Joe's reluctance as outright rejection, and when her fellow glee club members bring up their obvious chemistry,[15] she dismisses them out of hand: "Joe and I are just friends. Nothing else is going to happen.... It doesn't matter what I want. I've said goodbye to that part of my life. Joe took me to rehab the other day, we had a moment, and before we kissed, he pulled away. Grossed out by me and my chair.... Joe's not into me. I don't blame him. Who would be?" ("Dance with Somebody"). However, at her next rehab session, Quinn discovers that she is wrong; as Joe helps her do deep leg stretches, he gets an erection. Although Quinn is quick to reassure him that "it happens," he is mortified and tries to explain: "It's just that you are the prettiest, nicest, best-smelling girl I've ever met.... It's just that when I'm with you, I don't care what God says about sins of the flesh. I just want to know what it would feel like to be right up next to you" ("Dance with Somebody"). The latent queer potential in this relationship comes to the forefront as Joe tries to define what they are to one another: "So what is this? About you and me?" he asks, prompting Quinn to reply, smiling, "I don't know. Something new" ("Dance with Somebody").

Although Joe and Quinn's interaction avoids the major stereotypes about sexuality and disability, it nevertheless reinforces (albeit more obliquely) the same ableist, heteronormative standards upheld by other disabled character throughout the show. From a narrative perspective, Quinn's disability serves no real function; as a storyline, it takes her character nowhere she has not been before.[16] But while Quinn becoming disabled does not develop her character in any meaningful way, it does allow *Glee* to add new dimension to Joe, who experiences his own heteronormative epiphany—his physical and emotional attraction to women, as opposed to his mental and spiritual devotion to chastity—while in the company of Quinn's disabled body. Tellingly, this epiphany is not hinted at before Quinn becomes disabled, nor does the show follow up on it after the fact: after establishing the beginnings of a relationship between Quinn and Joe, *Glee* then drops that plotline almost entirely in the following episodes as she continues to recover from her disability. In other words, Quinn's disabled body—passive and flexible, laid out before Joe on a rehab mat—functions as both a literal and metaphorical means to bring about Joe's heteronormative epiphany. Having fulfilled that purpose, that body (like Sean's in Season 1) then begins to disappear, absorbed back into a storyline Quinn has gone through multiple times. Despite the queer promise of developing "something new," *Glee* ultimately returns once more to the preexisting heteronormative state.[17]

"There's always someone who's got it worse than you do": Jean Sylvester and Becky Jackson

Whenever I tell someone that I write about representations of disability on *Glee*, he or she usually responds by mentioning two specific characters—Jean Sylvester (Robin Trocki), the beloved older sister of Sue Sylvester, and Becky Jackson (Lauren Potter), a member of Sue's cheerleading squad.[18] The reasons for the comparison are plain: Jean and Becky are introduced in the same episode, they both interact primarily with Sue, and, most germane to this essay and to their respective plots on the show, they both have Down syndrome. But rather than focusing on the ways in which they are similar, I would like to conclude this essay by considering the ways in which they are dissimilar, the ways in which they represent both the best and the worst of *Glee*'s impulses in the on-screen depiction of disability.

Viewers first meet Jean and Becky in "Wheels," in which Becky tries out for—and wins—an open spot on Coach Sylvester's Cheerios (a decision that puzzles other characters— most particularly Mr. Schuester, who remains convinced that Sue has some nefarious purpose for letting Becky on the squad—but that the audience learns is motivated by Sue's feelings for her older sister). The show presents Jean from the outset as completely asexual and even somewhat infantilized,[19] positioning her squarely within the ableist cultural tradition that sexuality is not and should not be part of the lives of people with disabilities. The closest the show allows Jean to come to the queer is when she attends Sue's wedding to herself in "Furt," where she serves as ringbearer, but even then, her role is minimal and in itself reflective of ableist stereotypes of passivity and childishness. Throughout her five-episode run on *Glee*, Jean serves as a reminder to viewers of Sue's basic decency; several of Sue's more over-the-top plotlines are resolved through wisdom passed down from Jean.[20] And indeed, the decision to kill off Jean's character in the late second-season episode "Funeral" seems to have been motivated, at least in part, by the need to engender some sympathy for Sue's character in the audience after a season in which her behavior grew ever more outlandish. The larger thematic purpose of Jean's death, however, is actually to facilitate the romantic reconciliation of Finn and Rachel; even—or especially—in death, *Glee* coopts her for use as the site of Finn's heteronormative epiphany.

After Finn and Rachel break up in "Special Education" because she has cheated on him with Puck, Rachel spends the remainder of Season 2 trying to convince Finn to give her another chance, but he rejects her advances—at least for most of the latter half of the season— and instead begins dating his previous girlfriend, Quinn. By "Funeral," however, there have been numerous indications that Finn's feelings for Rachel are resurfacing, and those feelings come to a head over Jean's death. With Sue virtually incapacitated by grief, Finn takes the lead in planning Jean's funeral, and it is there that his heteronormative epiphany occurs. After Sue breaks down reading the eulogy, Mr. Schuester takes over, and the camera pans over the faces of the attendees, landing on Finn as Mr. Schuester reads, "When you love someone the way I loved her, they're a part of you. It's like you're attached by this invisible tether, and no matter how far away you are, you can always feel them" ("Funeral"). The look on Finn's face telegraphs his epiphany; he simply does not love Quinn as much as he loves Rachel. Immediately following the service, he tells Quinn so: "I shouldn't have done this with you. I thought I could fix everything from last year, but I—I can't. I just can't, and I—that feeling that Sue was talking about in there, of being tethered to someone, I just—I don't feel that way about you" ("Funeral"). Jean's final purpose on the show is thus to make it possible for Rachel and Finn to once again be together. Ultimately, like Sean before her and Quinn after her, Jean's disability exists on *Glee* to facilitate the heteronormative epiphanies of nondisabled characters.

By comparison, while Becky begins her run on the series in a somewhat similar fashion to Jean's, her character eventually grows and develops into a much more complex portrayal. Notably, she is the only disabled character on the show who does not play a major role in helping foment heteronormative epiphanies for nondisabled characters—a role that even Artie plays, at least once.[21] Furthermore, beyond being co-captain of the Cheerios and integrated into the classrooms of McKinley High, she also expresses sexual and romantic desire, which are treated as legitimate, healthy, and on par with those of other, nondisabled characters.[22] In fact, *Glee* devotes a substantial part of the third season episode "Yes/No" to exploring Becky's desire for a romantic relationship. In a long, sustained internal monologue voiced by Helen Mirren,[23] Becky considers and rejects several male McKinley High students before settling on Artie: "Now that's more like it. Sweet, sexy, and handi-capable, like me,[24] with a voice as velvety as my favorite Sunday church dress. It's decided. Artie Abrams, you're my new boyfriend" ("Yes/No"). She asks him out, and although he tries to pass off a glee club performance as the date she wants, they end up going to Breadstix together for dinner, culminating in Artie's realization that "[t]he more [he] get[s] to know [her], the more [he] like[s] [her]"—though his "like" is platonic, which she does not realize at the time ("Yes/No"). His apparent romantic interest leads Becky to send him suggestive cell phone pictures of herself as "a taste of what [he's] going to get on Friday night," when she plans for them to have sex ("Yes/No").

One could perhaps argue that Becky's portrayal in this episode falls under the stereotype of "excessive" sexuality (most frequently applied to those with developmental disabilities) in that Artie does not reciprocate Becky's desire and is in fact distressed by it. But as Sue points out when Artie goes to her for advice on how to handle Becky's naughty texts, similar behavior in his past relationships did not make him uncomfortable, suggesting that the real issue here is society's attitudes toward disability,[25] not the disability itself:

> SUE: Well, you dated Brittany. I'm sure she sent you titillating photos. That freak you out?

ARTIE: I guess not, but that was different.[26]
SUE: Well, did you go out to dinner with Becky?
ARTIE: Yeah, we had a great time.
SUE: Do you want to go out with her again?
ARTIE: No.
SUE: Well, here's a radical idea. Why don't you treat her like a real person and tell her? ... So why don't you tell her the truth so she can move on and maybe date someone who doesn't sound like one of those weird puppets they bring around to the grade schools to teach kids about sexual predators ["Yes/No"].

The most important aspect of this interaction is that it does not assume that Becky's failed attempt at romance with Artie means that any future attempts at romance are similarly doomed to fail or that Becky will remain trapped in heartbreak forever, both of which would fit with the ableist, heteronormative stereotype of the doomed or tragic disabled person, rendered forever undesirable by her disability. On the contrary, it suggests that Becky will get past the pain of Artie's rejection and that requited romantic and/or sexual love may very well be a part of her future[27]— impressions supported by Becky's actual reaction to Artie breaking up with her: disappointed, saddened, and realistic about the role her Down syndrome played in the break-up, but hardly devastated or tragic. And in fact, Becky's next major plotline, in "Prom-asaurus," supports this idea; when next viewers see her, she is apparently quite over Artie, confidently flirting with Puck at the "Anti-Prom" and eventually taking him as her date, albeit a platonic one, to McKinley High's official prom.[28] In this context, *Glee*'s representation of Becky's sexuality can be regarded as profoundly queer—a claim that can hardly be made of the show's other disabled characters.

Where Does *Glee* Go from Here?

Leonard Kriegel claims that "[i]t is important to point out that writers, by and large, view the world from the vantage point of 'normals.' Writers like to think of themselves as rebels, but the rebellions they are interested in usually reinforce society's conception of what is and is not desirable" (33). Had the preceding sentences not been written in 1987, one might almost suspect Kriegel wrote them with *Glee* in mind. For while *Glee* prides itself on portraying disability in sensitive and thought-provoking ways, in truth, the show often reifies the very stereotypes about disability that it purports to challenge. Its track record regarding issues of disability and sexuality is particularly poor, as *Glee* frequently denies or suppresses the sexuality of its disabled characters in ways that support ableist stereotypes about sexuality in people with disabilities. Without wishing to claim that any of *Glee*'s disabled characters are portrayed either wholly negatively or wholly positively, on balance, *Glee* provides its disabled characters with actions and plotlines that largely adhere to and/or support heteronormative, ableist societal standards, while far more rarely presenting material that allows for a queering of the norm. As the show moves forward, if it would seek to improve its representations of disabled characters, it could do worse than to follow the queer example of Becky Faye Jackson, "the hottest bitch at McKinley High School" ("Yes/No"), and develop disabled characters for whom sexuality is a visible, important, and everyday part of their plots, storylines, and lives.

Notes

1. It is by now well established that "queer," when used in the academic/activist sense of the word, names not a single sexual identity or way of desiring but rather a range of ways of desiring. The queer, then, threatens boundaries; although it has sometimes in the past been used as an antonym for heterosexuality, the queer more properly opposes (if such a dualistic conception may be said to exist) the heteronormative. Unlike what Gayle Rubin identifies as society's "Good, Normal, Natural, Blessed Sexuality"—sexuality that is "Heterosexual, Married, Monogamous, Procreative, Noncommercial, In pairs, In a relationship, Same generation, In private, No pornography, Bodies only, [and] Vanilla" (Rubin 13)—the queer embraces modes of sexual desiring and sexual expression that dare to venture beyond the prescribed bounds of heteronormativity.

2. See, for example, 1.9 "Wheels," 1.18 "Laryngitis," 1.19 "Dream On," 2.4 "Duet," 2.5 "The Rocky Horror Glee Show," 2.6 "Never Been Kissed," and 3.12 "The Spanish Teacher."

3. In fact, when Mr. Schuester decides to allow Kurt to audition, he does so by specifically referencing the similarity of Kurt's situation and Artie's: "I can't in good conscience preach about the importance of helping Artie, then reject Kurt's request out of hand" ("Wheels").

4. Two points here invite further commentary: One, Mr. Schuester's decision to have the glee club perform "Proud Mary" in wheelchairs is itself ableist, as it reinforces what Mollow and McRuer call "universalizing models of disability: everyone's a little disabled, really; we all face physical and mental challenges, but these can and should be overcome with hard work" ("Introduction" 22). This supports a claim Mr. Schuester makes in an earlier episode, "Throwdown," where he tells his students, "[Y]ou're all minorities. You're in the Glee Club." Two, it is ironic that Artie teaches others how to dance in the chairs when disability advocates such as Alice Sheppard, a dancer with AXIS Dance Company, have criticized how McHale moves in the chair: "There's an understanding of embodiment that's just not physical in McHale's portrayal of Artie, and for me, what I see is a huge gap between the body and the chair.... There's no rhythm, there's no feel, there's no understanding of the chair as part of his body.... And the sad thing about it is that McHale is a beautiful dancer, he's a really gorgeous mover, and, you know, he just can't make it work in the chair."

5. Prior to this moment, viewers have no idea if Artie was born or became disabled.

6. See, for example, the way the show treats Sean, the quadriplegic character it introduces in "Laryngitis," which I will discuss further later in the essay.

7. While there is a possible issue of infantilization here, Artie is clearly drawn to what Brittany is proposing: his face lights up in a sly, delighted smile.

8. When Artie says, "After my accident, we didn't know if I'd ever be able even to do that," his singular, emphatic 'that' refers specifically to vaginal intercourse, which erases the possibility of a practically infinite number of other forms of sexual expression, as well as the sexual lives and experiences of many disabled people. As Tobin Siebers notes: "Being able-bodied assumes the capacity to partition off sexuality as if it were a sector of private life: that an individual *has* sex or a sex life implies a form of private ownership based on the assumption that sexual activity occupies a particular and limited part of life determined by the measure of ability, control, or assertiveness exercised by that individual. People with disabilities do not always have this kind of sex life. On the one hand, the stigma of disability may interfere with having sex. On the other hand, the sexual activities of disabled people do not necessarily follow normative assumptions about what a sex life is. Neither fact means that people with disabilities do not exist as sexual beings" [39].

9. Nor does the show ever make it clear that Brittany was, in fact, only using him for his voice. Certainly she is drawn to him originally as a means to spite Santana, but at no point does she ever suggest that she is completely without feelings for him; on the contrary, when he breaks up with her, she is upset even before he brings up her apparent sexual betrayal. When he accuses her of only wanting a free dinner at Breadstix (the reward for that week's glee club assignment winners), she replies, "But I really wanted to go with you. I was gonna order us one really long piece of spaghetti, like in *Lady and the Tramp*. I've been practicing nudging the meatball across the table with my nose" ("Duets").

10. The show does condescend to have Artie later admit that "[he] was kind of mean to her when [he] blew her off," but he makes this admission to Puck, not to Brittany herself ("Never Been Kissed").

11. Seeing that his attentions are distinctly unwelcome leads Sean to immediately recast his prior behavior in the only way Rachel can, in fact, understand—as awkward attempts at humor: "They make me see a shrink. He says I compensate with humor" ("Laryngitis"). In doing so, Sean employs what Rosemarie Garland-Thomson calls a classic strategy by disabled persons "to manage relationships from the beginning [in hopes of being granted fully human status]. In other words, disabled people must use charm, intimidation, ardor, deference, humor, or entertainment to relieve nondisabled people of their discomfort" (13).

12. This is consistent with accounts by disabled persons of the erotic visual quality of stimulus of their or their partners' bodies, regardless of their ability to feel that stimulus. For examples, see Shakespeare, Gillespie-Sells, and Davies' *The Sexual Politics of Disability: Untold Desires* (1996), as well as, more recently, Sarah Smith Rainey's *Love, Sex, and Disability: The Pleasures of Care* (2011).

13. I specify "arguably" because one could read Quinn as queer (because nonheteronormative) outside of her disability plotline by focusing on her status as an unwed teenage mother.

14. For example, she tells her boyfriend Sam in "Never Been Kissed" that when they're Prom King and Queen it will feel just as good as the "little something something" sexual he wants from her.

15. After Mercedes and Rachel comment on how cute Quinn and Joe were together, Brittany adds, "I don't know, Joe's really pretty, but I heard she doesn't shave her armpits" ("Dance with Somebody"). This observation further hints at the queer potential of Quinn and Joe's relationship. Notwithstanding Brittany's limited mental gifts—she redefines the term "dumb blonde"—a major character on the show, herself involved in a queer relationship, reads Quinn and Joe's relationship as queer.

16. By this, I mean that Quinn's basic plot arc—from popularity-obsessed mean girl to a smart, wise young woman with dreams and plans beyond high school—is one that viewers see her repeat time and again on the show (for example, in Season 1, from head cheerleader who hates the glee club and actively plots its downfall to a fully participating

member of the Club who lives with Mercedes, one of its founding members; in Season 2, back to head cheerleader chasing Prom Queen glory and scheming to destroy the glee club after Finn breaks up with her for Rachel; and earlier in Season 3, before becoming disabled, trying to have her daughter's adoptive mother declared unfit before realizing that the glee club provides her with the family and sense of belonging she needs). Quinn's disability is used as a means to fulfill the Prom Queen dream she has carried throughout the years and then to teach her that she is better off giving up that dream, but this is a beat that has been hit several times over the course of the series.

17. This point is made explicit by Quinn's choice, once fully recovered from her disability, to rekindle—or at least strongly hint at rekindling—a romantic relationship with the hypermasculine Puck, rather than pursuing anything further with Joe.

18. In fact, Jean and Becky usually get mentioned before Artie, which is somewhat curious, given their comparatively small roles on *Glee*.

19. For example, her favorite activity is having Sue read to her from *Little Red Riding Hood*, her favorite book ("Wheels").

20. For example, when the glee club leaks an embarrassing video of Sue on the internet that leads to Sue's widespread social humiliation, Sue retreats to Jean's side, where Jean suggests that Sue might feel better if she did something for someone else for a while, such as volunteering at an animal shelter ("Bad Reputation").

21. In "The First Time," Artie encourages Ohio State University recruiter Cooter Mankins to try again to pursue a romantic relationship with McKinley High's female football coach, Shannon Beiste, who is convinced that Mankins has no interest in her and so has always been dismissive of his romantic overtures. Later in the season, in "Choke," it is revealed that Mankins has been domestically abusing Beiste for sometime.

22. For example, in "Silly Love Songs," when she gives Finn a candy heart and asks him to be her Valentine, he is flattered (though he does not reciprocate), informing viewers in voiceover that "[he's] been collecting a lot of hearts lately" before adding hers to the overflowing bucket of candy in his locker. Later in the second season, in "Prom," Becky attends prom with a date, Jason, who also has Down syndrome.

23. This can be regarded as simultaneously empowering and derogatory: Becky can be seen as taking control of her own narrative by deciding for herself how she wants to sound, or she can be read as internalizing societal oppression telling her that she needs to sound more "normal," even in her own head.

24. The disability rights community, it is worth noting, largely rejects the use of terminology like "handicapable," preferring to use simply "disabled" or "people with disabilities."

25. Artie's internalized ableist attitudes appear at various times throughout the show and are consistent with real- world accounts by some disabled persons regarding their feelings about disability in themselves and in others. As Shakespeare, Gillespie-Sells, and Davies point out, "[D]isabled people themselves are socialized within this dominant culture, and therefore hold conflicting views about desirable partners, and can have negative views about themselves" (49). For example, after the other glee club members confront Artie about his date with Becky, suggesting that he is "lead[ing] her on," Artie angrily dismisses their concerns: "What is she gonna think? That she's fun to be around, that I had a good time hanging out with her? ... I liked spending time with Becky. She knows what it's liked to be trapped by a disability.... She's really optimistic about life, which is really amazing considering what life has handed her" ("Yes/No"). Artie's ableism is two-fold here: one, he considers it impossible that she would think that their date was motivated by genuine romantic interest on his part, and two, he considers her (and by extension, himself) "trapped by a disability." Coming from Artie, who canonically struggles with feelings of diminished self-worth related to his disability, such projected opinions of Becky's quality of life make sense. Notably, however, Becky does not seem to share these feelings; she acknowledges her disability and the limitations it sometimes causes her, but she regards them just as parts of her life. Artie assumes that every day Becky lives with

a disability is a bad day for Becky, but she refutes that idea; some days are bad, certainly, but not all. For example, when Artie tells her he just wants to be friends, she responds in voiceover, "I didn't ask him what I wanted to ask him. I didn't ask if the reason he didn't want to be my boyfriend was because I have Down's. I didn't ask him because I know the answer is yes. *Some days*, it sucks being me" ("Yes/No," emphasis added).

26. Without wishing to imply that developmentally disabled people are unintelligent or that a lack of intelligence is synonymous with disability, I feel it deserves mention here that *Glee* more than once makes the point that Becky is smarter than Brittany, rendering Artie's comment of "that was different" even more problematic. For example, in "Wheels," it is revealed that Brittany frequently cheats off of Becky in math, and Sue comments in "The Spanish Teacher" that Becky is a better speller than Brittany.

27. Also notable is that Sue does not assume that any future partner of Becky's will necessarily be disabled.

28. It is important to note that the date is *mutually* platonic; Becky is no more seriously interested in dating Puck than he in dating her. She does, however, find him sexually attractive, luring him into a game of strip poker and mentally referring to him as a "hot piece of booty" ("Prom-asaurus").

References

"Bad Reputation." Episode 1.17. *Glee: The Complete First Season*. Twentieth Century–Fox, 2010. DVD.

"Big Brother." Episode 3.15. *Glee*. Fox Broadcasting Company. 10 April 2012. Television.

"Choke." Episode 3.18. *Glee*. Fox Broadcasting Company. 1 May 2012. Television.

"Dance with Somebody." Episode 3.17. *Glee*. Fox Broadcasting Company. 24 April 2012. Television.

"Duets." Episode 2.4. *Glee: The Complete Second Season*. Twentieth Century–Fox, 2011. DVD.

"The First Time." *Glee*. Fox Broadcasting Company. 8 November 2011. Television.

"Funeral." Episode 2.21. *Glee: The Complete Second Season*. Twentieth Century–Fox, 2011. DVD.

"Furt." Episode 2.8. *Glee: The Complete Second Season*. Twentieth Century–Fox, 2011. DVD.

Garland-Thomson, Rosemarie. *Extraordinary Bodies: Figuring Disability in American Culture and Literature*. New York: Columbia University Press, 1997.

"Hold on to Sixteen." Episode 3.8. *Glee*. Fox Broadcasting Company. 6 Dec. 2011. Television.

Kriegel, Leonard. "The Cripple in Literature." *Images of the Disabled, Disabling Images*. Eds. Alan Gartner and Tom Joe. New York: Praeger, 1987. 31–46.

"Laryngitis." Episode 1.18. *Glee: The Complete First Season*. Twentieth Century–Fox, 2010. DVD.

McRuer, Robert. *Crip Theory: Cultural Signs of Queerness and Disability*. New York: New York University Press, 2006.

Mollow, Anna. "Is Sex Disability? Queer Theory and the Disability Drive." *Sex and Disability*. Eds. Robert McRuer and Anna Mollow. Durham: Duke University Press, 2012. 285–312.

Mollow, Anna, and Robert McRuer. "Introduction." *Sex and Disability*. Eds. Robert McRuer and Anna Mollow. Durham: Duke University Press, 2012. 1–34.

"Never Been Kissed." Episode 2.6. *Glee: The Complete Second Season*. Twentieth Century–Fox, 2011. DVD.

"Preggers." Episode 1.4. *Glee: The Complete First Season*. Twentieth Century–Fox, 2010. DVD.

"Prom-asaurus." Episode 3.19. *Glee*. Fox Broadcasting Company. 8 May 2012. Television.

Rainey, Sarah Smith. *Love, Sex, and Disability: The Pleasures of Care.* Boulder, CO: Lynne Rienner, 2011.

Rubin, Gayle. "Thinking Sex: Notes for a Radical Theory of the Politics of Sexuality." 1984. *The Lesbian and Gay Studies Reader.* Eds. Henry Abelove, Michèle Aina Barale, and David Halperin. New York: Routledge, 1993. 3–44.

Shakespeare, Tom, Kath Gillespie-Sells, and Dominic Davies. *Untold Desires: The Sexual Politics of Disability.* London: Cassell, 1996.

Sheppard, Alice, et al. Interview on *The Largest Minority.* WBAI. New York City. 22 December 2010. Radio.

Siebers, Tobin. "A Sexual Culture for Disabled People." *Sex and Disability.* Eds. Robert McRuer and Anna Mollow. Durham: Duke University Press, 2012. 37–53.

"Silly Love Songs." Episode 2.12. *Glee: The Complete Second Season.* Twentieth Century–Fox, 2011. DVD.

"The Spanish Teacher." Episode 3.12. *Glee.* Fox Broadcasting Company. 7 February 2012. Television.

"Throwdown." Episode 1.7. *Glee: The Complete First Season.* Twentieth Century–Fox, 2010. DVD.

"Wheels." Episode 1.9. *Glee: The Complete First Season.* Twentieth Century–Fox, 2010. DVD.

Wilkerson, Abby L. "Normate Sex and Its Discontents." *Sex and Disability.* Eds. Robert McRuer and Anna Mollow. Durham: Duke University Press, 2012. 183–207.

"Yes/No." Episode 3.10. *Glee.* Fox Broadcasting Company. 17 Jan. 2012. Television.

Note: On September 18, 2012, Crip theorist Robert McRuer, whose ideas form the background for much of my analysis in this piece, published an article on Avidly.org about another show created by Ryan Murphy, *The New Normal*, which premiered in fall 2012 on Fox. McRuer's article, "The New Normal: Normal and Normaller," focuses on how *The New Normal* relies on ableist stereotypes to "normalize" the idea of two gay men becoming parents, and many of the arguments I make in this article bear a resemblance to ones McRuer makes in his. Although this article was submitted to this collection before McRuer's article on *The New Normal* was published, taken together, they establish a striking pattern in Ryan Murphy's televised representations of disability—one in which disabled characters serve little purpose other than to act as narrative conduits through which nondisabled characters may achieve "normality."

"So, is this the part where you judge me?"

Adolescent Sexuality

NIALL NANCE-CARROLL

From the beginning of its first season *Glee* was already heavily invested in portrayals of adolescent sexuality. Given early episodes that featured an unplanned pregnancy and a coming out story, it was no surprise that the show soon became a prime target of conservative critics such as Dan Gainor, who described McKinley High as "the gayest high school in America" and "a high school most parents would not want to send their kids to" (Fisher). Gainor's characterization of the show as "intentionally provocative" and his assertion that "controversy helps them promote their agenda," (Fisher) echoed similarly dire concerns over the sexual morality of earlier shows such as *Buffy the Vampire Slayer* and *Dawson's Creek*. Less predictable, however, was the criticism from other end of the political spectrum, which denounced *Glee* as overly conservative in its sexual politics. "Over the past two seasons," wrote Alyssa Rosenberg, "it's become impossible to escape the conclusion that Glee is an immoral show, but not for the reason cultural conservatives believe." Rosenberg called to task the show's creator, Ryan Murphy, as "a cynical exploiter of oppressed people who has very little actual interest in actually exploring their experiences in rich, complex, compassionate ways."

This essay examines both sets of claims, Right and Left, in light of the show's main sexual storylines, identifying the show's overarching stance on adolescent sexuality and considering its potential effects on an audience of adolescents and young adults. A note of caution is in order with regard to that first task. In their introduction to *Mikhail Bakhtin: Creation of a Prosaics* Gary Saul Morson and Caryl Emerson write, "Books about thinkers require a kind of unity that their thought may not possess" (1). Likewise, essays that seek to bring interpretive lenses to bear on a television show lend unity or coherence to a project involving a multitude of people and with them a multitude of agendas and perspectives. While *Glee's* moral and political outlook is largely consistent, there are certainly exceptions, and these are not limited to the actions or statements of individual characters or writers. At times the entire portrayal of a given character or issue may run contrary to the apparently progressive agenda of the show. While these exceptions will be acknowledged as they arise, this essay will argue that a largely coherent moral stance does emerge in *Glee*, especially on issues of sexuality.

When it comes to political agendas and aspirations, it is clear that questions of gender occupy *Glee's* center stage. While the show sometimes nods to issues of race and class, as many have noted, engagement with such issues is cursory, as when Tina commiserates with Mike on his grade of A-, an "Asian F" in the episode of the same name. When Sam's family is suddenly impoverished and lose their house, plotlines involving his poverty focus on temporary and relatively easily alleviated problems—the Glee club can buy back his guitar ("Rumors") and Rachel and Mercedes can arrange for him to go to Prom ("Prom Queen")—rather than on serious or long-term consequences of poverty. Conflicts due to race and class are typically resolved in a single episode. In contrast, Quinn's pregnancy, Kurt's coming out, anti-gay bullying, and various characters' decisions to have sex all receive extended plot treatment. Moreover, the show treats conflicts of race and class mainly as practical problems. Although *Glee* does (briefly) address directly some practical elements of sex education and pregnancy, it presents factual knowledge almost exclusively as the subject of humor. Rather than combining practical information about sex with discussions of sexual morality, the show separates the two topics. When practical matters are treated, the cluelessness of the characters pushes the bounds of believability: Finn and Mercedes think that Holly is explaining that condoms are necessary because cucumbers spread AIDS, and Brittany believes that storks bring babies ("Sexy"). Such responses reinforce the idea that lack of knowledge of sexuality is not only irresponsible but silly and immature. Likewise, when Finn asks Puck to recommend a brand of condom, Puck's unhelpful answer is that he never used them, and that it worked "ninety-nine percent of the time" ("The First Time"). Given the amount of time devoted to the pregnancy subplot, Puck's answer underscores the irresponsibility of unsafe sex, without sermonizing. Holly, the show's major source of formal sex education, conveys information about the risk of unprotected sex positively and with humor, as opposed to issuing stern warnings or admonitions. Such informational moments are rare, however: the majority of *Glee*'s plotlines on sexuality focus on moral judgments.

Glee devotes several episodes specifically to couples making the decision to have sex. In the first of these episodes, "The Power of Madonna," two of the couples, Will and Emma and Rachel and Jesse, decide not to. The third couple, Finn and Santana, is unsatisfied by their choice. "The First Time" features parallel plotlines with Rachel and Finn and Kurt and Blaine. When Rachel and Blaine set out to lose their virginity specifically to better portray dramatic roles, Finn and Kurt reject their respective partners. Only after Rachel and Blaine are no longer seeking to use their sexual experience for artistic improvement, are their respective partners interested in sex. In each instance the characters discuss their decisions in advance, and in both episodes Rachel seeks advice from the other girls of the Glee club. They advise her, even though they do not necessarily like her, and offer a range of opinions. Quinn provides the voice of warning, citing her own pregnancy as a reason why having sex is a bad idea. Santana, while generally in favor of having sex, advises Rachel not to sleep with Finn because he is bad in bed ("The First Time"). Tina explains that sleeping with Mike was a great idea—not because they will necessarily be together forever, she adds, but because they both felt like it was the right time ("The First Time"). The narrative of the episode supports Tina's advice, and Rachel's and Kurt's decisions. When sex is portrayed as negative, it is because one of the characters is using the other for social advancement. As long as both partners are on the same page, sex is portrayed as positive—providing, of course, that they use protection.

Quinn's pregnancy, the show's most obvious consequence of sex, is certainly not easy: *Glee* is not suggesting that it is a good idea to have a baby as a teenager. Quinn remains central to the show during her pregnancy, and members' families take her in when her father kicks her out of the house. While Finn and Puck are prepared to support Quinn whichever decision she makes, and while Puck intends (albeit ineffectually) to support their child, the baby does not serve to cement an ongoing romantic relationship between the young parents. Nor does the show suggest that Quinn's status as a mother will somehow make her an adult. She still remains fully an adolescent both during and after the pregnancy. Only in the third season, her senior year of high school, do others start insisting that she become more mature and stop acting childish. Although the show occasionally explores Quinn's second thoughts about giving up Beth for adoption, the impression is never that it would be a good idea for her to attempt to raise her daughter. Shelby explains, "I realized that no matter how much it hurt me, I did right by my daughter," referring to the her situation of giving Rachel up for adoption as a parallel to Quinn's experience ("I Am Unicorn"). Quinn does not initially take to this advice and attempts to sabotage Shelby's custody in "Pot O' Gold" and even considers having another child—an idea that even Puck rejects as being foolish ("I Kissed a Girl"). Even while portraying a level of support that reflects more the ideal than the reality of most pregnant teenagers' lives, *Glee* is careful not to tip the scales into suggesting that having a baby as a teenager is advisable. The right choice, *Glee* suggests, is to give Beth up for adoption. Not only does the show depict baby Beth with a loving adoptive mother who can take excellent care of her, depictions of Rachel's family further assure viewers that adopted children are well-loved and cared for. Finally, the show does not suggest that becoming pregnant forecloses Quinn's own future. As Kurt sums it up in "On My Way," "Sure you had a baby when you were 16 and you had a bad dye job for two weeks, but seriously, the world never stopped loving you, and you're going to Yale."

Kurt's comment, his response to Quinn's harsh judgment of a suicide attempt by Karofsky—the football team bully who drives Kurt out of McKinley High, but who turns out to be gay and eventually asks Kurt out—also reflects the relative emphasis placed by *Glee* on its two major sexual plotlines—teen pregnancy and coming out. In terms of screen time for issues of sex and gender, homosexuality is demonstrably more central to the show. Although early episodes center on Kurt's fears of his father's response to his sexuality, his anxiety turns out to be unfounded: Burt's matter-of-fact expression of love and acceptance wins him the title of "best dad on television."[1]

While Burt's response reflects the overall hopefulness of the show, it also reflects shifting social attitudes. Being working-class and from a small town no longer excuses homophobia, as Burt champions and defends Kurt. When Kurt temporarily attempts to return to the closet because he feels that Burt prefers spending time with Finn, Burt insists that even if it is difficult sometimes, it is his responsibility to work on it—not Kurt's ("Laryngitis"). His endorsement of his responsibility to his son and the assurance that this is not part of a reciprocal accommodation in which Kurt is expected to alter his self-presentation to be more traditionally masculine is essential to *Glee*'s view of orientation and presentation. Everyone has the right to be (and show) who he or she is.

Acknowledgment of that right on *Glee* does not result in utopian transformation, as apparent when both Blaine and Burt caution Kurt that his decision to wear a kilt to prom is likely to face homophobic responses, but it does assuredly "get better." As the club members reflect back on their years at Lima on the eve of graduation, Kurt is congratulated on having made the school safer for "tadpole gays" ("Goodbye"). At every pass Kurt's journey has been more difficult than that of the straight characters, with the result that his arrival with Blaine at the parallel episode with Rachel and Finn is itself a sort of victory. Even after he comes out and meets Blaine, Kurt is initially not only uncertain about having sex, he does not even want to hear about it. When Blaine broaches the topic, Kurt goes so far as to cover his ears and ask Blaine to leave; Blaine responds by approaching Burt and asking him to have "the sex talk" with Kurt ("Sexy"). While Burt tells Blaine that he is overstepping his bounds, Blaine insists that Kurt's peers are not an adequate source of sex education; that Burt himself needs to talk to his son ("Sexy"). It is only after that awkward endorsement that Kurt feels free to make his own decision. Even after all is going well with Kurt, with a handsome boyfriend and plans for a promising future in New York, *Glee* takes pains with the Karofsky plot to emphasize that homophobia and its tragic consequences for adolescents have not been vanquished from Lima. "Fag" is spray-painted on his locker, he is subject to hateful online messages, his friends stop talking to him, and his mother tells him he has a "disease" ("On My Way"). Even though he lives through his suicide attempt, the show does not imply that his troubles have come to an end; "I'm not gonna lie to you," Kurt tells him, " it isn't going to be easy and there will be days when life just sucks" but he also assures him that he will have support ("On My Way").

These three storylines—decisions to have sex, teenage pregnancy, and the consequences of coming out—do not exhaust the show's treatment of sexuality, which also extends to student- teacher relationships, romantic relationships between students' parents, and occasionally to intersections of sexuality and disability. Nevertheless, they serve as a fair illustration of the attitudes toward sexuality that the show appears to endorse. Summed up, *Glee*'s message is that the decision to have sex should be up to only those involved. Ethical sexuality requires honesty, consent, and protection. By extension, violations of sexual ethics would include instrumental use of another person, overly aggressive sexual advances, and denial of the others' rights to express and act on their own sexuality. Under these rules, Puck and Shelby's student/teacher one-night stand entails no serious ethical breach and thus requires no narrative punishment. By this measure, the sexual rules of *Glee* are considerably more liberal than those of *Dawson's Creek* where a similar student/teacher relationship between Pacey and his teacher ended in him having to (falsely) claim that he had invented the entire episode, permanently damaging his social status ("Baby"). Certainly *Glee* does not suggest that a relationship between a teacher and one of her students is appropriate, but neither does it suggest that it is necessarily exploitive. Puck was of age, interested in her, and neither one of them was attempting to use the other. For purposes of the show, they were in the clear, and Quinn's threat to tell others about the relationship is presented as petty and part of an ill-advised scheme to get Beth back.

Clearly, the Right-wing critics are correct that the show does not support extremely conservative values such as abstinence-only sex education and anti-homosexuality. There is no surprise here; *Glee* never claimed to promote such values. Indeed, conservatives can reference the show as shorthand for liberal values, as Bristol Palin did when criticizing Barack Obama's endorsement of gay marriage; Palin wrote that the endorsement was "merely reflecting what many teenagers think after one too many episodes of *Glee*." On the other hand, *Glee* does seem to be respectful (if a bit skeptical) of religious reservations about sexuality, as exemplified in the third season by a conversation between Sam and Joe regarding Quinn; Sam asserts that while he's "a good Christian, there's just no way a dude's gonna be able to resist" and asks Joe to decide if he wants to be "closer to god or closer to her?" ("Dance with Somebody"). Quinn asks Joe, "Would you give up your faith to be with me?" but then says that she is not asking him to, eventually defining the relationship between them as "something new" ("Dance with Somebody").

A response to claims from the Left—that *Glee* has failed to live up to its potential of promoting tolerance and diversity—is more complicated. As noted earlier, the fictional world of *Glee* is far from perfectly tolerant and diverse. Some of the show's apparent conservatism is no doubt a consequence of commercial constraints or of insufficient ideological purity on the part of writers and producers, and Jennifer Mulligan is no doubt correct that while the show has critiqued some of the stereotypes that it has initially perpetuated, "*Glee* has room to grow as a television show critiquing common stereotypes of race, ability, and sexuality." For instance, while the show attempts to take a non-judgmental stance on promiscuity, those characters who engage in promiscuous sex are presented as stupid (Brittany), rather heartless (Santana and Sebastian), or immature (April Rhodes and Holly Holliday). Brittany and Santana's promiscuity comes to an abrupt end when they are paired up in a monogamous relationship, suggesting that promiscuity is not a stable state but rather a phase. Emma does call Will a "slut," but generally promiscuity is presented as a trait that is only notable in women, reflecting society's well-known double-standards. This instance, though, of Will being judged and deemed a "slut" suggests that *Glee* is interested in critiquing those standards. At the risk of stating the obvious, *Glee* is commercial television and subject to corresponding constraints; only shows that promise to attract sponsors are likely to be picked up for prime time on Fox. Nevertheless, I will argue, some of elements of the show cited by the Left as shortcomings may paradoxically contribute to *Glee*'s potential to change the world.

Both groups' criticism of *Glee*, Left and Right, is underpinned by a common assumption, that a TV show has real-world effects on its audience. In this they are probably both correct, but the evidence bears examination. Can *Glee* change the world? While the question may suggest either a hyperbolic claim about the impact of prime-time television or else a critique of the moralizing of the show as heavy-handed and ineffective, I would instead cautiously assert that *Glee* can change the world, but only gradually and only in concert with many other forces at work on society.

Gary Saul Morson and Caryl Emerson observe that, in the view of Bakhtin, "novels ... occupy a special place in ethical education," and that novels "are powerful tools for enriching our moral sense of particular situations" (27). The genre of the novel grants readers detailed insight into an event and into other people; it grants them information that is impossible to access in real life (the inner lives of others). Serial television offers a similar potential because of the sustained storylines and characterization; watchers are able to come to know these characters in depth and, in doing so, they come to appreciate the particularities of the characters' lives. The appreciation for these particularities is key to developing empathy in lasting and useful ways.

Blakey Vermule asserts that "literary characters circulate, levitate, and generally become famous because they help us reason about the social contract under conditions of imperfect access to relevant knowledge" (55). Lisa Zunshine's *Why We Read Fiction* addresses the specific ways in which the novel engages "Theory of Mind" (one's ability to imagine the inner life of another person); however, she is careful to note that this is not merely a product of the novel, or of the written word. Even though the examples that she primarily draws on are modernist novels, she asserts that television shows likewise "require the full exercise of the viewer's Theory of Mind" (11). Zunshine theorizes on what makes fiction in general compelling, and inherent in this is curiosity as to the inner lives of others. While much of the interest in the moral effects of reading novels is used to justify something inherently important about *reading* fiction, Zunshine's observations suggests that other forms of fiction that require similar mental processes may produce the same effects. *Glee* is just as capable of providing the audience with the opportunity to improve their ability to theorize about other people's lives as any novel, and this interest in understanding other people is precisely what allows interactions to extend beyond mere contests of power and provide a space for ethical action.

While *Glee* has often handled some ethical issues with nuance, it has at times handled them with a decided lack thereof. In this regard, occasionally the show engages in self- correction—taking an issue that it has previously failed to address properly and explicitly addressing its previous problem, as in the episode where Santana (rightly) accuses Will of ignorantly perpetuating stereotypes about Latinos in the name of teaching about another culture ("The Spanish Teacher"). This is not to suggest that all of *Glee*'s retrograde moments are part of character development or are eventually resolved—only that social justice and responsibility are apparently central to the show's self-perceived mission. Keren Eyal and Dale Kunkel observed in their study of attitudes towards sexuality and popular culture that the portrayal of negative consequences in popular television shows for emerging adults produced negative attitudes much more strongly than the portrayal of positive consequences produced positive attitudes. Their test also reconfirmed viewers' attitudes several weeks after viewing, and the evidence suggested that the changes in attitude were at least modestly durable. Given that watchers of serial television shows will also have these attitudes reinforced many times over the course of a season, there is every reason to believe that television shows do contribute significantly to the attitudes of young adult viewers. These shows both reflect and construct the youth culture and thus the attitudes they support become part of the range of attitudes that young people perceive as normal or even possible. "Research results have been consistent and robust: fiction *does* mold our minds," Jonathan Gottschall observes (148). Gottschall explains not only that relatively straightforward correlations emerge (such as those in Eyal and Kunkel's experiment), but that indeed "studies have shown that people's deepest moral beliefs and values are modified by the fiction they consume" (151). He notes that when "white viewers see a positive portrayal of black family life—say, in *The Cosby Show*—they usually exhibit more positive attitudes towards black people generally" (151). Such studies support the assertions of critics of varying political outlooks that fictional representations matter.

The consistent access to the opinions and motivations of a range of characters provides a variety of points of identification for the audience. This is not to assert that there is a direct route from watching a program to espousing its politics, much less acting on them. *Glee* likely influences its audience less than the Right fears or the Left hopes. While fiction does have potential effects, they are not direct. Moreover, any real political agenda will bring its own practical constraints. The show can be ideologically pure or it can be effective, but probably not both.

As mentioned above, the program could not have started out so radical as to not be marketable, nor could the characters have been so "good" as to not invite identification. When they watch the show, adolescent audiences need, in some sense, to see themselves. The fictional world of *Glee* is constructed to hold a particular appeal for an adolescent audience. The concerns of *Glee* are typically exaggerated and simplified versions of many standard adolescent experiences. Perry Nodelman asserts that characters in adolescent fiction "live ordinary lives, but see them in terms of melodrama" (qtd. in Trites 3). Roberta Seelinger Trites describes Nodelman's view as dismissive but notes that he reacts "to the profound seriousness that many of these characters express in their first confusion about social institutions" (3). *Glee* wears its moralizing heart on its sleeve, and while certainly much of the show features topics that some might view as melodramatic, the microcosm of small town life and of high school renders such small issues matters of great importance to those involved.

The small world of McKinley provides the arena not only to model behavior but also to discuss and explore moral viewpoints, and ultimately to form them. When it comes to sexuality the characters spend far more time talking about, arguing about, and judging behavior, both others' and their own, than they spend actually having or even pursuing sex. Individually and collectively, they consider future actions and reevaluate the past. While certainly Karofsky undergoes the most dramatic change of heart, even the main characters are presented as works in progress when it comes to attitudes towards sexuality and ethics. Finn's casual use of the word "faggy" regarding Kurt's curtain choice for their shared room requires him to seriously reconsider whether he might be acting homophobic ("Theatricality"). In the same incident, after Burt has chastised Finn for his language, he also calls Kurt out for being dishonest about his attraction to Finn. While Kurt typically acts as the progressive and enlightened character on issues of sexuality, he reacts to Blaine's exploration of his feelings towards Rachel in ways that Blaine identifies as prejudiced against bisexuals ("Blame It on the Alcohol"). It is precisely this unfinished quality that makes the characters especially useful in an ethical project. *Glee* works, to the extent that it does work, by encouraging its viewers to consider the perspectives of others and to measure themselves against the same moral yardstick by which the show measures the characters.

Glee emphasizes unfinalizability,[2] not only through the transitory nature of high school and the potential to leave it, but also through the redemptive storylines for even characters that have previously seemed to be caricatures of cruelty. This unfinalizability is at the heart of *Glee*'s interest in judgment; plotlines are steeped in judging and in learning to judge better, but *Glee* emphasizes that such judgments must be temporary and contingent—based on how people act toward others, not who they are. When Kurt affirms that this is not the part where he judges Karofsky, it is because Karofsky is exploring his sexuality and not causing harm to others ("The First Time"). Karofsky explains that he feels accepted at the club, although he is remaining in the closet at his new school and asks "is this the part where you judge me?" but Kurt replies "No. As long as you're not beating people up, I'm all for being whoever you have to be at your own speed" ("The First Time"). He also asserts that he would never have told anyone, as he has previously told Karofsky, "I don't believe in denying who you are, but I don't believe in outing, either" ("Born This Way").

The characters in the glee club are subject to frequent bullying, and their location seems to foreclose upon their dreams and on the possibility of happiness. However, for many of the characters, their anticipation of an impending exit from Lima suggests that it is merely rural Midwestern America that is a problem, and that there is a place for them in the world at large. This is an ultimately hopeful vision for adolescents; while there remain pockets of hatred, overall, the larger world holds a place for them. Ultimately, as Kurt explains to Karofsky when they meet at the bar in "The First Time," this is expressly *not* the part where he will be judged.

Emphasis on the temporary nature of high school and of bigoted attitudes keeps *Glee* focused on hopeful matters even as it runs occasionally bleak storylines. Kimberley Reynolds notes that "many writers, editors, publishers, and critics argue strongly that whatever happens in the course of books, and no matter how realistically it is presented, if they are intended to be read by children, books should end on a note of optimism or at least hope" (89). An unrelentingly bleak outlook would be considered inappropriate not only for a comedy, but also for an adolescent audience.

Glee ultimately supports the assertion that sexual morality is contextual rather than systematic. It portrays a wide variety of relationships as appropriate as long as they are founded on consent and honesty; only nonconsensual, dishonest, or instrumental uses of sexuality are considered to be inappropriate. This is not to suggest that some of the portrayals of sexuality in *Glee* are not either problematic or troubling; however, *Glee* has consistently used its position as a popular network television show to endorse this broader vision of acceptable sexualities. This essay suggests that sexual morality in *Glee* is founded primarily, if not solely, upon the motives of the individuals involved, rather than on cultural values or norms.

In *Disturbing the Universe,* Trites observes that the norm in young adult fiction is the "ideological message that sex is more to be feared than celebrated" (85). Typically works for adolescents "assume that the reader has a sexual naiveté in need of correction" and are often "heavy-handed in their moralism" (85). As Kimberley Reynolds asserts in *Radical Children's Literature,* "social attitudes to including sexual content ... have become less proscriptive" (122). While *Glee* is a moralistic show, it is often self-conscious about these moral lessons, allowing the members of the club to respond to pluralism, and typically to embrace it, rather than attempting to assert a singular moral truth.

Notes

1. As Chris Colfer described him in a *Vanity Fair* interview.
2. The term "unfinalizability" comes from the work of Mikhail Bakhtin. He argues that even if optimism is not the correct attitude that at least open-endedness is necessary for a truly ethical perspective.

References

"Asian F." *Glee.* Fox. 4 Oct. 2011. Television.
"Baby." *Dawson's Creek.* WB. 24 Feb. 1998. Television.
"Blame It on the Alcohol." *Glee.* 22 Feb. 2011. Television.
Colfer, Chris. Interview. *"Glee's* Chris Colfer Wants to Show You His Ass." *Vanity Fair.* 27 April. 2010. Web. 7 Nov. 2012.
"Dance with Somebody." *Glee.* Fox. 24 April 2012. Television.
Eyal, Keren, and Dale Kunkel. "The Effects of Sex in Television Drama Shows on Emerging Adults' Sexual Attitudes and Moral Judgments." *Journal of Broadcasting & Electronic Media* 52.2 (2008): 161–181. *Academic Search Complete.* Web. 31 Aug. 2012.
"The First Time." *Glee.* Fox. 8 Nov. 2011. Television.
Fisher, Luchina. "'Glee': 'Born this Way' Episode has Sparks Flying." *ABC News.* 26 April 2011. Web. 20 August 2012.
"Goodbye." *Glee.* Fox. 22 May 2012. Television.
Gottschall, Jonathan. *The Storytelling Animal.* New York: Houghton Mifflin, 2012. Print.
"I Am Unicorn." *Glee.* 27 September 2011. Television.
"I Kissed a Girl." *Glee.* 29 Nov. 2011. Television.
"Laryngitis." *Glee.* Fox. 11 May 2010. Television.
Morson, Gary Saul, and Caryl Emerson. *Mikhail Bakhtin: Creation of a Prosaics.* Stanford: Stanford University Press, 1990. Print.
"On My Way." *Glee.* 21 Feb. 2012. Television.
Palin, Bristol. "Hail to the Chiefs—Malia and Sasha Obama." *Bristol's Blog.* Patheos. 10 May 2012. Web. 20 October 2012.
"Pot O' Gold." *Glee.* 1 Nov. 2011. Television.
"The Power of Madonna." *Glee.* 20 April 2010. Television.
"Prom Queen." *Glee.* 10 May 2011. Television.
Reynolds, Kimberley. *Radical Children's Literature.* New York: Palgrave Macmillan, 2007. Print.

Rosenberg, Alyssa. "Glee is an Immoral Television Show and it's Time to Stop Watching." *Thinkprogress.* 2 May 2012 Web. 20 August 2012.

"Rumors." *Glee.* Fox. 3 May 2011. Television.

"Sexy." *Glee.* Fox. 8 March 2011. Television.

"The Spanish Teacher." *Glee.* Fox. 7 Feb. 2012. Television.

"Theatricality." *Glee.* Fox. 25 May. 2010. Television.

Trites, Roberta Seelinger. *Disturbing the Universe.* Iowa City: University of Iowa Press, 2000. Print.

Vermeule, Blakey. *Why We Care About Literary Characters.* Baltimore: Johns Hopkins University Press, 2010. Print.

Zunshine, Lisa. *Why We Read Fiction: Theory of Mind and the Novel.* Columbus: Ohio State University Press, 2006. Print.

Let Me Get This Straight

Attraction and Actions

CHRISTINE L. FERGUSON

Fan engagement is a huge part of *Glee*'s phenomenal success, buoying the show up even when critical reception is mixed and allowing for prolific and profitable tie-ins and ready renewal of the series' contract with the network. It is also a source of some of the strongest and most passionate criticism of the show's characters and storylines, putting to shame the idea that fannish enthusiasm equates to uncritical acceptance of the text as truth, either as the way things are and should be or as the one right answer to the various problems presented through both individual plots and the characters' overall narrative arcs.[1] This is crucially important both as the founding concept for this anthology and because I am a fan of the show before I am a scholar of it and this analysis thus has its origins in a place of passion for an often contradictory, problematic, but also incredibly popular and enjoyable show.

Like many others in the *Glee* fandom, part of why I was drawn into the show was that finally, at last, there was someone like me on the screen. It was amazing as well as a relief to have this happen at all, especially as I still had little idea if there was anyone else out there like me period and so there was a massive sense of "I am not alone and maybe I *am* okay after all." Not only that, but this personal first in terms of media representation was happening on a primetime broadcast series that, as the show's success has now proven, could potentially reach a very large portion of the American public and without them specifically having to seek out "niche" programming, educational documentaries, or cable television series. I found

and still find many of the characters and their experiences personally identifiable to varying degrees, Kurt and Santana in particular being personal
avatars of my experiences, personal development, and personality. The
part of my identity and experiences I want to engage with in the context
of this analysis, however, is my status as a romantic asexual woman and
thus I turn now from the show's student body to McKinley High's guidance
counselor, Emma Pillsbury.

I believe that the show's increasingly problematic treatment of her
attractions and actions, specifically her changing relationship with glee
club coach Will Schuester, provides a particularly useful platform for
exploring some of the ways in which the show interacts with and often
reinforces standard cultural scripts and attitudes about how best to conduct and evaluate relationships and how to characterize and value sex.
With that, I also want to delve into how these supposed "truths" and ways
of relating to the world and to each other might be revised and improved
through expanded views on different types of attractions and intimacies
and through more inclusive, comprehensive views of what it means to be
sex-positive, a "good" feminist or empowered woman, and a "good" partner. These issues are complex and require far more extensive treatment
than can be given here, but hopefully by using the lens of Emma's asexuality and its treatment and mistreatment on *Glee*, I can give a starting
point for a larger discussion of improving representations in the media
and of altering and improving views of what is possible interpersonally
and also community wise as people invested in the values that *Glee* tries
to, and does not always succeed in, promoting.

In keeping with these limitations and that goal, I will not be conduct-
ing an exhaustive analysis of the series as a whole. Instead, I will choose
to highlight select episodes and overall characterizations and developments in order to chart Will and Emma's changing dynamic as well as
other instances of *Glee* using Emma to engage with the intersections
between representations and conceptions of asexuality and matters as varied as abstinence-only education, sex-positivity, and female empowerment. To go with my first premise, that of expanding what intimacy means
and can include and exploring how sexual attraction, as well as actions,
may not be the end-all, be-all of starting and maintaining relationships,
specifically those also involving romantic attraction since the show
includes no aromantic characters of any sexual orientation, I want to start
off this discussion with the series' first two episodes and the different
interpersonal dynamics they establish. Concomitant with that, I want to
open what is likely a first encounter with asexuality[2] for some readers of
this anthology not with a definition and discussion of sexual attraction,

but rather with one for and of *emotional* attraction. I believe understanding that facet of the complex ways in which humans can be attracted to and intimate with one another is the key to how Emma's storyline and romance with Will started off so engaging, went and continues to go so wrong, and yet can also still give hope and insight into what can make real-life mixed-orientation relationships, as well as ones that do not involve an asexual spectrum individual at all, work in a fair, functional, and enduring manner that respects the personhood of everyone involved.

The most striking element of Will and Emma's relationship from the time they are introduced as a dyad in the show's pilot episode is the clear and meaningful level of connection and communication between them. It is not directly dependent on their romantic, and in Will's case also sexual, attraction to one another or on whether they can or will act on those feelings. What the two of them share is its own separate, but not exclusive or exclusionary, category of attraction that can exist independently of, and also rate more strongly in terms of intensity, durability, and importance to relationship longevity than, those two more commonly known types of attraction and intimacy, which are themselves often conflated with one another. Now, as to the actual definition of emotional attraction, it is, in the words of sex-positive feminist blogger Semiel, "the desire to really get to know the other person, and to share in their life. It involves a desire to be vulnerable with the other person, and for them to be vulnerable with you. It can include sharing secrets, taking care of each other, and talking about feeeeeelings until the wee hours of the morning."[3] These qualities are crucial in close relationships and yet, especially in "traditional" relationships where sexual and romantic attraction and activities are both assumed as defining *and* essential terms, are often overlooked in favor of such criteria as the "spark" that is said to start relationships and to end marriages if it is "lost," formal vows and bonds and the alleged requirement that they be adhered to at all costs, including emotional and physical health, and of course the actions, such as sexual intercourse and the exchange of kisses, that are associated with being "in" a relationship but which can also be done in a "going through the motions" manner as opposed to a genuine, heartfelt one. This is *the* key point to remember, both when considering whether mixed-orientation relationships are feasible and fair in the "real world" and when evaluating the varying and evolving adult relationships portrayed on *Glee*, because it explains why Will's marriage was so unhealthy, why his friendship with Emma worked so well, why Ken was a bad match Emma never should have settled for, and why turning friendship to romance is working out so poorly for Emma and Will due to his relationship experiences and lack thereof and where he looks to for guidance in order to correct his perceived deficits and ensure success this time around.

Will's marriage to Terri is a classic example of having those more traditional outward signs of a "real" relationship without having that deeper level of trust, understanding, and respectful sharing based in emotional intimacy to underlie, or even exist in lieu of or follow after, the romantic and sexual attraction and intimacy that started, and possibly still exist to some degree in, the relationship. Underneath the attempts at keeping a good face for others and even for themselves to sustain the delusion that their marriage is not failing are actions such as Terri hiding the full extent of her spending and acquisition habits, which actually border on addiction besides on an obsession with outward markers of status, and always turning arguments against Will. Note that these are unproductive verbal conflicts, not constructive discussions that at least work on, if not resolve, issues in a fair and equitable manner. Instead, Will mentioning Terri's aforementioned problems gets turned around by her into complaints about how hard she works at her three shifts a week at Sheets 'n Things and how Will does not understand what Terri *deserves*, namely to have her needs for large amounts of money and the ability to turn herself into the appropriate high status married woman using those riches, or at least turn herself into the Lima, Ohio, version thereof, met by Will and by his working a well-paying, prestige-type job regardless of whether he is personally passionate about it.[4]

All of this is said and expected by Terri while also ignoring or denigrating how hard Will works as a full-time teacher and how passionate he is about his coaching of the glee club and the kids he is able to mentor, or attempt to mentor, through it. Terri talks at Will but not with him and she certainly does not truly listen to him or respect his feelings and viewpoints, even or especially when it comes to matters that are personally important to him. In contrast, Will's original friendship with Emma, which I will discuss more below, is characterized precisely by all those often overlooked but critically important characteristics filed under emotional attraction and intimacy, and that friendship and those valuable traits come prior to and are at the foundation of Emma and Will's later romantic relationship. This set of facts *should* set them up for far more success as a couple than many others in the "real world" and than Will and Terri in-narrative. As I will discuss later, however, Will's lack of direction after having been in this one emotionally unhealthy relationship his entire adult life, as well as during his formative teenage years, means that he looks to common cultural narratives and other popular sources of advice on how to get it "right" and on what a "healthy" relationship should look and be like once he becomes romantically involved with Emma and *that* is what starts to move them from a healthy functionality to a dysfunctional one, not the simple fact of them having changed status from friends to romantic partners.

Back to the early "glory days" of the Will-Emma relationship,[5] however, and to why I was so fond of them as a dyad regardless of what specific social role or label their relationship took, the whole complex of actions and attractions under the umbrella of emotional intimacy is a, or possibly, *the*, key to, and a clear part of, their original dynamic in Season 1. Again and again in those first episodes we see two people who may not consciously know *why* they are sharing long-ago incidents and serious personal problems with one another but who are confident and secure in that sharing of confidences and in trusting that what they share will be received respectfully and kept as something that exists between the two of them in their own special narrative space. Along with that, both Will and Emma are shown to have a greater willingness to take actions, both tangible, as in helping Will with his attempts at cleaning his first night as a janitor,[6] and intangible, giving Will his courage and his faith in himself back so that he does not settle for switching to a job he hates in order to have the "appropriate" money and status that society and Terri say he should,[7] on one another's behalves and at each other's behests than they are with others. That latter example is especially apropos as an illustration of this point since Will only agrees to career counseling because *Emma* asks him and because *she* is the one to give it. No one else would be able to get him to agree to it or to successfully convince him to follow his own heart instead of Terri's and society's directives about what he "should" want. As well, this extra propensity to help and to listen is located in a relationship between two characters who are both, although Emma has it to the greater and more consistently successful degree, defined in part on the show by their helpful, caring, and giving natures. What they have together is thus particularly special and meaningful while also coming naturally to them as part of their inherent personalities and as part of their relationship dynamic as it stands at this point in the show's narrative arc.

Emma and Will's early relationship does not involve "keeping score" or one-upping each other in terms of caring acts or other expressions of sentiment and attachment or false shows thereof that are meant to "prove" feelings and reaffirm roles. It also does not involve attempting to conform to other social norms, largely because it is impossible for their relationship, whether read as intense male-female friendship, unfulfillable romance, or both, to do so. Instead, clear communication, understanding, and trust with a decided lack of judgment or of a need to go to someone else in order to "fix" the problem instead of having an actual talk with the person involved are its foundation and its substance because there are no other options and because it is a natural part of the fabric of their relationship as it stands early on in Season 1. They "use their words," as the relationship advice blog Captain Awkward terms it,[8] and respect and honor boundaries and limits. This is not done perfectly, but, especially in the context of the show's various other relationships, both Will and Emma manage quite well in their attempts at it during this early period in their relationship. Will's invitation to Emma during "Showmance" to help him clean classrooms again during his night-time shift as a janitor and proud display of the new kind of sanitizing wipes he found is as clear as, and possibly more meaningful than, directly saying, "I accept and respect you for who you are." The same is true of Emma's offer of half her sandwich and a listening ear about Will's relationship with his wife past and present while they wait to see Carmel High's glee club performance in the pilot episode. He could easily judge her for her anxiety disorders and she could offer quite likely called for but hard to hear and unsolicited advice about needing to end his marriage for his own sake but neither of those things happens. Instead, in that scene, as well as in other interactions early on in the series, they both offer listening without judgment and acceptance that is not predicated upon perfection or upon changing or compromising sense of self or the desire to stick to one's guns even if, as with Will's attempts to make his marriage "work," it is not entirely advisable or wise in the long-run.

This packaging of attractions and actions is a marked contrast with football coach Ken's treatment of Emma when she repeatedly tries to rebuff and then directly refuses his advances and even more of a stark contrast with Will's later treatment of Emma once their romantic, and Will's sexual, attraction becomes a site not of potentiality but of actuality. The problems that ensue there are prefigured in the Ken-Emma dynamic and then magnified in Emma's later attempt at a "traditional" relationship with Will because she *is* romantically attracted to *him* and is thus invested in succeeding. This repetition and intensification of the troubling dynamic between Ken and Emma is also, and even more largely, due to Will's desire to get *this* relationship "right" not only because Emma is important to him but also because he feels he has something to prove due to his "failed" first marriage. That is decidedly not how you should approach a relationship and neither is Ken's method of "wooing" Emma, which I will turn to now as a way of explaining where and how Will later begins to go wrong in terms of his treatment of Emma.

What Ken does with Emma and what she later does in settling for him in order to not be alone and to take the best she can get, besides rendering her "harmless" and forcing her to abandon her romantic interest in Will, is horrific and not how anyone, not just a woman and not just an asexual woman, should be treated or should think she needs to act in accordance with in order to get by, to fit in, to be maybe some kind of happy in the world. Tellingly, Ken always goes to another man, Will, and one that he can clearly tell is emotionally intimate with Emma and reciprocally attracted to her on that axis, in order to pursue his cause of wooing Emma and to deal with any perceived failures in the plan, which failures are never his and which never have to do with the fact that Emma is not attracted to him and has explicitly told him as much. In Ken's grand plan to "win" Emma, Will is meant to put in a good word for him in exchange for being allowed to speak with the football team about joining glee club, then is the one at fault once Emma finally puts her foot down with Ken, and finally is an obstacle to be threatened and overcome when Ken decides willing help is not going to be forthcoming and that he will have her at any costs and by any means.[9]

The way Ken's interactions with and treatment of her are framed within the narrative, Emma is a passive object to be exchanged between men and to be dealt with as problematic and in need of fixing and indulging in turn by men as well, such as when Ken tells Emma that she does not have to live with, have sex with, or even have non-sexual physical intimacy with him if she agrees to marry him or when, once they are together again in the latter part of Season 2, Will "convinces" Emma to go on medication and also tries to pressure her to put "OCD" on her shirt for the episode entitled "Born This Way." This approach is deeply discomfiting and is a pattern that does not stop when Emma calls off her wedding with Ken and he leaves McKinley entirely at the end of the first season. Instead, Will, and, while he is on the show, Emma's fiancé and then spouse and now ex, Carl, increasingly take over the task of passing Emma back and forth and of trying to "shelter" her from the world while also "fixing" her, which leads this discussion back around to sexual attraction and actions. That area of focus is at the crux of where the Emma-Will relationship goes wrong and where portrayals of asexuality in general take a turn for the worse. It is also where very wrong-headed and damaging notions about what is and is not possible, fair, and "right" for asexuals to desire and to view as real possibilities in life originate, particularly although not exclusively when romantic asexuals and the idea or potential reality of romantic relationships with non-asexual spectrum individuals are involved.

I started this discussion with a definition of emotional attraction and exploration of it in terms of why and how Emma and Will's *friendship* functioned so well precisely because that type of attraction is a vital component of the more hopeful truth behind the widely held and very damaging idea that sex is key to the happiness and success of, as well as the defining characteristic of, romantic relationships and that the absence thereof, no less entering into a romantic relationship when you do not experience sexual attraction and also do not engage in what is traditionally considered "sex," is somewhere between unfair and unjust to downright abusive towards your partner.[10] Emma never directly voices this opinion about herself and about what she, especially as a particularly caring, compassionate person, can want out of life and from others without causing them any degree of harm. The myths and misconceptions surrounding and supporting it, however, repeatedly crop up in the show's narrative, especially during "special education" episodes such as Season 1's "Power of Madonna" and Season 2's "Sexy," and Emma is clearly distressed at the idea of being unfair towards her partners as well as at the tendency to treat her as the butt of jokes, shame her, and otherwise not treat her as a different but not "broken" or "abnormal" person based on her orientation and sexual activity or lack thereof.

Now, that Season 1 episode does allow Emma some self-agency and also support from her partner when she ultimately decides not to have sex with Will and, when she tries apologizing to him for her "failure" the next time they see each other, he tells her that her saying no was just as empowering as a yes would have been. That end choice and reaction are healthy and a good model for any relationship, not just mixed-orientation couples and not just in the context of romantic relationships or possible sexual activity: You do not owe anyone sex and both "no" and "yes" are valid and empowering answers in or out of the bedroom.[11] What is not worth modeling behavior and expectations on, but which is unfortunately an idea pervasive in mainstream culture, are the events preceding that exchange. Allowing Emma to say no and have that no both respected and lauded as empowering does not erase the framing of sex as something that Emma "needs" to do in order to be a "good"/"empowered" woman and a good girlfriend, or as something that from her point of view is a task to be gotten over with as quickly as possibly to minimize the unpleasantness. Sex should not be viewed as akin to removing a stuck-on band-aid from a wound but this is precisely what both allegedly "sex-positive" *and* abstinence-only narratives have led Emma to believe and to view as being the One Right Way.[12] This is further emphasized by Season 2's "Sexy," which sets up false dichotomies between abstinence- and celibacy-inclusive education and sex-positivity. As part of this, it also frames the latter approach, which again is not in reality antithetical to including both abstinence and celibacy as valid choices,[13] as being "sexy" and as a way for women to "empower" themselves while characterizing both Emma, which by extension means asexual women, and those who choose abstinence or celibacy as "prudish," "frigid," and unappealing and even laughable. The substitute health and wellness teacher, Holly Holliday, even outright calls Emma "frigid" and jokes about Emma's lack of sexual activity while herself being framed as the "whore" opposite to Emma's "virgin." No one wins in this view because Holly's sexual knowledge, which she can then share with the students, and also with the adults, including Emma's on-again, off-again love interest Will and her current, though soon to be ex-, husband Carl, comes at the price of not knowing what "romance" is, and Emma's relationship is doomed because there is no sex in it. *Glee* is trying to be and to promote a sexually "liberated" view of both teenage and adult life but in the process is reaffirming old dichotomies and beliefs, as well as alienating, and affirming stereotypes about, asexuals and promoting the view that romantic asexuals can never have successful relationships with non-asexual spectrum partners.

Instead of functioning as a discussion of their desires and limits that allows Carl and Emma to come to a mutual understanding of and conclusion about their compatibility as individuals and the likelihood of a continuing romantic relationship being fair and workable for both of them, the scene of Holly "counseling" Carl and Emma instead serves as an object lesson in what *not* to do when resolving relationship issues and when dealing with differing desires and interests between partners. Carl and Holly, because Emma is consistently talked over and otherwise not allowed to express what *she* wants and needs and thinks, come to the conclusion that the absence of sex in the marriage, which Carl views as a problem and Emma does *not*, is due to Emma's continuing interest in Will. The marriage clearly needs to and does end due to this, not due to personal incompatibility, which can happen in any relationship and for many reasons, or so the show's narrative states and would have us accept as "truth." With this, presumably Emma not experiencing sexual attraction *and* not being interested in sex is a "problem" that will "fix" itself and her along with it when she is paired up with the "right" person, namely Will.

This is a deeply troubling piece of subtext because it reinforces the idea that the "right" person can "cure" someone of his or her orientation. It is even more unsettling because it is coming from a show that is in a sense at the forefront of queer representation on mainstream television and in American popular culture. *Glee* would never permit that view, when aimed at a homosexual character (the show's problematic treatment of bisexuality would require an essay of its own), to exist in narrative unless it were called out and proven as both harmful and wrong, but it allows and perpetuates it when aimed against an asexual character. Increasing this problematic characterization of asexuality and location of it in outside factors instead of acknowledgment, even in an unspoken manner, of it as a legitimate orientation is the fact that the show's narrative later transfers the alleged source of this supposed "problem" over to Emma's mental illnesses involving cleaning and contamination. First her desires and lack thereof are related to denial of feelings, romantic but also presumably sexual, and now to a mental disorder. What manner of lesson, or, rather, set of lessons, is someone like Emma or myself, or our adolescent and teenage counterparts, supposed to take away from the show and from the real-life sources that its approach is a reflection of? With that, what are romantic asexuals in particular, since Emma is one, likely to receive as the takeaway message not just from this episode but also from the overall Emma-in-romantic-relationships narrative arcs?

According to the show, irreconcilable differences and relationship failure are the default for mixed-orientation relationships and they should therefore not be entered into at all, and if one does enter into one it will be doomed, or at least doomed to a perpetual state of not working like it "should"-ness, because it is not fair or kind and is possibly even abusive to the non-asexual spectrum person. Emma and Will are still together as of Season 3 but the relationship is not untroubled and there is still the "problem" of Emma being a virgin.[14] Non-sexual physical intimacy, such as Emma and Will waking up in bed together in the season premiere, is "not enough," and neither is the less than it was before emotional intimacy. As a sign of how far the latter type of formerly strong attraction and connection has dissolved, in Season 3 Will takes such actions as inviting Emma's parents over unannounced for dinner in "Asian F" when she has explicitly said that she does not want to see them or to have Will meet them and, in a later episode, "Yes/No," going to them to ask for Emma's hand in marriage when he has not yet asked Emma herself and when he knows, via his own severe mistake and ignoring of Emma's limits and boundaries, that they have a horrible relationship with her and one that has affected and still affects her mental health negatively.

I have far from given up on the show but the seemingly storybook, especially to someone who grew up hearing precisely what Emma has been led to believe about herself and the way the world works, romance between Emma and Will has told me more about why my view of how the world works and how long it took me to be able to question it with certitude occurred than it has about how such a relationship can be successful or about how I am a different but still very much normal person and one worthy of respect and also of respectful treatment by others. Again, the show does so very much for queer representation and handling of difficult and important issues in the mainstream media, including bullying and teen pregnancy, but it is not perfect and lauding it does not mean having to love every thing in and about it. Hopefully reading this essay is a way to introduce others to some of the show's problematics while also showing what it does right, because it *does* get it right and often in subtle ways such as with the emotional intimacy present in the early Will-Emma friendship, which is desirable and wonderful in *any* relationship and something worthy of emulating. As well, pointing out the show's problems is not the end point or an action done simply for its own sake or to feel "good." It is a way of beginning dialogues and of pointing out paths to improvement, not necessarily for the show to take but for its viewers and those they interact with to take in "real life." Knowing you are not alone and not destined and doomed to be alone and that you are as normal and acceptable as any and every one else can mean the world to anyone, but especially to young people with little opportunity to hear that about themselves and about the possibilities that life might and can hold for them and that is the spirit, if not always the letter, of *Glee*.

Notes

1. Finding examples of this is as easy as checking the *Glee* tags on Tumblr after a new episode has aired or during one of the show's hiatuses as fans debate such issues as screen time for and public displays of affection between the queer couples as opposed to those for and between couples such as Finn and Rachel.

2. For a very accessible, well-written 101-type introduction to asexuality, see kinky aromantic ace Venn's blog posting on that topic. A brief, scholarly overview of what the world can be like for asexual individuals is provided in MacInnis and Hodson's article in *Group Processes & Intergroup Relations*, "Intergroup Bias Towards 'Group X': Evidence of Prejudice, Dehumanization, Avoidance, and Discrimination Against Asexuals." Those two sources are far from exhaustive but they will begin to give an idea of the difficulties asexual-spectrum individuals have in terms of having their orientation acknowledged and validated and in explaining it to others and in terms of how they are viewed and treated socially and by larger social mechanisms.

3. For an introduction to other types of attraction, see the posting on Semiel's blog that the definition of emotional attraction was taken from.

4. The specific incidents mentioned here occur in the show's pilot, which is included in a "director's cut" version on the Season 1 DVD, although the general tenor of their interactions continues throughout Will and Terri's marriage, which ends in divorce in the twenty-first episode of Season 1, "Funk."

5. Will and Emma's relationship has never been problem-free but their interactions prior to the finalization of Will's divorce in "Funk" and especially towards the early part of Season 1 are significantly better than they later become. Besides Emma's career advice to Will at the end of the pilot episode, reminding him how much he loves coaching glee club and how miserable he would be quitting that and teaching to become an accountant,

and her listening but non-judgmental ear about his marriage to Terri while they chaperone a glee club trip to see their rivals at Carmel High perform, there are also moments such as Will's rescue of Emma from, and non-judgment of her reaction to, used chewing gum stuck to the bottom of her shoe in the series pilot. That is very different in attitude and feel from his later attempts to get her to "own" her "problems," get therapy, start taking drugs, and otherwise treat Emma like she is a problem and even ignore her triggers. They are still a charming fairytale not-couple at this point and Will even refers to Emma as Cinderella once he finishes removing the gum and returns her shoe, still on her foot, to her.

6. Season 1, Episode 2, "Showmance."

7. Season 1, Episode 1, "Pilot."

8. As a specific example of how that concept is applied see Jennifer P.'s response to a letter asking how you let someone know you are interested in them and where to go from there, including the sample scripts she provides of how to clearly communicate your needs and desires in a fair, functional manner.

9. All of these events occur in the pilot episode and Ken's desire for revenge against Will and success with Emma continue up until his failed wedding to Emma in the mid-season finale, "Sectionals," after which point his character does not reappear, having quit his job at William McKinley High School due to his distress over Emma not being in love with him and having no real desire to "settle" for him as a husband.

10. For examples of "sex as success," turn to any popular women's magazine for a wealth of articles focused on sex and (male) sexual pleasure as the keys to catching and keeping a man, or to relationship help guides that often focus on more sex and "better" sex as the answer to relationship troubles. On mixed-orientation relationships, especially monogamous ones, as ranging between inherently and always in all cases unfair to downright "abusive," see, for example, advice columnist and advocate Dan Savage's "Savage Love" columns when the topic hits upon matters involving asexuals in relationships and also look at the Pick-Up Artist blog Heartiste's response to a *Guardian* article profiling a mixed-orientation couple in a monogamous long-term relationship. The commentary from their followers is also illuminating, although particularly triggering in the case of the Heartiste blog posting where they also attempt to pick apart and question the asexual woman's mental health and truthfulness and her non-asexual- spectrum male partner's "manliness," among other unpleasantries that they feel are true and feel that asexuals "need" to be told and to be accused of so they can mend their ways and mend their "brokenness."

11. For an elaboration on this idea and related topics, see Holly P.'s discussion of what a culture of consent might look like and what we can do to help build one.

12. Abstinence-only education not only frames virginity as a gift to be given in marriage and sex as the culmination of one's path to marriage, but also frames sex as the defining feature for romantic relationships and the way to tell them apart from friendships. In lieu of the printed student workbooks my peers and I were given as young teens, see SIECUS' summation and review of the program, which is *still* in use with students today, as well as the reviews of other such abstinence-only education programs that can be found under the "Return to Curricula and Speaker Reviews" tab at the top of the web page.

13. See Charlie Glickman, as well as the sources cited within his blog posting, for asexuality-inclusive takes on sex-positivity and sex education.

14. The writing of this essay was completed before the Season 3 finale aired, wherein Emma "gives" her virginity to Will via penis-in-vagina penetrative intercourse essentially as a victory prize for the glee club winning nationals and for Will winning a teaching award. I have chosen to leave my discussion as-is to preserve what proved to be a sadly accurate prediction of where the show would go with Emma's character and her relationship with Will.

References

"Asian F." *Glee: The Complete Third Season*. Writ. Ian Brennan. Dir. Alfonso Gomez-Rejon. Twentieth Century–Fox, 2012. DVD.

"Born This Way." *Glee: The Complete Second Season*. Writ. Brad Falchuk. Dir. Alfonso Gomez-Rejon. Twentieth Century–Fox, 2011. DVD.

Glickman, Charlie. "Sex-Positivity and Asexuality: Bringing Them Together." *Charlie Glickman: Adult Sexuality Education*. Charlie Glickman. 25 January 2011. Web. April 2012.

Heartiste. "Beta of the Month: Asexual Purgatory." *Chateau Heartiste ... Where Pretty Lies Perish*. Heartiste. 2 February 2012. Web. April 2012.

Holly P. "Consent Culture." *The Pervocracy: Sex. Feminism. BDSM. And Some Very, Very Naughty Words*. Holly Pervocracy. 18 January 2012. Web. April 2012.

Jennifer P. "#231: How do I learn to say the right thing at the right time to people I'm interested in?" *Captain Awkward*. Jennifer P. 19 April 2012. Web. April 2012.

"Pilot." *Glee: The Complete First Season*. Writ. Ryan Murphy, Brad Falchuk, and Ian Brennan. Dir. Ryan Murphy. Twentieth Century–Fox, 2010. DVD.

"Power of Madonna." *Glee: The Complete First Season*. Writ. Ryan Murphy. Dir. Ryan Murphy. Twentieth Century–Fox, 2010. DVD.

Savage, Dan. "Savage Love: I'm An Asexual! (Well, Minimally Sexual, But Still)." *Savage Love*. Washington City Paper, 4 February 2011. Web. April 2012.

_____. "Savage Love: SL Letter of the Day: A Sexual Reflects on a Nearly Asexual Ex." *Savage Love*. The Stranger, 3 February 2011. Web. April 2012.

Semiel. "Towards a Better Model of Attraction." *Intimacy Cartography*. Semiel. 1 June 2011. Web. April 2012.

"Sexy." *Glee: The Complete Second Season*. Writ. Brad Falchuk. Dir. Ryan Murphy. Twentieth Century–Fox, 2011. DVD.

"Showmance." *Glee: The Complete First Season*. Writ. Ryan Murphy, Brad Falchuk, and Ian Brennan. Dir. Ryan Murphy. Twentieth Century–Fox, 2010. DVD.

SIECUS. "Summary: Siecus Review of *Passion & Principles*." *Community Action Kit*. SIECUS. 2008. Web. April 2012.

Venn. "Ramp Up Essay: Being a Kinky Ace." *Verbs Not Nouns: Wrong In All the Right Ways*. Venn. 22 May 2011. Web. April 2012.

"Yes/No." *Glee: The Complete Third Season*. Writ. Brad Falchuk. Dir. Eric Stoltz. Twentieth Century–Fox, 2012. DVD.

No Substitute for Comprehensive Sex Ed

Analyzing Sexual Ethics

JANE B. MEEK

In the small town of Lima, Ohio, where *Glee* is set, viewers can assume that the public school system of McKinley High, similar to most in the country, is hurting for funding, evidenced by Principal Figgins constantly cutting corners in ways that threaten the existence of the glee club. In such a state, we might also assume that McKinley High's sexual health program received no extra funding other than what the government provided from 1996 to 2009, namely the $1.5 billion in federal and state funding for abstinence-only-until-marriage programs. According to the Sexuality Information and Education Council of the United States (SIECUS), such programs "fail to teach teens how to prevent pregnancy or sexually transmitted infections (STIs), including HIV/AIDS," and therefore do not reduce the amount of teen pregnancies, such as *Glee* character Quinn Fabray's. Furthermore, instructors of these programs are federally mandated to "adhere to a strict eight-point definition of 'abstinence education' that ... promotes marriage as the only acceptable family structure; ostracizes lesbian, gay, bisexual, and transgender (LGBT) youth; stigmatizes youth who have been sexually abused; and denies information to sexually active youth" ("End Funding"). Under these programs, then, the lives of Quinn (whose out-of-wedlock child was adopted by a single mother), Kurt (gay and child of a single parent), Finn (child of a single parent and sexually active), Santana (queer or sometimes lesbian and sexually active), Brittany ("bi-curious" and sexually active), Rachel (child of gay parents and sexually active), indeed, almost all of the *Glee* characters, would be treated as shameful and given little to no helpful sexual health information.

Since *Glee* tackles tough social issues of the times, Season 2's episode "Sexy" featured the feminist and sex-positive guest character Holly Holiday—a substitute teacher who exposes the results of such abstinence-only-until-marriage curricula for students. According to her assessment, the students of the glee club are wildly misinformed about the facts of life, perhaps due to the limited education they have received from abstinence-based programs. From Finn's belief that he impregnated Quinn in a hot tub without penetration to Kurt's extreme aversion to seeking out education on gay male sex, the teenage characters of this sexually- charged series are, at least in Seasons 1 and 2, as sexually uneducated as many of their teen fans. But, in Season 3 when the star couples—Rachel and Finn, Kurt and Blaine—respectively decide to lose their virginity within their loving, monogamous relationships, some viewers (like conservative watchdog group the Parents Television Council) expressed outrage and renewed a national conversation about depictions of teen sexuality on prime-time television.

This essay, therefore, reviews research studies about media's influence on teen and young adult's understanding of sexuality and relates this to the shifting political and cultural landscape of sexuality education in the U.S. The theoretical framework for analyzing particular episodes draws on the "sexual super-peer" theory and Sut Jhally's theory of the pornographic imagination to examine the sexual ethics of the show as a whole and evaluate *Glee*'s influence as a sexual peer of young audiences.

Glee as a Sexual Super-Peer

> HOLLY: We gotta shake things up, you know. Information is power! Oh and by the way, Will, some of your kids in Glee Club are the most clueless.... We gotta educate these kids!
> EMMA: I strongly disagree. I don't think we need to barrage these kids with graphic information. They're kids. I don't want to steal their innocence.
> HOLLY: Are you like some sort of crazy Pope lady? Think about the images these kids are exposed to. I mean, think about what they have access to.
> EMMA: That doesn't make it okay. And it shouldn't change the message that they get from us, which is this is serious stuff and it's not for kids and it's not for adults.
> HOLLY: Okay well I think that's a little naïve. And now, if you'll excuse me, I'm off to have crazy sex because I'm crazy informed about it! Kidding ["Sexy"].

In this scene Holly Holiday, subbing for McKinley's Health and Wellness teacher, addresses the need for teachers to supplement the hyper-sexed media that students are consuming with medically-accurate sex education but finds resistance from the sex-phobic school counselor Emma Pillsbury, head of the school's Celibacy Club. The irony of this scene is that when the dialogue asks viewers to "think about the [sexualized] images these kids are exposed to," *Glee* is one obvious answer—an especially troubling answer for those members of the conservative Culture and Media Institute who cite the show's "lesbian fantasies, gay kissing, [and] teen pregnancy as 'immorality-promoting content'" (qtd. in E. Brown). *Glee* is indeed one of those cultural texts exposing youth to sexualized images and narratives, its popularity and cross- platform marketing making it one of the shows that sets the cultural tone for how youth might view teen sexuality. Therefore, the show qualifies as an important sexual super-peer, a term born of media critics who theorize that "media personalities may become 'super-peers,' engaging youths' aspirations, demonstrating how fictional teens think and act, and functioning as virtual role models for those who are figuring out who they are and how they should behave as sexual beings" (qtd. in Rich 20). And, since "less than one percent of the sexual content [on television] could be construed as portraying healthy sexual behavior" (J. D. Brown 7), such super-peers are in consensus when it comes to sexuality: "media are like powerful best friends in sometimes making risky behaviors seem like normative behavior" (Strasburger, Jordan, & Donnerstein 758). In a recent interview, the president of the conservative Parents Television Council cited the super-peer theory to blast *Glee* for its portrayal of teen sex: "Research proves that television is a teen sexual super peer that can, and likely will, influence a teen's decision to become sexually active. Fox knows the show inherently attracts kids; celebrating teen sex constitutes gross recklessness" (qtd. in Hibberd par. 3).

Though *Glee*'s rating of NC-14 ("Parents Strongly Cautioned") urges parents to "exercise greater care in monitoring this program and [take] caution against letting children under the age of 14 watch unattended," many parents do not review ratings ("Understanding the TV Ratings"). Pediatrician Victor C. Strasburger, a leading researcher of media influence on children and adolescents, concedes, "Most parents don't watch television with their children.... Parents don't want to fight with their children about media; it's far easier to park them in front of the television set or drop them off at the mall to see a movie (even one with a rating that would indicate it is inappropriate for them). In short, many parents are clueless" (110). Strasburger argues that parents should be more aware of the sexual content a TV super-peer can promote: "There are dozens of studies that show that the media function essentially as a 'super peer' group, making teenagers believe that everyone out there is having sex but them, that sex is without risks or consequences, and that birth control is completely unnecessary" (109–110).

To contextualize this debate further, consider communications scholar Jennifer Stevens Aubrey's research that found evidence for a direct relationship between TV content and viewers' "sexual self-concept," which she defines as "an individual's perception of his or her 'qualities' in the sexual domain ... giv[ing] guidance for sexual behavior" (qtd. in Aubrey 158). To measure this relationship, Aubrey and others rely on a "cognitive information-processing model, which suggests that people create and store in their memories programs called 'scripts' to guide a variety of social behaviors, including sexual behaviors" (160), and Strasburger confirms that "media present youth with common 'scripts' for how to behave in unfamiliar situations such as romantic relationships" (Strasburger, Jordan, & Donnerstein 758).

But, as Aubrey and others conclude, it is vital to understand that these sexual scripts are interpreted differently by viewers according to their backgrounds:

> Youth approach and respond to media from their own life experiences, so ethnicity, gender, class, and developmental stage all influence their media choices. Although some adolescents do not see people or lives such as theirs reflected in the media, when teens do see people or images in media to which they relate, they are more likely to be influenced [Rich 24].

Therefore, the most impressionable viewers of *Glee*'s sexual scripts are those who rarely see themselves represented in mainstream media—the types of youth *Glee*'s characters are based on, the "misfits," as Fox affectionately calls them ("*Glee*: The Complete"). A show as popular as *Glee* developing multi-dimensional characters who grapple with their outsider status, vulnerable to bullying and social isolation, is a beacon of hope and pride for many youth and young adults considered "at-risk,"[1] and the show thus serves as a potential source of valuable cultural scripts for them to follow. Since the show's creators likely understood this appeal to minoritized youth, they might have also felt a responsibility to make their sexual scripts healthier and more educational than the average prime-time show. After all, it is not a small leap to assume that at-risk youth might also be engaging in what is labeled "high-risk" sexual behaviors. A study from the Centers for Disease Control confirms this about at-risk LGBT students: "Sexual minority students, particularly gay, lesbian, and bisexual students and students who had sexual contact with both sexes, are more likely to engage in health-risk behaviors than other students" (Kann).

For these reasons, one major focus of this analysis is the sexual scripts given to those *Glee* characters with whom at-risk or minoritized youth might closely identify, particularly the show's empowered females and sexual minorities. Such characters do indeed explicitly deal with their sexual self-concept issues, particularly their sexual and romantic worthiness or sexual self-esteem (Aubrey 158), salient issues to questioning and LGBT teens looking for role models: "As young people grapple with their own emerging sexual identities, they may seek out models in the media, wrestling with their initial attraction-repulsion to sexual issues, evolving into virtual relationships with celebrities, and finally attraction to others in real life" (Rich 24). More than most TV shows, *Glee* develops storylines that explore student's sexual self-concepts head on, from the show's "Pilot" to "The Power of Madonna," "Showmance," "Laryngitis," and others that I will include in my analysis below.

Surveying *Glee*'s Sexy Scenes

Employing these theoretical perspectives, this section will examine some choice scenes to investigate *Glee*'s sexual content with an emphasis on sexual ethics, queer sex, and the role of teachers in promoting a responsible curricula regarding sexuality. As other studies have defined it for the purposes of research, "sexual content" includes any depiction of talk or behavior that involves sexuality, sexual suggestiveness, or sexual activities/relationships" (Cope-Farrar & Kunkel 63). Let us begin with "Sexy," the one episode devoted to sex education within a public high school. The episode covers new ground in depicting queer youth receiving adult guidance and support (though mostly in private), and it emphasizes the fact that most sex ed programs not only withhold information for sexual minorities but "may communicate the message to LGBTQ students that their sexual orientation is unacceptable and incompatible with cultural and social norms" ("What Programs"). However, on the whole, this episode fails to depict teachers educating students about sex in an inclusive, responsible, and comprehensive fashion. When Will Schuester admits to Holly that his glee club students are indeed misinformed, Holly replies, "We have really got to educate these kids." Will's response is a classic sexphobic trope that many politicians and parents use: "How are we gonna do that without being too graphic? I want to educate them, not titillate them" ("Sexy"). As numerous studies have found, the sex-education-as-titillation discourse and its influence on policy-makers is not helping youth, especially considering how sexually-saturated media is for this generation of adolescents, 93 percent of whom are online (Strasburger, Jordan, & Donnerstein 757). The hyper-sexualized atmosphere of high school culture is established in *Glee*'s pilot when, in a meeting of the Celibacy Club, Jacob Ben Israel exclaims, "I think I'm going to kill myself. I'm serious. We're bombarded with sexual imagery every day—beer ads, those short skirts. I'm supposed to be surrounded by temptation and not be able to do anything about it?"

In such an atmosphere, Holly's response to Will's above question is disheartening: "All we have to do is find a way to sneak in the sex education lesson in a less provocative way.... Let me come to Glee Club this week and I'll show you what I mean. The kids will think they're getting ready for regionals, but really I'll slip in a little lesson about how to avoid STD's" ("Sexy"). Instead of a straightforward conversation that could have fleshed out some of the students' sexual confusion, Holly visits the club wearing a skin-tight, black leather outfit to perform the following scene:

> WILL: Along with preparing for our regional next week, I want to spend the week educating ourselves about some of these ... intricacies [of adult relationships].
> RACHEL: Is this the appropriate forum for that?
> WILL: Look, whenever we've had issues in the past that are on our minds or giving us problems, it's always helped us to sing about it. So this week I've invited a special guest, Ms. Holliday.
> HOLLY: Okay, sex: it's just like hugging, only wetter. Artie: Yeah it is.
> HOLLY: Okay, so, let's start with the basics. Finn, is it true you thought you got your girlfriend pregnant via hot tub?
> FINN: I have always been dubious.
> HOLLY: And, Brittany, you think storks bring babies?
> BRITTANY: I get my information from Woody Woodpecker cartoons.
> HOLLY: Well, that's all gonna end right here, right now because today we are gonna get under the covers all together and get the ditty on the dirty.
> RACHEL: Uh, what about those of who choose to remain celibate?
> HOLLY: Oh, well, I admire you. Although I think you are naïve and possibly frigid, I do admire your choice.

Holly then performs the rock anthem "Do You Wanna Touch Me? (Oh Yeah)"[2] with Brittany and Santana. All the students ultimately join in, but the girls' sexually suggestive dance moves include repeatedly ripping open their jackets seductively while the boys cheer, give thumbs up, and high-five each other. The entire number equates sex with rock 'n' roll, fun, and coolness and ends with a flushed Holly exclaiming, "So, just remember: whenever you have sex with someone, you are having sex with everyone they have ever had sex with. And everybody's got a random" ("Sexy").

Several elements of this scene reinforce the fact that Holly's plan to covertly "slip in" sex ed was unrealistic and irresponsible, and her lesson provides no medically-accurate information to counter Finn and Brittany's misinformation or to address "STD's" appropriately. Judging by Puck's comment during the scene, "I'm so turned on right now," this performance ultimately fulfilled Will's (and parents') fear that by its very nature, a lesson on sex will titillate students. *Glee* as a super-peer so far, then, seems to be insinuating that celibate teens like Rachel and Quinn are extremely uncool ("naïve" and "frigid," as Holly calls them), and that casual teen sex with multiple partners is a norm—"everybody's got a random" ("Sexy").

By this point in the episode, Holly has twice acknowledged celibacy as "valid" and admirable but then immediately dismissed it as a naïve and outdated practice. But this is not the first time *Glee*'s writers have made a mockery of abstinence at McKinley High. To revisit the first season, Quinn—president of the school's Celibacy Club—leads the other members to observe Santana twirling in her short cheerleading skirt in their meeting and declares, "God bless the perv who invented these. Remember the power motto, girls: it's all about the teasing and not about the pleasing" ("Showmance"). This quip was set up by the previous scene where Jacob Ben Israel complains how the cheerleaders' short skirts are torturing him sexually, and Puck replies, "Are you kidding? Those skirts are crunchy toast. Santana Lopez bent over in hers the other day, and I swear I could see her ovaries." When Rachel attends her first meeting and is instructed by Quinn to participate in the "Immaculate Affection," where couples dance with balloons between their crotches, she exclaims,

> This is a joke. Did you know that most studies have shown celibacy does not work in high school? Our hormones are driving us too crazy to abstain. The second we start telling ourselves there's no compromise, we act out. The only way to beat teen sexuality is to be prepared. That's what contraception is for. You wanna know a dirty little secret that none of them want you to know? Girls want sex just as much as guys do ["Showmance"].

This assessment of abstinence as "a joke" is a potentially dangerous message to young viewers, especially since Rachel's passionate decree advances teen sex as inevitable—and scores her cool points with the hunky Finn Hudson. Thus, one lesson embedded here for "nerdy" girls like Rachel is that being vocal about sexual desire will attract the attention of popular boys.

Though Rachel's reference to research studies is partially accurate, the real issue at hand is hinted at when Finn narrates, "I'm still on the fence about the Celibacy Club. I mean, I only joined to get into Quinn Fabray's pants. Still, it is a productive way for us guys to get together and talk about sexual issues" ("Showmance"). The Celibacy Club, therefore, serves as the only public space where (heterosexual) students can talk openly about their developing sexualities. The club's meetings pop up sporadically in various episodes as the place where Glee students go when they are grappling with their sexuality and relationships, leaving viewers to assume that these students do not have a sex ed class where they can openly ask questions and receive medically-accurate and ethical responses. The Celibacy Club becomes their only haven, but as Rachel finds out, the meetings have a strict yet superficial grounding in a Christian faith, an unappealing aspect to religious minorities (like Rachel and Jacob Ben Israel) and an unsafe space for those students questioning compulsory heterosexuality (like Kurt, Santana, Brittany, Blaine, and Karofsky). Besides its lack of actual sex education, what makes the club a joke to Rachel is the feigned self-righteousness and hypocrisy of its female members and the males' obvious lack of interest in abstinence. But the sexual script young viewers might hear in her speech is that all boys want sex from girls unabashedly, and apparently all girls lust after boys with equal fervor but have to resist and taunt them publicly in order to maintain a righteous reputation.

What is easily missed in these scenes is the portrayal of how Quinn and her crew of cheerleaders negotiate the cultural constraints of female sexuality. They clearly possess a highly sophisticated sense of the modern gender-sexual power dynamic, as they promote sexualizing their bodies for display as their "power motto." But audiences come to find out that Quinn has broken her celibacy vow, making her behavior seem like an enactment of some complex sexual script, a script that cultural critic Sut Jhally might say is shaped by the "heterosexual, male pornographic imagination," or, "thinking of women as being defined *only* through their sexuality and that sexuality to be at the service of men's desires" (5) [emphasis added]. Jhally's theory is that, originating in music videos, today's most popular sexual script in all media relies on the creation of a "dream world" for a target audience—the heterosexual male—where "women are nothing but sexualized bodies who live for male attention ... [and] find their own identities in terms of how pleasing and desirous they are to men" (7–8). But, when such scripts for women and girls are repeated across all media platforms—to the point that the "pornographic imagination monopolizes virtually all of our media terrain"—female viewers are likely to internalize this pornographic script and present their sexual availability in ways that garner attention and (false) power, while male viewers feel entitled to this kind of access to females (Jhally 7). As Jhally describes, "These images and stories have worked their way into the inner identities of young women who view their own sexuality through the eyes of the male authors of that culture" (10).

Where traditional, sexist gender stereotypes have "males as sexually obsessed" and females setting the balance by being "responsible for access and consequences" (Hust, Brown, & L'Engle 19), the pornographic imagination of the dream world cares nothing for consequences and thus never depicts them: to do so would wake the viewer from the dream. Women and girls fall prey to this dream simply by trying to fit in: "The price of female entry into what is considered the mainstream of the culture is to accept the vision of the pornographic imagination; that the only things of value about women are their bodies and their sexuality and their willingness and desire to act out male fantasies" (Jhally 11). For instance, when Quinn and her fellow cheerleaders thank God for the their short skirts, they are reinforcing this script, affirming that women and girls "want to be possessed by the gaze of the watcher. Far from objecting when men look at them in sexual ways, the women of dream world revel in the attention" (Jhally 8).

The dangers of this sexual script to young female viewers are obvious; and though Rachel's speech could be interpreted as reclaiming girls' rights to express their sexual agency, some adolescents might see it as reinforcing the dream world script they have encoded, where women's sexual interest is rewritten as a "one dimensional definition of femininity based on a single story of ... objectification of a passive sexuality whose only goal is to please men, being told over and over again so it becomes the only way in which femininity is thought of" (Jhally 9). When this script is normalized, it justifies to many male teens their sexual harassment of and assault against girls, women, and feminine men; and to many female teens, it develops a cultural pressure to view their sexual power as not theirs to examine and understand but to display and ultimately give away, without a focus on self-empowerment and self-respect. Furthermore, because of the direct connection between misogyny and homophobia, the teens most vulnerable in this dream world are girls (regardless of sexuality) and feminine or feminized males—the majority of our beloved *Glee* characters. This essay's analysis must therefore question how often this unethical and heterosexist story of female sexuality and male entitlement is being told in *Glee* and how often it is being refuted.

In my analysis, I find that the stereotyped sexualities of the pornographic imagination are indeed present, most fundamentally in their molding of a theme that emerges from the very first episodes: sex and sexual attraction are weapons, wielded by male and female characters to enact social revenge, gain popularity, manipulate other's feelings, and control romantic relationships. Affirming the reality and saliency of the dream world, sex has become the most central plot device for the show's comedic and dramatic storylines. By the middle of Season 3, it has been explicitly confirmed that every glee club member is sexually active, except perhaps Sam and Mercedes, whose relationship Mercedes describes vaguely as a "fling" ("Yes/No"). When only 47 percent of high school students have had sex (National Center), why make at least 90 percent of *Glee*'s cast sexually active? Simply put, tapping into the pornographic imagination seems the easiest way for *Glee*'s writers to both conjure up the sexy glamour of popular music videos and develop their misfit characters' storylines in complex and provocative ways.

 Glee's sexual scripts therefore treat sex and sexual attraction as a type of social capital that is bartered for and laundered. When Quinn becomes pregnant after cheating on Finn with Puck, she wants to keep the popular quarterback as her boyfriend rather than admit the father is a "Lima loser" ("Preggers"). She therefore uses Finn's lack of sex education to convince him he impregnated her when he ejaculated near her in a hot tub while they were wearing swimsuits: "Ask Jeeves said a hot tub is the perfect temperature for sperm; it helps it swim faster." She then attempts to shame Puck into silence over their affair: "I had sex with you because you got me drunk on wine coolers and I felt fat that day. But it was a mistake" ("Preggers"). When Quinn is exposed and loses her social status, she secretly posts the "Glist" around the school, a list that ranks the "hotness" of the Glee students "based on sexual promiscuity," with herself at number one, hoping to regain some attention ("Bad Reputation"). Other glee club members see the Glist as their opportunity to make a name for themselves: Rachel plans to make a sexy video, saying, "In today's culture of bad boy athletes and celebrity sex tapes, a good reputation is no good at all." Brittany is stunned at her number four ranking, explaining, "I made out with everyone in this school—girls, boys, Mr. Kidney the janitor. I need to do something to get into the top three." Quinn seeks to reinforce the dream world of the pornographic imagination and insist that she and other Glee members are enacting its sexual scripts, knowing that teens view this behavior as a type of rule-breaking coolness to marvel at, if not admire.

 Furthermore, in Season 1's "Laryngitis," Puck convinces Mercedes that they should "join forces" and pose as a couple in order to help Puck "spice up his image" ("Laryngitis"). When Mercedes' first response to his scheme is, "Baby, I just am not attracted to you cause I know what you do to the girls you date: you knock them up and then you hang them out to dry," Puck retorts, "You can't tie me down. I'm a sex shark: if I stop moving, I'll die." Puck is the most sexually active of the male characters, and this line defines his sexual self-concept. When Mercedes is describing to Quinn why she ultimately agreed to enter this fake relationship with Puck, she sadly admits, "I know he's using me. But in a way, it's even better. I'm not you: I've never had a guy like me for anything. But now I'm such a steaming mug of hot chocolate, one of the studliest guys in school wants to use me to harvest some mojo" ("Laryngitis"). To promote the idea that students who become outsiders, freaks, misfits in their school community should resort to sexual blackmail and dishonesty to improve their social status is reinforcing a negative sexual self-concept to those young viewers who relate to Quinn as a teen mom, to Rachel and her nerdy ambition, to Brittany's bi-curiosity, to Puck as a fatherless bad boy, or to Mercedes' unappreciated (and stereotyped) Black diva attitude. If Jhally's theory is correct, though, it may seem more important for teens to appear to be living according to the pornographic imagination rather than by their own values. According to Jhally, "this male, heterosexual, pornographic imagination based on the degradation and control of women ... has colonized commercial culture," and this colonization includes *Glee* (7). One reason *Glee* is so vulnerable to perpetuating this dream world comes from its musical performances. Jhally argues that, as the origin of the pornographic imagination, the music video and "the sexual imagery that came to define it as a genre ... have moved from the margins of the culture ... to its very center" (1). The show's songs and dance choreography therefore cannot help but replicate to some degree the dream world of typical music videos, such as the glee club's performance of Salt-N-Pepa's "Push It" at a pep rally. This performance in Season 1 is complete with the girls grinding on the boys' crotches and crawling on the floor towards them and is received by the student body with ecstatic cheers and a standing ovation ("Showmance").

Besides musical numbers, the dream world's depiction of women as always sexually available shows up in "The Power of Madonna," when Rachel gathers the glee club girls for sex advice, describes her encounter with a guy she is dating who suggested they "do it" because, as he described it, "It's no big deal." When Rachel replied, "It is for a girl," he leaves her, acting "crabby" and non-communicative.

RACHEL: I just want to be ready. I know I'm getting older and these things are gonna happen someday, but how do I stop a guy from being mad at me for saying no?
SANTANA: Just do what I do—never say no.
BRITTANY: Oh, totally. I mean, what's the worse that could happen? Sorry, Quinn.
MERCEDES: Look, girl, don't ask me ... I can't wait to get a guy being mad at me for saying no.

Santana and Brittany's comments would be taken as completely serious since their sexual reputations are the cornerstone of their characters, and their words thus imply that they believe they must be always sexually available to men. This behavior again smacks of Jhally's dream world where "women never say no and passionately welcome masculine aggression"

(12). *Glee* writers would likely dismiss any viewer taking these ideas to heart by excusing these lines of dialogue as campy, tongue-in-cheek humor. On this point, however, numerous media scholars agree that humor is often employed by writers to shirk any responsibility for how viewers might interpret and enact the scripts they write as entertainment. In a recent study of the sexual health messages in teen media, communications scholar Stacey Hust and colleagues hold that "[t]he infrequent content about sexual health topics was often ambiguous and inaccurate, reinforced traditional gender stereotypes, and used humor to undermine sexually responsible behavior" (19). Take for example Puck's response to Finn's question about condoms in Season 3: "As for condoms, don't know, never use 'em. Worked for me 99 percent of the time" ("The First Time").

As in these scenes, often the at-risk glee club students, and especially those who have what experts deem "multiple risk factors" (Kominski, Jamieson, & Martinez), are the ones whose risky and negative sexual behavior serve as comedic punch lines. Another instance is when Brittany casually mentions her first sexual experience: "I lost my virginity at cheerleading camp. He just climbed into my tent. Alien invasion" ("The First Time"). Making comedy out of what sounds like a highly risky and coercive sexual situation is dangerous writing, especially since Jhally observes that "the use of humor gets men off the hook from having to take responsibility for the violence that is so prevalent in the real world" (qtd. in Media Education 39). In another episode Jacob Ben Israel sexually harasses Rachel, threatening that if she doesn't show him her bra he will write a bad review of her performance in the school's play: "Oh but I'll post my scathing review online. You'll be finished on the high school stage. Now get those sweater puppies out of their cashmere cage" ("The Rhodes Not Taken"). Not only is this scene cast as comedic, but the outcome actually reinforces this negative behavior: instead of reporting the incident, Rachel is seen in a later episode still being harassed and actually relenting to Jacob's demands, giving him a pair of her panties ("Throwdown").

Though its progressive storylines often overshadow these smaller scenes and quips, it is clear from my comprehensive review of *Glee*'s episodes that the show's humor still depends on traditional gender stereotypes and irresponsible sexual ethics. Therefore, the sex ed episode "Sexy" carries even more weight in establishing how conscious the writers are of sexual scripts. To return to my analysis of this episode, the "Do You Want to Touch Me?" scene is the only extended look at a teacher attempting to offer a sex ed lesson outside the health class forum, a vital, interdisciplinary move that more teachers must make if sexual ethics are ever to be thoroughly taught rather than glossed over. However, Holly's lesson offers next to no substantial information, and for the rest of the episode, scenes dealing with sex ed are not based on classroom instruction but are all private discussions, many featuring Holly advising couples who seek her out privately.

One subtle move this episode makes is having Holly—a transient substitute teacher not looking for a permanent position—be the only faculty brave enough to take the professional risk of promoting a more comprehensive and frank approach to sex ed. Other faculty and staff seem to think they are too culturally and contractually confined to address this curriculum, but in *Glee* these authority figures are themselves too uninformed and sexually dysfunctional to address sexual health appropriately. Will's fear of student titillation makes him too timid to even say the word *sex*, and he has already been reprimanded by Principal Figgins for the club's sexualized performances—one causing a "sex riot" at a pep rally ("Britney/Brittany"). Emma shows her extreme sex phobia in the Celibacy Club scene, avoiding answering Rachel's questions about sex; and Coach Beiste's asexuality, based on her poor sexual self-concept, silences her on the subject. Ultimately, though, Holly does pay the price for going beyond the bounds of the federally funded Title V abstinence-only curricula, which strictly prohibits sex ed instructors from "any mention of condoms" or demonstrating how to apply one ("What Programs"). She is fired due to "some parent complaints" ("Sexy"). This realistic depiction does draw attention to the shifting legalities of this sensitive topic, and since the airing of the episode, Holly's vision of comprehensive curricula has been upheld by President Obama's Personal Responsibility Education Program (PREP) that shifts the majority of federal funds to support comprehensive sex education and only a small amount for abstinence-only programs ("End Funding").

Other elements of the episode should be considered successful, at least in their departure from the pornographic imagination. First, there is a rare look into Santana and Brittany's private interactions, showing their struggle to make sense of their relationship ("Sexy"). As the most sexually active female characters, Santana and Brittany have always enacted a dream world sexual script for laughs, presenting the most troubling high-risk sexual behavior, but this aspect of their relationship goes unaddressed in their sex ed scenes with Holly. They begin to come to terms with their romantic relationship when Brittany suggests they seek advice from Holly—the first authority figure they trust as sex-positive and open. Though Holly focuses perhaps too much on identity labels (asking if either one thinks she is a lesbian) and not enough on their promiscuous past and sexual ethics, this scene does model how helpful it is for questioning youth to talk with adult allies. Puck and Lauren Zizes also seek Holly's guidance about the sex tape they are planning on filming, and she warns them that such activity between minors is in fact illegal—another important message for young viewers. After their talk with Holly, Santana professes her love for Brittany, but they find themselves in different places in the relationship, as characterized by a sex advocate blogger: "Santana is struggling with identity and peer pressure, and Brittany is struggling with having feelings for more than one person. Santana is worried about being bullied, and Brittany is worried about being a cheater and breaking someone's heart" (AFY_Abby). This scene is thus "representing relationships between [queer] young people for what they really are—meaningful and complex, just like everyone else's relationships" (AFY_Abby).

But the scene that perhaps garnered the most attention is Burt Hummel's sincere sex speech to his gay son Kurt, lovingly urging him to treat sex as a way "to connect to another person" ("Sexy"). Burt's journey of accepting Kurt's sexuality is indeed praiseworthy, but it's worth noting that this sex speech was not his idea: Kurt first prompted his dad in the previous episode, saying, "Maybe you could step outside your comfort zone and educate yourself so if I have any questions, I could go to my dad like any straight son could" ("Blame It"). And Blaine prompts a still resistant Burt again after Kurt refuses to openly discuss sex between men even casually with Blaine, his own boyfriend. In urging Burt to talk openly with his son, Blaine apologizes for "overstepping" but tells Burt that he is worried because his school doesn't offer sex ed: "Most schools don't. And the ones that do almost never discuss what sex is like for gay kids" ("Sexy"). Blaine admits that his father would not discuss sex with him, leaving Blaine to search the Internet for help.

Convinced by Blaine's pleas, Burt delivers a sex speech that some fans say they want to use in educating their own children (Bierly). Burt's speech is noteworthy because he gives Kurt pamphlets that he picked up at the free clinic on the "mechanics" of gay male sex and instructs Kurt to read them and come back for a follow-up conversation, showing that comprehensive sex ed cannot be covered in one sitting ("Sexy"). After referring to some off-putting stereotypes about males experiencing sex as purely for fun while females connect it to emotions, Burt finally tells Kurt, "Don't throw yourself around like you don't matter. Because you matter, Kurt." By the time Kurt is ready to lose his virginity, he has taken this advice to heart and denies Blaine's drunken attempts to seduce him in "The First Time" and waits until they are both sober and ready. Also in that episode we find Finn saying no to Rachel's plea for sex and Tina describing how she and Mike waited to have sex and "talked about it for a while" until it felt "absolutely perfect, no regrets" ("The First Time").

Though it's staggering how little abstinence is happening with these teens, *Glee* seems at its best when dealing with storylines that do not fall into tropes of the pornographic imagination, when it ventures outside the heteronormative and treats sex and sexual ethics as more than comic relief. Knowing that institutionalized abstinence-until-marriage sex ed has stigmatized sexual minorities long enough, *Glee*'s writers did well in handling Kurt's situation, but the female characters—the most at-risk being the queer female characters—have further to go in developing a healthy sexual self-concept. Though Season 3 contains more scenes where female characters like Rachel and Tina become sexually active within loving, monogamous relationships, the few scenes depicting this mature approach to sex could not make up for the first two seasons so filled with references to unsafe, casual sex and unethical sexual situations. As more females encode the script of the pornographic imagination that reduces women to sexualized bodies, *Glee* is doing a disservice in making jokes out of teen girls' sexual activity and treating it with the type of nonchalance due a commonly-accepted cultural stereotype.

As federally-funded sex ed turns a new corner in history, it is vital that parents, teachers, and communities follow suit and come to terms with the evolution of sexuality in modern American culture. Like many teachers in public schools, Will Schuester does not view sex education as part of his pedagogical domain, despite the fact that his core curriculum involves lessons on performing (heterosexualized) sexiness itself. When sexuality and the drama surrounding teen relationships and sex are major themes in nearly every glee club meeting, why does Will shirk his responsibility to address sex education directly himself? And why aren't more schools and parents investing in teaching media literacy to adolescents who spend on average more than seven hours a day consuming some form of media (Kaiser)? If *Glee* is any indication of the level of sexual content in such media, then adolescents are in need of some serious guidance, some serious sex and healthy relationship education that goes beyond even what current comprehensive programs offer. As psychologist Sharon Lamb and other feminist advocates promote, sex ed should be less self-focused and more community-minded and ethics-based: "Grounded on two ethical ideals, justice and caring for the other person ... sex can be explained to teens as an activity in which rules regarding justice and equality can be applied ... [and] is designed to educate the whole teen as a decision maker, a sexual citizen, and an ethical human being" (88). With TV shows like *Glee* as super-peers, teens indeed need a stronger ethical framework to navigate the tides of popular media's sexual content.

Notes

1. Educators often employ the controversial term "at-risk" broadly to indicate students whose backgrounds make them more at risk for academic failure or drop-out. Their high risk conditions vary greatly but tend to fall along similar lines as those mentioned earlier who are stigmatized in traditional abstinence-only programs: LGBTQ youth, youth from single-parent households, abused youth, as well as poor and homeless youth, youth with disabilities, youth who have a "lack of psychological attachment to school," and "whose cultural backgrounds don't mesh easily with the dominant culture at school" (Ormrod 1).

2. Controversy arose by this scene's use of Gary Glitter's song and the royalties he would earn from boosted sales. Glitter being a convicted pedophile, the children's advocacy and charity group Kidscape called *Glee*'s use of the song "wholly inappropriate," considering the episode's "Sexy" theme ("Gwyneth Paltrow").

References

AFY_Abby. "Reflections on *Glee*'s 'Sexy' Episode." *Amplifyyourvoice.com: Blog.* Advocates for Youth. 23 Mar. 2011. Web. 2 Aug. 2012.

Aubrey, Jennifer Stevens. "Does Television Exposure Influence College-Aged Women's Sexual Self-Concept?" *Media Psychology* 10 (2007): 157–181. Print.

"Bad Reputation." *Glee Season 1.* Dir. Elodie Keene. 20th Century–Fox, 2010. DVD.

Bierly, Mandi. "*Glee* Sex Talk: Let's Hear It for Burt Hummel! (And How Did Your Sex Education Compare?)." *Pop Watch.* Entertainment Weekly. 9 Mar. 2011. Web. 18 July 2012.

"Blame It on the Alcohol." *Glee Season 2.* Dir. Eric Stoltz. 20th Century–Fox, 2011. DVD.

"Britney/Brittany." *Glee Season 2.* Dir. Ryan Murphy. 20th Century–Fox, 2010. DVD.

Brown, Erin. "*Glee*: Sex, Songs, and Sleaze." *Culture and Media Institute.* Culture and Media Institute 3 Feb. 2011. Web. 29 July 2012.

Brown, Jane D. "Introduction: The Media as Sex Educators for Youth." *Managing the Media Monster: The Influence of Media (From Television to Text Messages) on Teen Sexual Behavior and Attitudes.* Ed. Jane D. Brown. Washington, D.C.: National Campaign to Prevent Teen and Unplanned Pregnancy, 2008. 6–17. Web.

Brown, Jane D., Jeanne R. Steele, and Kim Walsh-Childers. *Sexual Teens, Sexual Media: Investigating Media's Influence On Adolescent Sexuality.* Mahwah, NJ: Lawrence Erlbaum, 2002. *eBook Collection (EBSCOhost).* Web. 29 July 2012.

Cope-Farrar, Kristie M., and Dale Kunkel. "Sexual Messages in Teens' Favorite Prime-Time Television Programs." *Sexual Teens, Sexual Media.* Mahwah, NJ: Lawrence Erlbaum, 2002. 59–78. *eBook Collection(EBSCOhost).* Web. 29 July 2012.

"End Funding for the Failed Title V Abstinence-Only-Until-Marriage Program." *SIECUS Fact Sheet.* Sexuality Information and Education Council of the United States. Apr. 2010. Web. 19 July 2012.

"The First Time." *Glee Season 3.* Dir. Bradley Buecker. 20th Century–Fox, 2011. DVD.

"*Glee*: The Complete First Season DVD." FoxShop.com. Twentieth Century–Fox Film Corporation. 2012. Web. 29 July 2012.

Glitter, Gary. "Do You Want to Touch Me? (Oh Yeah)." By Gary Glitter Gary and Mike Leander. *Touch Me.* Bell Records: New York, 1973. *MetroLyrics.* N.d. Web. 31 July 2012.

"Gwyneth Paltrow in Gary Glitter Controversy over *Glee*." *The Telegraph.* The Telegraph. 11 Mar. 2011. Web. 31 July 2012.

Hibberd, James. "*Glee* Teen Sex Slammed by Protest Groups." *EW.com.* Entertainment Weekly, 8 Nov. 2011. Web. 19 July 2012.

Hust, Stacey J. T., Jane D. Brown, and Kelly Ladin L'Engle. "Boys Will Be Boys and Girls Better Be Prepared: An Analysis of the Rare Sexual Health Messages in Young Adolescents' Media." *Mass Communication and Society* 11 (2008): 1–21. Print.

Jhally, Sut. "*Dreamworlds 3*: Desire, Sex & Power in Music Video Transcript." *Video Store: Dreamworlds 3*. Media Education Foundation. 2007. Web. 28 July 2012.

Kaiser Family Foundation. "Daily Media Use Among Children and Teens Up Dramatically from Five Years Ago." *News Release*. Kaiser Family Foundation. 20 Jan. 2010. Web. 3 Aug. 2012.

Kann, Laura, et al. "Sexual Identity, Sex of Sexual Contacts, and Health-Risk Behaviors among Students in Grades 9–12: Youth Risk Behavior Surveillance, Selected Sites, United States, 2001–2009." *Morbidity and Mortality Weekly Report*. Centers for Disease Control and Prevention. 10 June 2011. Web. 29 July 2012.

Kominski, Robert, Amie Jamieson, and Gladys Martinez. "At-Risk Conditions of U.S. School Age Children." *Population Division*. U.S. Bureau of the Census. June 2011. Web. 2 Aug. 2012.

Lamb, Sharon. "Toward a Sexual Ethics Curriculum: Bringing Philosophy and Society to Bear on Individual Development." *Harvard Educational Review* 80.1 (2010): 81–105. Print.

"Laryngitis." *Glee Season 1*. Dir. Alfonso Gomez-Rejon. 20th Century–Fox, 2010. DVD.

Media Education Foundation. "Writing About Media: Transcript." *Writing About Media: DVD Compilation & Curriculum Kit Developed by Peter Elbow*. Media Education Foundation. n.d. Web. 30 July 2012.

National Center for HIV/AIDS, Viral Hepatitis, STD, and TB Prevention. "Press Release: Dramatic Decline in Sexual Risks among Black Youth Since 1991 But Progress among Students Overall Plateaued in Last Decade." *NCHHSTP Newsroom*. Centers for Disease Control and Prevention. 24 July 2012. Web. 1 Aug. 2012.

Ormond, J.E. "Characteristics of Students at Risk and Why Students Drop Out." Education.com. Pearson Allyn Bacon Prentice Hall. 2008. Web. 30 July 2012.

"Pilot." *Glee Season 1*. Dir. Ryan Murphy. 20th Century–Fox, 2009. DVD.

"The Power of Madonna." *Glee Season 1*. Dir. Ryan Murphy. 20th Century–Fox, 2010. DVD.

"Preggers." *Glee Season 1*. Dir. Brad Falchuk. 20th Century–Fox, 2009. DVD.

"The Rhodes Not Taken." *Glee Season 1*. Dir. John Scott. 20th Century–Fox, 2009. DVD.

Rich, Michael. "Virtual Sexuality: The Influence of Entertainment Media on Sexual Attitudes and Behavior." *Managing the Media Monster: The Influence of Media (From Television to Text Messages) on Teen Sexual Behavior and Attitudes*. Ed. Jane D. Brown. Washington, D.C.: National Campaign to Prevent Teen and Unplanned Pregnancy, 2008. 18–38. Web. 2 Aug. 2012.

"Sexy." *Glee Season 2*. Dir. Ryan Murphy. 20th Century–Fox, 2011. DVD.

"Showmance." *Glee Season 1*. Dir. Ryan Murphy. 20th Century–Fox, 2009. DVD.

Strasburger, Victor C. "Anything Goes! Teenage Sex and the Media." *Journal of Obstet Gynaecol* 30.2 (Feb. 2008): 109–111.

Strasburger, Victor C., Amy B. Jordan, and Ed Donnerstein. "Health Effects of Media on Children and Adolescents." *Pediatrics* 125 (2010): 756–67. Web. 18 July 2012.

"Throwdown." *Glee Season 1*. Dir. Ryan Murphy. 20th Century–Fox, 2009. DVD.

"Understanding the TV Ratings." *TVGuidelines.org*. TV Parental Guidelines.

Ward, L. M., B. Gorvine, & A. Cytron. "Would That Really Happen? Adolescents' Perceptions of Sexuality According to Prime-Time Television." *Sexual Teens, Sexual Media*. Mahwah, NJ: Lawrence Erlbaum, 2002. 95–124. *eBook Collection (EBSCOhost)*. Web. 29 July 2012.

"What Programs Much Teach." *NoMoreMoney.org*. Sexuality Information and Education Council of the United States (SIECUS). Nov. 2010. Web. 6 Aug. 2012.

"Yes/No." *Glee Season 3*. Dir. Eric Stoltz. 20th Century–Fox, 2012. DVD.

Glee and the "Ghosting" of Musical Theatre Canon

BARRIE GELLES

Alright guys, we're doing a new number for sectionals. I know that pop songs have sort of been our signature pieces, but I did a little research on past winners and it turns out that judges like songs that are more accessible, stuff they know, standards, Broadway.—Will Schuester, "Wheels"

Picture yourself standing in front of a full audience, belting out the final song of one of the greatest musicals of all time.—Kurt Hummel, "New York"

The critical investigation of Broadway musicals, arguably America's most popular theatrical genre, is gaining new ground within theatre studies. While the form has begun to find its place within the academy among other genres of serious consideration, it has also begun to find a new niche in mass popular culture. The form is embedded in media culture, especially in recent years with a resurgence of popular movie musicals, movies about making musicals, and television series that either borrow tropes and elements of the musical or showcase talents requisite in musical theatre performance. One of the most recent, successful cross-sections of media culture and the Broadway musical is the run-away hit *Glee*. Although *Glee* features other music genres (e.g., pop, rock and roll, funk) as often as it does songs from the musical theatre canon, the use of the latter genre offers a particularly interesting opportunity for analysis as it blends two forms of popular culture: the Broadway musical and a hit television show. Applying the concept of "ghosting," as defined in Marvin Carlson's *The*

Haunted Stage: Theatre as Memory Machine, I propose that the use of the musical theatre canon in *Glee* can sometimes offer a more complex reading of a given plot point and/or of character development. Furthermore, the ghosting of Broadway musical songs can often (as Carlson suggests) "complicate [the reception] process significantly" (Carlson 7). When showtunes such as "Defying Gravity," "Rose's Turn," and "Not the Boy Next Door" are used within the storylines of *Glee*, they bring with them their original context. This inquiry, focusing on the character of Kurt, a musical theatre aficionado and a devout Broadway fan, will consider where the ghosting of the original Broadway musical enhances plot and character within *Glee* and where it fails to do so. What is there to gain from doubled layers of implications when these songs are performed? In particular, how are the traditional interpretations of Broadway showtunes being subverted to foreground issues of gender and sexuality? How is *Glee* employing the "ghosts" of musicals to reemphasize our understanding of gender and sexuality?

"Here's what you missed on *Glee*"

Amid the overarching story of the "New Directions" annual competitive show choir season, *Glee* focuses on the trials and tribulations of high school life—first love, lost love, bullying, identity formation, and other social struggles. There are also plots involving the adult characters—their complicated love lives, work place rivalry, professional battles, and personal victories. This structure would not be all that different from your standard teenage television drama, but the thing that makes it unique within that genre is, not just the music, but the way it employs music to enhance the stories and characters (more on that later). There have been television series that embedded musical numbers within most or all of their episodes: *Fame* (1982), *Cop Rock* (1990), and *Eli Stone* (2008) to name a few. There have also been television shows that have musical episodes, such as "Once More with Feeling" (*Buffy the Vampire Slayer*, 2001). There have been some shows that parody songs from musical theatre (*South Park*, *Sesame Street*, *Animaniacs*) and shows that feature a showtune in a particular instance (*Ally McBeal*, *Pushing Daisies*). *Glee* stands apart because it uses Broadway showtunes repeatedly, regularly, and *as* Broadway showtunes. Part of the appeal of *Glee* is the imbedding of the Broadway musical theatre culture. As Rachel, the star of the show choir, puts it, "A guy came to glee club to talk to us about dreams. Luckily, I've known mine since I was four. I am going to play three parts on Broadway: *Evita*, *Funny Girl*, and Laurey in *Oklahoma*" ("Dream On").

Ghosting and Integration

In his book, *The Haunted Stage*, Carlson describes the phenomenon that he names "ghosting" as related to, but other than the operations of genre:

> Unlike the reception operations of genre [...,] in which audience members encounter a new but distinctly different example of a type of artistic product they have encountered before, ghosting presents the identical thing they have encountered before, although now in a somewhat different context. Thus, a recognition not of similarity, as in genre, but of identity becomes a part of the reception process, with results that can complicate this process considerably [Carlson 7].

Ghosting seems to be the exact process that is instigated when *Glee* employs songs from musical theatre, and the exact phenomenon encountered when musical theatre is consumed as such.

But, let us take this one step further. Applying Carlson's definition of ghosting, we can see that *Glee* uses musical theatre showtunes as the "identical thing [the audience has] encountered before, although now in a somewhat different context" (Carlson 7). The process does not end there, however, and I suggest that, in *Glee*, ghosting is the beginning of a recontextualization that includes the process of "de-integration" and "reintegration." That is to say that when *Glee* plucks a showtune from its original script, the *"integrated" book and score*, the song becomes de-integrated. When this song is then inserted into the episode of *Glee*, it must be reintegrated to fit the purposes of the story. Musical theatre showtunes are not stand-alone pieces of music; they are one part of an integrated piece of theatre. With that understanding, what is being removed from the song during the de-integration? How does the song change when it is reintegrated? And, the biggest conundrum: where does this process leave those ghosts?

At this point, I feel that it is necessary to clarify my use of the term "integration." Scott McMillin, in his book *The Musical as Drama*, questions the use of integration theory in the analysis of musicals:

> The American musical has been accompanied by a theory easily believed so long as it remains unexamined. The theory is that of the "integrated musical," according to which all elements of a show—plot, character, song, dance, orchestration, and setting—should blend together into a unity, a seamless whole [1].

McMillin further explores the notion of "difference" in relation to integration:

> When a musical is working well, I feel the crackle of difference, not the smoothness of unity, even when the numbers dovetail with the book. It takes

things different from one another to be thought of as integrated in the first place, and I find that the musical depends more on the differences that make the close fit interesting than on the suppression of difference in a seamless whole.... Integration theory would say that songs and dances advance the plot. I can think of songs and dances that do advance the plot.... But, most song and dances do not advance the plot. Usually the book sets forth the turn of plot and the number elaborates it, in the spirit of repetition and the pleasure of difference. Most songs and dances do not further characterization, they change the mode of characterization—difference again [2 and 7–8].

D.A. Miller, in his book *Place for Us: Essay on the Broadway Musical*, speaks of the pleasure of difference:

What [was] consequently sought in the Broadway musical was the very thing that those who despised it also found there: not the integration of drama and music found on the thematic surface, but a so much deeper formal disconti- nuity between the two that no makeshift for reconciling them could ever manage to make the transition from one to the other less abrupt, or more plausible [3].

The way I am using the term "integration" does not refute the difference inherent in the musical theatre form, nor does it deny the resulting pleas- ure. I employ the term integration purely to mean that the songs in musicals are intermixed or intermingled with the book, plot, characters, dialogue, and dances. I do not suggest that the elements are blended together, but that the musical numbers are part of a mixed form in which all the elements enhance the story in *different* ways. The songs of a musical theatre piece belong to that show; they were created for the purposes (be it elaboration of plot, or plot advancement; a heightened mode of characterization, or the furthering of characterization) of a contextualized moment. Musical theatre may not be an integrated form, but most individual musical theatre pieces tell an integrated story. We must then consider the original context of the songs within their original piece of musical theatre and compare that with their re-contextualized appearance in *Glee*, noting where the "ghosting" of the original Broadway musical is employed and to what effect.

The Use of Music on *Glee*

Unlike musical theatre, the majority of the music used in *Glee* is diegetic.[1] The songs are typically featured as part of a rehearsal, perform- ance, or presentation of a song as part of the weekly assignment from their teacher, Mr. Schuester (e.g., flops, theatricality, funk). Frequently, these songs have a double meaning, reflecting back thematically on the events of the episode, and it is to be understood (or we are simply told) that the song choice is revealing something about the storyline or character(s).

McMillin explains the term diegetic as it relates to musical theatre:

> The term diegetic, borrowed from film criticism, is coming to be used for numbers that are called for by the book. It is meant to cover the backstage musicals plus any other occasions on which characters deliberately perform numbers for other characters.... The diegetic number is not a case of someone "bursting into song." Rather, someone has a song to sing, according to the book, and goes ahead and sings it! [103].

Not all the songs in *Glee* are diegetic. Whereas non-diegetic songs are the exception to the rule in *Glee,* most songs in musical theatre are not "called for by the book" and are, instead, non- diegetic and therefore presented in a non-realistic manner. Because this latter type of song is the norm in musical theatre, it seems odd to refer to it as *non*-diegetic. As McMillin points out, "We need a phrase to distinguish the diegetic number from the usual kind, where characters burst into song" (112). Unfortunately, there doesn't seem to be a consensus on what that term should be. McMillin suggests, "When characters burst into song or dance the number seems to come from out of the blue. That will do for our phrase. Out-of-the-blue numbers ... are forms of spontaneous expression by the characters" (112). For the most part, *Glee* shies away from "out-of-the-blue" numbers; rarely do characters burst into song as a way of conveying emotions or thoughts. When they do, the song is often split so that it begins as a spontaneous eruption of emotions, presented in a non-realistic manner, and then transitions (using cuts) to a diegetic performance of that same song as part of a rehearsal or performance.

There is another layer of interpretation that is useful in understanding the use of songs in *Glee.* Each song, whether it is diegetic or out-of-the-blue, has a contextual purpose once it has been re-integrated into the story of the episode. Some of the songs are simply used in a performative manner, sung as part of a rehearsal or performance to showcase vocal talent or to complete a set list. Other songs are chosen to enhance plot points or characterizations. Whereas the type of song (diegetic or out-of-the-blue) conveys the function of the showtune, the usage of the song (it is performative or it enhances characterization/plot) signals to us whether or not we should be searching for double layers of interpretation.

"Defying Gravity": Ghosting as Underscoring and Pointed Difference

In the episode "Wheels," when Will Schuester decides that New Directions must add a "classic" Broadway standard to the repertoire to be more competitive at sectionals, he selects "Defying Gravity." This song, from the musical *Wicked* (2003), is the finale of the first act and is one of the strongest and most direct "I Am" songs in contemporary Broadway Theatre. One of the main characters, Elpheba, having been an "other" her whole life, has just been severely disappointed by her childhood hero. Her whole life she has been pressured to suppress that which made her different in an effort to be accepted. Now, she realizes that she must fully embrace her true identity and nature, and what is more, use that which makes her different to change the very world from which she has hidden her gifts. The song is empowering and uplifting; by the end of the number, her magical powers are at their strongest and she flies. This song is a declaration of self, of intent, of promise, and of a future of fearless existence.

In *Glee*, Kurt, the openly homosexual student with an extraordinarily beautiful soprano voice, asks to audition for the chance to sing "Defying Gravity" in the upcoming glee club sectionals. Mr. Schuester explains that he feels it is better suited to be sung by Rachel, their resident female soprano soloist, as the song was intended for a female. Kurt is extremely disappointed, as this song resonates with him on a personal level; he even has "an entire iPod shuffle dedicated exclusively to selections from *Wicked*" ("Wheels"). He explains his sadness to his father, "We are doing this amazing song for sectionals, a personal favorite of mine, and Mr. Schuester won't give me a chance to sing it" ("Wheels"). His father, a blue-collar, football playing, heteronormative man, who is fiercely supportive and accepting of his son, demands that Kurt be treated fairly and not suffer gender discrimination. Mr. Schuester agrees and decides to solve the problem by holding a competition between Kurt and Rachel where they will sing the song in front of the glee club peers who will then vote for whomever sings the song best. A few scenes prior to the sing-off, Kurt's father gets a phone call—an anonymous voice says, "Your son's a fag" and hangs up ("Wheels"). Kurt tries to ease his father's distress, "Well, that's not a big deal. I get that all the time" ("Wheels"). His father replies, "Now look, Kurt, I try to do right by you, you know, open some doors. What father wouldn't do that for his kid. And I know it's good for you to be out there with all this glee club stuff, I just, I don't want you to get hurt" ("Wheels"). His father assures him that he still wants him to sing the solo and congratulates him on hitting his "high F" during practice.

The "diva off" is filmed showing Kurt and Rachel alternately singing (a diegetic number), eliminating the redundancy of the same number sung twice and creating a montage effect. It has another stunning effect though, one that is much more narrative. It creates a comparison between the way in which the two characters sing it—not just the difference in their vocal quality but also the difference in their performance and emotional conveyance of the song. For Rachel, this is a number in which she can showcase her remarkable voice—it is performative. A devoted Broadway fan, she would know *Wicked* well and performs the song perfectly—with both vocal flourish and the appropriate acting technique to convey the emotions of the scene in the musical from which this song originates. In other words, she performs it as would be expected if she were playing the role of Elpheba in the production of *Wicked*. Kurt's performance is notably different, and far more poignant—it enhances characterization. From the very beginning, it seems clear that he is not playing a role but singing this song in his own voice, conveying what he needs to say through this song. Kurt is expressing his own sentiments when he sings.[2] The lyrics have real relevance to Kurt. Rachel plays the climax of the song with bravado, but as Kurt sings the part he seems hesitant and more fearful. Kurt has a lot more at stake; he is actually defying the constraints put upon him—to be closeted, to act "masculine," to behave like everyone else. This song features lyrics that resonate with his personal trials, but that is not all. The ghosting of the song, of its original context in which Elpheba claims her "otherness" and allows it to empower her, is evident in this scene, not just to the audience (if familiar with *Wicked*) but to the character of Kurt. As he sings, Kurt falters in the final moment, tears brimming in his eyes and sings the last note off-key, though we know it is "well within his range" ("Wheels"). Later, Kurt explains to his father: "I blew the note. I wanted to lose.... I have known who I was when I was five, I adapted. Being different made me stronger. At the end of the day its what's going to get me out of this cow town. You never had to do that" ("Wheels"). His father replies, "I can handle myself just fine" ("Wheels"). Kurt continues:

> No you can't. Not about this. That phone call was just the beginning. Especially if I get up in front of a thousand people to sing a girl's song. When I saw you right after you got the call and you were so hurt and so upset, it just killed me. I'm not saying I'm going to hide in the closet. I'm proud of who I am. I am just saying that I love you more than I love being a star ["Wheels"].

The use of "Defying Gravity" in *Glee* is not only consciously aware of the original context and narrative of the song within *Wicked* but uses it as an underscoring of the issues within the episode. The audience members who are familiar with *Wicked* will recognize the song as the exact thing they have seen before but in a different context. The song has been de-integrated from its original context; it is no longer about Elpheba and her bravery as she proclaims that the world must accept her, differences and all. The song has been reintegrated and is now about Kurt, a young boy who wants to be "through accepting" the heteronormative limits he feels constrained by, but ultimately, he doesn't defy them. Kurt purposefully sings the climactic note off-key because he wants to throw the competition and thereby forfeit his chance to sing this song in front of thousands of people. It is so near and dear to his own personal struggle, that he is not yet ready to make himself, and by extension, his father, vulnerable publicly. Although Kurt is inspired by "Defying Gravity," he is not yet ready to "trust [his] instincts, close [his] eyes and leap" ("Wheels").

"Rose's Turn": Ghosting as Appropriation and the Issue of Alteration

In the episode "Laryngitis," Kurt's father and Finn's (the quarterback and lead male singer) mother have begun dating. At first, Kurt is very excited, until he begins to feel ignored and recognizes that he may not be ready to share his father's attentions with Finn. Kurt's father, Burt, and Finn become fast friends due to their shared interest in sports, cars, and other hegemonic "masculine" pastimes. Kurt, jealous of their connection, begins to imitate Burt's behavior and lifestyle—wearing a trucker hat and flannel rather than his usual unique combination of high fashion and doc martens; dating a girl despite being openly gay; and singing a John Mellencamp song instead of a Broadway showtune. Despite his best (if misguided) efforts, this strange transformation does not get the desired results. Kurt's father shows up at school to pick up Finn for an evening of free hoagies at the motorcross, and Kurt asks why he isn't being invited along. Burt reminds Kurt that Finn doesn't have a father and that Finn is going through a tough time and could use a buddy right now—Burt is filling that void. As Burt walks away to find Finn, Kurt is crushed and begins to sing "Rose's Turn," out of the blue.[3]

Originally from the musical *Gypsy*, "Rose's Turn" is one of the best known and most beloved eleven o'clock numbers (Styne and Sonheim). Rose, a fervent stage mother, has dedicated her entire life to trying to make her daughters stars. Now, her daughter, Louise (Gypsy Rose Lee), is a phenomenal success, and it seems as though Rose's dreams have finally come true. The tragedy of this situation is that Rose's genuine dream, her heart's desire, was to be famous herself. Rose wanted to be a performer and had she had the support that she foisted upon her daughters, she would have been. Living vicariously through her daughters, forcing them into show business, Rose is constantly accused of selfishness. Having lost almost everyone she loves along the road to success, now about to lose Louise, she walks onto an empty stage in front of an empty house, and finally lets loose. Rose finally admits her motives, her real desires, and her sadness. "Rose's Turn" is a song of unrequited dreams, of feelings of failure, of mourning the life that wasn't. The song begins as a fantasy, held dearly by Rose, of what she would be like as a performer, it is a bawdy jazz number meant for the burlesque stage. It then descends into a recognition of loss, an agitated ballad expressing frustration at the unfairness of the world.

When Kurt sings this song he is standing in a hallway filled with people, but feeling very much alone. He begins to sing, out-of-the-blue, in a defeated and saddened manner, moving through the hallway, into the auditorium, and eventually onto the stage. The song isn't used in its entirety but begins in the second part, the descent into loss. The opening lines of this song do not really fit the situation, but let us assume that Kurt begins to sing this song because he is trying to express his feelings of being overlooked by his family. In that sense this song, used to express characterization, is ghosted, in part, by Kurt's application of a Broadway moment to his current situation. In fact, some of the lyrics are changed to reflect Kurt's particular situation, singing to his father and Rachel rather than the characters from the musical. This altering is uncomfortable because it is disconcerting that the *Glee* version of "Rose's Turn" should have different lyrics and only half the song. The use of the song *attempts* to convey Kurt's frustration at failed attempts to please his father and a decision to reclaim his identity but, for those who know this song and are susceptible to the ghosting, it is a very complicated layering of contexts and usage.

The initial layer of the ghosting focuses on the song within its original context, the musical *Gypsy*. The song is not quite the "identical thing" that has been encountered before; the lyrics have been changed. The "somewhat different context" is radically different in this layer of the ghosting. At this layer, "Rose's Turn," having been de-integrated from its original context, seems to be awkwardly re-integrated into this moment. Kurt, feeling neglected by his father, suspects that those things about him that are different from his father (being gay, enjoying musical theatre, interested in fashion) will result in the eventual dissolution of their relationship.

"Rose's Turn" may be, in part, a song about lost relationships, but it is ultimately a song written as a declaration of desperation and an awareness of missed opportunities. Rose, a middle aged woman, never fulfilled her dreams, is completely alone, and has only herself to blame—this song conveys her devastation and her attempt to reclaim her life.[4] Kurt is a young boy, is scared of losing his father, and has foolishly abandoned his sense of self to please his father (who accepted him all along!). Considering the original context of this song, the application does not seem particularly well suited to this moment, but the ghosts of "Rose's Turn" are not limited to the original context. This song offers another layer of ghosting that enhances characterization and explains its usage in this moment.

"Rose's Turn" is also a song about admitting one's true identity and no longer suppressing one's sense of self. It is one of the reasons that this song has often been used in queer and drag performances,[5] the other reason being that the song is associated with the actresses who are gay icons who played Mama Rose—Ethel Merman, Bette Midler, Patti LuPone. This additional layer of ghosting provides a particular aspect of characterization for Kurt: his anthem of identity and freedom from suppression was chosen for its context in queer culture. As Kurt finishes singing the song, he realizes that his father has been standing in the auditorium watching (as previously mentioned, *Glee* will often transition an out-of-the-blue song into a diegetic one). Burt explains that he changed his plans with Finn because he could tell that Kurt was "bent out of shape." Kurt insists that he is fine and his father replies: "Kurt, I'm dumb, but I'm not stupid. And I have no idea what that song was about, but 'fine' don't sing like you just sung" ("Laryngitis"). Burt reassures Kurt that he doesn't need to change his clothes, date a girl, or take on a new taste in music to be loved: "Your job is to be yourself, and my job is to love you no matter what" ("Laryngitis"). The scene is heartfelt and is very progressive in terms of a television script dealing with heteronormativity and acceptance. Certainly, the scene is enhanced by a song, and the choice of "Rose's Turn" is an interesting one. The ghosting of the song's original context within *Gypsy* may seem an imperfect fit, but the ghosting of the song's associations with the liberation of true identity are well utilized.

There is still a lingering discomfort in the use of "Rose's Turn," and the strangeness comes from the alteration of the song. Kurt is a musical theatre aficionado, and the songs that he sings tend to be ghosted in such a way that they belay his knowledge of musicals and his understanding of apt appropriation. His use of "Defying Gravity" certainly indicates the character's ability to recognize the intent of a song and parlay it to his current situation. In Season 2, Kurt sings "Le Jazz Hot!" (*Victor/Victoria*) as a play on duality and duets, "Don't Cry for Me Argentina" (*Evita*) as a plea to be adored and chosen as a soloist, and "As If We Never Said Goodbye" (*Sunset Boulevard*) as a nostalgic tribute when he returns to the glee club. The reintegration of these songs is most interesting when they remain unaltered and the ghosting functions to allow them to be appropriated in the context of the *Glee* episode. Part of the pleasure derived from this process is that the character Kurt seems aware of the appropriation, as if each song is simultaneously creating a new context and offering tribute to its original source. Audience members who had never previously heard "Rose's Turn," who are unfamiliar with *Gypsy*, may never even realize that the lyrics have been changed and that the song has been cut in half—after all, "Rose's Turn" appears in its revised form on the *Glee* albums. Audience members who know, and perhaps love, *Gypsy*, will undoubtedly note that the song was unnecessarily altered in an attempt to tailor it to the story and will, perhaps, object to the changes in this version. Ironically, the character of Kurt, being a musical theatre connoisseur, would belong to the latter group.

A Coda: "Not the Boy Next Door"—Ghosting as Repetition and Recognition

But what about those other ghosted showtunes that Kurt sings? In *Victor/Victoria*, "Le Jazz Hot!" is sung by a character who is a woman playing a man performing in drag as a woman, and Kurt sings this song solo as his contribution to the "duet" assignment, playing on the idea of mutable gender and sexuality. In *Evita*, "Don't Cry for Me Argentina," is a song of mutual adoration between the exceptionally feminine Evita and her people; Kurt selects this song to gain admiration, choosing it for its apropos content, regardless of the fact that it is sung by a female character. Even in non-performative moments, when Kurt sings an out-of-the-blue "As If We Never Said Goodbye" (*Sunset Boulevard*), he does so instinctively while channeling his emotions, identifying with the sentiments of the song, rather than considering that it is also traditionally sung by a woman. Kurt frequently chooses to perform songs that are intended for female characters.

In the episode "Funeral," Kurt sings "Some People" (*Gypsy*) as his audition for the coveted position of soloist. At the end his audition, Jesse St. James condescendingly asks, "Kurt, you do know that song was meant to be sung by a woman, right?" ("Funeral") Kurt responds, "Yes, I'm aware. And the glee club sort of dealt with that whole boys sing songs that were meant for girls … it's kind of old news" ("Funeral"). In Season 3, Kurt auditions for the McKinley High's production of *West Side Story* with "I'm the Greatest Star," a song from *Funny Girl*, made famous by Barbra Streisand ("I Am Unicorn"). There is a complicated duality in the selection of these songs: within the world of *Glee*, the character, Kurt, selects these songs because of his affinity for Broadway musicals and his love of the leading ladies (who typically get the best songs in musicals); in reality, these songs are selected by the writers, presumably to show off the actor's impressive vocal range but also as a signifier of the character's queerness.

Considering this history of song selection, it is particularly interesting that, in one of the final episodes of Season 3, during a defining moment for the character, Kurt sings "Not the Boy Next Door" (*The Boy From Oz*).

In the episode "Choke," the day has finally arrived when Rachel and Kurt will audition for the school of their dreams, the (fictional) New York Academy of Dramatic Arts. They will have one chance, and one chance only, to audition in front of newly appointed dean of "vocal performance and song interpretation" at NYADA, Carmen Tibideaux (perhaps a musical theatre reference to the lead character in *Caroline, or Change*, Caroline Thibodeaux). In the beginning of the episode, Kurt plans to sing "The Music of the Night" from *The Phantom of the Opera*. He chooses this song, ostensibly, to showcase his voice and because it is a safe selection from the musical theatre canon—though, it seems incongruous with what has previously been established as Kurt's musical theatre tastes. As Kurt announces his selection to Dean Tibideaux, he notices her unenthusiastic response. He apologizes, "It's a safe and standard choice" but then quickly recovers ("Choke"). He continues, "Which is why I have decided to change things up a bit. Here, in the eleventh hour, I have decided to go in a different direction, something that is a little more out there, but much more me—'Not the Boy Next Door' from the Peter Allan bio-musical, *The Boy from Oz*" ("Choke"). Kurt, obviously having planned this song as an alternate selection, invites his back-up singers on stage and begins the number. As Kurt performs, he is clearly comfortable and confident in this role. As he sings lines about a hidden identity he tugs at his tear-away tux to reveal another costume—a fitted black button-down shirt and gold lamé pants.

This is a defining moment for the character: Kurt, during this crucial audition that will shape his future, has decided to perform a song that clearly transmits his identity, in a manner that displays his exuberance, and with the enthusiasm of one who truly loves musical theatre. This is also a notable moment of characterization within the trajectory of Kurt's character: rather than have Kurt sing a Broadway showtune that, while suited to his voice, is intended for a female performer, this time, the character is finally given a song that suits him. Much like Kurt tears away the superfluous costume to reveal something more fitting underneath, the extraneous signifiers of Kurt's queerness have been removed to reveal a more honest characterization. "Not the Boy Next Door" is used in the same way in both its original context and in *Glee*—this is a song about an openly gay performer revealing and reveling in his identity. As Kurt sings we are reminded of the quieter boy Kurt used to be and all of the struggles he faced in the previous two seasons of the show. Now, as the character is about to graduate and move on from the glee club and high school, this song feels like a vindication of sorts—a moment for the character to truly relish being loved for exactly who he has become. *Glee*'s use of "Not the Boy Next Door" is employing ghosting purposefully: not only is this the "identical thing" that has been encountered before, but the "somewhat different context" is not all that different. As Kurt sings the climax of the song, we do not believe that he is at all apologetic for being himself. We get the feeling that he has no desire to return to his previous existence. In what is arguably the character's eleven o'clock number, *Glee* uses ghosting, by way of repetition and recognition, to affirm Kurt's identity, his sexuality, and his pride.

In this final example of the ghosting of Broadway musical theatre, we see clearly what is to be gained from the double layers of implications when showtunes are performed within the context of *Glee*. Though watching Kurt succeed at his audition with any other song would still be a delightful triumph for the character, the ghosting of "Not the Boy Next Door" foregrounds the issue of sexuality and pride. The story is complete because *Glee* is employing the "ghosts" of musicals to reemphasize our understanding of Kurt's character. Just as Kurt revels in the performance of the song, we derive joy from the selection of the song—through the ghosting of musical theatre, we share a deeper pleasure.

Appendix 1: The Use of Musical Theatre in *Glee*, a Data Analysis

Musical Theatre Songs from Season 1

Total Songs in Season 1: 132
Songs from Musical Theatre: 17
Songs from Movie Musicals: 3
Percentage of Songs from Musicals: 15%

Song	*Musical*	*Episode*	*Type*	*Usage*
"Where Is Love?"	*Oliver*	1	diegetic	performative
"Mr. Cellophane"	*Chicago*	1	diegetic	performative
"On My Own"	*Les Miserables*	1	diegetic	performative
"Sit Down, You're Rockin' the Boat"	*Guys and Dolls*	1	diegetic	performative
"You're the One That I Want"	*Grease*	1	diegetic	performative
"Tonight"	*West Side Story*	4	diegetic	performative
"Maybe This Time"	*Cabaret***	5	diegetic	performative
"Cabaret"	*Cabaret*	5	diegetic	performative
"I Could Have Danced All Night"	*My Fair Lady*	8	diegetic	enhances characterization
"Defying Gravity"	*Wicked*	9	diegetic	performative (for Rachel) enhances characterization (for Kurt)

Song	Musical	Episode	Type	Usage
"You're the One That I Want"	Grease	11	diegetic	enhances characterization
"Hair"	Hair	11	diegetic	performative
"And I Am Telling You I'm Not Going"	Dreamgirls	13	diegetic	enhances characterization
"Don't Rain on My Parade"	Funny Girl	13	diegetic	performative
"Home"	The Wiz	16	diegetic	performative
"Rose's Turn"	Gypsy	18	out-of-the-blue/ diegetic	enhances characterization
"Lady Is a Tramp"	Babes in Arms	18	diegetic	performative
"Big Spender"	Sweet Charity	19	diegetic	performative
"I Dreamed a Dream"	Les Miserables	19	diegetic/ out-of-the-blue	enhances characterization
"Funny Girl"	Funny Girl	20	diegetic	performative
"Over the Rainbow"	The Wizard of Oz*	22	diegetic	performative

Musical Theatre Songs from Season 2

Total Songs in Season 2: 138
Songs from Musical Theatre: 23
Songs from Movie Musicals: 7
Percentage of Songs from Musicals: 22%

Song	Musical	Episode	Usage	Type
"Getting to Know You"	The King and I	1	diegetic	performative
"Listen"	Dreamgirls	1	diegetic	performative
"What I Did for Love"	A Chorus Line	1	out-of-the-blue	enhances characterization
"Papa, Can You Hear"Me?"	Yentl*	3	out-of-the-blue	enhances plot
"Le Jazz Hot!"	Victor/Victoria	4	diegetic	performative
"Sing!"	A Chorus Line	4	diegetic	performative
"Science Fiction/ Double Feature"	The Rocky Horror Show	5	diegetic	performative
"Over at the Frankenstein Place"	The Rocky Horror Show	5	diegetic	performative
"Dammit Janet"	The Rocky Horror Show	5	diegetic	performative
"Hot Patootie"	The Rocky Horror Show	5	diegetic	performative
"Sweet Transvestite"	The Rocky Horror Show	5	diegetic	performative
"Touch-a, Touch-a, Touch-a, Touch Me"	The Rocky Horror Show	5	diegetic	enhances characterization

Song	Musical	Episode	Usage	Type
"Time Warp"	The Rocky Horror Show	5	diegetic	performative
"Make 'Em Laugh"	Singin' in the Rain*	7	out-of-the-blue	enhances plot
"Nowadays/Hot Honey Rag"	Chicago	7	diegetic	performative
"Singin' in the Rain"	Singin' in the Rain*	7	diegetic	performative
"Ohio"	Wonderful Town	8	diegetic	performative
"Don't Cry for Me Argentina"	Evita	9	diegetic	enhances characterization
"The Most Wonderful Day of the Year"	Rudolph the Red Nosed Reindeer*	10	out-of-the-blue	enhances plot
"We Need a Little Christmas"	Mame	10	diegetic	performative
"My Funny Valentine"	Babes in Arms	12	diegetic	enhances characterization
"Take Me or Leave Me"	Rent	13	diegetic	performative
"I Feel Pretty" (with "Unpretty")+	West Side Story	18	out-of-the-blue/ diegetic	enhances characterization
"As If We Never Said Goodbye"	Sunset Boulevard	18	out-of-the-blue/ diegetic	enhances plot
"Some People"	Gypsy	21	diegetic	performative
"My Man"	Funny Girl***	21	diegetic	performative
"Pure Imagination"	Willy Wonka and the Chocolate Factory*	21	diegetic	enhances plot
"New York, New York" (with "I Love New York")+	On the Town	22	diegetic	enhances plot
"Bella Notte"	Lady and the Tramp*	22	diegetic	enhances plot
"For Good"	Wicked	22	diegetic	enhances characterization

Musical Theatre Songs from Season 3

Total Songs in Season 3: 145
Songs from Musical Theatre: 27
Songs from Movie Musicals: 1
Percentage of Songs from Musicals: 19%

Song	Musical	Episode	Usage	Type
"Big Spender"	Sweet Charity	1	diegetic	performative

Song	Musical	Episode	Usage	Type
"Ding Dong, the Witch Is Dead"	*The Wizard of Oz**	1	diegetic	performative
"Anything Goes" with "Anything You Can Do" ++	*Anything Goes* and *Annie Get Your Gun*	1	diegetic	performative
"Somewhere"	*West Side Story*	2	diegetic	enhances characterization
"I'm the Greatest Star"	*Funny Girl*	2	diegetic	performative
"Something's Coming"	*West Side Story*	2	diegetic	performative
"Cool"	*West Side Story*	3	diegetic	performative
"It's All Over"	*Dreamgirls*	3	diegetic	enhances characterization
"Out Here on My Own"	*Fame*	3	diegetic	performative
"Tonight"	*West Side Story*	5	diegetic	performative
"A Boy Like That"	*West Side Story*	5	diegetic	performative
"I Have a Love"	*West Side Story*	5	diegetic	performative
"America"	*West Side Story*	5	diegetic	performative
"One Hand, One Heart"	*West Side Story*	5	diegetic	performative
"Buenos Aires"	*Evita*	8	diegetic	performative
"My Favorite Things"	*Sound of Music*	9	diegetic	performative
"Summer Nights"	*Grease*	10	out-of-the-blue/ diegetic	performative
"You're the Top"	*Anything Goes*	13	diegetic	performative
"The Music of the Night"	*Phantom of the Opera*	18	diegetic	performative
"Cell Block Tango"	*Chicago*	18	diegetic	performative
"Not the Boy Next Door"	*Boy from Oz*	18	diegetic	performative
"Don't Rain on My Parade"	*Funny Girl*	18	diegetic	performative
"The Rain in Spain"	*My Fair Lady*	18	out-of-the-blue/ diegetic	enhances plot
"Always True to You in My Fashion"	*Kiss Me, Kate*	20	diegetic	performative
"Pinball Wizard"	*The Who's Tommy*****	21	diegetic	performative
"Starlight Express"	*Starlight Express*	21	diegetic	performative
"Sit Down, You're Rockin' the Boat"	*Guys and Dolls*	22	diegetic	performative

* Movie Musical

** From the movie musical of *Cabaret* but was included in the 1998 revival of the stage version.

*** Although this movie was based on the stage version of *Funny Girl*, the song "My Man" was not part of the original score of the musical. It was created for the film.

**** *The Who's Tommy* was originally a concept album, released in 1969. It was not staged as a musical until 1992; it was billed as a rock opera.

\+ These songs were used as part of a mash up, combined with another song that is similar in content. Neither were featured more than the other.

\++ These songs were used as part of a mash up, combined with another song that is similar in content.

Musical Theatre Numbers Available on Albums

These songs are available on the *Glee* albums. They can be bought in CD format, downloaded through any service as part of an entire album, or downloaded through any service individually. Songs from movie musicals are not included in this list.

"Defying Gravity"	*Glee: Volume 1*
"And I Am Telling You I'm Not Going"	*Glee: Volume 2*
"Don't Rain on My Parade"	*Glee: Volume 2*
"The Lady Is a Tramp"	*Glee: Volume 3*
"I Dreamed a Dream"	*Glee: Volume 3*
"Home"	*Glee: Volume 3*
"Take Me or Leave Me"	*Glee: Volume 5*
"Sing"	*Glee: Volume 5*
"I Feel Pretty" (with "Unpretty")	*Glee: Volume 6*
"As If We Never Said Goodbye"	*Glee: Volume 6*
"We Need a Little Christmas"	*Glee: The Christmas Album*
"Science Fiction/Double Feature"	*The Rocky Horror Glee Show*
"Over at the Frankenstein Place"	*The Rocky Horror Glee Show*
"Dammit Janet"	*The Rocky Horror Glee Show*
"Hot Patootie"	*The Rocky Horror Glee Show*
"Sweet Transvestite"	*The Rocky Horror Glee Show*
"Touch-a, Touch-a, Touch-a, Touch Me"	*The Rocky Horror Glee Show*
"Time Warp"	*The Rocky Horror Glee Show*
"Don't Rain on My Parade"	*Glee the 3D Concert Movie*
"Somewhere"	*Glee: Volume 7*
"Tonight"	*Glee: Volume 7*

Musical Theatre Numbers Available to Download as Singles

These songs are not available as part of an album, but they are available to download from www.gleethemusic.com as singles.

"On My Own"	Season 1
"Maybe This Time"	Season 1
"Hair"	Season 1
"Rose's Turn"	Season 1
"Funny Girl"	Season 1

"Over the Rainbow"	Season 1
"What I Did For Love"	Season 2
"Papa Can You Hear Me"	Season 2
"Le Jazz Hot"	Season 2
"Make 'Em Laugh"	Season 2
"Nowadays/Hot Honey Rag"	Season 2
"Singin' in the Rain"	Season 2
"Ohio"	Season 2
"Don't Cry for Me Argentina"	Season 2
"Some People"	Season 2
"For Good"	Season 2
"New York, New York" (with "I Love New York")	Season 2
"Anything Goes" and "Anything You Can Do, I Can Do Better" performed as a mash-up	Season 3
"I'm the Greatest Star"	Season 3
"Something's Coming"	Season 3
"Somewhere"	Season 3
"Cool"	Season 3
"Out Here on My Own"	Season 3
"A Boy Like That"	Season 3
"America"	Season 3
"One Hand, One Heart"	Season 3
"Tonight"	Season 3
"Buenos Aires"	Season 3
"Summer Nights"	Season 3
"You're The Top"	Season 3
"Cell Block Tango"	Season 3
"Not the Boy Next Door"	Season 3
"The Rain in Spain"	Season 3
"Pinball Wizard"	Season 3

Musical Theatre Numbers
Available on the DVD *Glee Encore*

Glee Encore is a compilation DVD of selected music numbers, excerpted from the episodes. The advertisements instruct fans to "Put on your dancing shoes and get ready to Gleek Out." This DVD offers Season 1's "most sensational musical numbers," and invites spectators to take on performance roles as they sing and dance along with their favorite numbers from *Glee*.

"Defying Gravity"
"Don't Rain on My Parade"
"Rose's Turn"

Musical Theatre Numbers Available
on the DVD *Glee: The Concert Movie*

The most recent DVD release from the *Glee* franchise is *Glee: The Concert Movie* (2011). Originally screened in 3D in movie theatres nationwide, it is a live performance of their most recent tour, filmed for distribution.

"Don't Rain on My Parade"   Season 1

Appendix 2: Recommended Viewing

This list of links is intended to enhance the reading of this essay by suggesting that watching and "reading" the songs offers a more thorough understanding of the argument. All links are available to be accessed, but while some are free (YouTube), some require membership (Netflix, Hulu), and some have episodes available for purchase (iTunes).

For "Defying Gravity"—Ghosting as Underscoring and Pointed Difference

The 2004 Tony Awards performance of "Defying Gravity" from *Wicked*: http://www.youtube.com/watch?v=3g4ekwTd6Ig
"Defying Gravity" from the *Glee* episode "Wheels": Netflix—http://movies.netflix.com/WiPlayer?movieid=70177133&trkid=3325854 iTunes—http://www.apple.com/itunes/charts/tv-shows/glee/wheels/

For "Rose's Turn"—Ghosting as Refusal and Dismissal

The 2003 Tony Awards performance of "Rose's Turn" by from the revival of *Gypsy*: http://www.youtube.com/watch?v=4_eD1btsIAE
"Rose's Turn" from the 1993 movie musical of *Gypsy:* http://www.youtube.com/watch?v=zsZ9_rzmLjg&feature=related
"Rose's Turn" from the *Glee* episode "Furt": Hulu—http://www.hulu.com/watch/194819/glee-furt#s-p3-so-i0 iTunes—http://www.apple.com/itunes/charts/tv-shows/glee/furt/

For "Not the Boy Next Door"— Ghosting as Repetition and Recognition

The 2003 Tony Awards performance of "Not the Boy Next Door" from *The Boy From Oz*: http://www.youtube.com/watch?v=B3zU2IcVzbc
"Not the Boy Next Door" from the *Glee* episode "Choke" Hulu—http://www.hulu.com/watch/356212 iTunes—http://itunes.apple.com/us/tv-season/choke/id457167102?i=522971245

Notes

1. I am using the term diegetic as it is defined in musical theatre studies and theory. Although *Glee* is a television show, I have chosen not to use the term as is used in film

criticism because the frame of reference for this inquiry is musical theatre studies, rather than film or media studies.

2. This song is used in the *Glee* episode "Wheels." However, considering the point of this essay, I feel that it would be hypocritical not to cite its original source: Stephen Schwartz, "Defying Gravity" in *Wicked*, Soundtrack Recording (Universal Classics Group, a Division of UMG Recordings, 2003, iTunes, mp3), http://itunes.apple.com/us/album/wicked-original-broadway-cast/id4426862.

3. I am not addressing the issue of Kurt singing a song originally meant to be sung by a female, because that is addressed within the episode "Wheels." In fact, *Glee* episodes make frequent reference to that episode as a justification for Kurt's continued use of songs originally intended for female singers.

4. In the various Broadway productions, the end of *Gypsy* has been played differently. Some productions chose to allow a reconciliation between Rose and Louise, while others (most recently the 2008 revival) have Louise abandon her mother, leaving Rose alone and defeated.

5. D.A. Miller includes a thorough reading of the "'Turn' in 'Rose's Turn'" in *Place for Us: Essay on the Broadway Musical*.

References

Carlson, Marvin. *The Haunted Stage: The Theatre as Memory Machine*. Ann Arbor: University of Michigan Press, 2001. Print.

"Choke." *Glee*. Writ. Marti Noxon. Dir. Michael Uppendahl. 20th Century–Fox, 1 May 2012. *Hulu*. Web.

"Dream On." *Glee*. Writ. Ryan Murphy, Brad Falchuk, and Ian Brennan. Dir. Joss Whedon. 20th Century–Fox, 18 May 2010. *Netflix*. Web.

"Funeral." *Glee*. Writ. Ryan Murphy, Brad Falchuk, and Ian Brennan. Dir. Bradley Buecker. 20th Century–Fox, 17 May 2011. *Netflix*. Web.

"I Am Unicorn." *Glee*. Writ. Ryan Murphy, Brad Falchuk, and Ian Brennan. Dir. Brad Falchuk. 20th Century–Fox, 27 September 2011. *Hulu*. Web.

Krieger, Henry, and Tom Eyen. "And I'm Telling You I'm Not Going." *Dreamgirls*. Universal Music Enterprises, 2006.

"Laryngitis." *Glee*. Writ. Ryan Murphy, Brad Falchuk, and Ian Brennan. Dir. Alfonso Gomez-Rejon. 20th Century–Fox, 11 May 2010. *Netflix*. Web.

McMillin, Scott. *The Musical as Drama*. Princeton: Princeton University Press, 2006. Print. Miller, D.A. *Place for Us: Essay on the Broadway Musical*. Cambridge: Harvard University Press, 1998. Print.

"New York." *Glee*. Writ. Ryan Murphy, Brad Falchuk, and Ian Brennan. Dir. Brad Falchuk. 20th Century–Fox, 24 May 2011. *Hulu*. Web.

Schwartz, Stephen. "Defying Gravity." *Wicked*. Universal Classics Group, 2003.

"Sectionals." *Glee*. Writ. Ryan Murphy, Brad Falchuk, and Ian Brennan. Dir. Brad Falchuk. 20th Century–Fox, 9 December 2009. *Netflix*. Web.

Styne, Jule, and Stephen Sondheim. "Rose's Turn." *Gypsy*. Sony Music Entertainment, 2009.

"Wheels." *Glee*. Writ. Ryan Murphy, Brad Falchuk, and Ian Brennan. Dir. Paris Barclay. 20th Century–Fox, 11 November 2009. *Hulu*. Web.

III. THE COMPLEXITIES OF GENDER— OVERACHIEVERS, GOOD GIRLS, BAD GIRLS, AND TOUGH GUYS: "THAT ATTITUDE STARTS IN HIGH SCHOOL"

Gold Stars and Slushies
The High Cost for Overachieving Girls

KASEY BUTCHER

"Being part of something special makes you special" ("Pilot"). Rachel Berry (Lea Michele) gave the fictional glee club New Directions its mantra. Although mostly concerned with her own rising star, Rachel also recognizes that as a band of misfits, the glee club's differences, along with their talent, give them a competitive edge. While *Glee* has garnered praise for its portrayal of acceptance and diversity among teens of different races, creeds, and sexual orientations, one type of character is still regularly and unapologetically ridiculed on the show: the overachieving teenage girl. The show's self-proclaimed star, Rachel, demonstrates remarkable ambition, clearness of purpose, and drive toward achieving her goal of becoming a famous Broadway actress. Rachel, however, is bullied at school by jocks who throw slushies in her face, by her glee club teammates, and at times by Mr. Schuester (Matthew Morrison), all of whom feel her ruthless ambition and leadership style make her difficult to get along with. Through her quest for fame and her struggle with popularity, or her lack thereof, Rachel lives out many of the contradictory narratives pop culture and popular psychology tell about high-achieving girls and their femininity. Through Rachel, girls in the audience are given a portrait of a highly-capable, highly-driven girl in her successes as well as in the price she pays for expressing herself and fighting for her dreams. Still, however, on *Glee* achievement and popularity have a consistently inverse relationship that may undercut the positive example Rachel sets.

Gender, Leadership, and Schooling

For years, teachers, psychologists, and other specialists have focused on the self-esteem crisis among adolescent girls. In *Reviving Ophelia*, Mary Pipher famously explains, "[j]ust as planes and ships disappear mysteriously into the Bermuda Triangle, so do the selves of girls go down in droves.... They lose their assertive, energetic and 'tomboyish' personalities and become more deferential, self-critical and depressed" (19). A decade after Pipher's bestselling book, Linda Kreger Silverman argued that through the social pressures put on high achieving girls:

> The highly able young woman is faced with a Sophie's Choice: If she chooses to be true to herself, to honor her drive for achievement and self-actualization, she breaks some unspoken rule and faces disconnection, taunts, and rejection from both male and female peers. If she chooses to give up on her dreams, to hold herself back ... she is accepted and rewarded for her efforts [8].

On the other hand, research increasingly suggests that with the rising achievement level for girls in education, rather than the shrinking violets of *Ophelia*, many adolescent girls fit a new paradigm of "alpha" behavior. Dan Kindlon argues that "alpha girls" are confident leaders, shaped by a generation of strong female role models, more involved fathers, and strides toward equality in legal and social policies (xv). Kindlon defines alphas as those who have GPAs of 3.8 or higher, who are leaders in school clubs, student government, or honors societies, participate in extra curricular activities a minimum of ten hours a week, have high motivation for achievement, and rate themselves highly for dependability. He estimates that, based on the above criteria, around twenty percent of teenaged girls are alphas (xviii). Due to these high standards of achievement and the social climate of (alleged) equality, these girls exhibit an "equalist" mentality that assumes that girls are equal to, and as capable as, their male peers. Kindlon connects this attitude to the influence of third wave feminism (19) and also asserts that alpha girls do not struggle with the issues surrounding their appearance with which popular culture and advertising insist girls are obsessed (26).

Nonetheless, researchers of education and gender continue to find that students have gendered understandings of leadership and what a good leader looks like. Further, these gendered ideas place strict boundaries on effort in the classroom and proper gender performance (Francis 15): "Constructions of gender difference have themselves been shown to impact achievement in a variety of ways. It is dominant constructions of femininity that render high achievement potentially problematic for girls"

(Francis 6). Thus, although statistically girls continue to outperform their male peers (Silverman 8, Francis 10), this high level of success is still culturally understood as threatening to their femininity.

Success also has an enduring impact on a teenager's sense of self. For students who exhibit giftedness or leadership, these skills often become integral parts of their maturing identities in such a way that engagement in school activities facilitates the development of identity in teens. Therefore, Michael Nakkula argues that classroom interactions, especially with teachers, have a tremendous influence on a student's level of performance and understanding of community:

> Schools that promote positive identity development are rich in engaging activities in which students can invest their psychic energy, and they value the role of relationships at all levels of learning. Good teachers teach their subject matter well; great teachers engage students in the learning tasks of the moment and instill in them the desire to keep learning long after graduation. Teachers who have this kind of impact do more than impart knowledge; they engage their students' relationship to learning. The act of engagement is the key to identity development in schools, as elsewhere [9].

Glee demonstrates this sense of engagement through the lessons that coach Will Schuester teaches the teens via music. Rather than lecture the glee club, Will sets a theme for the week and allows his students to come to their own conclusions or exhibit their thoughts and feelings through the musical numbers they choose to perform. Nakkula argues, "transformational learning occurs when students sense that they too have moved their teachers—through their efforts and accomplishments and through their deep engagement in the learning process" (19). As Will coaches New Directions, his own life is touched as well.

The flip side of the way Will manages the glee club is that the lessons are frequently competitive. Researchers repeatedly find that while boys accept responsibility for their successes and brush off their failures as circumstantial, girls tend to blame themselves for failure and credit external factors for success (Galley 88–89). More troubling, competitive pedagogy runs counter to how girls are socialized (Galley 90–91). In glee club, the most successful girls tend to be the least popular while the most successful boys are the most popular. Because in traditional gender norms girls are supposed to be subdued, deferential, and nice, the drive to win makes Rachel unlikable and brands Quinn (Dianna Agron) a bitch. Meanwhile, despite her high levels of aggression,[1] Santana (Naya Rivera) maintains her coolness through sex appeal and a nonchalant attitude toward her academic success.

Finally, to reach both high levels of achievement and popularity, students are expected to do it all and make it look effortless. Putting too much effort into social interactions, school work, or extracurriculars makes a student look like a geek, while too much effort in leadership can make girls appear too masculine to their peers (Francis et al., 106–7). Further, "a number of studies have shown how popular girls have to balance trying to be 'nice' to everyone while simultaneously retaining the exclusivity of their friendship to those within the incrowd" (Francis et al., 117). Yet, behaving too "nice" or "good" toward authority figures can have the converse effect of making a girl a "goody-goody" or a suck up (Francis et. al., 117). Again, the social interactions must be effortlessly and perfectly balanced, especially for high-achieving young women.

Get It Right: Rachel Berry, Girlhood, and Leadership

As a highly talented, high achieving girl, Rachel faces the dilemma of this inverse relationship between success and popularity. Over the course of the series' first three seasons, Rachel struggles with striking a balance between pursuing her dreams and pursuing popularity. Early in the development of Rachel Berry, show creator Ryan Murphy drew inspiration from the film *Election*'s conniving overachiever, Tracy Flick (Reese Witherspoon), and in the first few episodes, the connection is readily apparent. Rachel is fast-talking, sharp-witted, and her desire for success is blinding. In the intensity of Rachel's speech and her cut- throat competitive spirit, it is clear from the pilot that the characteristics that make Rachel special are not loveable. While Santana's harshness, Brittnay's (Heather Morris) stupidity, and Finn's (Cory Monteith) cluelessness earn laughs, Rachel's punchlines are often as cringe-inducing as they are funny. For example, in "Funny Love Songs," Rachel tells Santana, "Okay, maybe you're right. Maybe I am destined to play the title role in the Broadway musical version of 'Willow,' but the only job you're going to have is working on a pole" and causes awkward silence before Santana storms out.

In struggling for balance, Rachel has two primary modes of operation: overconfidence and total insecurity. In her confident moments, she is hypercompetitive and will do seemingly anything to win or to get closer to achieving her goals. She says, "you might laugh because every time I sign my name I put a gold star after it,[2] but it's a metaphor and metaphors are important" ("Pilot"). As a diva-in-training, for Rachel everything is serious business. The good that comes from this side of Rachel's character is her demonstration of a goal-oriented, focused approach toward achievement. She is always aware that she will have to be dedicated and work hard to achieve her dreams. She does not expect stardom to just fall in her lap, and probably, this focus keeps her out of other kinds of trouble. She tells Finn, "We all have pressures, but you know how I deal with it? The natural way, with a rigorous diet and exercise routine. I'm up at 6:00 a.m. every day, I have my protein shake with banana and flaxseed oil, and by 6:10 I'm on the elliptical. You know how I motivate myself? Not with anything artificial, I set a goal and I won't rest until I reach it ("Vitamin D"). As Rachel explains her routine in voiceover, the audience sees her waking up in the morning, bright-eyed and full of energy. She exercises facing a picture of a Grammy with her name on it. Her dedication is laudable, but more than anything, the scene is hyperbolic. In these moments it is unclear whether the audience is supposed to admire Rachel or laugh at her.

When intensely focused on getting ahead, Rachel also does hurtful things, claiming that she's just trying to help. For example, in "Audition," she sends exchange student Sunshine Corazon (Charice Pempengco) to a crack house rather than have her audition for New Directions and compete with her for solos. This incident is particularly telling as Rachel defends herself claiming that she was trying to protect less featured members of the club. Even her claims that she got rid of Sunshine out of love have a competitive bite. She tells Tina (Jenna Ushkowitz) and Mike (Harry Shum Jr.), "what if Sunshine can dance? Then your contributions to glee club will be more insignificant than they already are" ("Audition"). Ultimately, Finn forces her to admit that she sabotaged Sunshine because she loved herself, not because she loved the club. Her closing number "What I Did for Love" leaves the episode ambiguous. Is Rachel singing about herself or about her teammates? Is she sorry because her plan backfired or because she hurt her friends? In moments like this, Rachel fails to strike the appropriate balance between ambition and effortless "niceness" that popularity demands, and the show portrays the tenuous nature of the conflict between gender norms and the rules of popularity in the high school setting.

When Rachel feels insecure, however, she functions on the other side of what Silverman calls a "Sophie's Choice": "preoccupation with boys, clothes, appearance, observing her tone of voice, choice of words and body language, remaking herself to become attractive to the opposite sex" (8). Recall when Rachel dresses like the sexy Sandy from the end of *Grease*, trying to seduce Finn ("Hairography"), or when she hosts a house party and ends up drunk and kissing Blaine (Darren Criss) ("Blame It on the Alcohol"), or when she considers getting a nose job ("Born This Way"). In these moments and many others, Rachel is incredibly unsure of herself.

She's needy and frightened, and focused on the ways in which her peers do not like her.

Rachel often gets stuck in her swings between overconfidence and insecurity. In "The Rhodes Not Taken," she quits glee club for the school musical when she is forced to share solos and returns when the director wounds her confidence. Perhaps the worst part of her relationship with Jesse St. James (Jonathan Groff) is that it brings out both her hypercompetitive side and her insecure side. Jesse taps into her desire to succeed by presenting himself as a capable duet partner and an older talent who can offer her support and guidance. She worries, however, about having sex with him and about the toll their relationship will have on her friendships ("Power of Madonna," "Laryngitis").

Nonetheless, Rachel is at her best when she is able to bridge the gap and compete with other people rather than against them. When she returns to the glee club in "The Rhodes Not Taken," she explains, "I realized being a star didn't make me feel as good as being your friend." During much of the first three seasons, Rachel moves back and forth between her higher-strung, more competitive side and her insecure, cooperative side, the switches between modes often hinging on her throwing fits over lost solos or her on-again, off-again involvement with Finn. Rachel's likability and the growth allotted to her character develop inversely to her confidence. As Rachel increasingly begins to doubt herself after Finn breaks up with her, her relationships with other glee clubbers such as Kurt (Chris Colfer) and Mercedes blossom.

In "Funny Love Songs," she decides to stop pursing Finn, focusing instead on her career, like other famous female musicians who reached stardom when they were single. During this time, Rachel argues that the glee club's best chance of winning Regionals is to compete with original songs, and with Finn's encouragement, she sets out to write the material. As Rachel struggles to write an original song, she doubts her ability, rather than barreling forward. During this string of five episodes, Rachel becomes less abrasive, but her increased likability is inversely related to her growing insecurity. Rachel's repeated failure to both follow her dreams and gain the affection of Finn and the rest of the glee club inspire her song. A conflict with Quinn produces a breaking point, as Quinn tells Rachel, "You can't write a good song because you live in this little schoolgirl fantasy of life. Rachel, if you keep looking for that happy ending, then you are never going to get it right." Rachel composes a song, "Get It Right," expressing her feelings that her "good isn't good enough" and that her "best intentions keep making a mess of things" ("Original Song"). In her song, Rachel makes it clear that no matter how much her ambition causes trouble for herself and for others, she does care and she will keep trying.

Though her social interactions cause her stress, Rachel never really experiences failure in her goals until her audition for the New York Academy of Dramatic Arts (NYADA) in her senior year. When auditioning for (fictional) Broadway legend Carmen Tibideaux (Whoopie Goldberg), Rachel twice forgets the lyrics to "Don't Rain on My Parade," the song she nailed at Sectionals in Season 1. The next episode, "Prom-asaurus" opens on Rachel's inner-monologue about her botched audition, thinking about how her dream has died: "I feel different. In some ways it's a relief. To be part of the crowd." A realistic observation tempers the pathos: "So I'm not going to get everything I ever wanted. It doesn't make me a loser." Rather than supporting Rachel in her sadness, as Rachel has done for others in the past, her peers continue to treat her as an outsider. Becky quips, "I don't want to catch your failure" while the glee club remains too caught up in prom to offer much support.

The nearness of prom also lends itself to connecting Rachel's failed audition to her worth in her social interactions. Finn and Quinn run for Prom King and Queen together, even though Finn is Rachel's boyfriend. To Rachel, the situation represents her failure to conform to norms of beauty and popularity. She believes that singing is all she had to offer and without it she is "just some sad little Jewish girl watching [Finn] get all the attention with the pretty blonde cheerleader" ("Prom-asaurus"). Later in the episode, Rachel is voted Prom Queen[3] and it is this vote of confidence from her peers that boosts her to try for NYADA and her dreams again. Thus, without career success, Rachel only finds her worth through the conventional tropes of high school popularity. Though her performance at Nationals earns her a second chance, the story of Rachel failing and then overcoming her embarrassment, let down, and self-doubt, adds nuance to the portrayal of her high-achievement, even if the show also connects her botched audition to her value in heteronormative social interactions.

Faberry: The Drama Queen and Prom Queen in Conflict

Also worth considering is the tense relationship between Rachel and Quinn Fabray. Dubbed by fans as "Faberry," Rachel and Quinn act as foils to one another. Both high-achievers in academics and extracurriculars, Quinn has the popularity that Rachel desires, but not Rachel's sense of self. Where Rachel favors her dreams over fitting in, Quinn continually strives to maintain or regain her popularity. In Season 1, Quinn finds that one unwise decision costs her everything she most values—her cheer captainship, her popularity, and her boyfriend. After getting pregnant, Quinn's peers mostly desert her and her family disowns her. In Season 2, however, after giving her baby up for adoption, Quinn strives to regain her position as the most popular girl in school. Quinn also bullies Rachel, and the relationship between the two girls further reflects the complicated politics of aggression that surround the relationships of teen girls, especially girls under pressure. In the second season, however, the growth Quinn experienced during her first season pregnancy seems to have completely reversed as she once again attacks Rachel and throws herself wholeheartedly into becoming Prom Queen. She tells Rachel, "I know you think it's hard to be you, but a least you don't have to be terrified all the time" ("Prom Queen"), revealing that she thinks her pretty face is her only asset and remaining popular her only hope for success. Season 3 produced another reversal as Quinn converts to the "bad girl" stereotype of pink hair, smoking, and punk rock clothing. When the adoptive mother of her child threatens to cut her out completely, Quinn abruptly snaps back to her prior "good girl" blonde hair and white dresses.

Instead of taking the time to portray this complicated girl's impressive journey from teen motherhood to Yale, the show gives the audience snippets of the process that lean heavily on stereotypes of good vs. bad girlhood. There are no gradients, no process. So many teachable moments are missed, moments that could have portrayed a girl—significantly a girl who is the strong, silent type—dealing with hardship and overcoming.

The conflict between Rachel and Quinn also complicates the connection between authenticity and popularity. Though popular teenagers must demonstrate leadership within the constraints of gender norms, niceness without trying to hard, and exclusiveness within their peer groups, authenticity also factors into the equation. A popular teenager must "do it all" while also coming across as genuine or authentically themselves; they cannot be phonies (Francis 123). While Rachel authentically expresses herself, she does not fit the norms of popularity because of her high-achievement and aggressive leadership. Further, she tries too hard to be popular. Before her pregnancy, Quinn was the "it girl" at school because she met all the qualifiers for popularity and did so effortlessly. After her pregnancy, however, Quinn fails to authentically recreate her pre-baby life. Her efforts to regain her popularity fall into the realm of trying too hard. Also, her attempts to reverse what happened to her life conceal the struggles she goes through emotionally. Thus, Quinn cannot achieve her popularity again because she lashes out or comes across as phony. The tipping point comes when she pretends that she still cannot walk after her car crash ("On My Way") in order to get the sympathy vote for Prom Queen. Her inauthenticity causes her date, Finn, to walk out on her. As with Rachel, the emphasis Quinn places on popularity and the gender norms it demands demonstrates the social pressures placed on high achieving adolescent girls. Unlike Rachel, the audience does not see Quinn striving for her other goals. She is not depicted in the classroom or cheerleading. She does not talk about her application process for Yale until after she gets accepted. Instead, *Glee* portrays Quinn almost entirely in stereotypes: the Queen Bee, the teen mom, the bad girl, the bitch. In doing so, the writers fail to create a suitable counterpart to Rachel Berry and the productive example the "Faberry" relationship could have provided is thwarted in favor of drama over boyfriends and tiaras.

(Mis)leading by Example: Female Role Models on *Glee*

To make matters more confusing, the poor treatment of high-achieving girls continues in the adult women on the show. For the driven girls of William McKinley High School, there does not seem to be much hope. Terri Schuester (Jessalyn Gilsig), Sue Sylvester (Jane Lynch), Coach Beiste (Dot Jones), and Emma Pillsbury (Jayma Mays) each represent different aspects of successful women who get criticized in the larger culture, depicting different possible futures for the girls.

With the help of speed, Terri Schuester was an overachiever in high school. In "Vitamin D," she tells Finn, "When I was in high school, I captained the cheerleading squad, achieved a perfect 4.0 GPA, cultivated my popularity and I maintained a loving relationship with the boy who would become my husband.... Wow, I don't even know how I did that" ("Vitamin D"). Her monologue closely resembles a statement Rachel makes at the end of the third season, explaining to Tina how much work it is just to be Rachel Berry ("Props"). Despite her previously high level of achievement, Terri grows up to be shrill, manipulative, and dissatisfied with her life. Whether she is explaining that she is not built to work five days a week or faking a pregnancy, Terri no longer has even a glimmer of achievement. Terri serves as a hyperbole of a demanding wife and her issues are perhaps more troubling because of her promising past.

Sue Sylvester, undoubtedly the epitome of high-achieving women on the show, is herself a bully and consistently portrayed as masculine, insensitive, and unattractive. The jokes made at the expense of Sue's femininity are numerous. She explains that she doesn't have children because "[I] don't have the time; don't have the uterus" ("Vitamin D"); in another episode she jokes that she doesn't menstruate. And let's not forget her numerous "You think this is hard?" one liners, including "You think this is hard? Try auditing for *Baywatch* and being told they're going in a different direction. That's hard!" ("Wheels"). Finally, Sue marries herself, wearing a blue tracksuit as a wedding gown ("Furt").

On the other hand, Sue has a soft spot for her sister, Jean. Growing up with an older sister who has Down syndrome made Sue sensitive to the limitations imposed on people with disabilities. In "Wheels," when prompted to diversify the Cheerios, she takes on Becky Jackson (Lauren Potter), a girl with Down syndrome. Afraid that she plans on destroying Becky's self- esteem, Will lectures Sue, who snaps back, "You know nothing about me." This is a Sue no one has seen before. The whole situation becomes more complicated, however, when Becky becomes Sue's sidekick of choice, an eager participant in many of Sue's meaner plots. There is no doubt the bonding is genuine, but whether it is in Becky's best interest is somewhat ambiguous. Although Coach Sylvester has her moments of vulnerability or sensitivity with Becky, she always returns to her hyper-aggressive self.

Like Rachel and Quinn, Coach Shannon Beiste serves as a foil to Sue. Because of her successful coaching record, the principal brings Beiste in to fix the school's pitiful football program, but unlike Sue, Beiste is friendly and sensitive. Her gentle, caring personality serves to highlight how conventionally unattractive she is. Played by a former pro-wrestler, Beiste is broad and masculine in appearance, despite her cherry lip color and short, curled hair. The early episodes featuring Beiste focused more on her appearance than on her coaching ability. In "Never Been Kissed," the boys of the glee club think of Coach in lingerie to prevent getting too aroused with their girlfriends. As the second season progresses, however, Will and Beiste develop a friendship and she becomes more beloved than belittled. Still, the very name of the character points toward the way her physical attributes stand out more at McKinley High than her coaching record or nurturing teaching style.

Finally, Emma Pillsbury, the guidance counselor, fits the norms of conventional femininity and "good girl" behavior. A virgin well into her thirties and after a failed marriage, Emma dresses primly, speaks in a soft voice, and views the world through doe eyes. Her submissive, docile personality is further highlighted by her struggle with Obsessive Compulsive Disorder, causing her to control and clean every aspect of her life. Over the course of the first three seasons, Emma struggles to overcome her OCD in order to have a successful relationship with Will. In this way, her own well-being is explicitly linked to her value in heterosexual mating, reifying the gender norms her character already embodies. Though Emma does get professional validation for her work with students and the pamphlets she creates, a project that was previously belittled by Will ("The Spanish Teacher"), she ultimately invests her worth fully to the relationship and to Will's needs, giving him her virginity as an implicit reward for winning Nationals ("Nationals"). Emma and Sue often butt heads, as they represent polar opposite stereotypes of successful femininity. Both, however, are hyperbolic. Sue symbolizes the defeminized successful woman while Emma represents success subverted to heteronormativity.

These conflicting portrayals work to confuse the message *Glee* sends about high-achieving women. In her struggles, Rachel further enforces the mixed messages, depicting real issues for adolescent girls. Silverman argues that in children and adolescents, girls are called bossy when they demonstrate traits that would be called leadership in their male peers. Worse, she found that girls are more likely to attribute their successes to luck, easy assignments, or teacher preferences and their failures to lack of ability (13–14). Though persistently reminded that her classmates disapprove of her leadership style, Rachel never silences herself. At a time when psychologists tell us girls are in danger of losing their individuality and their assertiveness in favor of fitting in, Rachel refuses to cave. In this way, the depiction of her struggle is realistic and valuable. Through Rachel, *Glee* shows the difficulty of sifting through conflicting messages about success and femininity, a problem that faces young women in an era of both "Alphas" and "Ophelias": "successful femininity now involves living a tension between exercising the traditional feminine mode of relationality and the exhibition of individualized agency previously associated with masculinity" (Budgeon 285).

Still, the ways that Rachel's peers deride her for having a voice, ambition, and a competitive spirit are cause for concern. By regularly presenting her as an unsympathetic, grating, or needy girl, the show undermines the strength other gifted girls might find by identifying with Rachel. Further, the persistently hyperbolic presentation of the inverse relationship between achievement and likability in other female characters reifies conservative tropes about successful women. Given the phenomenal popularity of *Glee* among a teenaged audience, the ways the show portrays the interaction of its teenage characters and their teachers can have a lasting impact on the very gender norms the show portrays. In fact, television has an active role in the way teens are socialized, as "teens often watch

TV in order to socialise, to have common frames of reference through which to talk to others, and their desire to view is frequently motivated by peer pressure and the need to 'belong' through a discussion of the media, rather than more conscious personal impetus" (Davis and Dickinson 2). Further, the very nature of teen television, its production, and the academic study of it are couched in the "precarious" nature of the genre itself. The target audience may grow out of the show and out of the ideologies the show promotes (4). Still, however, the genre is also largely controlled by capitalist aims on capturing the teen demographic and their disposable income. As with the large production of series-related merchandising, the shows produce the ideal teenagers, examples that the target audience emulates (9–10). Thus, as teen TV becomes a means of socializing, it also socializes its audience into proper ways to perform their commercial and personal subjectivity. As millennial teen programming increasingly draws on intertextuality and webs of cross-marketed media (as in the mashups of popular music released by the *Glee* cast on TV, iTunes, in concert, etc.) the community of teens engaged with media grows up along with the reach into their lives the media has (Wee 69).

My hope for girls on *Glee* as the series progresses is that the writers continue to explore the complex relationship between achievement, talent, and popularity, but that they do so in a way that shows evolving norms about gender and success. If *Glee* could stop leaning on stereotypes and on the inverse relationship between achievement and popularity for girls and women, perhaps the show could move forward discourse about gifted girls in the way it has begun to do so with issues about sexual orientation and other types of difference among adolescents.

Notes

1. Race and sexuality also play a key role in these dynamics as Mercedes (Amber Riley) often falls into the stereotype of the—sassy black friend and Santana's aggression later gives way to the storyline of her coming out of the closet. For the purposes of this essay, I am narrowing my focus to the ways that achievement and popularity are inversely related, which sacrifices more nuanced discussions of these two female characters.
2. Notably, Tracy Flick dotted her i with a star.
3. Santana and Quinn, both candidates for Prom Queen were selected to tally the votes because Sue thought their pettiness and competitive streaks would keep the tally honest if they were both in charge. Earlier in the episode, Rachel finally explained to Quinn how important their love-hate relationship had been to her on a personal level and as motivation to try harder. The tally reveals that Quinn beat Santana by one vote, but having finally won the crown, Quinn still feels unfulfilled. She points out to Santana that they have had dream high school careers and that they have the power to do something really special for someone else. They proceed to rig the election so Rachel wins.

References

"Audition." *Glee.* Writ. Ian Brennan. 21 Sept. 2010. Television.
"Blame It on the Alcohol." *Glee.* Writ. Ian Brennan. 22 Feb. 2011. Television.
"Born This Way." *Glee.* Writ. Brad Fulchuk. 26 April 2011. Television.
Budgeon, Shelley. "The Contradictions of Successful Femininity: Third-Wave Feminism, Postfeminism, and 'New' Femininities." Eds. Rosalind Gill and Christina Scharff. *New Femininities: Postfeminism, Neoliberalism, and Subjectivity.* Houndmills, Basingstoke, Hampshire: Palgrave Macmillan, 2011. Print.
"Choke." *Glee.* Writ. Marti Noxon. 1 May 2012. Television.
Davis, Glyn, and Kay Dickinson. *Teen TV: Genre, Consumption, Identity.* London: BFI, 2004. Print.
Francis, Becky. *Boys, Girls, and Achievement: Addressing the Classroom Issues.* London: Routledge Falmer, 2000. Print.
_____, Christine Skelton, and Barbara Read. *The Identities and Practices of High-achieving Pupils: Negotiating Achievement and Peer Cultures.* London: Continuum, 2012. Print.
"Furt." *Glee.* Writ. Ryan Murphy. 23 Nov. 2010. Television.
Galley, Michelle. "Who Am I as a Learner?: Would Girls and Boys Tend to Answer Differently?" *Adolescents at School: Perspectives on Youth, Identity, and Education.* Ed. Michael Sadowski. Cambridge, MA: Harvard Education Press, 2008. 95–98. Print.
Greene, Doyle. *Teens, TV and Tunes: The Manufacturing of American Adolescent Culture.* Jefferson, NC: McFarland, 2012. Print.
"Hairography." *Glee.* Writ. Ian Brennan. Fox. 25 Nov. 2009. Television.
Kreger Silverman, Linda. *Who Cares If I'm Smart, Am I Thin Enough?* Proc. of European Council of International Schools, The Hague, The Netherlands. Institute for the Study of Advanced Development. 1–19. Web. 15 Apr. 2011.
"Nationals." *Glee.* Writ. Allison Adler. 15 May 2012. Television.
"Never Been Kissed." *Glee.* Writ. Brad Falchuk. 9 Nov. 2011. Television.
"A Night of Neglect." *Glee.* Writ. Ian Brennan. 19 April 2011. Television.
"On My Way." *Glee.* Writ. Roberto Aguirre-Sacasa. 21 Feb. 2012. Television.
"Original Song." *Glee.* Writ. Ryan Murphy. 15 March 2011. Television.
"Pilot." *Glee.* Writ. Ryan Murphy, Brad Falchuk, and Ian Brennan. 19 May 2009. Television.
"Prom Queen." *Glee.* Writ. Ian Brennan. 10 May 2010. Television.
"Prom-asaurus." *Glee.* Writ. Ryan Murphy. 8 May 2012. Television.
"Props." *Glee.* Writ. Ian Brennan. 15 May 2012. Television.
"The Rhodes Not Taken." *Glee.* Writ. Ian Brennan. 30 Sept. 2009. Television.
Ross, Sharon Marie, and Louisa Ellen Stein. *Teen Television: Essays on Programming and Fandom.* Jefferson, NC: McFarland, 2008. Print.
Sadowski, Michael, ed. *Adolescents at School: Perspectives on Youth, Identity, and Education.* Cambridge: Harvard Educational, 2005. Print.
"The Spanish Teacher." *Glee.* Writ. Ian Brennan. 7 Feb. 2012. Television.
Wee, Valerie. *Teen Media: Hollywood and the Youth Market in the Digital Age.* Jefferson, NC: McFarland, 2010. Print.
"Wheels." *Glee.* Writ. Ryan Murphy. 11 Nov. 2009. Television.
"Vitamin D." *Glee.* Writ. Ryan Murphy. 7 Oct. 2009. Television.

"I'm a Slave 4 U" but Only When I Want to Be

Female Sexual Agency

MELISSA ESH

"Female insecurity in Hollywood is presented as devious, stupid, and needy." Therefore girls need to be engaged in conversations that "induce girls to think about what being a female means, how identity is formed, and how sexuality can be mis-created through intimidation and fear."—Steinberg 227

Heralded by Leah Wilson, Erin Balser, and Suzanne Gardner, authors of unofficial *Glee* guides, as simply some of the best television available, *Glee* is "multidimensional and surprising, entertaining and inspirational, outrageously implausible and yet in many ways more real than anything else on television. One that transforms both its characters and its audience on a weekly basis" (2). This possibility of transformation can work both positively and negatively. *Glee*, though criticized for its content by some, is one of the few shows that seems to be working to open conversations and present multiple possibilities for embodiment and choices. By portraying the difficult choices that adolescents face (such as the tension between popularity and loserdom) rather than moralizing with one-dimensional characters or situations, *Glee* serves as both a conversation starter and challenges its audience to think about the lives of adolescents in new ways.

In this essay, I argue that, while flawed at times, *Glee* works toward

200

breaking down boundaries and challenging the audience's prejudices. Issues such as homophobia, popularity, sex, being true to oneself, sexism, peer pressure, and parental pressure are addressed and no character is immune from problems. The show's depiction of the female characters' sexual desire and agency is this discussion's concern. Rather than preach that sex is simply forbidden or that anything goes without consequences, *Glee* illuminates the difficulties adolescent women face when navigating their own sexual identities, desire, and expression. Situated within cultural battles over female sexuality, *Glee*'s female characters and audience encounter narratives that reinforce females' desire only in terms of males' *and* those that empower them to take charge of their own sexuality and desires. As such the show provides a picture of a nuanced world that does not operate on a binary and examples of women who carry variety of attitudes toward their sexual desire and agency.

School as (Positively) Formative

McKinley High School is not wholly a typical high school. Studies of schools on television and film demonstrate that schools are usually depicted as adversarial to students. Paul Farber and Gunilla Holm's study found that schools as "social institutions [are] a hindrance, spectacle, or mere backdrop to the important story of how individuals break away, express themselves, and get on with their independent plans" (25). Teachers are typically portrayed as managers and drill sergeants, sexpots or sleazeballs, deranged or demented, and administrators are usually lame and weak. Generally, in the films studied, "virtually all forms of adult or institutional action are empty or intrusive, denying the social conditions of personal autonomy" (Farber and Holm 37). McKinley High School, at times, is an antithetical school. Will Schuester, Sue Sylvester, Shannon Bieste, and Emma Pillsbury all demonstrate care for their students albeit in vastly different ways. Even more shocking, some of them admit their mistakes and flaws to their students. Both McKinley High and the show itself offer space in which viewers can work to critique ideas about adolescence/ts while imagining more empowering models.

*Glee*ful S-E-X

One of the most controversial aspects of *Glee* is that it brings sex and talk about sex into the open. While the audience gets very few glimpses of a classroom setting in which sex is discussed, the informal school culture is filled with talk and deliberations about sex. As what the America Association of University Women calls the "evaded curriculum," sex education is usually nonexistent or irrelevant where students are given "a set of facts devoid of references to the complex personal and moral dilemmas they face in understanding and making decisions about critical facets of their lives" (361). The sex talk at McKinley serves as a de facto sex education class for characters and viewers. This facet of the show is what the Parents Television Council finds so objectionable:

> Research proves that television is a teen sexual super peer that can, and likely will, influence a teen's decision to become sexually active. Fox knows the show inherently attracts kids; celebrating teen sex constitutes gross recklessness [Winter].

The argument over adolescents and sex transcends concerns over *Glee*. The sex education battles reflect these opposing viewpoints about *Glee* because both discussions concern "struggles over knowledge: both the content of curricula—what students should know and when—and epistemological questions about what it means to know about sexual behaviors, desires, and identities" (Fields 148). That the talk happens outside of the formal classroom should be no surprise to anyone who is familiar with the informal culture of high school and the informal instruction regarding gender performances:

> Within the context of the schools much informal learning takes place concerning issues of gender and sexuality; the homophobia of young men, the sexual reputations of young women, and the pervasive presence of heterosexuality as an "ideal" and a practice mark out the terrain for the production of gendered and sexualised identities [Kehily 49].

The verisimilitude of this aspect of *Glee* benefits the show and the message of openness as beneficial. Teenagers think about and talk about sex—a lot. So the show depicts its characters *and teachers* talking about and negotiating the dilemmas that come with sex, which upends the norm of schools silencing talk sex while also disciplining students who fall outside the norm. This relatively sympathetic school, then, becomes the perfect backdrop for upending other assumptions about young adults.

Girl Power?

Inevitably, a mention of *Glee* and sex will result in someone bringing up the Britney Spears episode. Yet, a discussion about the Season 2 episode "Britney/Brittany" should also examine its sister episode from Season 1,

"The Power of Madonna," as each episode evokes strong reactions, both positive and negative, about female sexuality. While some critics, elevate Madonna as a better artist and more authentic icon, both women are cultural icons, sing about similar topics, and have been criticized in the same ways for the same things. And, each was used in similar ways in *Glee*.

For some, "The Power of Madonna" episode signaled a change in the way *Glee* treated its female characters: "About the time I was thinking I should write an essay about the show's mistreatment of the female characters—Rachel is abrasive, Sue is a villain, Santana is snarky mean, and Brittany is unbelievably stupid—the show redeemed itself with 'The Power of Madonna'" (Rusch 22). Indeed, Mr. Schuester has the glee club sing Madonna's songs because of her message of female empowerment, which in turn becomes the subject of the episode.

The first scene clearly identifies the problem. As the female members of New Directions chat in the choir room, Rachel tells them about a date where she and her boyfriend, Jesse, go to a concert then back to her house to make out in her room, which she describes as "erotic and romantic." But, when she tells Jesse that she does not want to have sex, he gets "crabby" and leaves.

> RACHEL: I just want to be ready. I know I'm getting older and these things are going to happen someday but how do I stop a guy from getting angry when I say no?
> SANTANA: Just do what I do—never say no.
> BRITTANY: Totally. What's the worst that could happen? [cut shot to pregnant Quinn] Sorry Quinn.
> MERCEDES: ... I can't wait to get a guy mad at me for saying no.
> TINA: We just have to accept that guys don't care about our feelings.

Tina tells them that Artie, her boyfriend, has informed her, "I'm going to need you to make a few changes ... maybe lose the vampire makeup and consider getting some tighter-fitting clothing. You've got the power and I believe you should work it if we are going to be an item." At this point, Mr. Schuester, who has been present for the entire conversation, says, "I'm sorry to interrupt your little sorority, but I couldn't help overhearing. Are you really having that much boy trouble?"

This scene is significant to the episode and the trajectory of the entire show. This is the first time that the tenor of the interactions between the male and female characters is addressed. The question of saying no or not saying no is one that preoccupies sex educators and adolescents alike; that the female members of New Directions have the same problems is significant. These young women are trying to find a way to respond to the male glee club members even though everything is framed in terms of what the guys want. Even Santana and Brittany, the whores in the virgin/whore binary that is formed in this conversation, equate sexual consent with not saying no. Despite the ongoing debates about what constitutes consent, not saying no is not the same as saying yes. Placing the focus on saying "no" to sex avoids the discussion of female sexual desire and agency. However, this conversation in "The Power of Madonna" mirrors the focus of many sex education programs that "teach girls negotiation and refusal skills because 'boys will be boys'—leaving girls responsible for maintaining the moral boundaries around sexual behaviors in male-female relationships" (Schroeder 4). The close parallels between the main message of many sex education classes and the opening conversation in this episode of *Glee* signal the show's stepping in as a sex educator.

Also of note in this conversation is Mr. Schuester's calling their conversation a "little sorority." While he is clearly concerned about their plight, his use of terms of diminishment serves to frame their discussion as trivial as does his calling it "boy trouble." His concern for his female students, however, does take him to the guidance counselor, Emma Pillsbury, for help. Yet, Mr. Schuester makes it clear that he views Ms. Pillsbury as incompetent regarding sex and relationships: "this area of interest is your blind spot but I want to help you so that the next time a girl comes in to talk to you, you'll be prepared." His comment to her puts him fully in control in that he sees her advice to the girls as inadequate and thinks he can do better. He then takes control of the conversation:

> MR. SCHUESTER: What this is all about is teenage girls feeling like they have no power.
>
> MS. PILLSBURY: Right. And that makes sense too. Look at their role models. You've got Britney Spears and her shaved head. Lindsay Lohan looks like something out of Lord of the Rings, Anne Coulter...
>
> MR. SCHUESTER: Let's work together to help make them feel more confident about themselves.
>
> MS. PILLSBURY: ... Yes, we will change the world one girl at a time.
>
> MR. SCHUESTER: ... and maybe along the way we can find a way to help you too.

In spite of the fact that the female glee members' discussion was about how their male counterparts are not respecting them, their feelings, and their opinions, Mr. Schuester identifies the problem as the females' confidence. Thus, the task is to change their behavior rather than the males'. This normalization of the male is typical in school settings from sex education to other experiences (AAUW). Over the course of two scenes, Mr. Schuester has taken charge of the situation, positioned himself as the carrier of knowledge, and turned the problem from the males' behavior into one about the females' confidence. Not only are the adolescent males not treating the adolescent females with respect, their teacher is doing the same. His sexism is veiled by his concern, however. The tension between paternalistic condescension and help continues throughout the episode, which highlights the subtle and sometimes unwitting ways males, schools, and broad cultural narratives (such as the vulnerability of women) work to systematically disempower women.

Stopping the episode there reveals a *Glee* that merely reifies the gender inequity and condescension in schools' and the media's treatment of adolescent females. Yet, the opening scenes of the episode perfectly frame an episode called "The Power of Madonna." After leaving Ms. Pillsbury's office, Mr. Schuester decides to have the glee club perform Madonna songs in an effort to empower the female glee club members. But the males do not want to sing her songs:

> PUCK: As a dude, Madonna makes me kind of uncomfortable.
> FINN: Yeah, she's smokin' and everything but can't some of us do the guy version of Madonna you know like ... Pantera?

Mr. Schuester then tells the male glee club members that it has come to his attention that they have not been very nice to the females in glee club lately:

> MR. SCHUESTER: You're disrespectful, bullying, sexist, and I hate to say it misogynistic.
> FINN: I have no idea what that means.
> MR. SCHUESTER: What it means is put yourselves in their shoes for a change.

He explains that Madonna's music is about being strong and confident and, more than anything, is about equality. During his speech, there are cut shots to the females and Kurt sitting up straighter, smiling, etc. while the other males look worried and he tells them "and that's something I think you guys need to work on." Interestingly, Mr. Schuester conflates their lack of confidence with the males' misogyny when he talks to Ms. Pillsbury, which likely has to do with his taking ownership of fixing her. Yet, he ultimately blames the males for their behavior.

Later, Emma, Finn, and Rachel all decide that they are ready to have sex. Each couple sings "Like a Virgin" as the visual cuts between the three couples getting ready to have sex. The singing and physical interaction simulates sex, which turns out to be only a shared fantasy. In the end, only Finn goes through with it. In response to Emma's decision to wait, Will takes charge as he did in the episode's first scenes. Even though he tells Emma that he is happy that she did take control of her body when she said she was not ready, he institutes a no dating policy until his divorce comes through and does so without asking Emma what she thinks and in spite of the fact that she tries to speak. Further, "while we're waiting, I want you to get some help for your problems." He then tells her that a counselor will come to her office. Again, he attempts to control her under the guise of helping her. In assuming her helplessness and his superior knowledge, he acts the role of the dominant male.

Yet once again, Mr. Schuester faults the adolescent males for behavior similar to his own and asks the male glee club members to sing "What It Feels Like for a Girl," Madonna's comment on female oppression. The song works to demonstrate that females, while expected to be sexy are also expected to act weak, hide both their strength and pain, and be a little less than their best. Mr. Schuester intends for the song to reveal the cultural expectations the young women are up against; the conversation after demonstrates that some of them get it while others actively feminize the ones that do.

> PUCK: I'm still not down with it. I like being a dude.
> FINN: That's because it's easy to be a dude.
> PUCK: Mr. Schue, I think we need a new baritone because Finn wants to become Finnessa
> MR. SCHUESTER: Finn's got a point. Haven't you noticed how low morale has been around here?

Finn explains that they have been objectifying, not listening to, and not caring about the females' feelings. Kurt then asks Mr. Schuester why he was singing with them, and he replies that he has to learn the lesson, too. At the end of the episode, Artie apologizes to Tina and tells her that she does not need to change unless she wants to. Likewise, Finn apologizes to Rachel. However, he and Jesse argue over who "gets" her. So, despite their apologies, they talk about Rachel as if she was not there and as if the relationship was to be decided only between them. Both Mr. Schuester's and Finn's contradictory attitudes demonstrate that overcoming embedded ways of speaking and acting is neither easy nor achieved only once.

The episode is significant because it does address sex, adolescent females' opinions about negotiating the males' desire, and draws attention to the embedded patriarchal practices in adolescent and school culture. As seen from the above description, there is also a deeper tension between efforts to protect or help the females, adolescent and adult, and males' taking control of them by imposing what they believe to be best for them. Not only does the females' opening conversation reflect common assumptions in sex education, Mr. Schuester's attitude of protection is also prevalent in abstinence-only sex education discourses that keep young people "within the 'sexually innocent' frame of childhood" (Powell 15). This infantilization of young women can be attributed, in part, to "fears that children and adolescents may be easily exploited and victimized by adults" (16). But, it strongly evokes a patriarchal discourse that gives men the mandate to decide what is best for women, particularly adolescent women, because females are supposedly weaker than men and thus more vulnerable.

Similarly, the episode explores cultural ambivalence regarding female sexual agency. In this episode, the female members of New Directions sing "Express Yourself" to the guys. They sing the song while wearing suit pants and jackets over teddies with the garter straps hanging outside the pants. Eschewing the traditional romantic gestures, the girls sing about the importance of non-sexual encounters with the opposite sex while the final pose is them grabbing their crotches. This performance demonstrates in microcosm the tension in this episode, the "Britney/Brittany" episode, the entire show, sex education, and U.S. culture in general between female empowerment and the expression of female sexuality. To some, the "Express Yourself" performance evokes the ideas of female self-objectification and in the final gesture, submission to male desire. However, the scene can also be read as their appropriation of masculine clothing, making it their own, and showing that females can want men to express their feelings *and* have sexual desire and agency.

"Britney/Brittany" brings this tension even more to the fore. Echoing Ms. Pillsbury's sentiment in "The Power of Madonna" that Britney Spears is a poor role model, Mr. Schuester quickly vetoes Kurt's idea that they perform a Britney Spears song. Later in a private conversation, Emma recants her former opinion of Britney saying that she is a model for the possibility of rebirth—she's reformed and has been raising two kids—but Will continues to adamantly refuse to let New Directions perform Britney Spears.

Meanwhile, Brittany dreams of herself singing Spears' "I'm a Slave 4 U." Her performance is a mash up of Britney Spears's videos for and revealing costumes from "Toxic," "Oops I Did It Again," the "I'm a Slave 4 U" performance from the 2001 MTV Video Music Awards, and "Baby One More Time." The song discusses the tension between what people expect and what the singer desires. The song reveals the tension between female agency (exercise of desire) and self-objectification (slavery to a male). The use of the song and the ongoing discussions of female sexuality in the show places *Glee* right in conversation with a heated cultural argument about whether such sentiments reflect females taking control of their own sexuality or whether it is self-objectification that situates them solidly within the patriarchal framework.

Madonna vs. Britney/Brittany

Clearly, the choice to use Madonna and Britney Spears episodes as the framework for discussions of adolescent female sexuality was deliberate. Madonna single-handedly accelerated the battle between opposing ideas of appropriate expression of female sexuality and desire. An early concert review positions the obvious sexual aspects of her performance as the center of the show

> but, for the most part, Madonna's singing was like a soundtrack to a more visceral display of herself, her persona, her nonstop dancing and her surprisingly explicit sexual dare, which included a visual climax—so to speak—to every song.
>
> Somehow, despite the hard-core moves, Madonna did not really come off as naughty or menacing so much as solicitous and good-hearted, a kind of flirtatious, sugary sex fairy whose outrageous poses were really just a gift for the kids, a fantasy offering to help them grow up [*Variety* 194–95].

The sexuality of her performances were the subjects of several, now iconic, cultural moments: her performance of "Like a Virgin" in a modified bridal gown with a "Boy Toy" belt buckle at the 1995 MTV Video Music Awards and the simultaneous release of her album *Erotica* and her book *Sex*.

Britney Spears concert reviews are startlingly similar to those for Madonna commenting on explicit sexuality and what the reviewers read as innocence, which may really be an example of a woman who refuses to validate the virgin/whore binary.

> Spears somehow conveys the innocent, gee-whiz facets of American childhood and adolescence—yet nearly all of her attire and song lyrics hype her up as the self-determined pop vamp, able to use whatever she's go to her advantage, *but never being taken advantage of* [Carter, emphasis added].

Britney Spears, like Madonna, is the center of now iconic performance moments. Her snake-handling at the 2000 MTV Video Music Awards and her performance and kiss with Madonna at the 2003 MTV Video Music Awards are as risqué and memorable as Madonna's.

Both Madonna and Britney Spears' videos, music, performances, and style angered conservatives and feminists alike. For Madonna in particular, both groups considered her the antithesis of true womanhood. Steve Allen in a particularly scathing article uses a highly sexist argument explaining that Madonna does not even measure up as a subject of male desire:

> Madonna's sexuality is, to put the matter quite simply, that of the professional prostitute. She does not really look like Marilyn Monroe. Her hair is black and her features considerably less than ideal; she simply *imitates* Monroe's true beauty.... Even as a sex object the young woman is simply not the real article [149].

More consequential than the unsurprising criticism by conservatives is the debate that still rages among feminists. Madonna and Britney Spears, and *Glee*, are parts of a much larger debate.

The Feminist Porn Wars

Many scholars posit these wars as a battle between second- and third-wave feminist ideologies that, while about pornography are also about popular culture because images previously deemed sexist are now being repurposed by women (Meltzer 25). At the heart of the argument is whether images and acts that have been dubbed acts of patriarchal power (e.g., sexualized females) will always signal objectification by the male gaze or if such images could be appropriated in empowering ways by females working to subvert the patriarchy. In their critique of feminism's engagement with popular culture, Joanne Hallows and Rachel Moseley position the war between second-wave feminists who claimed authority over appropriate female actions and third-wave feminists who criticized their predecessors for presuming they could speak for and somehow identify a single idea of "woman." This ideological battle comes down to whether anyone or any group can dictate the right way to be feminist or female or whether that is left up to individual women.

Applying these arguments to the subjects at hand evokes several questions: should Madonna and Britney and the *Glee* performances be criticized for objectifying women or should they be heralded as empowering? When the Madonna/the *Glee* cast sings "Like a Prayer" or when Britney/Brittany sings "I'm a Slave 4 U" while simulating sex and wearing a bikini, do audiences have a right to claim that the women are not in charge of her own sexualities, that their performances are inherently victimization? Brian McNair argues that such depictions can be read as subversive: to claim patriarchal objectification is to evoke "the familiarly patriarchal notion that nice girls didn't do such things, and that this particular woman was thereby a slut and a pop tart of the worst sort" (67) and that performers' reclamation of sexual images is a rejection of any dictated definition of woman and that anyone had power to dictate that they had to be "good."

However, Marisa Meltzer's discussion of Britney Spears identifies a potential flaw in McNair's argument by explaining that girls and young women may not see the sexiness as empowering and may not even be aware of the possibility of their own exploitation. M. Gigi Durham dubs this compulsive hypersexuality "The Lolita Effect" and argues that the rhetoric of empowerment masks something that actually serves the patriarchy by promoting a narrow view of sexual expression. Other critics in the vein of Meltzer and Durham point to the increased commodification that accompanies the sexual empowerment message as consumer culture capitalizes on the movement. Anoop Nayak and Mary Jane Kehily cite Angela McRobbie's argument that the message of sexual empowerment ends up serving consumerism by [re]subjecting females to the capitalist patriarchy under the guise of empowerment and self- determination (68).

Yet under this argument of unwitting objectification, females do not have many choices in the way they respond because it imposes restrictions just as narrow as they accuse the sexual empowerment camp of imposing. If females should not seem as though they are practicing self- objectification through compulsive hypersexuality, it seems that one of their only choices is to button up (literally); retreat into suppression of sexuality; or develop a cerebral sexuality that denies embodiment. Advocated by Durham throughout her book, a third, more positive, option is to promote open conversations about sexuality that acknowledge female desire and help adolescents make healthy choices about sex including sexual expression through embodiment. Discussing varying ways of embodiment is imperative because to limit sexual expression is to replace one system of oppression with another. Besides, argues McNair, it is more important that the artist "reserves control over what is shown and how, and exercises her power to represent her sexuality in the manner that *she* choose" (203). The preeminence of one's power over representation is echoed in the female glee club members' responses to their interactions with Britney Spears' music.

Britney/Brittany Revisited

After the initial performance of "I'm a Slave 4 U," Brittany and Santana recreate the "Me Against the Music" video, which is notable as a Britney Spears and Madonna collaboration. When they return to glee club Brittany informs the others that she realized what a powerful woman she truly is. Similarly, after Rachel's performance of "Baby One More Time," she exclaims that she feels freedom to feel good about herself. These expressions do not wrap up the story neatly nor do they mark a point at which Brittany and Rachel always have concrete and fixed answers in response to questions of agency or power over how their bodies are interpreted. In fact, the show demonstrates that power over interpretation and definitive answers are never fully achieved—there is a great deal of gray area that must be navigated as seen later in the episode. Rachel goes to school in the "Baby One More Time" schoolgirl outfit. When Finn sees her he covers her up and asks her if it is just a bit too much ("I think that guy just broke up with his girlfriend just so her could look at you"). Later in the conversation, Rachel asserts that they should not be trying to control each other. In this short scene, Rachel dresses provocatively in response to what she thinks Finn told her to do and is objectified by several males yet also asserts her right not to be controlled. The contradictory dynamics in this scene reveal how the issues of sexuality, empowerment, and objectification can play out in real life. Girl power of this kind recognizes that easy answers are usually simplistic rather "it delights in ambiguous gray areas" (Meltzer 144). Indeed, ambiguous gray areas are present throughout *Glee*.

Female Sexual Agency (Sometimes)

For several of the characters, "The Power of Madonna" marks the beginning of a trajectory toward sexual empowerment and realization of choice. As seen before, the opening conversation in the Madonna episode, positions Rachel as the virgin who does not want to have sex yet and Santana as the whore who never says no. Rachel ultimately choosing not to have sex with Jesse while Santana happily takes Finn's virginity only reinforces the binary as does the episode "Bad Reputation" (two episodes after "The Power of Madonna"). Throughout the episode, Rachel learns that sex is not only about saying yes or no, but it is also about how others perceive it. Wrapped up in multiple facets of adolescent life, sexuality and identity are portrayed as difficult to navigate, never the same for everyone, and far from simple.

Just as "Bad Reputation" is an important episode for Rachel's development, "Sexy" is crucial to turning the Santana as a whore theme on its head. "Sexy" delves more into the relationship between Santana and Brittany challenging what the audience and the glee club think they know about them. After disagreeing about how to address their feelings for each other, they take their problem to Holly Holliday (the substitute sex ed teacher) who asks them if either of them thinks that they might be lesbians (they reveal their relationship over the course of Season 3). In this episode Santana reveals her depth of thought and emotion particularly when she finally talks to Brittany: "I want to be with you but I'm afraid of the talks and the looks. You know what happened to Kurt at this school." "Sexy" marks a drastic shift in Santana's character from the stereotypical jaded "whore" to a young woman trying to navigate her sexual desire and agency. While her new position opens her up to more harsh critique, it empowers her to pursue what she wants. Again, like Brittany and Rachel, Santana does not undergo a complete character shift, but it does provide an alternative to compulsory heterosexuality and explores other ways to respond to questions of desire and agency.

"First Time"

Season 3 of *Glee* has seen even further growth of these two characters and a maturity in the way the show talks about sex, particularly female sexuality. In "First Time," two couples, Rachel/Finn and Kurt/Blaine, have sex for the first time. While the Kurt/Blaine relationship has garnered the most attention and their having sex is a milestone for television, the episode contains a brilliant conversation among the female glee club members that is a perfect companion to the conversation from "The Power of Madonna" because it shows just how far these girls and the show, have come. After their first attempt at sex is thwarted by Rachel's dishonest intentions, she asks for help. Santana, Brittany, Quinn, and Tina offer their advice: Quinn tells her to wait because she cannot get her virginity back, it makes everything more complicated; Santana tells her to wait because Finn is terrible in bed; and Brittany says she lost her virginity to a guy who crawled into her tent a cheerleading camp. When Tina speaks, however, Rachel and the audience are treated to a positive reflection about sex and relationships that is shocking in that female desire and agency is rarely depicted with positive consequences.

Tina tells them that losing her virginity was a great experience for her because she was with someone she loved. She and Mike talked about it for a long time because they knew it was something they were going to remember forever: "And when that moment came we just knew. It was right. It wasn't rushed. It was amazing. He's my first love and I'll always look back at that moment as absolutely perfect. No regrets." Tina's monologue is remarkable because she does not idealize her relationship as one that will last forever, and she and her boyfriend made the decision together. *And she enjoyed it. And she does not regret it.* Her revelation is a picture of adolescent female sexuality that few television shows ever depict or celebrate and argues that helping adolescents think through decisions about sex may be a more authentic education than cross-sectioned pictures of the female anatomy.

Glee in Perspective

Tina's account turns common narratives about adolescent female sexuality on their heads. Rather than seeing her "yes as the answer to someone else's desire, rather than as an affirmation of her own" (Corinna 182), we are told that she and Mike had equal agency. Most conversations about sex in school focus on dire warnings about "the real dangers of AIDS and adolescent pregnancy and parenthood associated with sexual activity" which deny "even the possibility that girls experience and must deal with their own sexual desire" (Tolman 251). Similarly media depictions of female sexuality tend to depict females as subject to the males' desires or voracious female sexuality. Thus, the choices become abstinence, sex for the sake of the relationship, or being "sexually active" which means having as much sex as you possibly can without thinking.

With the trajectory of the female characters and the show itself, *Glee* presents possibilities that acknowledge the dangers (teenage pregnancy is tackled in the first season and ignorance about safe sex is faced in the second season with "Sexy"), but also "manifest[s] something better than a woman's merely being able to say no; something that is an entirely different animal from scenarios that are positive only because we have escaped the most negative consequences or results" (Corinna 191). The show is one of a few that acknowledge female desire while also depicting the difficulties and nuances of navigating and acting upon that desire.

Where the show flounders, however, is in its treatment of the broader issues of power and inequity. *Glee* does not address issues of social class or social class and sexuality. While the middle-class adolescent females on the show have problems speaking their sexual desire, other women in more oppressed circumstances have more dire associated difficulties and dangers, which are part of a broader power structure that includes both race and gender. But *Glee* does represent an important step not only for its boldness in discussing female sexual desire but for its taking it seriously.

Ultimately, *Glee* works to provide a venue in which actual problems are addressed in both humorous and serious ways. In doing so it meets Henry Giroux's "ethical imperative to provide complex images, ideas, narratives, and sites of struggle that not only challenge conservative 'common sense' notions of the real but also demand from youth critical self- reflection, moral commitment, and social responsibility" (209) and challenges "a sophisticated media culture that encourages an objectified sexualization and a school culture that denies desire altogether" (Okun and Gause 49). At the very least, it is a springboard for conversations with adolescents and between adults about what it means to empower female sexuality.

References

Allen, Steve. "Madonna." *The Madonna Companion: Two Decades of Commentary.* Eds. Carol Benson and Allen Metz. New York: Schirmer Books, 1999. 144–60. Print.
American Association of University Women (AAUW). "The Evaded Curriculum." *The Jossey-Bass Reader on Gender in Education.* San Francisco: Jossey-Bass, 2002. 361–74. Print.

"Bad Reputation." *Glee.* Fox. 4 May 2010. Television.
Balser, Erin, and Suzanne Gardner. *Don't Stop Believin': The Unofficial Guide to* Glee. Toronto: ECW, 2010. Print.
"Britney/Brittany." *Glee.* Fox. 28 September 2010. Television.
Carlson, Dennis. "Introduction." Carlson and Roseboro 3–27. Print.
Carlson, Dennis, and Donyell Roseboro, eds. *The Sexuality Curriculum and Youth Culture.* New York: Peter Lang, 2011. Print.
Carter, Nick. "Spears" flashy show somehow innocent and sexy." *Milwaukee Journal Sentinel* 10 July 2000. Web. 17 December 2011.
"Concert review: Universal Amphitheater, Los Angeles." *Variety.* May 8, 1985. Benson and Metz 4–5. Print.
Corinna, Heather. "An Immodest Proposal." *Yes Means Yes! Visions of Female Sexual Power and a World Without Rape.* Eds. Jaclyn Friedman and Jessica Valenti. Berkeley: Seal Press, 2008. 179–92. Print.
Durham, M. Gigi. *The Lolita Effect: The Media Sexualization of Young Girls and What We Can Do About It.* Woodstock, NY: The Overlook Press, 2008. Print.
Farber, Paul, and Gunilla Holm. "Adolescent Freedom and the Cinematic High School." *Schooling in the Light of Popular Culture.* Eds. Paul Farber, Eugène F. Provenzo, and Gunilla Holm. Albany: State University of New York Press, 1994. 21–39. Print.
Fields, Jessica. *Risky Lessons: Sex Education and Social Inequality.* New Brunswick, NJ: Rutgers University Press, 2008. Print.
"First Time." *Glee.* Fox. 8 November 2011. Television.
Giroux, Henry. "Teenage Sexuality, Body Politics, and the Pedagogy of Display." Carlson and Roseboro 189–216. Print.
Hallows, Joanne, and Moseley, Rachel. "Popularity Contests: The Meanings of Popular Feminism." *Feminism in Popular Culture.* New York: Berg, 2006. Print.
Kehily, Mary Jane. *Sexuality, Gender, and Schooling: Shifting Agendas in Social Learning.* New York: Routledge Falmer, 2002. Print.
McNair, Brain. *Striptease Culture: Sex, Media and the Democratisation of Desire.* London: Routledge, 2002. Print.
Meltzer, Marisa. *Girl power: The Nineties Revolution in Music.* New York: Faber and Faber, 2010. Print.
Nayak, Anoop, and Mary Jane Kehily. *Gender, Youth, and Culture: Young Masculinities and Femininities.* New York: Palgrave Macmillan, 2008. Print.
Okun, Tema, and C.P. Gause. "What's Love Got to Do with It? The Imperative of Authentic Desire." Carlson and Roseboro 44–56. Print.
Powell, Anastasia. *Sex, Power and Consent: Youth Culture and the Unwritten Rules.* New York: Cambridge University Press, 210. Print.
"The Power of Madonna." *Glee.* Fox. 20 April 2010. Television.
Rusch, Kristine Kathryn. "Musical Promiscuity: The music of *Glee.*" Wilson 13–25.
Schroeder, Elizabeth. "What Is Sexuality Education? Definitions and Models." *Sexuality Education: Past, Present, and Future (Vol. 1).* Eds. Elizabeth Schroeder and Judy Kuriansky. Westport, CT: Praeger, 2009. 3–7. Print.
"Sexy." *Glee.* Fox. 8 March 2011. Television.
Steinberg, Shirley. "The Celluloid Sexuality Curriculum: Deconstructing Teen Films." Carlson and Roseboro 217–230.
Tolman, Deborah L. "Daring to Desire: Culture and the Bodies of Adolescent Girls." Ed. Janice Irvine. *Sexual Cultures and the Construction of Adolescent Identities.* Philadelphia: Temple University Press, 1994. 250–84. Print.
Wilson, Leah. *Filled with Glee: The Unauthorized Glee Companion.* Dallas: Smart Pop, 2010. Print.
_____. Introduction. Wilson 1–3.
Winter, Tim. "Statement on "Glee" from Parents Television Council President Tim Winter." Parents Television Council. 8 November 2011. Web.

"The Power of Madonna"
Unleashed?

REBEKAH LOBOSCO

The primetime television show *Glee* has transformed the relationship of music to mainstream media. The role and use of music in television had already begun changing in recent years, thanks to programming such as *American Idol*. It was not until the creation of *Glee*, though, that the performance of music in a television show was used as a main form/ source of both entertainment and communication.[1] Premiering in 2010, it is promoted and funded by Twentieth Century–Fox Film Corporation, a mainstream popular culture powerhouse in both television and film, and whether because of it or despite its origins, *Glee* is the first show of its kind and is an undeniable success.

In a "Behind the Scenes" session entitled "Deconstructing *Glee* with Ryan Murphy," Murphy, the creator and executive producer, explains his concept: "*Glee* is a one-hour comedy, musical, strange hybrid. I'd like to think of it as a reinvention of the musical, and its different, I think, from a lot of musicals that you think of, like *High School Musical* or those types of projects because people just don't sort of burst out into song." The show's creators also present their audience with serious issues, seemingly for the purpose to inform and to teach. The issues tend to be contemporary reflections of the issues other forms of mainstream media are focused on—bullying due to sexual orientation, teen pregnancy, and underage drinking, to name only a few. Within the show, Mr. Schuester usually writes an overarching lesson on the whiteboard of the chorus room, overtly outlining what the students, and audience, should be taking from each week.

In the first season, Episode 15 is entitled "The Power of Madonna" and is the first episode of the series to feature only the songs of one artist. The lesson of the episode is female empowerment via both Madonna's persona and music. In this article, I discuss how the themes of feminine power, feminism, sexuality, and gender roles are presented and interpreted. This includes how the show seeks to represent the so-called "power" of Madonna, while also discussing what feminism means for *Glee*. I posit that this episode is a strong example of how our culture now understands and deals with feminism and the issues surrounding it. Through a close reading of four of the musical performances from the episode, I argue that Madonna's message, as a feminist and boundary-pushing artist, does not empower the young generation of the show's glee club as it might have done when she was first popular.[2] A discussion of such matters also brings to light a generational gap that is made apparent by the episode, particularly in comparison to Episode 2 from the second season, which features almost solely the music of Britney Spears. Each episode seeks to focus on female empowerment, though each, in my reading, has a vastly different outcome. The most effective form of empowerment does not devalue others in the process—something the show, in this case, does not fully manage to accomplish.

The episode from Season 1 begins with a voice-over of the central adult antagonist of the main characters, Coach Sue Sylvester, as she writes in her journal: "Madonna. Simply say the word aloud makes me feel powerful, even in voice over. How I have worshipped her ever since I was a little girl. Sorry Angie Jolie, Catherine the Great. Madonna is the most powerful woman to ever walk the face of the earth" ("The Power of Madonna"). This moment sets up the focus for the episode, as Sue's love of Madonna leaks into the rest of the school; she makes the principal play *Madonna's Greatest Hits* on repeat over the school's PA system throughout the entire school day. After overhearing the girls of the glee club discuss their mistreatment by some of the boys, the club's director makes the musical assignment for the week a performance of a Madonna song. Mr. Schuester's goal is to give the girls the chance to be empowered while teaching the guys understanding and respect. As the character of Mr. Schuester says when talking the dilemma over with the school's guidance counselor: "What this is really about is teenage girls feeling like they have no power" ("The Power of Madonna"). On the face of it, this is a poignant and important line coming from a main character from a hit television show. Many of the audience watching, as young women themselves, might never have heard an adult advocating for their gender this way. To have it said by a person of authority (a teacher) on mainstream television is a way to validate frustration over gender inequality and make it okay to talk about because "they said it on *Glee.*"

The male students, with the exception of the openly gay character, protest when given the assignment. Mr. Schuester chides them, saying, "Put yourself in *their* [the girls'] shoes for a change. Culturally, Madonna's legacy transcends her music because by and large, the subtext of her songs are about being strong, independent and confident—no matter what your sex. But more than anything, Madonna's musical message is about equality, and that is something I think you *guys* need to work on" ("The Power of Madonna"). The episode then features Madonna songs, looking to feature moments of empowerment and a "new level of understanding" from the heterosexual male characters of the group.

The allusion to feminism is strong in the teacher's line, though the word itself is only uttered once in the entirety of the episode. Overall, there is a more constrained and easily digestible vocabulary used including words such as power, empowerment, equality, and understanding. Feminist writer Angela McRobbie finds this kind of word choice in today's mainstream media problematic. She refers to modern Western culture as being in a self-declared state of "post-feminism," where popular culture and the media in particular put forth a façade that no longer needs feminism and its message. She argues that feminism, as it is presented in popular culture currently, is made out to be undesirable, unnecessary, and out-dated. "Drawing on a vocabulary that includes words like 'empowerment' and 'choice' [elements of feminism] are then converted into a much more individualistic discourse ... as a kind of substitute for feminism" (1). Though likely done with the best of intentions, Ryan Murphy's presentation, as the director of this specific episode, creator of the program, of issues of gender equality falls into this trap of "individualistic discourse" through his choice of promoting the emancipation of the female solely through Madonna's music. Murphy, the self-proclaimed "biggest fan of Madonna on earth" ("Unleashing"), inadvertently highlights the issue that it was the artist's music that was put first, with the message of the episode serving the music rather than the other way around.

McRobbie's outlining of the post-feminist discourse continues: "[This new] 'feminism' is instrumentalized, it is brought forward and claimed by Western governments, as a signal to the rest of the world that this is a key part of what freedom now means. Freedom is revitalized and brought up-to-date with this *faux*-feminism" (1). Again, this is reflected by the overall effect of the episode—the show must quickly present and resolve this issue along with its lesson/moral so the overall storyline can move on. For *Glee* and its characters to do so, the feminism that is presented must be palatable to a large audience, complete with enjoyable and light dialogue. I argue that in his quest to accomplish all those goals, Murphy feeds into the post-feminist discourse without actually utilizing the opportunity to tackle a serious issue or critically examine new cultural norms.

Also, that the show does not use the word "feminism" until almost the end of the episode is indicative of an assumption that the audience is expected to already know what feminism is and means. This is further complicated by the assumption that *Glee*'s feminism represents *all* of feminism. As mentioned above, feminism is a concept that is likely newer to the show's audience, and their understanding of its definition cannot be taken for granted. It has a complex history in and of itself, which I believe has further been complicated by today's Western popular culture and media—*Glee* being a primary example of this. As McRobbie further posits, "[Through] an array of machinations, elements of contemporary popular culture are perniciously effective in regards to [the] undoing of feminism, while simultaneously appearing to be engaging in a well-informed and even well-intentioned response to feminism" (11).

In addition to the issues presented above, Madonna has a complex relationship with feminism herself. Karlene Faith summaries this well in her book *Madonna: Bawdy & Soul*, noting, "Feminists, given the diversity of our social, political, and personal identities and agendas, have mixed views in appraising Madonna's value or harm to women and young people[...]. On the one hand, Madonna's celebration of myriad sexual identities breaks down taboos and clears more cultural space for sex" (50). She continues by presenting the other side of the argument that Madonna's use of "sex [including] multiple partners, 'seductive' children, and sado-masochism with dark meanings underscored by religious symbols" (50) could confuse young adults, particularly in the 1980s and early 1990s. Faith's book was published in 1997 and was part of the third wave of feminist writings, entrenched in Madonna's musical career while it was still going strong. Faith clearly outlines that feminists do not always support Madonna and her actions but that there are many feminist-positive reactions to her as well. Ryan Murphy, born in 1965, grew up with Madonna, experiencing the rise of her career first-hand, its nuances, and, as her "biggest fan," likely knows at least some of the feminist discourse around Madonna ("Ryan Murphy Bio"). Even if Murphy was not aware of any of the dialogue surrounding Madonna's career, in choosing Madonna as his solo artist for the "female empowerment" episode declares definitively his stance on whether or not he finds Madonna's music and images a positive proponent of feminist discourse.

Posed as a tribute to the "Queen of Pop," the Madonna episode was considered particularly important by the creators. The extras, for example, in the DVD-box-set of the first season include a behind-the-scenes special about the making of this episode—the only one that this is done for. This mini-documentary is entitled "Unleashing the Power of Madonna" in which the music supervisor, PJ Bloom, discusses the episode: "We knew we wanted to do a one artist episode, a single artist episode … in terms of finding that artist that was just so unbelievably popular and broke through so many thresholds and crosses so many boundaries, it just made perfect sense to do a Madonna episode." Bloom's statement reveals that the concept of Madonna in relation to the show is identifying her being as a positive representation of female empowerment, while also reaffirming that the task of the producers and writers was to make the dramatic action and storyline work for the music, instead of vice versa.

The first musical number performed by the glee club is "Express Yourself," done by the six girls of the group. They are angry and hurt as a result of the way most of the boys have been treating them and because of this, partly use the performance to counter the argument that the Madonna assignment is a bad idea. Successfully performing Madonna's music would mean the girls could show that her music does in fact "translate" to show choir. The performance also potentially serves to help the girls be and feel empowered. Musically, the performance of "Express Yourself" in the episode is a shortened version of the original. They begin with spoken lines then directly follow with the chorus. The girls sing the first verse and another chorus, then jump to the bridge. The bridge leads back into the chorus followed finally by the outro, and ends with a strong a cappella statement of the words "express yourself."

After the spoken intro, which takes place in the high school's choir room with the characters dressed in street clothes, they are transported into the school's auditorium for the rest of the performance, the girls on the proscenium-style stage and the rest of the club with their teacher in the audience, watching the performance. The girls, for their performance on stage, are dressed in matching charcoal/ black tailored suits with brightly-colored, satin corsets (each character in a different color), a monocle around their necks on a gold chain, and their hair styled in finger waves. They are an updated, interpreted version of Madonna from the video when she is in her iconic tailored suit with black lingerie underneath. The outfits, though signifying an embracing of feminine sexuality by way of the corsets, feature garter straps that are much too long to be functional in reality. Their costumes are therefore just that—a caricature of Madonna's outfit from her 1989 video. Their look does not embrace or show control over their femininity as Madonna did; it instead highlights the fantastical elements of their performance.

The potential for the girls to be empowered by this song is undermined from the start in multiple ways. Aside from the unrealistic costumes, though they appear confident with their powerful and angular dance movements and strong in stage presence and posture, when the camera switches back to the male characters in the audience, only the teacher and the gay character, Kurt, are attentive and smiling. The other five male characters are pointedly distracted, looking anywhere but the stage, overly bored, and fidgeting in their seats. When the performance is finished, the girls look tired but pleased, having put significant energy into the performance. Yet only Mr. Schuester, who gives them a standing ovation, and Kurt clap in appreciation. The rest of the boys remain seated with dejected expressions on their faces. The indifferent male audience quickly overpowers the performance itself.[3] The boys make it clear that the girls were not successful, while also denying that the music might be relevant to their situations.

"Express Yourself" was a huge hit for Madonna, "a feminist call to arms, complete with muscular brass-playing and soulful voice. Here Madonna is the anti-material girl, exhorting her audience to respect themselves[...]. Like a female preacher, Madonna emphasizes each word of the chorus, invoking God and the power of orgasm" (O'Brien 132). If this is the legacy of the song, it does not align with the performance within the show, especially when considering the majority of the reaction, or lack thereof, from the boys in the audience. With almost no positive reaction at all, the power of this Madonna song falls flat in the teenage characters' hands; the message of gender equality is not allowed past the edge of the stage. Aside from the issue that a "triumph of gender equality" could not be achieved at the beginning of the episode's dramatic arc, I argue that it is indicative of a deeper issue. Their costumed sexuality and fantastical performance are entertaining, but there is a lack of a true sense of ownership over the music and therefore themselves during the performance.

Connected to the issues of ownership of Madonna's music and message is the remake of the "Vogue" video with Sue Sylvester singing the solo and portraying the Madonna role in the video. The lead up into the performance helps contextualize and justify it. Kurt and the only black female character of the glee club, Mercedes, are sitting with Sue in her office. Sue is lamenting her lack of a fashionable hairstyle when Kurt offers to help. "Mercedes is black, I'm gay. We make culture ... we're working on an exciting new project and would like to use the Cheerios [the cheerleading squad Sue coaches]." Mercedes continues, "We can help you find a new look" ("The Power of Madonna"). The next time the characters are shown is in the "Vogue" video, shot in black and white, and the production is close to a frame-for-frame of the original. "The sets were built exactly the same, the costumes ... I actually think the feathers that wipe [at the beginning and end of the video]—I think they are the actual ones that were used in the 'Vogue' video that our prop guys found in some prop house deep in the bowels of Sony somewhere" ("Unleashing"). Again, the song is shortened for the show, with the structure now: opening, first verse, second verse, chorus, bridge, chorus, the interpolated spoken/rap section, and outro. The only lyrical changes made are in the rap section where two ending lines are altered to personalize it slightly for the characters of the show.[4]

The purpose of the video is to use Madonna as a springboard for personal empowerment for Sue, to help her find a new style that would make her feel more confident about herself, inside and out. It is worth noting, also, that the only gay character and the only black female character are the ones with the idea and desire to help this happen. Using these characters as the main supporting roles in the "Vogue" music video recalls Madonna's original and her feature of the "voguing" dance/lifestyle.[5] In the original, the dance floor is identified as a safe place, a place of freedom. It is where marginalized communities can fully be themselves, freed from normal cultural restrictions (Metz and Benson 299). The song creates an acceptable space for reinvention, albeit fleetingly, for all three of the main characters involved.

The fact that the producers sought to be so meticulously close to Madonna's original is unusual for the show. The songs used in *Glee* are obvious remakes of the originals, shaped to fit the needs of the show, the characters, and each episode's plot. For example, earlier in the episode, main characters Rachel and Finn sing a duet that features a mash-up between the two Madonna hits "Borderline" and "Open Your Heart." The mixture of the two catchy pop tunes is not done with the pretense of potentially empowering for either character—the performance instead serves only as a vehicle for the imagery presented as the singers' backdrop: there are a slew of high school students in the hall dressed in different iconic Madonna styles (i.e., styles from "Material Girl," "Human Nature," "Frozen," "Open Your Heart," etc.). Yet the producers wanted the performance of "Vogue" to exactly mimic the original with a focus on the video *and* the music. "A song like 'Vogue' was direct homage to Madonna. I mean, we wanted that to sound absolutely as identical as we possibly could. And so the backgrounds, I was trying to match it exactly, the lead vocals— I was trying to get [the actress who portrays Sue] to sing like Madonna" ("Unleashing").

The next time Kurt and Mercedes see Sue, they are surprised to see that she returned to her original style. In explanation, the scene cuts to a flashback, where Sue is in the principal's office, wearing her signature tracksuit and the Madonna cone bra from the "Vogue" video on top of it. To this, the principal says: "Sue, you're a powerful woman. You don't need to copy anyone else. You're an original, just like Madonna. Don't lose that quality" ("The Power of Madonna"). Building off that extra encouragement, Sue explains to Kurt and Mercedes, "See kids? Sue Sylvester realized she doesn't need to reinvent herself" ("The Power of Madonna"). The high school girls, whom the episode is specifically supposed to be empowering, do not ever get the verbal support Sue does. The music seems to momentarily provide a positive sense of empowerment for the characters, as in the "Express Yourself" performance, but what really drives the message home is what happens in the surrounding scenes. For the high school students, the message is fleeting due to a lack of their peers' respect, but the female adult's empowerment is reinforced by her interaction with another character. Sue also already feels a thorough connection and ownership over Madonna and her music. There are a number of moments throughout the episode in which she outright claims the right to bestow or take away the presence of Madonna's music in any given situation.[6]

Sue, instead of reinventing herself, declares that she will instead remake everyone else, starting with Mercedes and Kurt. The following scene shows that the two characters have been made part of the cheerleading squad, performing Madonna's 2008 hit "4 Minutes" (which originally featured singer Justin Timberlake and producer Timbaland) at a pep rally in front of the entire school. The marching band plays the brass riffs of the original, the Cheerios dance, and Kurt sings Madonna's part while Mercedes sings Timberlake's. In the gender role switch (there are no gendered words in the lyrics, so the switch is not overly apparent), the gay and black female characters are given a performance that is received with accolades and great applause from the large crowd of the entire high school student body.[7] The positive reinforcement is short-lived, though. Mr. Schuester comes down from the stands and immediately deflates their triumph, chastising them for essentially switching over to the "dark side," as Sue and Mr. Schuester are rivals. Mercedes and Kurt defend their decision but walk away upset by his reaction. The difference in how the two generations of the show are dealt with and supported creates the idea that Madonna's music only truly belongs to those who grew up with her.[8] Though the girls and Kurt sing Madonna's music, other characters purposefully bring their performances down.

To approach the generational gap from a different angle, the second episode of the second season focused on the music of Britney Spears. Unlike the Madonna episode, it was the students' idea to perform her songs, rather than the idea coming from the teachers. Kurt brings up the issue when Mr. Schuester begins to hand out a song by Christopher Cross: "I think I speak for all of us when I say it's not that we don't love the idea of spending a week on this silky smooth adult contemporary—it's just that, as teens, this is not the easiest music for us to relate to" ("Britney/Brittany"). The idea was squashed throughout the episode, with Spears labeled as a "bad role model" for the students without much discussion of why, and it remained a point of contention between the teachers and the students. The character of Mr. Schuester is surprised and skeptical when the girls of the club announce that they feel empowered by Spears partly because they grew up with her music and images. What about Madonna's boundary pushing is positive empowerment, while Spears' boundary pushing behavior is inappropriate? Who gets to make that decision?

There are enough parallels between the careers and public image of these two female artists that would plausibly legitimize placing Spears in a positive light along with Madonna. The major difference, for the purposes of the present essay, is *when* these strong women, with their myriad of iconic looks took over the radio and music video scene. Because Madonna influenced the strongest adult female character on the show, she is a role model to idolize—even though Sue never touches the imagery of many of the more openly sexualized videos ("Justify My Love," for example) or Madonna's book, *Sex*, and how that might be inappropriate for those under eighteen years of age. On the other hand, all that Sue and Mr. Schuester choose to see Britney Spears doing is promoting sex, which is deemed immediately inappropriate for high school students.

Another factor to consider when discussing how the show handles the teenagers' empowerment is the fantasy versus non-fantasy context of the performances when comparing the two episodes. The empowering moments of the "Britney/Brittany" episode are all fantasies the students have while drugged as a dentist works on their teeth. Each member, as they have the fantasy of performing an iconic Britney Spears song, comes back to glee club, altered by their confidence in different ways.[9] These moments, then, serve as confidence boosters for the characters because through their hallucinatory pop performances, they have complete control over a situation. They control their musical fantasy scenarios. The one male who has a Britney Spears performance fantasy even has a mini-scene as an introduction to the performance of the song where Spears herself makes an appearance, high-fiving him as he says he is "stronger" than pining over his ex-girlfriend. The Madonna episode, however, features performances that happen within the frame of the show's reality, presented mostly as something put on for fellow students. From this direct comparison, the fantasy performances allow the singers to have control over the situations, where their voices are actually heard, instead of a possibility of an onscreen audience's detraction of it (as in "Express Yourself" and "4 Minutes").

Sue, like Ryan Murphy himself, grew up with Madonna and therefore Sue feels an ownership over Madonna, claiming a deeper understanding and appreciation for her music and message. The glee club, conversely, is not allowed the same kind of knowledge and possession of Madonna— the performances of her music are undermined in one way or another. The students, when they perform Britney Spears numbers, feel good about themselves—with some boys even experiencing something positive, too. A lack of appreciation for why or how Spears' music could help empower the students causes the adults to fear what they do not understand. For example, without even trying to understand what it might mean to the younger generation, Sue deems Spears' music inappropriate. Mr. Schuester tries to understand but does so by performing a Britney Spears number *with* the students. When it does not work out the way he had planned, he figures that the music was the problem, rather than his selfish motivation for joining the performance.

To return to the Madonna episode, the last number that is central to this essay is the song performed by the male characters only. Performed more than two-thirds of the way into the episode, "What It Feels Like for a Girl" is done with the six guys standing around the piano in the choir room with Mr. Schuester joining them, guiding them through reading the music. The boys' appropriation of Madonna's song was meant to be a pivotal moment for the male characters, ending with the realization that they have been mistreating the girls of the club. With a close reading, though, the message is ineffective, undermined by the script and context within the episode.

Of all the performances, "What It Feels Like for a Girl" is the most altered in the episode from its original form recorded by Madonna, transposed to a different key for the men's voices and markedly truncated. During the intimately staged moment around the piano, Puck—the character that proclaimed Madonna made him uncomfortable in the beginning of the episode—looks judgmental and pessimistic throughout the song, even when he is singing. He cuts off the music by stating loudly: "I am NOT okay with this. I *like* being a dude." When Finn, the main male character, responds, "That's because it's easy to *be* a dude," Puck lashes back, saying: "Uh, Mr. Schue, I think we're going to need a new baritone because Finn would like to become Finn*essa*" ("The Power of Madonna"). Though it seems like a knee-jerk reaction out of the character's mouth, the writers had a specific reason for including the line. Throughout the episode, comments like this are made and thrown away—they are not dealt with head-on or they are ignored. Puck's comment about "Finnessa" is not even recognized as an issue by the teacher—it is not addressed at all for what it is. Was it meant to actively highlight how jokes emasculating men are hurtful, degrading to women, and an easy response within our culture? It is close to impossible to say one way or another if the line was meant to be something more than a laugh-line. Yet, when taking in the episode as a whole in conjunction with how the comment is dealt with, it does not seem to be more than a way to lighten the mood. The song was meant to be a moment for the guys of the glee club to really think about how they were treating their female teammates and to try and imagine the hardships they might come across due to their gender. Instead, the effort is immediately negated by a need to have a comedic moment.

Within the context of the episode, this performance and the dialogue that occurs afterward are especially poignant. For a second time the girls of the club are not valued like the adult female characters. This scene is the only moment in the episode in which the male characters are alone, without the girls. Instead of making this a moment for a productive, respective dialogue about what it means to help empower their female counterparts, the writers chose to include a laugh-line that deliberately does the opposite. For the audience, there is no resolution to Puck's sour faces or derogatory language when dealing with gender equality issues. Even a comment by another male character, Artie, is problematic, partly because it is *supposed* to evince a level of understanding of the female plight. After the teacher asks, "Haven't you noticed how low morale has been around here?" Artie replies, "I think the way I was objectifying Tina [his love interest and a fellow glee member] may have sent her over the edge" ("The Power of Madonna"). There is then a flashback to an earlier moment as Artie is in the school hallways, passing Tina and calling out: "Hey girl." Tina whips around and shouts: "My eyes are up here. I am a person with feelings—get out of my grill! And I am a powerful woman and my growing feminism will cut you in half like a righteous blade of equality" ("The Power of Madonna").

This reaction is exaggerated for its own sake, perpetuating an unhealthy representation/stereotype of feminism. Artie's scared and disturbed reaction by the unexpected outburst appears justifiable. It is in this context that the one use of the word "feminism" appears. Because of this, "feminism" is associated with something unnecessary and undesirable.

Tina's response can then be perceived as an overreaction to Artie's two-word greeting. This is a direct example of the McRobbie idea that even a well-intentioned presentation of feminism in a post-feminist context does little other than work to undermine a more productive form of the concept.

The use of the "angry feminist" stereotype undermines positive associations with the idea of feminism. Seen as a display of animosity and contempt, the "angry feminist" is one that commands attention but also ridicule (Tomlinson 114). Put in other terms, the moment is made to be outrageous and unreasonable by the phrasing, the context, and Artie's reaction. Tina's behavior is further made ridiculous by the scene following the performance of "What It Feels Like for a Girl." Artie and Tina are sitting alone at the piano in the choir room, and Artie is trying to apologize. Tina does not want an apology; rather, she needs a confirmation that Artie is interested in her. By this framing Tina's "angry feminist" outburst is blamed on her female insecurities.

In the end, the male characters who apologize only do so to their respective romantic interests. Puck, the character who expressed discomfort and lashed out at other male characters because they displayed "softer" emotions, does not appear in a scene for the rest of the episode, with the exception of the final performance. He appears in the final number of "Like a Prayer" with the rest of the glee club at the end of the episode, but he is mostly in the background with no specific attention given to him. The episode itself can be wrapped up nicely because the students act like they have all come to an understanding, jubilant at the end of their performance, which closes the show with a bang.

In a blog entitled "The Guy's Guide to Feminism," writer Tyler Haney says of the episode: "Even in the media, buzzword saturated world we live in, I think it's safe to assume that 'The Power of Madonna' episode was the first time many young females *and* males heard the word feminism ... this was the first time these kids heard and understood feminism in a kind of institutionalized sense. Feminism means x ('because that's what they said on *Glee*')." As a viewer, if I did not understand what feminism was before watching the episode, I would still be unsure after watching it. The female students get disrespected and undervalued throughout the episode, and Sue, as the only woman who was fully autonomous to begin with, is the only one who remains so throughout. Madonna's music, billed as a vehicle for "empowerment no matter what gender," does not make all that much of a difference in the end.

The show is a reflection of American popular culture. It is shaped by a number of facets of mainstream media, and in turn, the relationship is becoming increasingly symbiotic. The jokes that are off-color ("Finnessa") are there because the *Glee* writers construct their scripts according to what will be effective. McRobbie's criticism of Western societal media and popular culture is then manifested in this episode, which is particularly apparent when balanced with the issues brought to light in the later Britney Spears episode. The latter's message inadvertently devalues the students' judgments about their own autonomy and self worth, especially when taken in conjunction with the former. Though statistics still prove otherwise, the Madonna episode presupposes that female empowerment, choice, and gender equality have already become automatically inherent in modern Western culture, simultaneously pointing *Glee*'s audience towards the idea that feminism is no longer important or necessary.

Notes

1. It should be noted that the Disney *High School Musical* (*HSM*) franchise is *Glee*'s predecessor, but the two are different in many ways. The most important difference is that while the latter is a weekly, one-hour show, the *HSM* installments were three movies, with only the first two premiering on television—the last was released to theaters first. Another major difference is that *HSM* is geared towards a younger audience (generally "preteen," or "'tween").

2. When I compare the *Glee* performance with the Madonna "original," I am referring to the official music video released for each song.

3. Related to the issues at play here is that of the "male gaze." Due to the fact that the concept is not without its own complicated history, it is outside the scope of this essay to do the topic full justice as it is related to the show.

4. The lines become "Sue Sylvester/ dance on air" and "Will Schuester/ I hate you."

5. Georges-Claude Guilbert goes into detail about Madonna's use of "voguing" and "voguing culture" in *Madonna as Postmodern Myth*, 123–126 (see bibliography for full citation).

6. For example, Sue has the PA speaker in Emma's, the guidance councilor, office disconnected, which means Madonna's hits are played throughout every room in the school but hers. When Emma questions Sue's motives, Sue states that Emma does not deserve "the power of Madonna."

7. I see the gender role switch having to pertain more to the voice part: Mercedes is given Justin Timberlake's line as he has more of an R&B kind of pop singing style, making the runs in his vocal line natural in her voice (the character is known for her agile vocal styling). Kurt represents Madonna, then, in his straightforward tone and manner. It seems purposeful that a white, gay character represents Madonna (and her music) while the black character represents Timberlake (and his music) in the confines of this song.

8. Though disrespected by Sue, Emma is empowered, Mr. Schuester supports in decisions about her embracing her sexuality. Her character goes through a down and up pattern in the episode, but her last scene is one where she is supported and encouraged to take control and make her own decisions.

9. For example, Brittany has more confidence about her singing, and Rachel gains confidence in her outward appearance.

10. The spoken dialogue reads: "Girls can wear jeans, cut their hair short, wear shirts and boots 'cause it's okay to be a boy. But for a boy to look like a girl is degrading 'cause

you think that being a girl is degrading. But secretly you'd love to know what it's like, wouldn't you, what it feels like for a girl."

References

"Britney/Brittany." *Glee*, Season 2, Episode 2. Dir. Ryan Murphy. Perf. Lea Michele, Cory Monteith, Matthew Morrison. 20th Century–Fox Television, 2011. DVD.

"Deconstructing *Glee* with Ryan Murphy." *Glee*, Season 1 DVD Extras. Dir. Ryan Murphy. 20th Century–Fox Television, 2010. DVD.

Estes, Mark O. "Glee—'The Power of Madonna' Review." *TV Overmind*. Last modified April 21, 2010. http://tvovermind.zap2it.com/fox/glee-tv-news/glee-the-power-of-madonna-review/22446.

Faith, Karlene. *Madonna: Bawdy & Soul*. Toronto: University of Toronto Press, 1997. Print. Guilbert, Georges-Claude. *Madonna as Postmodern Myth*. Jefferson, NC: McFarland, 2002. Print.

Haney, Tyler. "Madonna, *Glee*, and Critical Thinking." *The Guy's Guide to Feminism Blog*. Ed. Marie Chesaniuk. http://guysguidetofeminism.blogspot.com/2010/05/madonna-glee-and-critical-thinking.html.

Lealos, Shawn S. "Glee—*The Power of Madonna* Review." *411mania*. http://www.411mania.com/music/album_reviews/136816/Glee—The-Power-of-Madonna-Review.htm.

McClary, Susan. *Feminine Endings: Music, Gender, and Sexuality*. Minneapolis: University of Minnesota Press, 1991. Print.

McRobbie, Angela. *The Aftermath of Feminism: Gender, Culture, and Social Change*. Los Angeles: Sage, 2009. Print.

Metz, Allan, and Carol Benson, eds. *The Madonna Companion: Two Decades of Commentary*. New York: Schirmer Books, 1999. Print.

Middleton, Richard. *Studying Popular Music*. Philadelphia: Open University Press, 1990.

Miller, Neil. "Review: Glee: 'The Power of Madonna.'" *Film School Rejects*. http://www.filmschoolrejects.com/tv/review-glee-the-power-of-madonna.php.

O'Brien, Lucy. *Madonna: Like an Icon*. New York: Harper Entertainment, 2007. Print.

"The Power of Madonna." *Glee*. Dir Ryan Murphy. Perf. Lea Michele, Cory Monteith, Matthew Morrison. 20th Century–Fox Television, 2010. DVD.

Raven, Charlotte. "How the 'New Feminism' Went Wrong." *The Guardian Online*. March 6, 2010. http://www.guardian.co.uk/books/2010/mar/06/charlotte-raven-feminism-madonna-price.

"Ryan Murphy Bio." *Tribute Magazine Online*. http://www.tribute.ca/people/ryan-murphy/16123/.

Tomlinson, Barbara. *Feminism and Affect at the Scene of Argument: Beyond the Trope of the Angry Feminist*. Philadelphia: Temple University Press, 2010.

"Unleashing the Power of Madonna." *Glee*, Season 1 DVD Extras. Dir. Ryan Murphy. 20th Century–Fox Television, 2010. DVD.

Whiteley, Sheila. *Women and Popular Music: Sexuality, Identity, and Subjectivity*. London: Routledge, 2000. Print.

Doppelgängers in Lima
Gendered Identities and Divided Selves
SHERYL LYN BUNDY

One self does what the other self can't. One self is meek while the other is fierce. One self stays while the other self runs away.—Karl Miller 415

Since Fox first began airing episodes in 2009, the television show *Glee* has championed the underdog: the misfit clambering for status in a socially confining environment. More than anything, the New Directions kids that *Glee* primarily follows want to be seen and accepted for who they are. Often, that "real" self is hidden behind a stereotypical one the characters wish to shake off. In fact the show often explicitly packages its characters *as* types—the Diva, the Juvie, the Jock, the Dumb Blonde— then presents new layers to those characters to make them more three-dimensional to the viewer. For instance, in the third-season episode "I Am Unicorn," Diva Mercedes Jones proclaims to Mr. Schuester that her role is to "park and bark," to merely stand and sing while the rest of New Directions dance around her. Mercedes projects an even more extreme version of the Diva elsewhere in "A Night of Neglect," as her "Manager" Lauren Zizes confers with Rachel Berry about the accouterments of Mercedes' backstage room before a benefit concert:

RACHEL: As you can see, we have followed your exact specifications.
MERCEDES: Hey—where's my puppy?
LAUREN: She specifically asked for a puppy.
MERCEDES: This is unbelievable. How am I supposed to work like this?

229

Rachel: Don't worry. Puckerman is out right now scouring pounds for the perfect Pomeranian!

Despite Mercedes' over-the-top Diva antics, the episode later works to expose the confines of the character's appointed type, as Mercedes wonders to Rachel, "Why are you a bigger star than me?" She continues,

Mercedes: Everyone actually *likes* me ...
Rachel: That's your biggest problem! I would rather be a star than be liked ["Night of Neglect"].

Here, the girls' exchange offers insight into the sacrifices accompanying celebrity; at the same time, it provides a glimpse of Mercedes as notably different from the type she represents.

While characterization beyond stereotypes certainly helps an audience connect more deeply with the inhabitants of a narrative, there are two *Glee* characters in particular who seem to be more than just "types with added layers": Quinn Fabray and Blaine Anderson. Both are preppy, clean-cut teens who present a front of wholesomeness, morality and manners, and do so in a way that is often decidedly old-fashioned. Quinn is a proper young lady in a sweater set and knee-length A-line skirt, while Blaine is a dapper bow-tie-wearing gentleman. That Quinn and Blaine *present a front* is a key distinction between this pair and the rest of New Directions. Quinn and Blaine aren't the obvious underdogs many of the other *Glee* kids are. They both know what it's like to fit in; in fact both characters' abilities to *act* a type allow them to do so when necessary. And unlike Mercedes' Diva or Tina's Goth, what Quinn and Blaine seem to epitomize and struggle with are broader expectations derived from binary gender roles.

On the surface, for instance, Quinn often tries to project that she's the Good Girl, and Blaine, the Sweet Boy. But, that's not all that they are. Rather, I would argue that both Quinn and Blaine go beyond the other characters' "not *just* a diva," "not *just* a jock" types-with-added- layers representations and into something more akin to literary doubling. Quinn, the Good Girl who desires a Prom Queen tiara and a man who can provide for her, finds her double in Bad Girl Quinn, a pink-haired Skank who lights pianos on fire and is willing to plant evidence to unseat her daughter's adoptive mother. In parallel fashion, Blaine's Tough Guy aggressive version of himself, represented by the tousled boxer, is kept primarily hidden while the more compliant Sweet Boy reigns. Quinn and Blaine's internal wars continually push the characters to be the "good," i.e., hegemonic version, of the gender. The ways in which these battles play out are grounded in the tradition of the double, as two selves fight to be visible or hidden, embraced by the character or suppressed. But, what is being suggested through these characters' doubling narratives, and through Quinn and Blaine's respective choices to accept or reject their second selves? And, given *Glee*'s focus on being true to one's self, what can be attained by these characters who embody competing hegemonic notions regarding what it "means" to be a man or woman? Ultimately, Quinn's and Blaine's character development thus far suggests that where gender is concerned, *performing a role*—the "right" role—leads to acceptance by others, acceptance of self, and agency.

When examining Quinn and Blaine through the lens of the literary double, it's worth noting that these characters aren't doppelgängers of the variety found in Mary Shelley's *Frankenstein* or even Robert Louis Stevenson's *Dr. Jekyll and Mr. Hyde*. "Duality," perhaps, is a more general term we might employ, as it's "a word which means that there are two of something, and which has also meant that some one thing or person is to be perceived as two" (Miller 21). The doubling that occurs on *Glee* is closer, perhaps, to David Fincher's film *Fight Club*. In the film, Jack's double Tyler Durden is an imagined one, and Jack is largely unaware of his dual nature. The film, referenced in *Glee*, interestingly, by Blaine himself ("Hold on to Sixteen"), is a relevant touchpoint, since "drama and narrative based on split identity has an important resonance for cultural anxieties surrounding identity, masculinity, the body and gender" (Ruddell 494). Such anxieties in the guise of a literary double can be heightened, as "part and counterpart are both perceived to be true" (Miller 21). Since Quinn's and Blaine's doubles center around what Betsy Crane and Jesse Crane-Seeber term the "four boxes of gendered sexuality" (2), namely the Good/Bad Girl roles as well as the Tough/Sweet Guy, for *all* of the roles to be "true" is especially problematic, since, as Crane and Crane-Seeber posit, "Each of these 'boxes' is a trap providing only limited space for people to be themselves" (2). For *Glee*, and its focus on being one's self, Quinn and Blaine (and their respective doubles) offer a set of competing, contradictory notions worth sorting through.

Internal Battles: Public and Private Selves, Agency, and Gender

> *Who are you? I don't recognize you at all.*—Russell Fabray ("Ballad")

> *I'm searching, okay? I'm honestly just trying to figure out who I am.*—Blaine Anderson ("Blame It on the Alcohol")

When we first meet Quinn Fabray in "Pilot," she's engaged with the other Cheerios in cyberbullying Rachel Berry. "If I were your parents," she types in response to Rachel's *MySpace* video, "I'd sell you back" ("Pilot"). Quinn initially seems to be the typical Popular Girl, happy to assert her status. However, the rest of her character profile is more complicated, as evidenced by the series' second episode, "Showmance," where we experience her as Good Girl for the first time—as head of the Celibacy Club. Ironically, during the same episode Quinn uses her sexuality as a tool to manipulate Finn to leave New Directions: "If you quit the [glee] club, I'll let you touch my breast," she offers ("Showmance"). Maintaining her status at the school is what motivates her: Quinn wants to be Prom Queen, and Finn, King. That said, by the end of the episode, she's joined New Directions herself in part to keep a jealous eye on Finn and Rachel but also to help Cheerios coach Sue Sylvester undermine the club by spying on it. However, when asked about her interest in joining New Directions she says sweetly, "What kind of girlfriend would I be if I didn't support [Finn]?" before auditioning with Dionne Warwick's "I Say a Little Prayer," a song about a woman who is emotionally dependent on her lover. In a single episode, then, we are presented with a character who publicly presents herself as the Good Girl, who desires status in visible ways. She's a girl who doesn't go too far with her boyfriend, and supports him in his efforts even if she doesn't always agree with his actions. Her faith is an important (and again, public) guide in her life. And yet, in more private moments, she's the Bad Girl: she withholds from her boyfriend her true intentions, she makes deals with an outside party she knows is bent on dismantling the club her boyfriend respects, and she's willing to use her body as a tool to get what she wants. Quinn's character, in fact, is rather similar to the teenage femme fatale figure that emerged in films such as *Cruel Intentions* during mid–90s, a figure that "demonstrate[s] the complexities of trying to live as a teenage girl in a space which insists that girls' only power lies in their sexuality, and yet judges and vilifies them for utilizing it publicly" (Farrimond 83).

While Quinn's dual nature is apparent from our initial encounters with her, she herself seems to find no conflict between her public and private selves. Once the actions of the Bad Girl become public, however, in this case through an unplanned pregnancy ("Preggers"), Quinn seems aware and frustrated by the contradictory roles she's mediating. Not only has Quinn had sex, but she also cheated on her boyfriend to do so. To complicate matters, Quinn lies about who the father is—choosing the more respectable Finn over Puck—thus attempting to hide her Bad Girl actions with as close to a Good Girl narrative as she can craft. In keeping with that narrative, she expects her man to be her provider. "Somewhere in that pea brain of yours is a man," she tells Finn, while explaining that medical bills will be piling up soon. "Access him, and tell him to prove to me I chose the right guy to have a baby with" ("Wheels"). Quinn's home life further pressures her to meet the Good Girl standard. Against a backdrop of strong Christian faith, Quinn's mother and father play out very traditional gender roles themselves. For instance, Quinn's father tells the story of attending an Indians' game, and how "all the other dads brought their sons," while Quinn's mother cleans up after her husband, saying, "I don't want you to have to lift a finger for me—I'm your wife" ("Ballad"). Both parents expect Quinn to follow suit: "Speaking of getting married, how's that boy you're dating?" ("Ballad"). When faced with the news of the pregnancy, Quinn's father cannot accept his daughter's dual nature. "I don't recognize you at all," he claims, as he turns her out of the house ("Ballad").

While Quinn herself seems initially accepting of her dual nature, we find her male counterpart Blaine less so. When Blaine is introduced early in *Glee*'s second season, he's identified as a Sweet Boy ("Never Been Kissed"). In his Dalton uniform, he appears identical to his classmates, but unlike Quinn, seems unconcerned with status, despite having plenty as the Warbler's lead vocalist.[1] Blaine is courteous above all and tries to put a spying Kurt at ease: "Next time don't forget your jacket, new kid," he says. "You'll fit right in" ("Never Been Kissed"). The Sweet Boy persona is maintained even when Blaine is confronted and shoved into a fence by David Karofsky, Kurt's bully. Rather than take a Tough Guy, aggressive tack, Blaine's approach is to tell a closeted Dave, "You should just know that you're not alone" ("Never Been Kissed").

Beneath the non-confrontational persona, however, we find Blaine's private self desires to be the Tough Guy at times. As he explains to Kurt why he ended up at Dalton in the first place, Blaine admits, "I ran, Kurt. I didn't stand up. I let bullies chase me away and it is something I really, really regret" ("Never Been Kissed").

In some ways Blaine has the additional complication of a *split* persona: his musical-performance persona showcases the sexually assertive side of the Tough Guy. In contrast, Quinn's performances tend to be Good Girl projections, as her songbook initially includes artists from an earlier era, like Warwick, mentioned earlier, The Supremes, and James Brown ("Showmance," "Throwdown," "Funk"). Blaine's early songbook is full of contemporary artists like Katy Perry, Robin Thicke and Pink singing explicitly about sex, drinking, and interestingly, confronting others ("Never Been Kissed," "Silly Love Songs," "Original Song"). In performance,

Blaine projects the image of an experienced man, willing to take what he wants or take on those in his way—all of which counters his otherwise compliant Sweet Boy persona.

If Quinn seems initially unaware of any conflicts between the Good Girl image she projects and the Bad Girl behaviors she displays less publicly, Blaine seems the opposite—in fact, he characterizes his inability to unleash the Tough Guy (even the sexually assertive one) as a shortcoming on his part. In "Silly Love Songs," for example, Blaine brings the Warblers as backup so that he can serenade a boy he's just gotten to know. Before his big moment, Blaine hesitates: "This is insane—I don't even know what I'm doing. We've never even gone out on a date. We shouldn't do this." Kurt replies, "Okay. Come on, come on. Man up. You're amazing. He's gonna love you" ("Silly Love Songs"). After the song turns out to be a disaster, Blaine laments, "Look, Kurt. I don't know what I'm doing. I pretend that I do—and I know how to act it out in song, but the truth is, I've never really been anyone's boyfriend" ("Silly Love Songs"). Blaine's sexually assertive side makes another disastrous appearance—after a lot of drinking—in the episode "Blame It on the Alcohol." After a drunken kiss with Rachel, Blaine finds himself wondering if he's even gay to a vexed Kurt:

> BLAINE: Why are you so angry?
> KURT: Because I look up to you. I admire how proud you are of who you are. I know what it's like to be in the closet, and here you are about to tip toe back in!
> BLAINE: I'm really sorry if this hurts your feelings or your pride or whatever, but however confusing it might be for you, it's actually a lot more confusing for me. You're 100 percent sure of who you are: *fantastic*. Well, maybe we all can't be so lucky ["Blame It on the Alcohol"].

At the heart of these internal wars leaving both characters befuddled with who they are is the level of agency inherent in the Good Girl/Sweet Boy vs. Bad Girl/Tough Guy roles. In a study exploring the connection between gender stereotypes and social roles, researchers Alice Eagly and Valerie Steffen define "agentic qualities [as] manifested by self-assertion, self- expansion, and the urge to master" (736), qualities which seem in keeping with the Bad Girl/Tough Guy roles. The Good Girl/Sweet Boy, on the other hand, aligns with what Eagly and Steffen term "communal qualities," which are "manifested by selflessness, concern with others, and a desire to be at one with others" (736). Quinn's Good Girl and Blaine's Sweet Boy—their default personas—seem grounded in more communal, less agentic modes of being. Those more agentic qualities which Quinn and Blaine either hide or can't seem to bring to the fore *do* finally surface, however, and with them, each character's differing attempt to narrow the gulf between his or her split selves.

The Double in Physical Form: Of Skanks and Fighters

I've finally found myself.—Quinn Fabray ("Purple Piano")

Don't act so surprised. After getting bullied so much I took up boxing. I also started the Dalton branch of Fight Club, which I obviously can't talk about.—Blaine Anderson ("Hold on to Sixteen")

When Quinn and Blaine are at their most vulnerable, the agentic half of their dual nature surfaces. No longer content with private action, in Quinn's case, or with musical performance, in Blaine's, the Bad Girl/Tough Guy presents itself literally, through the characters' appearance. For Quinn, that point comes during the episode, "The Purple Piano Project," where she appears as a pink-haired Skank who confidently narrates, "Senior year, and I've finally found myself. I'm not sure what the tipping point was— dying my hair, the nose ring, my ironic tattoo of Ryan Seacrest—but one thing I know. I'm never going back." This Quinn, who wears dark eyeliner and a spiked black belt, bullies younger students for lunch money and smokes under the bleachers. While it's true that Quinn's earlier Bad Girl involved manipulating others, lying, and cheating, her goal was always status-oriented; she desired improving her reputation. Now that her double is so publicly exposed, her actions seem to have no underlying motivation, nor do they allow her true agency.

When faced with Quinn's new, more aggressive appearance, the female characters in particular question it; they don't believe it's really Quinn, in spite of her protestations[2] ("Purple Piano"). "Everyone needs to leave me alone," Quinn tells Shelby, "because this is who I *am*" ("I Am Unicorn"). The women seem to be trying to guide her back to the Good Girl; she needs to at least *look* the part. Shelby is especially insistent in this regard. "Clean up your act," she says to Quinn, as an ultimatum for granting Quinn the chance to see her daughter Beth ("I Am Unicorn"). When Quinn responds that she's never going back to being "Little Miss Perfect," Shelby asks, "Were you ever really that girl? Would that kind of girl get pregnant in the first place?" ("I Am Unicorn"). On the surface, these questions might be Shelby's way of asking Quinn to let go of the Good Girl standard; however, the comment simply adds more pressure, just like the reprimands she receives from Brittany, Santana, Rachel and Sue. And, so Quinn is still stuck between two roles at war with each other. Discarding one leaves her without agency; discarding the other leaves her censured by other females.

The next we see Quinn, she's meekly asking to rejoin New Directions. She's dyed her hair back to its original color, and dons a conservative white dress ("I Am Unicorn").[3] While it might appear she's repressed Quinn the Skank, she explains to Puck, "I have to get [Beth] back. If that means dying my hair blonde and pretending that I think I'm special, that's something I'm willing to do" ("I Am Unicorn"). For all the times she'd told her friends that she finally was presenting her "real" self, Quinn chooses to hide it so that she can have power again in the world. In fact, Quinn seems *aware* in a way she wasn't before of performing the part of the Good Girl, and becomes a more desperate manipulator willing to slander a teacher (and her daughter's adoptive mother) to regain custody ("Pot o' Gold"). When she finds out that Puck and Shelby have become intimate, Quinn has even more power; she could use the secret to finally dethrone Shelby, who challenges, "Just because you take out your nose ring and dye your hair blonde again … doesn't make you any less lost" ("Hold on to Sixteen").

Ultimately, Quinn finds peace but only after she lets go of most of her Bad Girl behaviors—especially her ferocity—and only after she's physically punished by way of a car accident. Perhaps because she'd let the Bad Girl take control so publicly, punishment comes, and she finds herself in a wheelchair ("On My Way"). The crash seems to finally eradicate the Bad Girl. This new Quinn asks Sue for her spot back on the Cheerios instead of manipulating her way there ("On My Way"). If Quinn does manipulate, it's to achieve more *communal* goals, like propping up Rachel by awarding her Prom Queen, after Rachel compliments "the new Quinn— the still beautiful, but humbled and inspiring Quinn" ("Prom-asaurus"). She still hides things, but with a new Good Girl motive of putting others at ease because of her condition. "Don't," she says. "I could've easily become one of those creepy memorial pages in the yearbook, but, by the grace of God, I'm here. Believe it or not, this is the happiest day of my life" ("Big Brother"). Literally assisted by "Teen Jesus" Joe Hart ("Heart"), Quinn seems to shift her focus away from small victories and onto a larger picture, as Joe reminds her, "I don't pray for you to walk. I ask God to help you accept what your journey may be" ("Big Brother"). And yet, while it seems as if Quinn is simply more mature, that she's cast off behaviors that are wholly negative, it feels a bit like assimilation, with the more confident parts of Quinn's double, the ferocity, seemingly eradicated. She seems whole in body and spirit, but at what cost?

Like Quinn, Blaine's double manifests itself physically when Blaine is most vulnerable, but while Quinn's journey involves more or less obliterating the Bad Girl from her system, Blaine's involves making the Tough Guy increasingly visible and public. In fact, that side of Blaine becomes manifest as various men—who are of higher status, more aggressive sexually, or more attractive—call into question Blaine's masculinity. In the episode "Hold onto Sixteen," for instance, we see Blaine's Tough Guy double appear physically for the first time. Where normally Blaine is so neat he wears shirts buttoned all the way up to their collars, Blaine's boxing Tough Guy is sweaty and disheveled, in a low-cut tank and loose-fitting shorts, his hair messy and curly. This first appearance of the boxer is the result of Finn Hudson asserting his authority over Blaine in glee club on several occasions ("Purple Piano Project," "Mash Off"). When Finn makes it seem as if he's offering a solo to Blaine, only to suggest Rory, for instance, Blaine avoids public conflict and keeps up his gentlemanly ways as he responds, "You're totally ready, Rory. You'll kill it—we'll all help you. I think it's a great idea, Finn" ("Mash Off"). The breaking point comes when Sam insults Blaine's dance moves (i.e., his more confident performance persona) and directs the glee club toward a more suggestive body roll. While Blaine is no stranger to emanating sexual energy in performance, he directs his anger at Sam, telling him that he doesn't want to do the move because he's "not for sale" ("Hold on to Sixteen"). He walks out and boxes privately until he's accosted by Finn, who seems shocked by his appearance and intensity. He shouts at Finn, "What is your problem with me anyway?" but the conflict doesn't escalate, as once Finn says he needs Blaine's talent and support to *help the group*, a calm Blaine asks simply, "What do you need me to do?" ("Hold on to Sixteen").

While Quinn is punished physically for letting her double be *too* visible, Blaine is punished—via a doctored slushie to the eye—for not letting his double emerge *enough* during his dealings with Sebastian Smythe. Sebastian is all Tough Guy: he's assertive and dominating to the point of being manipulative and aggressive. He doesn't want a relationship—just a sexual conquest—and his ease in stating those desires is disarming to Blaine:

BLAINE: You're just so, you know, *out* there.
SEBASTIAN: And your whole bashful schoolboy thing? Super hot.
BLAINE: Look, Sebastian—I have a boyfriend.
SEBASTIAN: Doesn't bother me if it doesn't bother you.
BLAINE: No—I mean, I really care about him.
SEBASTIAN. He doesn't need to know.
BLAINE: I just never want to mess my thing up with him—in any way. He's really great ["The First Time"].

In spite of Sebastian's advances, Blaine is unable to confront him directly. He seems to quietly ignore Sebastian's attempts to communicate online ("Hold on to Sixteen") but still answers his phone calls ("Michael"). The conflict deescalates only because Sebastian stops pursuing Blaine ("On My Way").

Even after Blaine's punishment is doled out, his masculinity continues to be questioned— and his Tough Guy double appears, albeit still in private. When his brother Cooper comes to visit in "Big Brother," he finds his friends—male or female, gay or straight—fawning over Cooper, particularly his appearance:

> KURT: Blaine, your brother's the best looking man in North America.
> BLAINE: Um, Coop and I are gonna—
> SUE: [approaching Cooper] Excuse me, Gaston, if I could pull you away from these ladies for a minute, there's something I'd like to ask you.
> BLAINE: Yeah—that's why I never really talk about my brother ["Big Brother"].

Labeled a "lady" by Sue, Blaine once again finds himself boxing angrily alone, unable to directly confront his brother.

Interestingly, Blaine *does* seem able to confront others through his musical performances. In "Michael," he performs a fight-as-dance with Sebastian and the Warblers through Michael Jackson's "Bad," while he settles his differences with Cooper during a duet of Gotye's "Somebody That I Used to Know" ("Big Brother"). However, one conflict brings Blaine's aggressive double out in a very public way, minus the disheveled appearance, when Blaine suspects his boyfriend Kurt of cheating on him, thus calling their relationship into question ("Dance with Somebody"). While Blaine sings a Whitney Houston song about cheating, "It's Not Right, But It's Okay," furiously to Kurt in the choir room, it's clear from the looks on the others' faces that they've never seen this "side" of Blaine before. Despite being able to show some anger publicly, albeit in performance, Blaine's internal battles aren't over.

The Gender Binary, Identity, and Popular Television

> *In all its variations, the double arises out of and gives form to the tension between division and unity. It stands for contradiction within unity, and for unity in spite of division, the likeness expressing the unity of the individual, the doubleness or complementarity expressing division within the personality.—Herdman 2*

In the end, *Glee* itself has its own split identity, as it simultaneously affirms certain stereotypes or notions about gender while subverting them. Perhaps the show's own duality as well as its location on prime-time network television lend themselves to issues of agency, too, just as with Quinn and Blaine. In one study on gender roles and social roles on television, for instance, Martha Lauzen examined the social roles played out by female and male characters on prime-time, broadcast network programs, comparing them to a similar study done fourteen years prior. She found that male and female characters were still "operating in the same spheres," with female storylines focused on romance, family and friends, and male storylines focused on work- related roles (Lauzen 211). "Such portrayals," Lauzen concludes, "illustrate the ongoing network tendency to paint characters in the broadest of gender strokes" (211).

If we consider further that "the basic social roles enacted by characters contribute to viewer expectations and beliefs about gender" (Lauzen 202), then for *Glee*, a show about misunderstood misfits, underdogs—kids who strive to be accepted for who they are, who want their identities acknowledged—where do characters like Quinn and Blaine leave us? Quinn's story of maturation ends with her graduation from McKinley High, and shapes her into a perfect woman, as far as binary gender roles are concerned. That means The Good Girl, but one who has agency not tied to sexuality; one who has views about gender and rights, but still has what would be described as communal goals. She's not as tough, but she's liked and fully accepted—and her motivations are no longer tied to the men in her life. But, her ferocity is gone, even if she might still see herself at times as a "self-obsessed bitch" ("Dance with Somebody"). Instead, Quinn has incorporated what traits from the double allow her to retain agency and acceptance and her reward for doing that is a spot at Yale University.

As for Blaine, not only does he battle with competing notions of what it means to be a man, but he does so as an out, gay young man, who his boyfriend Kurt accuses of being "the Alpha Gay." Kurt elaborates, "Even Rachel wanted to make out with you" ("Dance with Somebody"). As a gay young man who can pass as straight, Blaine's ability to ultimately act on the Tough Guy self is further complicated, especially on prime-time television. He can't, according to Kathleen Battles and Wendy Hilton-Morrow, writing on mainstream television's limitations where gay characters are concerned; such behavior would make him too threatening to the straight guys around him, and follows "a heteronormative logic that requires clear demarcation between gay and straight masculinity" (200). Again, while Quinn seems able to find a way to find peace within (in spite of giving up some of her ferocity to make herself acceptable to society), Blaine's ability to do the same is complicated, and Miller's comments about the literary double seem particularly apt: "We are brought to feel that he is engaged in the impossible task of trying to escape from himself, or to separate himself from someone whom he can't help resembling or repeating" (Miller 47).

As *Glee* enters its fourth season, Quinn has moved on to Yale and into the background, while Blaine has become a central character. Already in several storylines, Blaine attempts to make more public his private self. A more assertive Blaine pursues a position of leadership in New Directions as well as in the student body as class president ("The New Rachel," "Makeover"). At the same time, the more sexually assertive version of Blaine's Tough Guy has re-emerged and taken a page out of Sebastian's book when it comes to engaging in a random hook up with a boy ("The Break Up"). Significantly, Blaine's actions in this case stem not from a desire to display dominance or sexual prowess but instead are rooted in insecurity and dependence. The guilt over his behavior seems to dismantle his performance persona; during a rendition of "Teenage Dream," Blaine crumbles while singing to Kurt in a completely public place ("The Break Up"). It is yet to be seen how Blaine will reconstruct himself, and with what ramifications—or compromises. In addition new characters like Wade/Unique have the potential to continue Blaine's exploration of self. In some ways, Wade and Unique are literary doubles, too, but unlike Blaine, who keeps sides of himself separate for performance or private, Wade and Unique are *both* public. *Both* perform. And importantly, the versions of self seem to present themselves not due to vulnerability but simply at the behest of their owner.

In an essay called "Gender Treachery: Homophobia, Masculinity, and Threatened Identities," Patrick Hopkins describes the particular challenges a binary gender system lends to one's sense of self:

> Individuals' sense of personhood, their sense-of-self, is largely a result of their construction as members of particular social groups within society-at-large: religions, ethnicities, regional affinities, cultural heritages, classes, races, political parties, family lineages, etc. Some of the most pervasive, powerful, and hidden of these identity-constructing "groups" are the genders; pervasive because no individual escapes being gendered, powerful because so much else depends on gender, and hidden because gender is uncritically presented as a natural, biological given, about which much can be discovered but little can (or should) be altered.... To a very large extent, what it means to be a member of society, and thus what it means to be a person *is* what it means to be a girl or boy, a man or woman [Hopkins 113].

Because Quinn and Blaine, through their respective doubles, straddle both sides of a binary gender system, we see how difficult it is for them to do what *Glee* presents as one of its major themes: accept yourself, *be* yourself. For Quinn and Blaine, such unity is achieved only through compromise. Hopkins continues to explain the nature of identity, echoing language we might use to describe the literary double:

> Identity is fundamentally relational. What it means to have a particular identity depends on what it means not to have some other identity, and by the kinds of relationships one has to other possible and actual identities. To have personhood, sense-of-self, regulated by a binary sex/gender system means that the one identity must be different from the other identity; a situation

requiring that there be identifiable, performative, behavioral, and psychological characteristics that allow for clear differentiation [Hopkins 113].

Ultimately, both Quinn and Blaine are locked in a complicated performance. They can't neatly separate these elements of self, but the pressure is great to do so, as they face either acceptance or condemnation for the choices they make about presenting themselves or exercising agency. Their own awareness of the cage they find themselves in is key, however. Otherwise they are merely trapped like the warbler Pavarotti, singing perhaps, but simply surviving.

Notes

1. Of course Quinn wears a uniform too—the Cheerios uniform—which, like Blaine, allows her to fit in and achieve status socially.

2. Santana, Brittany, Rachel and Sue all question Quinn's appearance and choices. In "The Purple Piano Project," Brittany and Santana remind her, "We joined Cheerios together, we joined Glee Club together, we all slept with Puckerman the same year. We're, like, Besties for Life." Santana's comments highlight the communal role Good Quinn played as a way to encourage her to rejoin them. She continues, focusing on how Quinn's appearance needs to change: "I've got a bar of soap and a bottle of peroxide with your name on it in my locker." In the same episode, Rachel also emphasizes community: "We need you…. We're a family and this is our year to get it right." And, when Sue accosts Quinn in the bathroom in "I Am Unicorn," she emphasizes the ways Quinn has compromised her status: "You've never looked worse. You lost your child, your boyfriend, your rep and worse—your high pony."

3. Quinn also wears an all-white, mid-length dress when preparing for the Chastity Ball in "Ballad" and again in "Hold on to Sixteen," after she's finally abandoned her plans to oust Shelby. The color and style of dress is certainly symbolic of purity, even though Quinn appears to merely be acting the part at times.

References

"Asian F." *Glee.* Dir. Alfonso Gomez-Rejon. Fox Broadcasting Company. WMAQ, Chicago, 4 October 2011. Television.

"Ballad." *Glee.* Dir. Brad Falchuk. *Netflix.* Web. 16 June 2012.

Battles, Kathleen, and Wendy Hilton-Morrow. "Nobody Wants to Watch a Beacon: *Will & Grace* and the Limits of Mainstream Network Television." *Queers in American Popular Culture.* Ed. Jim Elledge. Vol. 1. Santa Barbara: Praeger, 2010.

"Big Brother." *Glee.* Dir. Eric Stoltz. Fox Broadcasting Company. WMAQ, Chicago, 10 April 2012. Television.

"Blame It on the Alcohol." *Glee.* Dir. Eric Stoltz. *Netflix.* Web. 24 July 2012.

"The Break Up." *Glee.* Dir. Alfonso Gomez-Rajon. Fox Broadcasting Company. WMAQ, Chicago, 4 Oct. 2012. Television.

Crane, Betsy, and Jesse Crane-Seeber. "The Four Boxes of Gendered Sexuality: Good Girl/Bad Girl & Tough Guy/Sweet Guy." *Sexual Lives: A Reader on the Theories and Realities of Human* Eds. R. Heasley and Betsy Crane. New York: McGraw Hill, 2003. 196–217. *Indiana University of Pennsylvania.* PDF File.

"Dance with Somebody." *Glee.* Dir. Paris Barclay. Fox Broadcasting Company. WMAQ, Chicago, 24 April 2012. Television.

Eagly, Alice, and Valerie Steffen. "Gender Stereotypes Stem from the Distribution of Women and Men into Social Roles." *Journal of Personality and Social Psychology* 46.4 (1984): 735–754. *Academic Search Complete.* Web. 26 July 2012.

Farrimond, Katherine. "Bad Girls in Crisis: The New Teenage Femme Fatale." *Women on Screen: Feminism and Femininity in Visual Culture.* Ed. Melanie Waters. Hampshire, England: Palgrave Macmillan, 2011. 77–89. Print.

"The First Time." *Glee.* Dir. Bradley Buecker. Fox Broadcasting Company. WMAQ, Chicago, 8 Nov. 2011. Television.

"Funk." *Glee.* Dir. Elodie Keene. *Netflix.* Web. 18 June 2012.

"Heart." *Glee.* Dir. Brad Falchuk. Fox Broadcasting Company. WMAQ, Chicago, 14 Feb. 2012. Television.

Herdman, John. *The Double in Nineteenth-Century Fiction: The Shadow Life.* New York: St. Martin's Press, 1991.

"Hold on to Sixteen." *Glee.* Dir. Bradley Buecker. Fox Broadcasting Company. WMAQ, Chicago. 6 Dec. 2011.

Hopkins, Patrick. "Gender Treachery: Homophobia, Masculinity, and Threatened Identities." *Rethinking Masculinity: Philosophical Explorations in Light of Feminism.* Eds. Larry May and Robert Strikwerda. Lanham, MD: Littlefield Adams Quality Paperbacks, 1992. 111–131. Print.

"I Am Unicorn." *Glee.* Dir. Brad Falchuk. Fox Broadcasting Company. WMAQ, Chicago, 27 Sept. 2011. Television.

Lauzen, Martha. "Constructing Gender Stereotypes through Social Roles in Prime-Time Television." *Journal of Broadcasting & Electronic Media* 52.2 (2008): 200–214. *Academic Search Complete.* Web. 20 July 2012.

"Makeover." *Glee.* Dir. Eric Stoltz. Fox Broadcasting Company. WMAQ, Chicago, 27 Sept. 2012. Television.

"Mash Off." *Glee.* Dir. Eric Stoltz. Fox Broadcasting Company. WMAQ, Chicago, 15 Nov. 2011. Television.

"Michael." *Glee.* Dir. Alfonso Gomez-Rejon. Fox Broadcasting Company. WMAQ, Chicago, 31 Jan. 2011. Television.

Miller, Karl. *Doubles: Studies in Literary History.* London: Oxford University Press, 1985. Print. "Never Been Kissed." *Glee.* Dir. Brad Falchuk. *Netflix.* Web. 24 July 2012.

"The New Rachel." *Glee.* Dir. Brad Falchuk. Fox Broadcasting Network. WMAQ, Chicago, 13 Sept. 2012. Television.

"A Night of Neglect." *Glee.* Dir. Carol Banker. *Netflix.* Web. 17 June 2012.

"On My Way." *Glee.* Dir. Bradley Buecker. Fox Broadcasting Company. WMAQ, Chicago, 6 Dec. 2011. Television.

"Original Song." *Glee.* Dir. Bradley Buecker. *Netflix.* Web. 18 June 2012. "Pilot." *Glee.* Dir. Ryan Murphy. *Netflix.* Web. 15 June 2012.

"Pot o' Gold." *Glee.* Dir. Adam Shankman. Fox Broadcasting Company. WMAQ, Chicago, 1 Nov 2011. Television.

"Preggers." *Glee.* Dir. Brad Falchuk. *Netflix.* Web. 24 June 2012.

"Prom-osaurus." *Glee.* Dir. Eric Stoltz. Fox Broadcasting Company. WMAQ, Chicago, 8 May 2012. Television.

"The Purple Piano Project." *Glee.* Dir. Eric Stoltz. Fox Broadcasting Company. WMAQ, Chicago, 20 Sept. 2011. Television.

Ruddell, Caroline. "Virility and Vulnerability, Splitting and Masculinity in *Fight Club*: A Tale of Contemporary Male Identity Issues. *Extrapolation* 48.3 (2007): 493–503. *Expanded Academic ASAP.* PDF File.

"Showmance." *Glee.* Dir. Ryan Murphy. *Netflix.* Web. 22 June 2012.

"Silly Love Songs." *Glee.* Dir. Tate Donovan. *Netflix.* Web. 3 July 2012.

"Throwdown." *Glee.* Dir. Ryan Murphy. *Netflix.* Web. 21 June 2012.

"Wheels." *Glee.* Dir. Paris Barklay. *Netflix.* Web. 18 June 2012.

IV. "I know what *Glee* is. I'm a
total Gleek": The Cultural
Reach of *Glee* and the Many
Roles of Its Fandom

Glee Literally Means Glee
The Queer Art of Community's *Parody*
Nicholas Alexander Hayes

Three-quarters of the way through the *Community* episode "Regional Holiday Music," the fair-skinned, blonde-haired Britta runs from her friends in her Greendale Community College study group. They have been infected with gleeful musicality. The urge of song has overwhelmed their ability to cynically dissect the world, as they normally would. The transformation terrifies Britta. In the midst of her flight, she runs into the handsome and white Jeff Winger who she believes has not been infected. He turns. She sees his plastic, generic smile and realizes he, too, has been infected with glee. His mouth gapes, and he begins to sing. A single note escapes before the camera zooms into his deepening maw. The scene cuts. His incomplete song serves to remind the viewer that the worst horrors are never depicted. The Greendale study group faces the horror of an alien and incompatible ethos as members join the glee club. The study group's conversion represents a shift away from a critical understanding of the social environment as illustrated in *Community* to an emotional one as illustrated in *Glee*. *Glee* derives much of its poignancy through the musical depiction of emergent identities. When *Community* parodies its rival, it questions this approach to identity formation. The satiric scenes and episodes challenge *Glee*'s ethos as it undermines and reconstructs its own comedic modes, relations to setting, and characters' identities.

When the sitcom *Community* parodies *Glee*, it tries to prove the smug superiority of its ethos over the dramedy's. The sitcom turns its critical gaze on *Glee* repeatedly[1] in this effort. Yet in trying to prove this point,

Community reveals the pervasiveness of *Glee*'s influence for even those who are dismissive of the show. Jeff Winger's musical fantasy that introduces the third season of *Community* (the same season as the much more acerbic "Holiday Regional Music") is in fact an homage to the show's loathed rival. *Community* destabilizes its own narrative as much as it challenges *Glee*'s through parody. Parody forces the imitator into a grave form of repetition. In *Difference and Repetition,* Gilles Deleuze makes the case that "[r]epetition belongs to humour and irony; it is by nature transgression or exception, always revealing a singularity opposed to the particulars subsumed under laws, a universal opposed to the generalities which give rise to laws" (5). In making fun of the original, *Community* must replicate it, transgressing its own logic and locating itself in the same psychological plane. And, this is where *Community* finds itself negotiating its simple comedy into something much more injurious to itself. The study group must act with the sincerity, which *Glee*'s students use to exhibit the show's potency.

Community, as a show that focuses on media criticism, often takes an adversarial stance toward popular culture. The repeated parodic assaults on *Glee* are not surprising, but the vociferous antagonism is more intense than in other pieces the sitcom criticizes. In the episode "Basic Genealogy," Jeff Winger encapsulates the overall antipathy for the musical series. Jeff cries, "I hate *Glee*." Hatred becomes a meaningful way that *Community* engages with *Glee*. Martin Buber, in *I and Thou,* reveals the importance of such hate: "Yet whoever hates directly is closer to a relation than those who are without love and hate" (68). Replicating and hating *Glee* destabilizes any type of normative actions *Community* would seem to advocate. In critiquing, *Community* critiques itself, revealing the non-normative, queer, impulse of the parody.

Some of the energy for the parody comes from the Oedipal and pre–Oedipal comedic modes of the narratives and the ways they create identity. In *In a Queer Time and Place: Transgender Bodies, Subcultural Lives,* Judith Halberstam says of Oedipal comedy, "The plot involves the boy's accession to maturity which is marked by the beginning of a heterosexual romance with an acceptable female love object; the love object may find the funny boy humorous but not ridiculous, and this distinction allows him access to the illusion of mastery" (136). Mr. Schuester who directs the glee club New Directions[2] has a long narrative arc in his pursuit of Emma Pillsbury. This romance fits within the general framework for Oedipal comedy. His quirky niceness drives him, his students and his colleagues into a kind and productive maturity. The various romances at McKinley follow this pattern with slight variations.[3] Likewise in the musical introduction of the *Community* episode "Biology 101," Jeff Winger expresses a desire for this type of narrative. This is particularly evident in the lyric, "We're going to sleep together," which is sung by Jeff and his sometimes love interest Annie.

This musical interlude promises an emphasis on normative narrative structures. The zaniness of the characters will be downplayed so that heterosexual pair bonding will drive the narration. However, Annie wakes Jeff from his fantasy. This single incident indicates that *Community's* overall comedy belongs to a different mode since this heteronormative drive is thwarted by narrative disjunction. Andrew Horton, in *Comedy/Cinema/Theory*, explains, "Pre- Oedipal comedy has much in common with a spirit of carnival" (12). Halberstam provides a similar definition and further explains that this mode of comedy "...almost refuses narrative coherence" (136). *Community's* various narrative intrusions resist psycho-sexual maturity even as it alludes to it. Such a stance by the study group helps explain why they have such disdain for the various manifestation and proxies of *Glee*.

The comedic modes have a deeper implication for the way the narrative's structure utilizes fantastical intrusions. The musical and performative interjections in *Glee* often advance the narrative but stand outside of it by occurring in the floating world of the stage or by occurring in the alternate chronological structure of the montage. One such intrusion of the floating world occurs in "The Power of Madonna." The interjection of the performance of "Like a Virgin" serves as the vehicle in which the couples question their sexual engagement. Another occurs in "Sexy." Mr. Schuester's attempt to turn Prince's "Kiss" into a tango transforms a classroom into a candlelit, curtain draped dance studio. In the fantastical space, the substitute teacher Holly Holliday and Mr. Schuester struggle against their open desires and its potential manifestations. The song and dance in the fantastical plane allow the two educators to surface the tension and underlying elements that will allow them to enter into a relationship.

These interjections ultimately serve the normative drives of *Glee's* narratives. In contrast, the fantastical interjections in *Community* are built into the narrative and do not act as a narrative bypass. These fantasies destabilize *Community's* attempts at direct and stable plots. The Christmas parody changes styles of intrusion as the story comes closer to its object of ridicule. Abed challenges the first *Glee*-style of interruption by asking, "How's your piano still playing this song?" The glee club director Mr. Radisson sings, "Glee is the answer when the questions are wrong. You'll understand if you just sing along 'cause glee is the gift that you need." In the larger infection of *Glee* into Greendale, the interruptions cannot be scrutinized for being ridiculous. *Community* loses its critical ethos through this change.

The characters in *Glee* and *Community* struggle to adapt to their environments. In both comedic series, the academic setting is the crucial platform for expressing the ethos through the projection of identities. *Glee* presents an environment in which students must act with sincerity. Their school is a transformative space. Students must see the world in new ways because of their experiences in the school. The lessons they learn (especially the musical assignments given by Mr. Schuester) have signification in the development of the student's identity through cathartic musical release. Involvement in New Directions allows characters to move past their limitations as they grow to accept themselves. The paraplegic Artie Abrams, for instance, realizes that he can never be a dancer but can still entertain. He even finds his strength and new dream of directing in the episode "I Am Unicorn." He is able to overcome his limitations because of the workings of the academic environment.

Greendale's study group has a less favorable attitude to their school. Its cynicism insulates the members' real lives from the absurd interjections that the academic environment propagates. The functions of the two academic settings accentuate the dissonance between the worldviews that set the stage for *Community*'s parodic assault on *Glee*. In general, the school is separate from the larger world. The bizarreness of academia is rooted in such separateness. Greendale's academia is even stranger because of the faculty's ineptness. The failure of knowledge leaves Greendale a college only in the empty forms of classroom behavior. The show often reveals the students are "queer"[4]compared to their expectations of students at other institutions. *Community* approaches the academic setting with cynicism and impotent hostility. For the Greendale study group, identity is something that exists outside of the school and was formed before the narrative. The environment is transitional and disruptive as they seek a way to return to their adult lives.[5] They view the workings of the academic environment as an empty form. Jean Baudrillard, in "Value's Last Tango," describes such attitudes thus:

> The exchange of signs (of knowledge, of culture) in the university, between "teachers" and "taught" has for some time been nothing but a doubled collusion of bitterness and indifference (the indifference of signs that brings with it the disaffection of social and human relations), a doubled simulacrum of a psychodrama (that of a demand hot with shame, presence, oedipal exchange,[6] with *pedagogical incest* that strives to substitute itself for the lost exchange of work and knowledge) [155].

To exist in this environment without succumbing to its excessive and ludicrous nature the Greendale study group members must insulate their outside lives from the empty exchanges that happen on campus. They must balance a sincere effort at working through the motions of education without ever fully buying into the excess of the bureaucratic fantasy. They preserve their outside identities with their cynical analysis of the irrational regulation of Greendale Community College.

The social environments of the schools provide another challenge to identity and location of conflict for the parody. *Community's* hostility mirrors the hostility toward New Directions shown in the first season of *Glee*. In *Glee*, the main adversaries, the cheerleading squad and the football team, harass the club members. This social hierarchy dominates and dictates the possibility of heteronormative expectations of McKinley. Cheerleaders date football players, and both groups are permitted unofficial authority to harass those peers who do not fit into this social framework. The tension produced by the conflict between popular cheerleaders and unpopular glee club members indicates an ethos entrenched in clearly demarcated social positions. The glee club becomes a place for outcast people to come and emotionally bond. The members of the club tacitly accept this power structure since the glee club is sanctioned by the administration and placed under the authority of a director.[7]

Community repeatedly returns to its adversarial representation of *Glee* to deride an overtly emotional understanding of the world. In the parody, *Community* attacks *Glee* more viciously than the slushie-wielding cheerleaders. The study group also represents a diverse body of students that is comprised of outcasts. Dean Pelton recognizes the group as the most diverse on campus, even without Latino members.[8] In addition, the study group has a less hierarchical structure and derives its sense of authority through cooperation and cynical resistance to Greendale's administration. So when they turn their acerbic glare to Greendale's glee club, the ingenious proxy for the other show, it emphasizes a logical and non-emotional approach to the social environment. It also represents an entity truly capable of resisting the excesses of the academic bureaucracy. Jeff Winger justifies their hostility by saying, "Not liking glee club doesn't make us bullies, and implying that is reverse bullying." He acknowledges the struggle of the glee club but differentiates the abuse from the socially permissible violence perpetrated in *Glee*. *Community's* assaults against the glee club are multifarious. For instance, one incarnation is offhandedly killed in a bus crash. The study group outguns another incarnation in paintball. However, the most devastating weapon of all comes in the form of a legal injunction. Issued with the confidential tip of Jeff Winger, which will prevent them from singing any copyrighted music.[9] This is a particularly successful jab at *Glee* because so many of their episodes revolve around the music of a celebrity or a music group who is well-entrenched in the corporate system of music. The formal injunction, a weapon that can only be utilized by someone who understands the logical underpinnings of the legal bureaucracy causes the members of the Greendale glee club to break down. Their world ruled by emotions is deprived of the music from which they build meaning. The riot that ensues reveals a fracture in the glee club's ethos. They are left without a means to process the world, suffer a mental breakdown and are committed to a mental hospital. Logic, skepticism and petty disdain come to fruition through legal and logical intervention.

The split between the mechanics of logic and engagement through emotion is crucial to identity in *Glee* and *Community*. In *Glee*, those who use logic (or pseudo-logic) are cast as villainous or potentially hostile neutral centers of power: Sue Sylvester and Principal Figgins loom over and threaten the glee club as budgets and time tables are created and revised. *Glee*'s reliance on emotion is revealed in the importance of music and its required surrender to pathos. The philosopher Maurice Blanchot reminds us that Kafka, the master of irrational yet regulated order, considered his non-musicality one of his greatest strengths (430). It is a short stretch to see the sneering face of Jeff Winger or the docile visage of Abed Nadir reflecting this sentiment since they prize their logical detachment. In *Community*, surrender to emotional lines of flight— as is often done by Dean Craig Pelton—represents a movement into the ridiculous or grotesque. As "Regional Holiday Music" adopts the tropes of *Glee* and the characters lose their detachment, music and its emotional expression impose revision on the identity of characters.

Many people use music as the analogue for their personal identity. High school and college students in particular use it as a way in which they get to know somebody. A choice in music reveals something about the person in a way that the facts of their lives cannot. In examining music, we so often find ourselves pursuing something akin to the essence or soul of the performer and audience. Perhaps this is one reason why *Glee* has become so powerful. Young people facing the crucible of identity formation in the hothouse of high school are allowed to express something true about themselves through the miracle of song. Mr. Schuester's glee club assignments to choose a song are a direct outgrowth of the belief that music can express some innate personal truth. In the episode "The Rocky Horror Glee Show," the club and Mr. Schuester try to stage a production of *Rocky Horror Picture Show*. They find themselves plagued by the obscenity of the piece, but they also find themselves faced with the salve of the music that has helped many straight and queer outsiders find themselves. Eventually they perform the show, but they perform for themselves. This allows them to experience the power of the music without the crisis of a public performance. In many ways, the music allows the singers to become themselves. When Will Schuester and Emma Pillsbury sing "Toucha, Toucha Me," Brittany and Santana watch on—echoing the scene from the original movie. They join in the song when appropriate. The educators and the students play out their erotic struggle as they sing. Brittney and Santana dart from the voyeurism into the halls continuing their own erotic play through the lyrical interlude after their educators race around the classroom performing both the script of the musical and their libidinal dramas. The tacit desires and identities of the characters are made explicit. In "Sexy," a similar phenomenon occurs. Santana sings "Landslide" with and to Brittany. In this rendition of the song, Santana allows herself to publicly display her emotions for the girl she loves. However, after the song is finished she quickly retreats into prosaic protections. Brittany asks Santana if the song truly expresses her sentiment. But when Rachel praises Santana for "exploring the uncharted world of Sapphic charm," Santana defensively rejects the label. The rejection indicates that out of the performance she must publicly distance herself from her innate identity.

Community resists the identity formation inherent in music because it contains the imperative that this approach is beneficial for everyone. *Glee* insists this in its infectious seduction. McKinley cheerleaders eventually join the club. And, in "The Sue Sylvester Shuffle," the entire football team is required to temporarily join the club. The process of seduction of antagonists is a similar mechanism to that used in "Regional Holiday Music." The Greendale's study group's skepticism of and cynicism towards the glee club is weakened by the persuasive power of song. In the first song of the parody, Abed reveals, "Glee is what I'll spread to my friends like a virus that sends them to a healthier place." The infectious conversion is heightened by the fact each member of the group is presented a song tailored to their identity. These songs act in two ways. The first is that they target the foibles of the characters. The friends use their intimate knowledge of each other to disrupt and break down the other's cynical protection from the glee.[10] Secondly, the songs act in such a way that they hyper-accentuate the qualities of the singers and listeners. In essence, the songs make the characters caricatures.

Stupidity emerges as a dominant characteristic in the parody as it renders the characters flat. This stupidity is reflected in the first time the study group takes the glee club's place.[11] The lyrics of their song are "Sing-a-ling-ling, Ding-Dong" and "Sing, sing, sing, sing, sing." No words are necessary since they can perform in blank bliss. *Community*, in this episode, utilizes strategies of forgetting and stupidity similar to those described in Judith Halberstam's *The Queer Art of Failure*. In discussing *Dude, Where's My Car?* Halberstam explains:

> [The protagonist's] tolerance is revealed to be part and parcel of their stupidity, and their stupidity is represented as a likeable absence of critical judgment which relieves them of being either politically sensitive (aware of their own biases) or politically biased (homophobic). The amnesiac circularity within which the dudes coexist casts them as bound to forget what others around them remember all too well [63].

The study group's stupidity makes them self-destructively tolerant the second time they fill in for glee club. They accept the single-minded plan to go to regionals while forgoing their own holiday plans and long-term goals since as Mr. Radisson informs Abed the glee club is their life now. This submissive stupidity damages the normal modes of *Community's* narrative. Normally, the study group remembers events for the audience and other members of the Greendale community. To this end, the show sometimes utilizes the trope of the clip show to depict the importance of memory. Unlike other iterations of the clip show, *Community* relies on footage not present in previous episodes. In effect, they remember what the audience cannot. They prove the importance of their critical intelligence through such actions.

The study group's critical intelligence is flattened after they join glee club. They seem unable to speak except about the performance and the ambiguous regionals. All other attempts at communication reveal fundamental misunderstandings and stupidity. These misunderstandings in turn show how identity as well as intelligence has been flattened. When Abed seduces his Jehovah's Witness friend Troy into joining the club and celebrating Christmas,[12] he reveals an inability to understand the deeper religious aspects of his friend's psyche. In seducing the baby-boomer Pierce, Abed and Troy reveal their larger cultural ignorance. The two young men equate "fake butter and AIDS and *Twin Peaks*" and offer them equally as the "amazing" inheritance left by the post-war generation. The transformation ushered by the music is most clearly seen in the performance of "Teach Me How to Understand Christmas." Annie allows her innocent sexuality to erode her intelligence as she serenades Jeff. Her naiveté subsumes her penultimate quality of intelligence as her lyrics devolve from coherent sentences into unintelligible baby talk.[13] The musical dumbness permits religion to become nominal, reveals generational differences are simple, goofy misunderstandings, and demonstrates that sexuality is comically grotesque. The main markers of identity are exaggerated.

In the songs that Troy, Abed, Pierce and Annie (and later Britta) sing they all embody stupidity through exaggerated identities. Yet the nature of this exaggeration is not equitable. The performances are situated in a gendered context. In *The Queer Art of Failure*, Halberstam analyzes the way in which stupidity is gendered:

> Stupidity is as profoundly gendered as knowledge formations in general; thus while unknowing in a man is sometimes rendered as part of masculine charm, unknowing in a woman indicates a lack and a justification of a social order that anyway privileges men. Though we both punish and naturalize female stupidity, we not only forgive stupidity in white men, but we often cannot recognize it as such since white maleness is the identity most often associated with mastery, wisdom, and grand narratives. In other words, when a white male character in a film or novel is characterized as stupid or unknowing, this is quickly folded back into his general appeal as a winning form of vulnerability [55].

Even though Troy and Abed are not white, their performance does signify the way in which they have mastery over others. In fact, the whole premise of infection of music from Abed's first song represents his overarching desire to control the study group's holiday plans. Yet, when Annie and Britta sing,[14] they become merely foolish. Their songs illustrate this by the deterioration of language skills: Annie's song becomes mere gibberish, Britta's song lacks basic grammatical sentence structure ("Me so merry. Me so Christmas"[15]). Annie's willful coyness takes on Ubuesque dimensions by the end of the song. Winger even comments on its failure in one of the shows many metatextual comments: "Look, eventually you hit a point of diminishing returns on the sexiness." In "Transsexuality," Jean Baudrillard observes, "After the demise of desire, a pell- mell diffusion of erotic simulacra in every guise, of transsexual kitsch in all its glory" (22). Annie's performance embodies such a diffusion; her sexiness is clearly not sexy as her baby talk increasingly resembles real baby talk. Clearly, her crawling toward Jeff has the motions of seduction, but they are empty. The movement into empty enactment of characteristics (sexuality, spirituality, age) is increasingly visible as the study group succumbs to their roles in the glee club. An absurd characteristic becomes dominant for each singer as they perform. The subtleties of their personality are eclipsed by this exaggerated quality. Annie's sexual presentation through song serves to counterpoint the sexuality revealed in *Glee*'s music.

Glee, in presenting music as a positive force, forgoes this particular pitfall of gender positionality. In *Glee*, musical performance bolsters sexual identity. In "The Power of Madonna," Emma Pillsbury and Will Schuester, Santana and Finn, and Rachel and her then boyfriend Jesse St. James bridge a variety of initial sexual encounters through the song "Like a Virgin."[16]

The unrelenting sincerity of the characters prevents them from seeing the subtle irony that the singer of the lyrics cannot actually be a virgin since she is only "like a virgin." Similarly in "Sexy," the Celibacy Club's choice of the song "Afternoon Delight" reveals an almost willful ignorance of sexuality. Emma Pillsbury insists that the song is about a dessert and not sexual activity. Despite the lack of clear understanding, the characters embrace the emotion of the song and allow the subsequent fantasy of performance to bridge and expedite the complex interpersonal scenarios that accompany of the loss of virginity. In this context, the misreading of the lyric is not stupid; it is merely irrelevant. The emotional content of the music subsumes the denotative value of the lyrics. Thus the logical disconnection between the emotion and the words supports the general worldview of *Glee*.

Eventually, Abed becomes aware that such uncritical, musical interludes are untenable and destructive to the study group and their identities precipitated on the eventual return to the world outside of school. He realizes he must end the study group's transformation into the glee club by ruining the Christmas Pageant. To do this, he tells Britta to take a central role in the performance. When she doesn't know the lyrics, he responds that the lyrics are in her heart. Infected by glee, she embraces the tautology and improvises her awkward little song. Music does not flow through her. The degeneration of language and the allusion to situational prostitution in her lyrics make the song uncomfortable to listen to. Mr. Radisson is infuriated because their chance of going to regionals is over. Losing control, he spontaneously confesses he staged the bus crash that killed the last club because they were unwilling to take the steps necessary to win. Vicious ambition underneath the supposed joy of music is revealed.

Mr. Radisson's true and tacit confession is the revelation that he is an agent of the cynical and plotting world of *Community*. The communicability of music is unable to create community. During the last scene, *Community* frees itself from the infection of *Glee*. Complex individuality returns as the power of music dissipates. The emancipation from the glee club points towards the ethical superiority of *Community*. The seeming victory of this worldview is bittered when the celebration lulls and the impact of the glee club director's actions sinks in. The episode ends with the group joining Abed in his apartment. The group reconciles as they watch a terrible Christmas special of Abed's favorite show. Instead of recoiling, they embrace their opportunity to ridicule something else. Their disdain and their criticism are joyous. But much like their disdain of *Glee*, it reveals the instability of themselves, their selves, signifying the inherent queerness of ridicule and parody.

Notes

1. These episodes include "Regional Holiday Music," "Paradigms of Human Memory," "Modern Warfare," and "Biology 101."
2. This is a crucial role because in directing the glee club Mr. Schuester influences the actions of everyone in the show.
3. Kurt Hummel and Blaine Anderson, and Finn Hudson and Rachel Berry engage in relationships that strive for normative stability
4. In this context, the word is being used to indicate strangeness and non-normativity.
5. This aspect of the show is best represented by the character of Jeff Winger, a disbarred lawyer, who is trying to get the college credits he needs to practice law again.
6. This simulated Oedipal exchange is internal to the narrative and does not affect the overall external pre–Oedipal mode of the narrative.
7. The same is true for Greendale's glee club.
8. The audience could add that the study group also lacks gay, lesbian, or bisexual members despite Pierce Hawthorne indicating that Jeff Winger's narcissism queers him.
9. Sue Sylvester makes a similar feint in the "Original Song" episode of *Glee*.
10. By logically and musically targeting obvious character traits, these songs threaten identity by appealing to identity. Troy's childlike enthusiasm is turned against his religious devotion in "Jehovah's Secret Witness." Pierce Hawthorne's Baby Boomer narcissism is played against him in "Baby Boomer Santa." Jeff Winger's sexual vanity is used against him as the ingénue Annie lyrically seduces him with the song "Teach Me to Understand Christmas." Shirley's evangelical Christianity is manipulated by the song "Happy Birthday Jesus."
11. The study group first replaces the glee club in a clip from the episode "Paradigms of Human Memory."
12. Troy's religion prohibits him from celebrating Christmas.
13. Her naiveté in the Christmas song originates from two sources. The first source is her sexual innocence. The second is her Judaism. Much like Troy, she rejects her religious obligations and norms to sing Christmas carols.
14. The one woman who escapes such musical degradation is Shirley. Perhaps as the only African American woman she is allowed to forgo the dismissive script so that the show can avoid the complicated power relations in the interplay of race and gender.
15. The inherent sexuality of this line echoes the line "Me so horny" from Stanley Kubrick's film *Full Metal Jacket*.
16. In this scene, Rachel and Emma preserve their virginity despite the seductions of Jesse and Will. However, Finn succumbs to Santana.

References

Baudrillard, Jean. "Transsexuality." *The Transparency of Evil: Essays on Extreme Phenomena*. Trans. James Benedict. New York: Verso, 2002. 23. Print.
_____. "Value's Last Tango." *Simulacra and Simulations*. Trans. Sheila Faria Glaser. Ann Arbor: University of Michigan Press, 1994: 155–157. Print.
"Biology 101." *Community*. By Garrett Donovan and Neil Goldman. Dir. Anthony Russo. NBC. 22 Sep. 2011. Television.
Blanchot, Maurice. "Reading." *The Station Hill Blanchot Reader*. Ed. George Quasha. Trans. Lydia Davis. Barrytown, NY: Station Hill, 1999. Print.
Deleuze, Gilles. *Difference and Repetition*. 1968. Trans. Paul Patton. Reprint, New York: Columbia University Press, 1994. Print.
Halberstam, Judith. *In a Queer Time and Place: Transgender Bodies, Subcultural Lives*. New York: New York University Press, 2005. Print.

_____. *The Queer Art of Failure*. Durham: Duke University Press, 2011. Print.

Horton, Andrew. *Comedy/Cinema/Theory*. Berkeley: University of California Press, 1991. Print.

"I Am Unicorn." *Glee*. By Ryan Murphy. Dir. Brad Falchuk. Fox. 27 Sep. 2011. Television.

"Modern Warfare." *Community*. By Emily Cutler. Dir. Justin Lin. NBC. 6 May 2010. Television. "Original Song." *Glee*. By Ryan Murphy. Dir. Bradley Buecker. Fox. 15 Mar. 2011. Television. "Paradigms of Human Memory." *Community*. By Chris McKenna. Dir. Tristram Shapeero. NBC. 21 Apr. 2011. Television.

"The Power of Madonna." By Ryan Murphy. Dir. Ryan Murphy. *Glee*. Fox. 20 Apr. 2010. Television.

"Regional Holiday Music." *Community*. By Steve Basilone and Annie Mebane. Dir. Tristram Shapeero. NBC. 8 Dec. 2011. Television.

"Rocky Horror Glee Show." By Ryan Murphy and Tim Wollaston. Dir. Adam Shankman. *Glee*. Fox. 26 Oct. 2010. Television.

"Sexy." *Glee*. By Brad Falchuk. Dir. Ryan Murphy. Fox. 8 Mar. 2011. Television.

"Everything is Klaine and nothing hurts"

Klaine Fandom and Explorations of Teen Sexuality by Female Fanfiction Writers

EMILY HAMILTON-HONEY
and AMY PATRICK

On November 9, 2010, *Glee* aired the sixth episode of its second season, titled "Never Been Kissed." In the episode, openly gay McKinley High glee club member Kurt Hummel, played by Chris Colfer, is sent to spy on the Dalton Academy Warblers, a rival group to McKinley's New Directions. While searching around Dalton for the Warblers, Kurt happens to run into a boy on the stairs, Blaine Anderson (played by Darren Criss), who promptly leads him to the Warblers' "impromptu performance in the senior commons." As Blaine pulls Kurt into the room, he adjusts Kurt's shirt collar, gives him a cheeky wink, and cheerfully takes up the lead in the Warblers' song, much to Kurt's astonishment.

Thus, a new couple and a new fandom were born: Kurt and Blaine, known affectionately the world over as "Klaine." Kurt had already won a large following among *Glee* fans as a sharp-tongued yet vulnerable gay student in a homophobic Midwestern town, and with the addition of Blaine, *Glee* writers added a whole new dimension to the show's exploration of gay teens. While homophobia and bullying had been a central part of Kurt's storyline from the beginning, in Season 2 of the show those problems escalated, as Kurt received physical abuse and death threats from classmate Dave Karofsky. When Kurt meets Blaine in "Never Been Kissed," he discovers that Dalton's lead singer has also experienced bullying for being gay, and the pair of them become friends through sharing their struggles. As their friendship slowly evolves into romance, Kurt and Blaine develop a committed, caring relationship that helps them weather both internal and external hurdles on their road to adulthood.

The Klaine fandom is vast, covering many websites and all kinds of media, including fiction, original artwork, digital images, and videos. Klaine fans, known in fandom as "Klainers," are also a vocal group, doing a great deal to promote non-profits like The Trevor Project, which runs a 24-hour suicide and counseling hotline for LGBTQ teens. Most recently, two fans on Tumblr known as Teej and Heather took it upon themselves to raise money for Project Angel Food, a Los Angeles charity that makes and delivers meals to individuals and families living with HIV/AIDS and other life-threatening illnesses. Project Angel Food was auctioning off the script of Episode 3.09, "Extraordinary Merry Christmas," which contained a Klaine gift-giving scene that ended up on the cutting room floor. Fans have been insatiably curious about what was contained in the missing scene. If enough money was raised to win the script, Teej and Heather promised a PDF file of the script to any Klaine fans that donated $25 or more. The Klaine Fandom Charity Giveaway, also known around the fandom as "The Box Scene Project," won the script and raised a total of $14,000 for Project Angel Food.

As another measure of the size of the Klaine fandom, as of October 18, 2012, there were 20,367 Klaine stories in 22 languages filed on Fan-Fiction.net, one of the largest internet clearinghouses for fan-created stories. Fiction is one of the major mediums for Klaine fans, allowing them to pay tribute to the on-screen couple, dispel homophobia, and explore many aspects of sexuality. Fanfiction allows the young authors to have both ways to self-express and a place to engage with other young writers exploring many of the same questions and identity issues. All the writers who come into the various avenues of Klaine fanfiction begin to find answers and support. In the seminal book *Textual Poachers*, Henry Jenkins talks about fanfiction as a place where a "dialogue about the politics of sexuality may be conducted, and created opportunities where the social construction of gender may be explored with greater openness and self-consciousness" (221), and even though the book was written in 1992, it is an accurate description of the safe space that fanfiction still provides and the issues that Klaine fanfiction writers grapple with currently. Like many of the other fanfiction portals, the Klaine stories rely on a strong homosexual current, but what makes the Klaine stories more interesting is the fact that the characters are homosexual on their show. The layer of homosexual fantasy utilized by writers from previous fanfiction portals is gone from Klaine fandom, but because the writers are looking less at subtext and more at text, their explorations become more interesting.

Many Klaine fandom writers acknowledge a sexual attraction to Kurt and Blaine, and writing about the on-screen couple allows them to explore what they want in a relationship, both emotionally and sexually. Female writers in particular seem to utilize Kurt and Blaine in this way; girls can use gay crushes as a way to safely understand their own desires and wants. As fictional characters, Kurt and Blaine are a conduit for the female writers to explore their feelings in an even "safer" way than a real-life crush. Crushing on gay teen boys in real life still carries the danger of getting emotionally hurt and carries guilt with it. In fandom, that danger of emotional or sexual hurt involved with a gay male-female crush is completely removed— a girl fan can love and admire Kurt and Blaine freely, explore her own sexuality, and know that she is neither going to get hurt nor hurt them.

In addition, Klaine fandom functions as a venue for the distribution of knowledge about various kinds of sexual activity. Like any large fandom, the quality of the information is sometimes suspect, but many Klaine writers take seriously the idea that teens need access to safe, accurate information about all kinds of sex, and they make a point of providing those facts in their fiction. If the teen female writers have been led to educational sources about sexual practices, they share those sources with their readers. Due to the level of honesty that the writers of *Glee* engage in about Kurt and Blaine's relationship, the fanfiction writers have a jumping off point that lets them look into sexual health and safety in conjunction with exploring sexual fantasy.

By acknowledging the needs for this kind of information and by openly sharing it, writers remove any self-consciousness readers may have about their own ignorance and curiosity. Fandom becomes a comfortable, semi-anonymous space for education and information exchange. These two poles of fanfiction become a place where a young female can learn more about her own sexuality and also begin to understand sexuality in the more abstract sense of education and knowledge about a variety of sexual behaviors and attitudes. The fans are able to traffic in their own "cultural economy" of creativity and in the sharing and trading of their knowledge to inform the other writers as well (Fiske 30). These young, female fanfiction writers are able to use Klaine fandom to learn more about themselves emotionally and physically while improving their writing abilities, engaging in friendships, and debating important topics.

One of the most striking traits of Klaine fanfiction is the forthright-ness with which the writers talk about the boys' relationship, their emo-tions, their desires, and even their sexual activity. After reviewing quite a number of stories, we felt that this openness was stemming from two sources: (1) Many of the writers of *Glee* fan fiction are younger than the average fan fiction writer, even when you add in the ages at the higher end of the spectrum. Most writers appear to be between the ages of 15 and 35, and this appears to affect the explicitness with which they write and their ease with more graphic gay content. (2) Since Kurt and Blaine's rela-tionship is already established canon on *Glee*, the fan writers do not have to do the work to make the boys' relationship plausible. In many cases of "slash" fandom writing, the relationships involved are pure speculation or are occasionally hinted at in canonical subtext. Thus, fan writers have to establish homosexual desires between particular characters as real, legit-imate, and possible, which can sometimes be the entire aim and content of a story. A good example of this is in the various iterations of the Sherlock Holmes fandom, in which establishing a sexual or romantic relationship between Holmes and Watson is tricky at best, given that the original char-acters were living in Victorian London. *Star Trek* and *Star Trek: The Next Generation* have also used the friendships between male characters (Kirk/Spock, Picard/Riker) to explore queer desire with as much contort-ing, even though the shows themselves take place in a world where all dif-ferences over sexual orientation have been reconciled. There are only small textual hints at any personal intimacy between any of these male pairs; fandom writers take those hints and try to create a framework for a romantic relationship.

For Kurt and Blaine, however, this problem has been erased. When Blaine is introduced in Season 2, it is made clear that he is gay, and he and Kurt quickly become close friends and progress into boyfriends. The boys *are* gay, *are* in love, and *are* together; that much is a *fait accompli*. The romantic and sexual content already exists in the show. In one sense, this takes away one of a fandom writer's tools; they don't need to establish a relationship where one is already established. In another sense, however, this seems to give writers a new point of departure. Kurt and Blaine are together and happy, which allows writers to delve into all of the cultural baggage that comes *with* a gay relationship and/or being openly gay: bul-lying, homophobia, parental rejection, domestic and familial abuse, loss of civil rights, self-esteem problems, and struggles with self-harm. Although Kurt and Blaine's relationship is functional and beautiful, there are many external cultural forces putting pressure on it and attempting to code their love as deviant or abnormal.

For example, in the story "Help" by a writer with the pseudonym katiek723, several of these issues are addressed in the plot. Just as Kurt and Blaine's friendship is warming up to a relationship in Season 2, Blaine is date-raped by an acquaintance and turns to Kurt's family for help. Over the course of the story, Kurt discovers that not only has Blaine been bullied at school, but also he has been living with parents who hate him for his sexual orientation and actively work to destroy his self-esteem. While living through the aftermath of the rape, Blaine also struggles to come to terms with his neglectful and emotionally abusive parents. Kurt, Kurt's father Burt Hummel, and Blaine's brother Cooper become the bulwarks against which Blaine rebuilds his life and sense of self. The continuous support that Blaine receives from his boyfriend, his brother, and others shows readers that it is possible to recover from physical and emotional abuse.

In something of a reversal, "Sketchy Relations" by female writer xxPandaLawlsxx has Kurt transferring to Dalton Academy after being sexually assaulted by a classmate at his public high school. Although Kurt does his best to keep his past a secret from his new friends, they gradually unravel his story on their own and offer him their own personal stories as a method of gaining his trust and friendship. Blaine opens up about his own experiences with bullying. Classmate Nick tells Kurt about being physically abused by his alcoholic father before he was sent to foster care and eventually to Dalton. In addition, Nick is in his own relationship with Jeff, and the pair serves as friends and positive role models for Kurt. All three boys are in the Warblers, and the group itself fosters Kurt's singing talent and gives him a cohesive social group to belong to. Thus, in this story, several negative social problems and positive social developments are addressed simultaneously: sexual assault and recovery, alcoholism and parental abuse, positive reinforcement of self-esteem, the importance of having trusted friends, and healthy, communicative gay teen relationships.

Even when writers decide to change the canonical storyline and give Kurt and Blaine a different way of meeting than they did in *Glee*, as "Sketchy Relations" does, it usually doesn't take long for the two boys to become friends and/or discover their attraction to one another. That part of their relationship is easy; what *isn't* easy is negotiating the reactions of the rest of the world. Sometimes this involves recalcitrant or prejudiced parents, sometimes it involves hostile classmates, and sometimes outside forces enter the boys' world and threaten them. How the boys react to and learn to contend with the various types of hostility form an important and almost continuous undercurrent in most of the stories.

In a more extended example, "Road to Love," by a 19-year-old female writer calling herself just-a-silly-romantic, has Kurt and Blaine meeting when Blaine comes to work for Kurt's father as a mechanic's assistant. The two boys are attracted to one another immediately and spend some time dancing around each other as they try to gauge one another's interest and sexual orientation. Much of each character's background is the same as on the show: Kurt still goes to McKinley and is still being bullied by closeted classmate Dave Karofsky. Blaine is still the lead singer for the Dalton Academy Warblers, still was bullied and beaten by his public school classmates, still has a father who refuses to acknowledge his sexual orientation, and still gets sexually propositioned by a fellow Warbler named Sebastian Smythe. However, Dave, Sebastian, and Mr. Anderson are all dealt with differently in the author's universe; each of them is given a chance to reform their behavior and mend their relationships with Blaine and Kurt. In the process, each creates a particular message about acceptance, friendship, and trust.

In *Glee* itself, Dave Karofsky bullies Kurt from the start of the series, even going so far as to threaten him with death. Eventually, it is revealed that Dave is also closeted and highly confused about his sexuality. He and Kurt have a confrontation in the locker room that results in Dave kissing Kurt, and while Kurt is horrified by the boy's actions, he sympathizes with how trapped his tormentor feels. Eventually, Dave mends fences with Kurt and transfers high schools to try and get a new start, but he is inadvertently outed when a classmate sees him asking Kurt out on Valentine's Day. He is subjected to the same kind of bullying and harassment that he inflicted on Kurt, and he attempts suicide but luckily fails.

In "Road to Love," Dave's outing to the student body is accelerated when a student who runs a gossip blog overhears and films Dave and Kurt's confrontation in the locker room. Dave, terrified of the consequences of his outing, turns to Kurt and Blaine for help. In this case, both Dave and Kurt end up transferring to Dalton in order to be safe from physical and verbal harassment. Blaine takes Dave in as his roommate and introduces him to members of Dalton's football team, one of whom is openly gay. Dave still harbors feelings for Kurt, but he puts them aside in favor of cultivating the friendship of both boys and gratefully acknowledges and returns their attempts at forging a positive relationship with him. Dave becomes much more comfortable at Dalton, and although Kurt eventually returns to McKinley, it is implied that Dave stays at the more tolerant school, happier in an environment where he is free to be himself without fear of retribution.

In the original storyline of the show, Sebastian Smythe is a playboy. Good-looking and smooth-talking, he makes his attraction to Blaine clear at their first meeting. He also makes clear his disdain for Kurt and for anything resembling committed relationships. He has no problem attempting to split up the two committed teens, and he eventually becomes aggressive enough that he physically injures Blaine in an attempt to humiliate Kurt. It is not until Dave Karofsky's attempted suicide that Sebastian's more humane side begins to appear. Initially, in "Road to Love," Sebastian is much the same. He still makes sexual overtures to Blaine, although this time he combines them with insults and propositions to Kurt. He threatens to expose Dave Karofsky's feelings for Kurt. He makes sexual conquests of his other classmates. It isn't until he falls romantically for one of those conquests (nearly at the end of the story) that he works up the courage to make amends with Kurt and Blaine, apologizing for his actions and explaining that he was profoundly jealous of their happy relationship. Kurt and Blaine offer their forgiveness and friendship, bringing Sebastian into their circle of friends. Although he is initially selfish and self-centered, friends and love make it possible for Sebastian to change the way he thinks and operates in the world.

Finally, Blaine's father Mr. Anderson is addressed more extensively in "Road to Love" than he has yet been on *Glee* itself. While the canonical Blaine has admitted that his father does not accept his sexuality, even going so far as to try and make Blaine straight one summer by forcing them to fix a vintage care together, Mr. Anderson has not appeared on the show, and no further explanation has been offered for his homophobia. In "Road to Love," just-a-silly-romantic delves into this absent backstory and creates a much more profound reason for Mr. Anderson's anger and fear: the fate of his older brother.

Edward Anderson explains to Kurt's father that his older brother, Daniel, had been gay and felt obliged to hide it from everyone—his parents, his classmates, and even his brother, until one day Edward caught Daniel kissing his best friend, Jack. Edward, then a freshman in high school when Daniel was a senior, decided that he didn't care whether or not his brother liked boys and told him so. From then on, he was the only one who knew Daniel's secret besides Jack.

However, one day Jack had his schoolbag rifled through by some bullies, and they found an unsigned note that Daniel had written him. The next day it was all over school that Jack was gay, and although Daniel defended him, the abuse to Jack escalated. He disappeared one morning and was found in the river two days later, with three stab wounds and a fractured skull. Daniel subsequently hanged himself in his bedroom.

Explained this way, Edward Anderson's apprehension and hostility toward Blaine's sexual orientation is not as simple as prejudice or homophobia. In fact, it is based in tragedy and fear: fear that what happened to

Daniel and Jack will someday happen to Blaine, that Edward's son will eventually be beaten, killed, or kill himself through the hatred of others. Edward has already had a terrifying experience regarding Blaine: when Blaine and a gay friend of his went to a public school dance together, some of their classmates beat them "half to death," leaving them both hospitalized. Edward is petrified that the next time, Blaine will be taken from him, as his brother was.

Through some firm and compassionate conversation, Burt Hummel is able to make Edward see that Blaine's happiness should be his first priority, that the world is slowly changing for the better. Kurt and Blaine have the chance to lead happy lives as they go to college together. Away from Lima and in the much larger city of New York, the two boys can be themselves without fear. Just-a-silly-romantic takes what could have been a simplistic narrative and turns it into a much more complex story, showing the progress from past to present and the hope for the future.

By creating the narrative possibility for redemption even in the most unlikable characters, and by drawing attention to issues like bullying, self-harm, parental neglect, sexual abuse, and social indifference, *Glee* fanfiction writers actively attempt to create social change through their fiction. The stories become outwardly focused, using Kurt and Blaine as a conduit to let readers know that there are others who experience the same problems they do, and to encourage those same readers to promote love and tolerance in all areas of their lives. The fanfiction becomes much more textual and analytical than some of the other standard slash fiction. The stripping away of the "forbidden fruit" aspect of the content allows the writers to explore topics that stretch the bounds of fanfiction and fan communities in general. The activist nature of the fanfiction moves the community away from simple adoration and into something more nuanced, almost like a collective that exchanges information, stories, and advocacy.

Promoting love is also very much a part of the romance and sex in Klaine fanfiction stories. In much of (heterosexual) fanfiction, romance and sexuality are separate issues even for the same paired couple, and different writers tackle one or the other. Although when most people think about fanfiction and fan communities, the dominant tone is homosexual themed, there are exceptions. Probably one of the most segregated "romance" versus "sex" contingencies that featured an explicit heterosexuality was the fan community of the 1980s television program *Beauty and the Beast*. The community became active almost with the first episode of the program. The community had around 50 fan clubs and 90 active zines and newsletters that focused on the romance inherent in the storylines. The zines themselves were split between erotic sexual fiction and that of a more romantic flair (Jenkins 140–141). In the majority of Kurt and Blaine fanfiction, on the other hand, writers intertwine the two concepts of romance and sex, exploring both aspects of the boys' relationship in the same story. The physical expression of their affection and love for one another becomes an integral part of their emotional development.

There are several possible reasons why sex and love are so interconnected in Klaine stories. The first is that sexual activity becomes a way of reaffirming the validity of the boys' gay relationship and their feelings for one another. On *Glee* itself, Kurt and Blaine are one of the two most stable couples on the show. Except for Mike Chang and Tina Cohen-Chang, the other members of New Directions are constantly switching partners and cheating on one another with their classmates. Kurt and Blaine, on the other hand, have thus far stayed with each other, working together through several moments of jealousy, insecurity, and attention from other potential boyfriends. They are, from the start, given a relationship that is more committed and communicative than the other relationships around them. By the same token, when Kurt and Blaine make love for the first time in Episode 3.05 (aptly titled "The First Time"), their discussion of intimacy and their decision to move forward with their relationship is given just as much examination and screen time as the same discussion and decision between Finn Hudson and Rachel Berry, the show's most popular straight couple. In some ways, the discussion between Kurt and Blaine is infinitely more poignant. As two boys who have been verbally and physically harassed and beaten for their sexual orientation, finding someone to love who can also love them back is something to be cherished. For them, having sex is about a larger commitment to each other. By making sex an act of love, Kurt and Blaine's relationship is verified as just as loving and legitimate—and perhaps *more* loving and legitimate—than a heterosexual relationship.

Also, it is possible that Klaine fanfiction writers are using their favorite couple as an avenue for wish fulfillment, particularly given the young age of some of the writers. They may believe that sex and love *should*, in an ideal world, always go together. They give Kurt and Blaine the kind of romance that they wish for in their own relationships. The writers are able to weave together romance and sexuality in a way that is different than much of slash and heterosexual fiction. Even when the boys do not begin a story as a couple, or when their relationship begins with physical rather than emotional intimacy, the emotional side of their relationship is always there, waiting to be developed, acknowledged, and brought into the open. Sometimes the emotions enter the story before physical affection, and sometimes it is the other way around, but no matter how Kurt and Blaine meet and become friends and boyfriends, writers almost always make clear their emotional connection along with their physical attraction.

In "Taking Chances" by female writer anxioussquirrel, Kurt and Blaine connect on an emotional level long before they become friends and then boyfriends. The backgrounds of both Kurt and Blaine are quite different from their history in the show. At McKinley, Kurt is a junior, but instead of being out and proud, he is closeted and popular, a head cheerleader who is feared and envied by the student body. He is also dating his female co-captain, Quinn Fabray. However, he notices Blaine in the halls. While Blaine's history at public school and Dalton is the same as in the show, he transfers to McKinley as a junior because his family cannot pay the Dalton tuition. Blaine has been pegged as a nerd for his colorful clothes, glasses, and high grades, and he suffers even more because he is openly gay. He is subjected to the same kind of bullying Kurt used to endure from the jocks: shoving, slushies, name calling, dumpster tosses, and verbal harassment. Though Kurt knows that being seen with Blaine would undo all of the work he has done to get on top of the school social ladder, he is intrigued:

> [T]here's something about Blaine that resonates within Kurt, though he wouldn't admit it to anyone. Being out and proud in high school requires insane amounts of courage—and doesn't come without a price. Sometimes, in the darkest night hours Kurt imagines being so courageous. Coming out to his dad and his friends instead of hiding it like the most shameful secret. Not pretending anymore. Being who he is. But then he remembers the cost of such freedom. Whenever he sees Blaine slushied or pushed into lockers, or tripped in the cafeteria during lunch—which happens all too often—Kurt's mind flashes back to the past he wants to forget ... whenever he looks at Blaine, he can't help but think, over and over again: *It could have been me* [emphasis in original].

Kurt identifies with Blaine, in this story, before he has ever met him. He understands what it is like to be bullied and tormented, though he has done everything he can since his middle school years to avoid that fate. He knows what it means to be gay in Lima and at McKinley, which is precisely the reason he is still in the closet. He empathizes with Blaine, and it is that empathy as well as curiosity and a desire for friendship that drive him to seek out Blaine.

When his history teacher assigns a partnered essay, Kurt asks Blaine to be his project partner in order to spend more time with him. The two of them form a close friendship that slowly builds into romance. Blaine proves to be understanding and compassionate about Kurt's fears and insecurities, someone to whom Kurt can show his true self without being judged. Blaine is the first person to whom Kurt reveals his sexual orientation, and while Blaine is completely supportive and caring, he is also unflinchingly honest about what he perceives to be the consequences of Kurt's dishonesty. Kurt is repressing parts of himself in order to fit in, he is unhappy that he hasn't told his father he is gay, and he is potentially hurting Quinn by being with her when he doesn't love her. Blaine forces Kurt to acknowledge that the façade he has created in order to survive McKinley might protect him from the worst of the bullying, but it is also suffocating him. As Kurt develops romantic feelings for Blaine, he finds that he is less and less able to hide who he really is, from himself or anyone else. His friendship with Blaine gives Kurt the strength to be honest about himself. That same friendship and honesty provide a strong foundation for a lasting romance.

"Take Off Your Colours" by fifteen-year-old female captain-ally places Kurt in an entirely different position at McKinley: he becomes the school's resident bad boy. Unlike the show's canon, a heart attack takes Burt Hummel's life a few months before Kurt's senior year, leaving Kurt on his own except for his stepmother Carole and his stepbrother Finn. Kurt no longer lives at home; he has his own apartment. He is a loner with tattoos on his wrists and ear and nose piercings. He is not at the top of the social ladder by any means, but he has managed to make people fear him, and he keeps the jocks' harassment to a minimum by making himself sexually (though not emotionally) available to them.

Blaine's backstory is also different in this tale. Blaine has become the brother of Rachel Berry, one of the leads of New Directions. He transfers to McKinley as a senior because his gay fathers (Rachel's adoptive parents on *Glee*, and here Blaine's parents as well) cannot afford to send him to Dalton for his last year. Blaine almost immediately becomes a bullying target for Dave Karofsky, but Kurt intervenes on Blaine's first day at school, getting the football player to back off. Blaine is immediately taken with what he sees: "[H]e was so enraptured by the face in front of him. It was exquisite. There was not a single blemish on the porcelain skin and the full lips were quirked into a smirk. He was an angel.... Kurt Hummel was the living manifestation of every fantasy and feeling of sexual desire he'd ever had before in his life. If he didn't know better, he'd say it was love at first sight." Blaine is overwhelmingly physically attracted to Kurt and intrigued by the boy who seems to push everyone away.

Though Blaine doesn't know Kurt, he feels drawn to his rescuer, and not only because he finds Kurt beautiful. He is determined to be let inside Kurt's walls. Blaine wants to be someone that Kurt can trust, and he knows that after losing both his parents and being bullied for a great deal of his school life, trust does not come easily to Kurt. When the boys spend a night out dancing and kissing, and Kurt ignores Blaine the next day at school, Blaine confronts Kurt about his fears:

> "Kurt, whether you like it or not, there's something between us. You can't deny it, or write it off as a one night stand because there's someone involved in this apart from you! You're not used to that, are you?" Kurt's eyes blazed and Blaine knew he'd hit a raw nerve. "You're not used to there being two people involved in something you start. You're used to being used and dumped. Well, guess what, Kurt? I'm not like those guys. And neither are you." ...
>
> "You don't know me!" Kurt shrieked, voice tearing through surprisingly high octaves in his rage. "Get that into your head. Tell me one thing you know about me!"
>
> Blaine didn't even stop to think. "You're a better person than you think you are."

What begins as physical attraction for Kurt and Blaine rapidly develops into an emotional connection; Kurt feels more than just lust for Blaine, and Blaine has wanted friendship and love from Kurt from the beginning. Blaine is determined to show Kurt that the person he hides from the world is worthy of being loved, and eventually, thanks to Blaine, Kurt comes to love himself again and show his real self to the rest of the world. He even acknowledges that his change of heart is thanks to Blaine: "'It feels good to be back to normal. No more hiding or pretending or putting up barriers. And it's all thanks to you.' Kurt's voice thickened with emotion and for once, he didn't swallow it away. His eyes bore into Blaine's, shining with unshed tears. 'I don't think you realize, but you saved me.'" Kurt and Blaine give strength and hope to each other by loving one another, despite the prejudice surrounding them for being gay. The stability, trust, and friendship that are such integral parts of their relationship are used by fanfiction writers to demonstrate that love between same-sex couples is just as passionate and fulfilling as love between heterosexual couples. Kurt and Blaine become the epitome of true love; they are best friends who fall in love and stay in love, despite all obstacles.

Glee has now been on television for three years. From almost the beginning, the fan community has been vocal and active in a variety of ways. The fanfiction community, like that of many other television programs, has many separate factions and engages in debates about what is canon. Fandom members disseminate their fiction on a variety of online portals for the enjoyment of other fans and to engage in debate about the material. Like many fan communities, they do "what even the most committed single fan cannot: accumulate, retain, and continually recirculate unprecedented amounts of relevant information" (Baym 118). However, what makes *Glee* fans a little different than most is that beyond the show, the information and knowledge they aggregate relates to larger issues in society, issues that are both directly and indirectly related to the show and their fandom.

The material that *Glee* fanfiction writers compile and discuss becomes more complex and issue-oriented because one tool in the fanfiction arsenal has been eliminated. The gay content is not subtext but in the text and canonical to the show. Many fanfiction communities rely on creating a subtext where male lead characters move from friendship to romance. Within the *Glee* community of writers, that first step is eliminated. The content of *Glee* fanfiction can take on more explicit sexuality and also more complicated plotting. By being able to skip the arduous process of courtship that many pieces of fanfiction engage in, the stories take on a dimensionality that is more complicated than most fanfiction. The stories begin to address problems that can be common in the LGBTQ youth community, such as bullying, abuse, and homelessness, and writers use their stories to open discussions and answer questions other fans might need to be answered.

The Klaine fandom represents an exciting new ground in the world of fan fiction. The majority of the fans are a little younger than members of other fandoms, and, because of their age, they come with more media savvy. These fans bring their wealth of media knowledge to their stories to examine more complex aspects of the human experience. The newness and youth of the community is a large part of why much of the fanfiction is so different from that of other fanfiction communities. Many of the Klaine fans and writers have lived in a culture where homosexuality has been mainstreamed, if not always accepted. By using fan fiction to explore other social issues alongside sexual preference and identity, Klaine fans are changing some of the standards of fanfiction communities. Klaine fanfiction writers are advocating for more acceptance and awareness through their inquiring, compassionate, and insightful discussions of love, romance, sexual orientation, and social injustices surrounding teens.

References

anxioussquirrel. "Taking Chances." *FanFiction.Net.* n. p., 19 Sept. 2012. Web. 18 Oct. 2012.

Baym, Nancy. "Talking About Soaps: Communicative Practices in a Computer-Mediated Fan Culture." *Theorizing Fandom: Fans, Subculture, and Identity.* Ed. Cheryl Harris and Alison Alexander. Cresskill, NJ: Hampton Press, 1998. 111–129. Print.

The Box Scene Project. Web. 19 Oct. 2012. theboxsceneproject.org.

captain-ally. "Take Off Your Colours." *FanFiction.Net.* n. p., 19 Sept. 2012. Web. 18 Oct. 2012.

"Extraordinary Merry Christmas." *Glee: The Complete Third Season*. Prod. Ryan Murphy, Ian Brennan, and Brad Falchuk. Writ. Marti Noxon. Dir. Matthew Morrison. Twentieth Century–Fox, 2012. DVD.

"The First Time." *Glee: The Complete Third Season*. Prod. Ryan Murphy, Ian Brennan, and Brad Falchuk. Writ. Roberto Aguirre-Sacasa. Dir. Bradley Buecker. Twentieth Century–Fox, 2012. DVD.

Fiske, Jon. "The Cultural Economy of Fandom." *The Adoring Audience: Fan Culture and Popular Media*. Ed. Lisa A. Lewis. New York: Routledge, 1992. 30–49. Print.

katiek723. "Help." *FanFiction.Net*. n. p., 19 Sept. 2012. Web. 18 Oct. 2012.

Jenkins, Henry. *Textual Poachers: Television Fans and Participatory Culture*. New York: Routledge, 1992. Print.

"Never Been Kissed." *Glee: The Complete Second Season*. Prod. Ryan Murphy, Ian Brennan, and Brad Falchuk. Dir. Bradley Buecker. Twentieth Century–Fox, 2011. DVD.

just-a-silly-romantic. "Road to Love." *FanFiction.Net*. n. p., 19 Sept. 2012. Web. 18 Oct. 2012.

xxPandaLawlsxx [Pseud.]. "Sketchy Relations." *FanFiction.Net*. n. p., 19 Sept. 2012. Web. 18 Oct. 2012.

About the Contributors

Sheryl Lyn **Bundy** teaches creative writing, composition and literature at Moraine Valley Community College in Palos Hills, Illinois, where she also serves as co-director of the Speaking & Writing Center. She has presented papers on collaborative teaching in the college classroom and on methods for the assessment of student writing.

Kasey **Butcher** is a Ph.D. student in English literature at Miami University where she studies girlhood and nationalism in twentieth-century literature and culture. She also teaches first-year writing classes, focusing on rhetoric and critical media literacy.

Anita M. **DeRouen** joined the Millsaps College faculty as director of writing and teaching and assistant professor of English after completing a Ph.D. at the University of Georgia. Her teaching and scholarship coalesce around issues of rhetoric, media studies, and racial identity formation.

Melissa **Esh** is a Ph.D. student in American studies at Purdue University. Her dissertation focuses on sexualities education in Indiana elementary schools. She co-wrote an essay on male adolescent identity crises in young adult graphic novels and is researching sex education trade books for young girls and the nature of good and evil in Stephen King.

Christine L. **Ferguson** holds a master's degree in advanced studies in American media and popular culture from Arizona State University. Her interests include representations of masculinities in the films of Tim Burton, women in science fiction, and representations of feminine desire and friendship in television and film.

Barrie **Gelles** is a fellowship student in the Ph.D. program in theatre at the Graduate Center at CUNY. Her scholarly areas of interests include

269

American musical theatre, theories of acting and directing in training and practice, and the interrelation of Jewish studies with theatre studies.

M. Shane **Grant** is a visiting assistant professor in the Department of Theatre at Millsaps College in Jackson, Mississippi, where he teaches classes on performance, theatre history, and dramatic criticism. His dissertation examined how recent mainstream representations of gay men simultaneously contain rhetorics of assimilationism and queer rebellion.

Emily **Hamilton-Honey** is an assistant professor of English and humanities at SUNY Canton. Her book, *From Spiritual Guides to Eager Consumers: American Girls' Series Fiction, 1865–1930*, was released by McFarland in 2013. Other research interests include *Harry Potter*, Louisa May Alcott, and Sherlock Holmes.

Tracy L. **Hawkins** earned a Ph.D. in women's studies and religion from Claremont Graduate University in 2011. Her work focuses on the formation of identity, gender, and sexuality in religion, in popular culture, and in social networking technologies.

Nicholas Alexander **Hayes** is an instructor at DePaul University's School for New Learning. He has taught courses in queer literature at Columbia College Chicago and gender representations and is the author of *NIV: 39 & 27* (2009) and *Metastaesthetics* (2012).

Rebekah **Lobosco**, a University of Toronto musicology Ph.D. student, investigates how the performance of femininity intersects with fictional representations of cyborg technology. She has presented papers at the Tufts's Women's Center Symposium on Gender and Culture and the International Association for the Study of Popular Music.

Erin Kathleen **Marshall** is a librarian with the American Theological Library Association in Chicago, with an interest in queer theory and how religion is portrayed in American media.

Jane B. **Meek** is an instructor of composition and rhetoric at the University of Mississippi. Her published research has focused on social movements, LGBTQ youth culture and queer pedagogy, and her teaching often includes units on media literacy and gender theory.

Taylor Cole **Miller** is a doctoral student in media and cultural studies at the University of Wisconsin–Madison where his primary areas of interest are queer and feminist television and production studies and media reception studies. He is also a contributor to the *Huffington Post*.

Niall **Nance-Carroll** is a Ph.D. student at Illinois State University specializing in children's and adolescent literature. His research interests include A.A. Milne, *Glee*, narrative theory, the ethics of the prosaic, medieval literature, Old English, and Latin.

Michelle **Parke** is an assistant professor of English at Carroll Community College in Maryland and holds a Ph.D. from Michigan State University. Her work primarily focuses on issues of gender and sexuality in contemporary American literature and television. She has published pieces on *The Wire*, *CSI*, and the works of Edgar Allan Poe.

Amy **Patrick** earned an MA in liberal studies at Empire State College where she focused on popular culture, gender studies, race theory, and the psychology and history of fan communities. She also has an MS in information science from the Pratt Institute.

Benjamin **Phelps** is a master's degree candidate in educational studies at Tufts University. His research interests lie at the intersection of education and media, particularly popular television.

Rachel E. **Silverman** holds a Ph.D. from the University of South Florida and is an assistant professor of communication at Embry-Riddle Aeronautical University. Her research focuses on Jewish and LGBT identities in popular culture, women's health, and social justice pedagogy. She has published articles in *Sexuality and Culture*, *Health Communication* and the *Journal of Religion and Popular Culture*.

Meredith **Wiggins** is a Ph.D. student in literature at the University of Kansas, where she focuses on African American literature and disability studies. Her academic interests include African American literature, disability theory, queer literature, feminist and queer theory, popular culture studies, and twentieth century feminist drama.

Index

ABC Network 11
Abed Nadir (character) 245, 248–252
abject 74–75, 78
able-bodied 30, 32, 34, 64, 69, 75–76, 121
ableist 108, 116–117, 119–120, 122
abstinence education 150; abstinence-based programs 151; abstinence-only programs 130, 138, 144, 148, 150–151, 162, 165
"Acafellas" 29, 37
acceptance 8, 12, 17, 24, 36, 42, 44, 47–48, 63, 65–66, 94, 115, 128, 137, 142, 176, 187, 231, 239, 241, 260, 267
achievement 7, 27, 47, 187–190, 194–195, 197–198
activism 41, 43, 91, 99
Adele 32
Adler, Max 3, 48, 67, 79, 94–96, 199
adolescent 2, 7, 125, 127, 133–134, 146, 165, 188, 195, 197, 199, 201, 204–207, 211–214, 269–270; see also girls
African American 63, 66, 253
AfterEllen.com 35, 37, 85, 95
AFY_Abby (blogger name) 163, 165
agency 7, 19–21, 44–46, 76, 88, 158, 197, 200–201, 204, 207, 210–212, 231, 234–235, 238–239, 241
aggression 35, 160, 189, 194, 198
Agron, Dianna 3, 10, 94–96, 189
Aguilera, Christina 75
All in the Family 28, 36
Allan, Peter 178; see also The Boy from Oz
Ally McBeal 168
alpha (behavior) 188, 197, 239
Alptraum, Lux 33
Althaus-Reid, Marcella 98–99, 104–106
ambition 160, 187, 191–192, 197, 252
American Idol 215
Anglican 79

Anglos 78
Animaniacs 168
Annie Edison (character) 245, 250–251, 253
anti-gay bullying 48, 51, 126; see also gay bullying
"anti-homosexual" 97
anxioussquirrel (pseudonym) 264, 267
appropriation 174, 176, 207, 224
April Rhodes (character) 57, 67, 86, 96, 130, 161, 166, 192, 199
archetype 8, 28, 30, 36, 100
Archie Bunker (character) 28
Armstrong, Jennifer 43, 52
Artie Abrams (character) 3, 18, 20, 23, 59, 67, 69–72, 75, 107–111, 115, 118–123, 155, 203, 206, 225–226, 246
Artist, Jacob 4
"As If We Never Said Goodbye" 176–177, 181, 183
asexual 7, 78, 108–109, 113, 117, 138–139, 143, 145–149, 162
Asian 54, 58, 61, 63, 66–67, 69, 72, 74–75, 82, 126, 135, 146, 149, 241
assimilation 70, 88, 236, 270
atheism 97, 101, 104
Aubrey, Jennifer Stevens 153–154, 165
authenticity 14–15, 19, 31, 194, 203, 212, 214
awareness 51, 175, 241, 267

backlash 11, 31
Bad Girl 8, 230–232, 234–236
"Bad Reputation" 18, 23, 86, 94, 122–123, 159, 165, 211, 214
Bakhtin, Mikhail 131, 135
Balser, Erin 200
Barna Group 97, 105
"Basic Genealogy" 244

Baudrillard, Jean 246, 251, 253
Baym, Nancy 266–267
Baywatch 196
beards 20, 31
"Beautiful" 75
Beauty and the Beast 262
Becky Johnson (character) 3, 82, 116–120, 122–123, 193, 196, 199
Benoist, Melissa 4
Berger, John 94
Beth (character) 128, 130, 235–236
Beyoncé 87
Bible 39, 103
bi-bullying 36
bicuriousity 26, 35
bi-erasure 25–26, 36
Bierly, Mandi 163
biphobia 25–26, 35, 37
The Bird Cage 94
bisexuality 6, 24–30, 33–37, 49, 69, 133, 145, 150, 153, 253; *see also* sexualities
blackness 42, 55, 61–67
Blanchot, Maurice 248
Bloom, PJ 219
Blythe, Teresa 98
Bones 11
"Borderline" 221
"Born This Way" 20, 23, 49, 56, 67, 87, 94, 134–135, 149, 191, 199
boundaries 5, 97–99, 105, 120, 142, 146, 188, 201, 204, 219
The Boy from Oz 177–178
boyfriend 3, 25, 27, 33, 79–80, 91, 100, 118, 121, 123, 129, 159, 163, 193–195, 203, 212, 232, 234, 237–239, 241, 251, 258–259, 263–264
Breadstix 78, 84, 118, 121
Brennan, Ian 1, 9, 24, 33, 35–36
Britta Perry (character) 243, 251–252
Brittana 34
Brittany Pierce (character) 3–4, 18, 20–24, 26, 29–36, 39, 44, 52, 59, 64, 69, 72, 77, 81, 84, 91, 103, 110–111, 118, 121, 123, 126, 130, 150, 155, 157, 159–163, 190, 203, 209–212, 227, 235, 241, 249
Britzman, Deborah 48
Broadway 7, 9–10, 15, 167–168, 170–175, 177–179, 186–187, 190, 193
Brody Weston (character) 4
Brook, Vincent 52
Brothers and Sisters 11–12
Brown, Erin 152
Brown, James 233
Brown, Jane D. 152
Buber, Martin 244
Budgeon, Shelley 197, 199
Buecker, Bradley 10, 67, 95, 106, 165, 186, 242, 254, 268
Buffy the Vampire Slayer 8, 10–11, 94, 125, 168

bullying *see* anti-gay bullying; bi-bullying; cyberbullying; gay bullying
Burke, Kenneth 92, 95
Burt Hummel (character) 4, 32, 71, 128–129, 133, 163, 174, 176, 259, 262, 265
Butler, Judith 19, 23, 95

Callie Torres (character) 29
Calvin Owens (character) 12
Carl Howell (character) 143, 145
Carlson, Marvin 167–169, 186
Carmen Tibideaux (character) 60, 63, 178, 193
Carole Hudson-Hummel (character) 265
Cassandra July (character) 10*n*4
categories 6, 25, 28, 40, 42, 44, 46, 62, 66, 69–70, 73–75, 78, 139; *see also* identity
Catherine the Great 216
Caucasian 78
CBS Network 37
celibacy 100, 145, 152, 155–157, 162, 232, 252
character(s), gay 25, 28, 32, 76, 85, 88, 98, 102, 217, 220–221, 227, 239
characterization 5, 40, 51, 82, 101, 114, 125, 131, 138, 146, 170–171, 173, 175–176, 178–182, 230
chastity 114, 116
Cheerios 3, 29, 32, 72, 75, 82, 117–118, 196, 220, 222, 232, 236, 241
cheerleader 3, 24, 29, 32, 72, 76, 87, 91, 98, 101, 107, 114, 116, 121–122, 156–158, 161, 193, 195, 212, 220, 222, 247, 249, 264
Cher Horowitz (character) 94
Cho, Sumi 41, 46–47, 52
Christianity 6, 97–98, 100–106, 115, 253
Christmas 181, 183, 245, 250–253, 256, 268
church 100–102, 118
Cinderella 148
class (economic) 2, 42, 52, 74, 99, 126, 128, 153, 213
classroom 56, 90, 93, 118, 142, 162, 188–189, 195, 199, 202, 245–246, 249, 269
closet/closeted 3, 6, 13–14, 21, 24–27, 29–37, 44–46, 48–50, 71, 76–77, 79, 99, 104, 128, 134, 173, 198, 233–234, 260, 264; *see also* LGBT; sexualities
Clueless 94
Colfer, Chris 3, 10, 40, 61, 82–83, 94–96, 107, 135, 192, 255
colorblindness 41–42, 55, 62, 65
comedy 1, 42, 134, 158, 161, 215, 225, 243–246, 254
commodification 30, 56, 209
Community 8, 243–250, 252–254
competitiveness 4, 55, 58–59, 64, 66–67, 70, 72, 82, 84–85, 92, 101–102, 109, 168, 172, 174, 187, 189–192, 197–198
complexity 9–10, 44, 46, 48, 50, 76, 232

conformity 9, 12, 79, 99, 141, 193
Connell, Robert 94–95
conservativeness 32, 102, 125, 130, 151–152, 197, 208, 213, 236
contraception 156
contradictions 76, 81, 87, 108, 137, 187, 199, 206, 211, 231–232, 238
controversy 27, 36, 125, 165, 201
conversion 98, 243, 249
Cooke, Janice 23
Cooper Anderson (character) 238, 259
Cooter Mankins (character) 122
Corinna, Heather 212–214
The Cosby Show 132
"Cough Syrup" 104
Coulter, Anne 204
Crane, Betsy 231, 241
Crane-Seeber, Jesse 231, 241
Crenshaw, Kimberlé 42, 52, 60, 67
"crip drag" 107
Crip Theory: Cultural Signs of Queerness and Disability 108, 123
Criss, Darren 3, 51, 94–96, 191, 255
Critical Race Theory Matters: Education and Ideology 55
cyberbullying 232

Dalton Academy 3, 48–49, 80, 92, 233, 235, 255–256, 259–260, 264–265
Daniel Anderson (character) 261–262
Dave Karofsky (character) 3, 17–18, 20–22, 31, 48–50, 71–72, 78–80, 82, 89–92, 104, 128–129, 133–134, 157, 233, 256, 260–261, 265
Davies, Dominic 108, 121–122, 124
deconstruction 43, 105, 214–215, 228
de-integration 169
"Defying Gravity" 109, 168, 171–174, 176, 179, 183–186
DeGeneres, Ellen 11
Deleuze, Gilles 244, 253
desexualization 81
desirability 48, 50, 113, 119, 122, 147
destabilization 73, 108, 244–245
deviance 17, 27, 32, 36, 99, 258
diegesis 2, 30, 170–172, 176, 179–182, 185
difference/differences 3, 41–42, 48, 51–52, 56, 64, 66–67, 70–71, 73, 81, 86, 88–89, 93–94, 96, 99, 103, 146, 169–173, 185, 187–188, 198, 222–223, 226–227, 238, 250, 253, 258
Difference and Repetition 244
disability 1–2, 6, 67, 70–71, 73, 75–76, 81, 107–109, 112, 114–124, 129, 165, 196, 271
discourse 40, 45–46, 48–49, 51, 61, 90, 94, 154, 198, 206, 217–218
discrimination 40, 48, 51, 55, 65, 92, 172
disempowerment 45, 62, 205
Disney 227
disownment 33–34, 194

Disturbing the Universe 135–136
diva/Diva 1, 30, 65, 75, 85, 160, 172, 190, 229–230
diversity 6, 8, 11, 41–42, 52, 61, 64, 69–70, 76, 102, 130, 187, 218, 247
divinity 99
"Do You Wanna Touch Me? (Oh Yeah)" 155
"Docile Bodies" (Foucault) 76, 82
docility 70, 76, 78–79, 81, 196, 248
Dr. Frank-N-Furter (character) 54
Dr. Jekyll and Mr. Hyde 231
Donnerstein, Ed 152–153, 155, 166
Donovan, Garrett 253
Donovan, Tate 23, 242
"Don't Rain on My Parade" 180, 182–185, 193
doppelgängers 8, 229, 231, 233, 235, 237, 239, 241
Dow, Bonnie 90, 95
Down syndrome 3, 116, 119, 122–123, 196
Dreamgirls 58, 180, 182, 186
duality 176–177, 231, 238
Dude, Where's My Car? 250
duet 30, 84–85, 89, 93, 101, 111, 120, 176–177, 192, 221, 238
"Duets" 17, 23, 30, 85–86, 89–90, 95, 110–111, 121, 123
Dumb Blonde 229
Durham, M. Gigi 209, 214
Dynasty 29

Eagly, Alice 234
education 1, 7, 44, 46, 55–56, 61, 63, 65, 131, 137, 151, 153, 188, 212, 247, 257; *see also* abstinence; sex education
Eli Stone 168
Ellen 11, 23
Ellen Morgan (character) 11
Elpheba (character) 172–173
embodiment 120, 200, 210
Emerson, Caryl 126, 131, 135
Emma Pillsbury (character) 4, 7, 54, 58–59, 66–67, 127, 130, 138–148, 151–152, 162, 195–197, 201, 204–205, 207, 227, 244, 249, 251–253
Emmys 2
empowerment 5, 7–8, 12, 18, 21, 23, 45, 49, 122, 138, 144, 154, 158, 172, 201, 203, 207, 209–211, 216–223, 226–227
equality 40, 42, 51, 55, 94, 164, 188, 205, 217, 220, 225, 227
erasure, of bisexuality 6, 25–26, 28, 34, 36, 42, 44, 54, 64
Eric van der Woodsen (character) 12
Erotica 208
eroticism 113, 121, 203, 249, 251, 262
Etheridge, Melissa 30, 35, 110
ethics 7, 129, 131–133, 135, 151, 154, 157, 161–162, 164, 213, 252

ethnicity 2, 6, 30, 34, 42, 55, 65, 78, 153, 240
ethos 24, 35–36, 42, 243, 246–248
evangelicalism 97, 100–101, 103, 253
Evita 94, 176–177, 181–182
Evita (character) 94, 168, 177
expression, sexual 108, 120–121, 128, 209–210
"Extraordinary Merry Christmas" 256, 268
Eyal, Keren 132, 135

Faberry 193, 195
fag 36, 71, 78, 172
"fag" 129
"faggy" 71, 87, 133
failure 34, 42, 46, 55–56, 63, 65, 143–144, 146, 165, 175, 189, 192–193, 197, 246, 251
faith 100–101, 103, 130, 141, 157, 232–233
Faith, Karlene 218, 228
Falchuk, Brad 1, 9–10, 23–24, 33, 35–36, 67–68, 94–96, 106, 149, 166, 186, 199, 241–242, 254, 268
Fame 168, 182
family 14, 25, 27, 44, 47, 79, 98, 104, 122, 126–128, 132, 150, 175, 194, 239–241, 256, 259, 264
fandom 2, 8–9, 137, 255–258, 267
fanfiction 8, 255–258, 262–263, 266–267
fantasy 175, 192, 205, 208, 223–224, 244–245, 247, 252, 257, 265
Farber, Paul 201, 214
Farrimond, Katherine 232, 242
Fausto-Sterling, Anne 94–95
femininity 87, 94, 158, 187–189, 196–197, 220, 270
feminism 7, 95, 149, 188, 199, 209, 214, 216–218, 225–228, 242
feminist 33, 60, 67, 87, 91, 94, 106, 138–139, 151, 164, 208–209, 216–218, 220, 226, 228, 270–271
Ferguson, Anne Arnett 48, 52
Field, Sally 75
Fincher, David 231
Fink, Ashley 3, 94–96
Finn Hudson (character) 3–4, 15, 20, 23, 26, 29, 32–35, 44–46, 49–50, 52, 59, 62, 67, 69, 71–72, 76–78, 81, 84, 87, 91–92, 98, 100, 112–114, 117–118, 122, 126–129, 133, 147, 150–151, 155–156, 159, 161, 163, 174, 176, 190–193, 195, 205–206, 210–212, 221, 224, 232–233, 237, 251, 253, 263, 265
"Finnessa" 206, 225, 227
Finocchiaro, Peter 5, 10
Fiske, John 73, 82, 257, 268
Flandez, Raymund 85, 95
football 3–4, 18, 28, 71–72, 78, 87, 89–91, 98, 100, 112, 122, 128, 142–143, 172, 196, 247, 249, 260, 265
Foucault, Michel 76, 82, 94–95

Frankenstein 231
Franklin, Aretha 57
Freaks Talk Back 27, 37
Freedman, Jonathan 88, 95
Friends 11, 94
Full Metal Jacket 253
"Funeral" 87, 117–118, 123, 177, 186
"Funk" 95, 147, 233, 242
"Funny Girl" 180, 183
Funny Girl 168, 177, 180–183
"Funny Love Songs" 190, 192
"Furt" 72, 82, 91–92, 95, 117, 123, 185, 196, 199

Gainior, Dan 125
Gamson, Joshua 27, 37
Gardner, Suzanne 200, 214
Garland, Judy 85
Garland-Thomson, Rosemarie 121, 123
Gary, Mary 23
gay bashing 31–32
gay bullying 3, 24, 29, 32, 36, 258; *see also* anti-gay bullying
"Gay Hogwarts" 48
"Gay Witch Hunt" 12, 23
gayness 25, 40, 44–45, 50, 52, 87
gay/straight binary 27
gender: discrimination 172; equality/inequality 205, 217, 220, 225, 227; identity 9, 97; neutral 45, 49; norms 189, 191, 194–195, 197; performance 88–89, 94, 188, 202; queer 105; and queerness 7; and race 46; representation 9; sexual 157; stereotypes 157, 161, 234
gender roles 216, 230, 233, 238–239; norms 189, 191, 194–195, 197
gender system, binary 240
"Gender Treachery: Homophobia, Masculinity, and Threatened Identities" 240, 242
genders 28, 105, 240
Gerbner, George 28
"Get Happy" 85
Geyer, Dean 4
ghost(s) 7, 168–169, 175, 179
ghosting 167–170, 173, 175–177, 178–179
Gillepsie-Sells, Kath 108, 121–122, 124
Gilman, Sander 94–95
Gilsig, Jessalyn 195
Gintis, Herbert 56
girl power 202, 211
girlfriend 34, 39, 44, 100, 103, 110, 114, 117, 144, 155, 196, 210, 223, 232
girlhood 194, 269
girls: adolescent 188, 197; teenagers 9, 164, 194, 204, 216
Giroux, Henry 213–214
Giving Account of Oneself 19, 23
GLAAD 9, 27
Gleek 184

Glickman, Charlie 148–149
"Glist" 159
Glitter, Gary 165
Goldberg, Whoopie 193
Golden Globes 2
Gomez-Rejon, Alfonso 23, 67, 94, 106, 149, 166, 186, 241–242
Good Girl 8, 230–236, 239
The Good Wife 29
"Goodbye" 56, 67, 129, 135
Goodman, Tim 1, 10
Gorton, Don 51–52
Gossip Girl 11–12, 23
goth 72, 230
Gottschall, Jonathan 132, 135
Grammy 191
Greek 12, 23
Greendale Community College 243, 245–250, 253
"Grilled Cheesus" 6, 100, 102, 104, 106
Gross, Larry 28
Grossberg, Lawrence 89, 95
Guilbert, Georges-Claude 227–228
Guinier, Lani 40, 52
"A Guy's Guide to Feminisim" 226, 228
Gypsy 174–177, 180–181, 185–186
Gypsy Rose Lee (character) 174

"Hairography" 29, 37, 191, 199
Halberstam, Judith 244–245, 250–251, 253
Hall, Stuart 52, 89, 95
Hallows, Joanne 209, 214
Halperin, David 71, 124
"handicapable" 122
Haney, Tyler 226, 228
Happily Divorced 11, 94
"Happy Days Are Here Again" 85
harassment 48–51, 109, 158, 260, 264–265
The Haunted Stage: The Theatre as Memory Machine 168–169, 186
Havrilesky, Heather 1, 10
Heartiste (blogger name) 148n–149
Heather (Tumblr username) 256
hegemony 29, 34, 40, 42–43, 47, 50–51, 70, 81, 87, 98, 102, 174, 230–231
Herdman, John 238, 242
Herman, Didi 88, 95
heteroflexibility 28
heterogenital 111
heteronormativity 6, 28, 34–35, 48, 79, 108–111, 114, 116–120, 164, 172–173, 176, 193, 197, 239, 245, 247
heterosexist 158
heterosexuality 14, 28–30, 36, 40, 45–46, 48–49, 64, 78, 81–82, 88, 98, 108, 120, 156–157, 160, 164, 197, 202, 211, 217, 244–245, 262–263, 266
Hibberd, James 152, 165

hierarchy 40, 47, 56–57, 60, 63, 78, 91, 247
High School Musical 215
Hill, Aaron 79
Hilton-Morrow, Wendy 87, 239, 241
Hispanic 34; *see also* Latina/Latinas; Latino/Latinos
HIV 150, 166, 256
Hodgson, Matthew 23, 106
Hodson, Gordon 147
Hogan, Heather 35, 37
Holly Holliday (character) 4, 130, 145, 151–152, 155, 211, 245
Hollywood 43, 77, 80, 87, 199–200
Holm, Gunilla 201, 214
homology 93
homophobia 31, 34, 36, 47–50, 71, 91, 104, 128–129, 133, 158, 201–202, 240, 242, 250, 255–256, 258, 261
homosexuality 24–32, 33–34, 36, 39–40, 45, 48–49, 88, 94, 109, 128, 130, 145, 172, 257–258, 262, 267
Horton, Andrew 245, 254
Houston, Whitney 115, 238
Hudson, Kate 10
"Human Nature" 221
humanity 99, 105
Hust, Stacey 158, 161, 166
hybrid 29, 37, 99, 215
hyperaggressiveness 196
hypercompetitiveness 190, 192
hypermasculinity 122
hypersexuality 209–210

"I Kissed a Girl" (episode) 18, 21–22, 33–34, 36–37, 44, 46, 52, 128, 135
"I Kissed a Girl" (song) 28, 33, 49
"I Say a Little Prayer" 232
identification 21, 32, 57, 62, 132–133
identity 2–3, 6, 8–9, 18, 19–20, 22, 24–25, 28–31, 36, 39–46, 42–44, 46–52, 56, 58, 60–62, 64, 65, 66, 67, 68, 70–71, 72, 73–76, 78, 80, 82, 85–91, 92–94, 93–95, 96, 97, 98, 100, 102, 104, 106, 108, 110, 112, 114, 116, 118, 120, 122, 124, 126, 128, 130, 132, 134, 136, 138, 140, 142, 144, 146, 148, 152, 154, 156–158, 160, 162–163, 164, 166, 168–169, 170, 172, 174, 175–176, 178–179, 180, 182, 184, 186, 189, 199–200, 201–202, 211, 214, 218, 228, 229, 231, 238, 239–240, 242–244, 246–252, 253, 256, 267, 269–270, 271; *see also* able-bodied; ableist; African American; bisexuality; blackness; identity, gay; Latina, gay; Latino/Latinos; male, gay, white
identity, gay 86–91
ideology 6, 25, 31–34, 39–42, 43, 45, 47, 51–52, 55–56, 68, 73, 89, 130, 133, 135, 198, 209

"I'm the Greatest Star" 177, 182, 184
imagination, pornographic 151, 157–160,
    162, 164
"Immaculate Affection" 156
immorality 7, 125, 152
inclusivity/inclusiveness 71, 73, 98, 102
Indigo Girls 31, 35
individuality 71, 197, 217, 252
inequality 48, 214, 217
inequity 40, 55–56, 60, 205, 213
infantilization 117, 121, 206
infection 150, 245, 251–252
injustices 86, 267
intercourse 111, 121, 139, 148
interdependence 99, 104
"Intergroup Bias Towards 'Group X': Evi-
    dence of Prejudice, Dehumanization,
    Avoidance, and Discrimination Against
    Asexuals" 147
"Intersection Theory: A More Elucidating
    Paradigm of Quantitative Analysis" 66–
    67
intersectionality 39–40, 42, 44, 47–48,
    50–52, 60, 62, 67, 99, 107
intimacy 19, 70, 80, 98, 109, 138–141, 143,
    146–147, 149, 236, 249, 258, 263
intolerance 23, 92
Irish 72, 78; see also Caucasian; Rory
    Flanagan (character)
irony 87, 93, 120, 152, 235, 244, 252
Isabelle Wright (character) 10
Isherwood, Lisa 104, 106
Italian 78; see also Caucasian
"It's Not Right, But It's Okay" 238

Jacob Ben Israel (character) 72, 155–157,
    161
Jagose, Annamarie 93, 95
Jake Puckerman (character) 4
Jamieson, Amie 161, 166
"Le Jazz Hot!" 84, 176–177, 180, 184
Jean Sylvester (character) 116–118, 122,
    196
Jeff Winger (character) 243–245, 247–
    248, 250–251, 253, 259
Jehovah's Witness 250, 253
Jennifer P. 148–149
Jesse St. James (character) 114, 177, 192,
    251
Jewishness 6, 62–63, 69, 78, 85–91, 93–
    96, 193, 270–271
Jews 86, 88, 90, 93–96
Jezebel 33, 37
Jhally, Sut 151, 157–158, 160–161, 166
JJ (blogger name) 30, 33–34, 37
jock 34, 50, 98, 100, 105, 187, 229–230,
    264–265
Jodie Dallas (character) 29
Joe Hart (character) 3, 39–40, 69, 98, 100,
    103–105, 115–116, 121–122, 130, 236

Jolie, Angelina 216
Jones, Dot-Marie 4, 95–96
"Journey to Regionals" 100, 106
Judaism 253
justice 42, 60, 86, 92, 104–105, 132, 164,
    227, 271

Kabbalah 94
Kafka, Franz 248
Kaiser Family Foundation 164, 166
Kalinda Sharma (character) 29
Kann, Laura 153, 166
Keck, William 102, 106
Keene, Elodie 23, 94–95, 165, 242
Kehily, Mary Jane 202, 209, 214
Kellner, Douglas 43, 52
kenosis 99–101, 105
Kidscape 165
Kindlon, Dan 188
kink 108, 147, 149
Kinnaman, David 97, 106
Kirk/Spock 258
"Kiss" 245
Klaine 8, 255–259, 261–263, 265, 267
Klainers 256
Kohlman, Marla H. 66–67
Kominski, Robert 161, 166
Kreger Silverman, Linda 188, 199
Kriegel, Leonard 119, 123
Kubrick, Stanley 253
Kumashiro, Kevin 48, 52
Kunkel, Dale 132, 135, 154, 165
Kurt Hummel (character) 3–8, 10, 15–17,
    22–26, 30–32, 35, 39–40, 42–44, 46–
    52, 57, 61–63, 66–67, 69, 71–72, 78–82,
    84–93, 95, 98, 100–102, 104–105, 107,
    109, 120, 126–129, 133–134, 138, 150–
    151, 157, 163–164, 167–168, 172–179,
    186, 192, 205–207, 211–212, 220, 222–
    223, 227, 233–234, 238–240, 253, 255–
    266

The L Word 11
Lady and the Tramp 121, 181
Lady Gaga 49, 71
Lamb, Sharon 164, 166
"Landslide" 30, 249
Lang, KD 35
Larsen, Samuel 3, 39, 97, 102–103
"Laryngitis" 37, 86, 95, 112–114, 120–121,
    123, 128, 135, 154, 159–160, 166, 174,
    176, 186, 192
Latina/Latinas 39, 45, 50–51, 53, 69, 76;
    gay 45, 51
Latino/Latinos 132, 247
Lauren Zizes (character) 3, 69, 72, 74–75,
    163, 229
Laurey (character) 168
Lauzen, Martha 238–239, 242
Law and Order 11

Lawrence, Charles 46, 53
LBGTQ 81; *see also*
  LGBT/LGBTQ/LGBTQIQ
leadership 187–190, 194, 197, 240
"Lebanese" 20, 34
Lengies, Vanessa 3
lesbian 11, 17–18, 20–21, 23, 26, 30–35,
  37, 39–40, 44, 47, 49, 52, 69, 76, 92, 103,
  105, 107, 110, 124, 150, 152–153, 162, 211,
  253; *see also* gay identity; identity
LGBT/LGBTQ/LGBTQIQ 4, 11–23, 25,
  32, 37, 40, 43, 45–52, 69, 81, 88, 90–92,
  107, 150, 153–154, 165, 256, 267, 270–
  271; *see also* bisexual; homosexuality;
  identity, gay; lesbian; male, gay
Liberalism 30, 40–41, 46, 51–52, 55–56,
  101, 129–130, 271
"Like a Prayer" 209, 232
Lima (Ohio) 2, 8, 37, 72, 100, 108, 129,
  134, 140, 150, 159, 229, 231, 233, 235,
  237, 239, 241, 262, 264
Lohan, Lindsay 204
"The Lolita Effect" 209, 214
Lopez, Alfred J. 74, 82
"Loser Like Me" 8, 101
Louise (character) 174, 186
Lowry, Brian 9–10
LuPone, Patti 176
Lynch, Jane 3, 82–83, 94–96, 195

MacInnis, Cara C. 147
Madonna 5, 7, 29, 37, 94, 127, 135, 144,
  149, 154, 160, 166, 192, 203–228, 245,
  251, 254
Madonna: Bawdy & Soul 218
Madonna's Greatest Hits 216
"Makeover" 240, 242
male/maleness 3, 6, 18, 20, 24–25, 29, 31–
  32, 35, 39–40, 43–50, 61–62, 80, 87, 101,
  105, 110, 118, 141, 148, 151, 157–160, 163,
  174, 188–189, 197, 201, 203–209, 211,
  213, 217, 220, 223–227, 233, 238–239,
  251, 257–258, 267, 269; *see also* gender,
  identity
male: gay 24–25, 27, 31, 35, 80, 87, 94, 101;
  white and gay 40, 43, 50
male sex, gay 151, 163
Mama Rose (character) 176
Mame 181
"Mapping the Margins: Intersectionality,
  Identity Politics, and Violence Against
  Women of Color" 60
marginality 25, 29, 40–41, 45–46, 48, 57–
  58, 60–63, 65–66, 74, 88–90, 99, 105,
  108, 221
Maria (character) 54, 58–59, 61
Marley Rose (character) 4, 69
marriage 84, 92, 130, 139–140, 142, 145–
  148, 150–151, 164–165, 196
Martinez, Gladys 161, 166

masculinity 24, 29, 52, 87, 94–95, 111, 128,
  160, 173–174, 190, 195–196, 197, 207,
  214, 231, 237–240, 242, 251, 269
"Mash-Off" 32, 35, 37, 44–45, 52, 59, 64,
  67, 77, 82, 237, 242
"Mash-Up" 29, 37
"Material Girl" 221
Mays, Jayma 4, 94–96, 195
McHale, Kevin 3, 94–96, 107, 120
McKee, Alan 43, 53
McMillin, Scott 169, 171, 186
McNair, Brian 209–210, 214
McRobbie, Angela 209, 217–218, 226–228
McRuer, Robert 107–108, 120, 123–124
"Me Against the Music" 210
Mellencamp, John 174
Meltzer, Marisa 209, 211, 214
men 27–29, 33, 37, 47, 49–50, 79, 81–82,
  87, 90–91, 102, 111, 143, 157–158, 160–
  161, 163, 202, 206–207, 224–225, 237,
  239, 242, 250–251, 258, 270; *see also*
  gender, norms; masculinity
Menzel, Idina 10, 95
Mercedes Jones (character) 3–4, 6, 15–16,
  23, 30, 39, 52, 54–67, 69, 72, 74–75, 84,
  101, 103–104, 121–122, 126, 159–160,
  192, 198, 203, 220, 222, 227, 229–230
merit 6, 55, 57–66
Merman, Ethel 176
Messerschmidt, James 94–95
Metz, Allan 213–214, 221, 228
Meyer, Michaela 28–29, 37, 93, 95
Meyer, Moe 93, 95
microaggression 56, 65, 68
Midler, Bette 176
Midnight Caller 29, 37
Mike Chang (character) 3, 23, 66, 263
Mikhail Bakhtin: Creation of a Prosaics
  126, 135
minority 6, 13, 16–18, 22–23, 25, 62, 65,
  67, 70, 73–74, 76, 90–91, 93, 99, 120,
  124, 153–154, 157, 164
Mirren, Helen 118
mis-gender 105
misogyny 35, 158, 205
Mr. Radisson (character) 245, 250, 252
Mittell, Jason 10
Modern Family 11
"Modern Warfare" 253–254
Molina-Guzmán, Isabel 50, 53
Mollow, Anna 107–108, 120, 123–124
monogamy 25, 27–29, 36, 79, 120, 130,
  148, 151, 164
Monroe, Marilyn 208
Monteith, Cory 3, 10, 44, 77, 82–83, 94–
  96, 106, 190, 228
"Moral Hazard" 13, 23
morality 7, 70, 125–126, 134, 230
Morris, Heather 3, 39, 94–96, 190
Morson, Gary Saul 126, 131, 135

Moseley, Rachel 209, 214
MTV 207–208
Mulligan, Jennifer 130
Murphy, Ryan 1, 9–10, 23–24, 26–27, 33, 35–37, 67–68, 95–97, 101–103, 106, 125, 149, 165–166, 186, 190, 199, 215, 217–218, 224, 228, 242, 254, 268
"The Music of the Night" 178
The Musical as Drama 169
musical theater/theatre 6–7, 167–186, 189–190
musicality 30, 35, 37, 243, 248
musicals 7, 54, 61, 66, 167–186, 192, 214–215, 227, 249

Nakkula, Michael 189
Nayak, Anoop 209, 214
NBC 8, 23, 29, 37, 94, 253–254
"Never Been Kissed" 48, 53, 90–91, 95, 120–121, 123, 196, 199, 233, 255–256, 268
New Directions 2–4, 7–9, 24, 32, 54–55, 59, 64, 67, 69–74, 76–77, 82, 84, 86–88, 168, 171, 187, 189, 191, 203, 207, 229–230, 232, 236, 240, 244, 246–247, 255, 263, 265
New York Academy of Dramatic Arts (NYADA) 4, 60, 178, 193
Newell, Alex 4
"A Night of Neglect" 74–75, 82, 199, 229–230, 241
Noah "Puck" Puckerman (character) 3–4, 10, 20, 23, 29, 69, 72, 89, 114, 117, 119, 121–123, 126–130, 156, 159–161, 163, 205–206, 224–226, 230, 232, 236, 241
Nodelman, Perry 133
nondisabled 107–108, 114, 118, 121; *see also* able-bodied; disability/disabilities
nonheteronormativity 108, 110, 121; *see also* heteronormativity
Norma Rae (character) 75
normativity 8, 28, 70–71, 80–82, 87–89, 94, 121, 152, 244–245, 253
Noxon, Marti 67, 186, 199, 268
NYADA *see* New York Academy of Dramatic Arts (NYADA)

Obama, Barack 41, 101, 130, 135, 162
OCD 143, 197
Oedipal 244–246, 253
The Office 12, 23
Okun, Tema 213–214
O'Malley, Mike 4, 95–96
"On My Way" 22, 78–79, 82, 98, 104, 106, 115, 128–129, 135, 195, 199, 236–237, 242
"Oops I Did It Again" 207
The Oprah Winfrey Show 27, 37
oppression 29, 47, 50, 55, 61, 71, 91, 99, 105, 108, 122, 206, 210

orientation, sexual 25, 28, 31, 40, 45–47, 103, 138, 154, 187, 198, 215, 258–261, 265, 267
"Original Song" 9–10, 101, 106, 192, 199, 233, 242, 253–254
Ormond, J.E. 165–166
Osborne, Joan 101
Oscar (character) 12
Otherness 50, 70, 74, 75, 76, 89, 173
outed 12, 18, 24, 34, 44, 49, 77–78, 104, 260; *see also* outing
outfits 90, 219
outing 14, 32, 35–36, 44–45, 64, 69, 76, 78, 134, 260; *see also* outed
Ovadia, Seth 66–67
overachiever 7, 187, 190, 195; girls 187–188, 190, 195, 197–198
Overstreet, Chord 3, 95
Oz 28

Pacey (character) 129
"Pairability" 102, 106
Palin, Bristol 130, 135
Paltrow, Gwyneth 4, 165
"Paradigms of Human Memory" 253–254
paraplegia 112, 246
Parents Television Council 151–152, 202, 214
parody 8, 168, 243–247, 249, 252
Pavarotti (character/animal) 241
pedagogy 52, 164, 189, 214, 246, 270–271
peer pressure 163, 198, 201
Pelias, Ronald 94, 96
Pellegrini, Ann 87, 94–96
Pelton, Dean 247–248
Pempengco, Charice 191
performativity 2, 171, 173, 179–182, 241, 245
Peron, Eva 94
Perry, Katy 1, 28, 33, 35, 49, 233
The Phantom of the Opera 178, 182
The Phil Donahue Show 27
Picard/Riker (character pairing) 258
Pierce Hawthorne (character) 253
Pipher, Mary 188
Poniewozik, James 85, 96
Popular Girl 232
popularity 3, 7, 8–9, 30, 33, 39–41, 43, 46, 49–50, 73, 76, 86–88, 94, 98, 100, 107, 114, 132, 121, 134, 137, 140, 145, 148, 152, 153, 156–157, 158, 159, 164, 167, 187–191, 193–195, 197–198, 200–201, 209, 214, 215–219, 226–227, 244, 247, 263–264, 269–271
pornography 120, 209
postcolonialism 74–75, 81–82
postfeminism 199
post-gender 6, 40, 42, 48, 51
postidentity 51
postracialism 40, 41, 43, 46, 49

"Pot o' Gold" 59, 67, 128, 135, 236, 242
Potter, Lauren 3, 95–96, 116, 196
poverty 56, 126
prayer 100, 104
"Preggers" 15, 23, 57, 100, 106, 114, 123, 159, 166, 232, 242
pregnancy 128, 150, 155, 159, 194, 203, 235
prejudices 40, 108, 133, 201, 259, 261, 266
Prince 245
Principal Figgins (character) 150, 162, 248
"Prom Queen" 31, 37, 122, 126, 135, 194, 199
"Prom-asaurus" 119, 123, 193, 199, 236, 242
promiscuity 27, 29, 36, 130, 159, 162, 214
"Props" 59–60, 62, 67, 195, 199
"Proud Mary" 120
"The Purple Piano Project" 59, 67, 72, 83, 235, 237, 241–242
Pushing Daisies 168

quadriplegia 112, 120
The Queer Art of Failure 250–251, 254
Quinn Fabray (character) 3, 8, 10, 23, 29, 64, 69, 72, 75, 85, 87, 91, 100, 103–105, 114–118, 121–122, 126–128, 130, 150–151, 156–160, 189, 192–196, 198, 203, 212, 230–241, 264–265

race, and gender 45, 47–49, 60–61, 213, 253
race/ethnicity–gender intersection 6, 55
Rachel Berry (character) 3–7, 10, 15, 17, 23, 25, 30, 44, 52, 54–64, 66–67, 69, 72, 76–77, 84–89, 91–94, 112–115, 117–118, 121–122, 126–129, 133, 147, 151, 155–164, 168, 172–173, 175, 178–179, 187, 189–198, 203, 205–206, 209–212, 214, 221, 227, 229–230, 232, 234–236, 239–242, 249, 251, 253, 263, 265, 271
racialization 50, 56
racism 41–42, 46, 47, 58, 62
Radner, Gilda 94
Rainey, Sarah Smith 110, 121, 124
"Raise Your Glass" 102
Rasmussen, Mary Lou 44–45, 48–49, 53
Reading the Popular 73, 82
"Regional Holiday Music" 243–244, 248–249, 253–254
relationship, interracial 60
religion 1–2, 6, 3, 39, 86, 97–100, 102–103, 105, 130, 157, 218, 240, 250, 253, 270
Reviving Ophelia 188
Reynolds, Kimberley 134–135
Riley, Amber 3, 39, 59, 61, 198
Rivera, Naya 3, 39, 44, 76, 94–96, 189
"Road to Love" 259–261, 268
"The Rocky Horror Glee Show" 54, 61, 68, 120, 180–181, 183, 248, 254
Rocky Horror Picture Show 248

Rory Flanagan (character) 72, 237
Rosenberg, Alyssa 125
Rubin, Gayle 120, 124
Ruddell, Caroline 231, 242
Rusch, Kristine Kathryn 203, 214
Rust, Rodriguez 28

Saint Foucault: Towards a Gay Hagiography 71
Salling, Mark 3, 94–96
Sam Evans (character) 3, 17, 20, 23, 56, 67, 69, 72, 84–85, 103, 109, 121, 126, 130, 159, 237
Santana Lopez (character) 3–6, 9, 18, 20–24, 26, 28–37, 39–40, 42–52, 59–60, 62–64, 66, 69, 72, 76–80, 82, 84, 88, 98, 103–104, 107, 110–111, 121, 127, 130, 132, 138, 150, 155–157, 160, 162–163, 189–190, 198, 203, 210–212, 235, 241, 249, 251, 253
"Saturday Night Gleever" 64
Saturday Night Live 94
Saul (charater) 12
Savage, Dan 52, 148–149
Savin-Williams, Ritch 28, 37
"Saving All My Love for You" 115
Schroeder, Elizabeth 204, 214
Schwartz, Stephen 2, 186
Scott, Jill 66
Screen Actors Guild 66
Seacrest, Ryan 235
Sean Fretthold (character) 112–114, 116, 118, 120–121
Sebastian Smythe (character) 78–79, 82, 130, 237–238, 240, 260–261
"Sectionals" 9–10, 23, 29, 37, 66, 98, 106, 110, 148, 186
Seitz, Matthew Zoller 48, 53
Semiel (blogger name) 139, 147, 149
Sesame Street 168
Sex 208
Sex and the City 94
sex education 4, 7, 126–127, 129–130, 148, 152, 154–155, 157, 159, 162, 164, 202, 204, 206–207
The Sexual Politics of Disability: Untold Desires 121, 124
sexuality 6, 11, 13–23, 94–95, 125, 134, 156, 158, 167, 209, 269
Sexuality Information and Education Council of the United States 150, 165–166, 202, 214
sexualization 50, 74, 152, 155, 157, 162, 164, 209, 213–214, 223
"Sexy" 20, 23, 30–31, 37, 80–81, 83, 126, 129, 136, 144, 149, 151, 154–156, 161–163, 165–166, 211, 213–214, 245, 249, 252, 254
Shakespeare, William 108, 121–122, 124
"shameful lesbian musicality" 30, 35, 37

Shane Tinsley (character) 67
Shankman, Adam 67–68, 242, 254
Shannon Beiste (character) 4, 17, 122, 162, 195–196
Shelby Corcoran (character) 10, 128–129, 235–236, 241
Shelley, Mary 231
Sheppard, Alice 120, 124
Sherlock Holmes 8
Sherlock Holmes (character) 258
Shirley Bennett (character) 253
"Showmance" 72, 83, 100, 106, 142, 148–149, 154, 156, 160, 166, 232–233, 242
showtune 66, 168–169, 171, 174, 177–179
Shum, Harry, Jr. 3, 94–96, 191
Siebers, Tobin 121, 124
SIECUS 148–150, 165–166
"Silly Love Songs" 122, 124, 233–234, 242
Sister Mary Constance (character) 101
Skanks 230, 235–236
"Sketchy Relations" 259, 268
Sloop, John 89, 96
Snarker, Dorothy (blogger name) 1–2, 5, 10
Snider, Kathryn 46–48, 53
"Somebody I Used to Know" 238
Sondheim, Stephen 2, 174, 186
Sontag, Susan 93, 96
"Sophie's Choice" 188, 191
South Park 168
"The Spanish Teacher" 63, 120, 123–124, 132, 136, 197, 199
Spears, Britney 2, 7, 202, 204, 207–210, 216, 223–224, 227
"Special Education" 64, 66, 68, 87, 92, 96, 117
Stamos, John 96
Star Trek 258
Star Trek: The Next Generation 258
STD 155–156, 166
Steffen, Valerie 234, 242
Steinberg, Shirley 200, 214
stereotype 12, 13, 18, 25, 32, 34, 36, 50–51, 56, 66, 75, 86–87, 90–91, 92, 96, 98, 103, 108–109, 111, 112, 116–120, 130, 132, 145, 157, 158, 160, 161, 163–164, 194–195, 197–198, 211, 225–226, 229, 230, 234, 238, 242
Steven Carrington (character) 29
Stevens Aubrey, Jennifer 153, 165
Stevenson, Robert Louis 231
STIs 150
Stoltz, Eric 10, 23, 67–68, 95, 106, 149, 165–166, 241–242
straight 13–14, 16–20, 22–24, 26–29, 32–34, 44–45, 50, 61, 64, 69, 76, 88, 90, 98–99, 103, 105, 129, 163, 238–239, 248, 261, 263; *see also* heterosexuality; sexuality
Strasburger, Victor 152–153, 155, 166
Stratton, Jon 88, 96

Streisand, Barbra 2, 85, 177
Styne, Jule 174, 186
"The Substitute" 75, 83
Suburgatory 13
Sue Sylvester (character) 3–4, 17, 29, 32, 62, 72, 82, 101, 116–117, 195–196, 201, 216, 220, 222, 227, 232, 248, 253
"The Sue Sylvester Shuffle" 249
Sugar Motta (character) 3, 69, 72, 82
suicide 3, 22, 24, 79, 82, 104, 128–129, 256, 260–261
Sunset Boulevard 176–177, 181
Sunshine Corazon (character) 66, 191
Supernatural 8
super-peer, sexual 151–153, 156, 202
The Supremes 233
Sweet Boy 8, 230, 233–234

"Taking Chances" 264, 267
Talton, Dijon 3
Tammy Jean Albertson (character) 98, 101
Teej (Tumblr username) 256
"Teenage Dream" 240
teenager, gay 24, 50, 86, 107, 255, 257, 259
Tegan and Sara 35
Terri Schuester (character) 140–141, 147–148, 195
Textual Poachers 256, 268
"Theatricality" 71, 83, 98, 106, 133, 136
Theba, Iqbal 94–96
theology 6, 97–106, 270
Thicke, Robin 233
"Throwdown" 62, 65, 68, 120, 124, 161, 166, 233, 242
Timbaland 222
Timberlake, Justin 222, 227
Tina Cohen-Chang (character) 3, 15, 23, 57, 59–60, 62–64, 66–67, 69, 72, 82, 84, 91, 109–111, 126–127, 163–164, 191, 195, 203, 206, 212, 225–226, 230, 263
Tinkerbelle 86
Tobolowsky, Stephen 95–96
Tolman, Deborah 213–214
"Toucha, Toucha Me" 249
Tough Guy 8, 230–231, 233–240
"Toxic" 207
transgender 11, 69, 82, 150, 244, 253; *see also* gender, identity
transgenderism 27
transsexual 251, 253
The Trevor Project 256
Trites, Roberta Seelinger 133, 135–136
Trocki, Robin 116
Tropiano, Stephen 29, 37
The Trouble with Normal: Sex, Politics, and the Ethics of Queer Life 70, 83
Troubletones/Trouble Tones 10, 32, 55, 59, 64, 67, 72, 77, 82
Troy Barnes (character) 250–251, 253
Tyler Durden (character) 231

Unique Adams (character) 4, 69, 82, 105, 240

United States of Tara 13

Ushkowitz, Jenna 3, 94–96, 191

Valdivia, Angharad 50, 53

"Value's Last Tango" 246, 253

VanDerWerff, Todd 33–36

Vanity Fair 135

Variety 9–10, 208, 214

Venn (blogger name) 147, 149

Victor/Victoria 84, 176–177, 180

virgin 29, 111, 127, 145–146, 148, 151, 161, 163, 196–197, 203, 208, 211–212, 252–253

virgin/whore binary 203, 208

"Vitamin D" 191, 195–196, 199

Vocal Adrenaline 10

"Vogue" 220–222

Warbler(s) 3, 78, 92, 233–234, 238, 241, 255, 259–260

Warner, Michael 70, 83

Warwick, Dionne 232–233

Watson (character) 258

Weinstein, Zack 112

"What It Feels Like for a Girl" 206, 224, 226

Whedon, Joss 186

wheelchair 67, 70–71, 75, 107–111, 115, 120, 236

"Wheels" 57, 63, 70–71, 83, 96, 109–110, 117, 120, 122–124, 167, 171–174, 185–186, 196, 199, 233, 242

whiteness 40–42, 44, 46–47, 50, 64, 70, 73–76, 78–82

whore 145, 203, 208, 211

Wieselman, Jarrett 85, 96

Wilkerson, Abby 108, 124

Will Schuester/Mr. Schue (character) 3, 32, 54, 57–58, 62, 70–72, 82, 84, 109, 117, 120, 138, 154, 164, 167, 170–172, 187, 189, 195, 201, 203–207, 215–217, 220, 222–224, 227, 229, 244–246, 248–249, 251, 253

Wilson, Leah 200, 214

Winfrey, Oprah 27, 37

Winter, Tim 202, 214

Witherspoon, Reese 190

womanhood 80, 87, 208

Wood, Natalie 59

Yale 128, 194–195, 239

Yoshino, Kenji 25, 28

Young the Giant 104

Zamudio, Margaret 55–56, 68

Zunshine, Lisa 131, 136